CLARENDON LIBRARY OF LOGIC AND PHILOSOPHY

*General Editor*: L. Jonathan Cohen, The Queen's College, Oxford

# CRITICAL SCIENTIFIC REALISM

*The Clarendon Library of Logic and Philosophy* brings together books, by new as well as by established authors, that combine originality of theme with rigour of statement. Its aim is to encourage new research of a professional standard into problems that are of current or perennial interest.

*General Editor*: L. Jonathan Cohen, The Queen's College, Oxford

*Also published in this series*

# Critical Scientific Realism

ILKKA NIINILUOTO

OXFORD

UNIVERSITY PRESS

# OXFORD

UNIVERSITY PRESS

Great Clarendon Street, Oxford OX2 6DP

Oxford University Press is a department of the University of Oxford.
It furthers the University's objective of excellence in research, scholarship,
and education by publishing worldwide in

Oxford New York

Athens Auckland Bangkok Bogotá Buenos Aires Calcutta
Cape Town Chennai Dar es Salaam Delhi Florence Hong Kong Istanbul
Karachi Kuala Lumpur Madrid Melbourne Mexico City Mumbai
Nairobi Paris São Paulo Singapore Taipei Tokyo Toronto Warsaw
and associated companies in Berlin Ibadan

Oxford is a registered trade mark of Oxford University Press
in the UK and certain other countries

Published in the United States
by Oxford University Press Inc., New York

British Library Cataloguing in Publication Data
Data available

Library of Congress Cataloging in Publication Data
Niiniluoto, Ilkka.
Critical scientific realism / Ilkka Niiniluoto.
(Clarendon library of logic and philosophy)
Includes bibliographical references and indexes.
1. Realism. 2. Science—Philosophy. I. Title. II. Series.
B835.N55 1999 149′.2—dc21 99–32396

ISBN 0–19–823833–9

1 3 5 7 9 10 8 6 4 2

Typeset by Best-set Typesetter Ltd, Hong Kong
Printed in Great Britain
on acid-free paper by
Biddles Ltd,
Guildford and King's Lynn

# Preface

The philosophy of science in the twentieth century has been a battlefield between 'realist' and 'anti-realist' approaches. The interpretation of scientific theories, and the dispute about the cognitive significance of their theoretical terms and claims, provided a major impetus for the work of the Vienna Circle in the 1920s. The demise of logical positivism was followed by the rise of scientific realism within the analytic philosophy of science in the 1950s, but anti-realist attitudes became fashionable again through the historical-relativist approaches in the 1960s and the new pragmatist turn in the 1970s.

Arthur Fine's recent declaration that 'realism is dead' seems utterly overhasty, however. In this book, I claim that realism is alive and well. I also argue that critical scientific realism can be successfully defended against its most important current alternatives (instrumentalism, constructive empiricism, Kantianism, pragmatism, internal realism, relativism, social constructivism, epistemological anarchism).

Fine's announcement is an expression of philosophical frustration. In fact, he is not the only one who feels that the two camps—the realists and the anti-realists, divided moreover into several sects—are producing endless sequences of more and more elaborate positions and technical arguments, but still the basic issues remain unsettled. But, as long as we are doing philosophy, no final consensus can be expected: the realism debate is one of its 'eternal' problems, since wholesale philosophical programmes cannot be proved or disproved by any single *pro* or *contra* argument. Such overall philosophical outlooks are able to survive even in hard circumstances—gaining new strength, or losing credibility, by novel insights and discoveries. This is, indeed, the pattern of progress in philosophy: the debate on realism has taught us many important new lessons in logic, ontology, semantics, epistemology, methodology, axiology, and ethics.

In brief, the case of realism vs. anti-realism is alive and philosophically fascinating, since it is *un*settled. Its vitality and continuing relevance can be seen in the fact that all major philosophical trends of our time can be located, in some way or another, in coordinate positions defined by the axes of reality, truth, and knowledge. This holds not only of the varieties of realism and anti-realism, but also of those 'minimalists' (like Fine) who try to get rid of the whole problem of realism.

My first attempt to contribute to the realism debate was given in the book *Theoretical Concepts and Hypothetico-inductive Inference* (1973). My colleague Raimo Tuomela and I were engaged in applying Jaakko Hintikka's powerful formal tools (distributive normal forms, inductive logic) to investigate the methodological gains brought about by the introduction and use of theoretical terms. The aim was to defend scientific realism against the famous Theoretician's Dilemma that Carl G. Hempel had formulated in 1958. The main result of my doctoral dissertation was a proof that theoretical terms can be logically indispensable for the inductive systematization of observational statements (just as Hempel had claimed, but was not able to sustain convincingly).

Those were the days: I was an Angry Young Realist. Today I am still a realist. In the meantime, new programmes both for and against realism have started to flourish.

Influenced by Wilfrid Sellars, including his whiff of American pragmatism (i.e. truth as assertability), Tuomela developed a position of 'causal internal realism', an improvement on Hilary Putnam's 'internal realism', where truth is an intralinguistic and epistemic notion. Here Helsinki Realism was split: after having taught model theory to mathematicians, I was convinced that Alfred Tarski's semantic definition gives for a realist the right kind of notion of truth as correspondence between language and reality.

Even though Karl Popper's criticism of induction was grossly mistaken in my view, I became convinced—partly through Charles S. Peirce's fallibilism—of the crucial importance of the concept of truthlikeness or verisimilitude. When Popper's conjectural definition of comparative truthlikeness was refuted in 1974, I started to work in this problem area. The definition of scientific progress in terms of increasing truthlikeness is developed in the essays collected in *Is Science Progressive?* (1984); the technical details of the project are fully exposed in *Truthlikeness* (1987a).

So my brand of scientific realism takes seriously, and also makes precise, the idea that good scientific theories typically are false but nevertheless 'close to the truth'. Here I agree with Larry Laudan's insistence that realism stands or falls with something like the concept of verisimilitude. While Laudan opts for the latter alternative in his 'confutation of realism', I have tried to answer his challenge by defending the former.

Armed with the theory of truthlikeness (and the related notion of approximate truth), we can develop a thoroughly fallibilist version of scientific realism. In my view, its great advantage is the possibility of arguing that the justified criticism of naively realist and foundationalist epistemological standpoints need not, and should not, lead to any forms of anti-realism. In this sense, I offer truthlikeness as a medicine for the disillusioned absolutists who are tempted to abandon realism altogether. Truthlikeness should be seen also as a tool for resolving some family quarrels within the realist camp. Here a number of alternative views are viable.

It is of course still possible to try to develop the realist view of science without this concept—using only notions like truth, information, and probability, as Isaac Levi (1991) and many other Bayesians do. Also some of Popper's followers, like John Watkins (1984), now prefer to defend realism in science without appealing to verisimilitude at all.

Some of the best books in the field, like Michael Devitt's *Realism and Truth* (1991), mention the idea of increasing verisimilitude, but openly acknowledge their difficulties with this notion. With disarming honesty, Devitt says that the 'very technical literature' about this topic 'finished (for me) with Niiniluoto (1978)'. This early paper of mine deals with the quite complicated case of distances between Hintikkian depth-d constituents; I only wish Devitt had read the later work on intuitively more accessible cases with quantitative statements and laws.

To my disappointment, perhaps the most typical approach of the realists has been to continue the use of terms like 'approximate truth', 'verisimilitude', and 'approach to the truth' *as if* their meaning were clear enough without a definition, failing to refer to the large body of post-Popperian literature on this subject since 1975. This is the case in such otherwise important works as Jarrett Leplin's *Scientific Realism* (1984), Nicholas Rescher's *Scientific Realism* (1987), and Philip Kitcher's *The Advancement of Science* (1993).

One reaction among fellow realists has been open hostility towards a logical treatment of verisimilitude. In a review of my book on scientific progress, Ernan McMullin (1987) ridicules my approach as 'D-formalization', where 'D' means 'dazzles but disappoints'. McMullin misunderstands the nature of my project—he mistakenly believes that I take quantitative similarity to be an undefined primitive notion. But, apart from this error of ignorance, McMullin's unfriendly rhetoric seems to condemn to the flames *any* formal approach in the philosophy of science. Even though the Carnapian virtues of the exact explication of concepts are not as popular as they used to be, for me McMullin's remarks sound dogmatic and old-fashioned. For example, who could seriously claim today that the quantitative approach to probability (in its various interpretations) is illegitimate? Why should not the treatment of verisimilitude be at least equally bold and enterprising in this respect?

Even though the endorsement of truthlikeness gives a special flavour to this book, I am not writing a logical treatise at this time. I shall not enter into detailed technical debates with authors (among them, David Miller, Graham Oddie, Theo Kuipers, Jerrold L. Aronson, R. Harré, Ilkka Kieseppä) who largely share the critical realist outlook, but have different views about verisimilitude (cf. Niiniluoto 1998*a*). Instead, I shall keep the formalism to a minimum, introducing it only to the extent that is needed to follow my arguments for realism. But I am working with a clear conscience: I even dare to hope that some readers of this book might be encouraged or provoked to consult and study the thick formalism of *Truthlikeness*.

Two further aspects of this book deserve attention here.

First, in spite of advocating the correspondence theory of truth, and thereby rejecting a key element of 'internal realism', I am not a 'metaphysical realist' in Putnam's sense. In fact, the much discussed distinction between metaphysical and internal realism is in my view a false dichotomy. (If it was not initially intended as an exhaustive dichotomy, it has been so treated by many subsequent participants in the debate.) As in my earlier books, I shall argue that different conceptual frameworks (*pace* Donald Davidson) may carve up the mind-independent world (*pace* Richard Rorty) in different ways into individuals, kinds, and facts. There is no a priori privileged or a posteriori ideal 'Peirceish' framework for describing the world (*pace* Sellars); truth is relative to the conceptualizations of reality. But this does not entail that truth is an epistemic notion (*pace* Putnam); rather, this is required or presupposed in the Tarskian version of correspondence theory. This conclusion does not give comfort to relativism or anti-realism; on the contrary, it gives grounds for a realism worth fighting for.

Secondly, many—perhaps even most—contemporary philosophers write about truth, language, and realism from a naturalist-nominalist-physicalist-behaviourist-causalist standpoint. The influence of the towering figure of W. V. O. Quine is here strong and, by my lights, pernicious.

My own favourite metaphysics is a version of emergent materialism which opposes reductionist physicalism by acknowledging the ontological reality of the human-made, socially produced 'World 3', containing as 'social constructions' abstract and cultural artefacts and institutions. I hope to be able to elaborate this idea in more detail in future work. Here I employ this conception in two directions: against those constructivists (like Nelson Goodman and Bruno Latour) who in effect are reducing the whole or a part of physical nature (Popper's World 1) to World 3; and against those physicalists who conversely reduce World 3 to World 1.

The latter point has here the following significance: not only languages, but also language–world relations, are human-made social products. Facts about semantics do not reduce to physics (*pace* Hartry Field), since they belong to the level of World 3. In emphasizing the triadic nature of signs, and the conventionality of symbols, Peirce's work (once again) supersedes many of the later ramifications of the philosophy of language. In particular, the attempt to 'naturalize' semantics has led to strange pseudo-problems and unfair criticisms of realist views.

The plan of the book is as follows. The introductory Chapter 1 distinguishes various problems of realism, and contrasts scientific knowledge with common sense, religion, and metaphysics. It gives a systematic survey of the main rival schools of the philosophy of science and outlines my own critical scientific realism. It also argues that the realism debate is today as alive, compelling, and momentous as ever.

The next five chapters explore realism in ontology, semantics, epistemology, theory construction, and methodology. The positive side of the argument supports the mind-independence of physical reality, truth as correspondence, truthlikeness as an aim of science, theoretical entities as referents of scientific theories, truth-seeking as a rationale for methodological norms and for the concept of cognitive progress, and the links between realism and the success of science. On the negative side, criticism is given of positivism, instrumentalism, Kantianism, pragmatist theories of truth, and non-realist accounts of scientific methodology and progress.

Chapters 7–9, respectively, evaluate and criticize versions of internal realism, relativism, and social constructivism.

The final Chapter 10 gives a glimpse over the various extra-scientific reasons that have been presented for and against realism. Such considerations—religious, moral, political, etc.—do not speak in favour or against the truth of realism, but still raise important philosophical issues. I conclude (*pace* Paul Feyerabend, Rorty, and the postmodernists) that critical scientific realism is in many ways a desirable philosophical outlook in a free, democratic, liberal society.

Nicholas Rescher once described his work *Scientific Explanation* (1970) as a combination of 'three generally distinct genres: the textbook, the monographic treatise, and the polemical tract'. I hope that the same can be said about my book.

I assume that my reader has some basic knowledge of philosophy, including elementary concepts of logic and probability. The book should be suitable for advanced courses in the philosophy of science, but its arguments should be interesting for professionals working in the fields of semantics, epistemology, philosophy of science, and science studies.

While all important philosophers and questions related to scientific realism cannot be dealt with in detail within one book, I still try to give a picture of the whole problem area. In addition to the key issues that I treat at some length, there are also brief passages, historical notes, and bibliographical references which give a broader perspective and hints to the reader for further investigations.

I have used, modified, extended, and rewritten parts of a number of earlier articles. I am grateful for permission to use excerpts or draw upon material from the following articles:

'Measuring the Success of Science', in A. Fine, M. Forbes, and L. Wessels (eds.), *PSA 1990*, i (1990). Permission from the Philosophy of Science Association.

'Science and Epistemic Values', *Science Studies*, 3 (1990). Permission from the Finnish Society of Science Studies.

'Realism, Relativism, and Constructivism', *Synthese*, 89 (1990). Permission from Kluwer Academic Publishers.

'What's Wrong with Relativism', *Science Studies*, 4 (1991). Permission from the Finnish Society of Science Studies.

'Scientific Realism and the Problem of Consciousness', in M. Kamppinen and A. Revonsuo (eds.), *Consciousness in Philosophy and Cognitive Neuroscience* (1994). Permission from Lawrence Erlbaum Associates.

'Descriptive and Inductive Simplicity', in W. Salmon and G. Wolters (eds.), *Logic, Language, and the Structure of Scientific Theories* (1994). Permission from the University of Pittsburgh Press.

'The Relativism Question in Feminist Epistemology', in L. H. Nelson and J. Nelson (eds.), *Feminism, Science, and the Philosophy of Science* (1996). Permission from Kluwer Academic Publishers.

'Reference Invariance and Truthlikeness', *Philosophy of Science*, 64 (1997). Permission from the Philosophy of Science Association.

The actual writing was started in the spring of 1993 during my sabbatical leave, made possible by a research grant from the Academy of Finland. Mr Sami Pihlström, who worked as my research assistant, gave me valuable help in collecting up-to-date material on realism. He has also given useful critical comments on my work (cf. Pihlström 1996; 1998). I am also grateful to an anonymous reader who gave very useful suggestions for the presentation and organization of the material in the book. In the final stage of preparing the electronic manuscript, with figures and indices, I have been assisted by Mr Jukka Appelqvist.

Finally, as always, I wish to thank my family for patience and encouragement.

I.N.

# Contents

# 1

# The Varieties of Realism

'Realism' is one of the most overstrained catchwords in philosophy. In this chapter, I make some distinctions between varieties of realism: for example, we may speak of ontological, semantical, epistemological, axiological, methodological, and ethical realism (Section 1.1), or of common-sense, scientific, and metaphysical realism (Section 1.2). Stronger and weaker forms of realism and anti-realism can also be separated from each other. These distinctions help us to make a plan for the next chapters of the book: a tree-form classification of the most important rival views about truth and science is outlined in Section 1.3, together with a preliminary formulation of the basic theses of critical scientific realism. Further comments on realism as a philosophical research programme and its relations to naturalism are given in Section 1.4.

## 1.1 The problems of realism

The word 'real' is derived from the Latin *res*, which means things both in the concrete and abstract senses. Thus, 'reality' refers to the totality of all real things, and 'realism' is a philosophical doctrine about the reality of some of its aspects. But, as philosophy is divided into several subdisciplines, the doctrines of realism are likewise divided into a number of varieties. For our purposes, without attempting to be exhaustive, it is appropriate to divide philosophy—and thereby the problems of realism— into six areas: ontology, semantics, epistemology, axiology, methodology, and ethics.

Ontology studies the nature of reality, especially problems concerning existence. Semantics is interested in the relation between language and reality. Epistemology investigates the possibility, sources, nature, and scope of human knowledge. The question of the aims of enquiry is one of the subjects of axiology. Methodology studies the best, or most effective, means of attaining knowledge. Finally, ethics is concerned with the standards of evaluating human actions and alternative possible states of the world.

Given these brief characterizations, it now seems easy to distinguish six different problems of realism:

*Ontological*: Which entities are real? Is there a mind-    (OR)
independent world?

*Semantical*: Is truth an objective language–world relation?    (SR)

*Epistemological*: Is knowledge about the world possible?    (ER)

*Axiological*: Is truth one of the aims of enquiry?    (AR)

*Methodological*: What are the best methods for pursuing    (MR)
knowledge?

*Ethical*: Do moral values exist in reality?    (VR)

It may also appear that these questions can be answered independently of each other: each of them has typical positive and negative answers whose supporters can be identified as 'realists' of the appropriate type, and their opponents as 'anti-realists'.

The situation is more complicated, however. The relationships between these six disciplines are a fundamental point of departure that divides philosophical schools. Such disagreement about the philosophical method is also an important source in the debates between realism and anti-realism.

Plato's theory of forms was a bold attempt to solve together the problems of ontology, semantics, epistemology, axiology, and ethics. The traditional view, formulated by Aristotle, takes ontology to be the 'first philosophy' and, hence, primary to epistemology.[1] However, many philosophers have followed Immanuel Kant in rejecting such an approach as 'metaphysical': the first task of philosophy is to study the possibility and conditions of knowledge by uncovering the innate structures of the human mind (see Section 4.3). Kant's followers have changed the mental structures to languages and conceptual frameworks. Analytic philosophy in the twentieth century has studied questions of existence through the 'ontological commitments' of conceptual systems and theories (Quine 1969). The pragmatist tradition has developed variations of Charles Peirce's proposal to 'define' reality and truth by the ultimate consensus of the scientific community. These approaches place epistemology and methodology before semantics, and semantics before ontology (see Section 4.6).

Similarly, many pragmatists have denied the fact–value distinction (cf. Putnam 1992), whereas the independence of OR and VR is often defended by 'Hume's guillotine' (i.e. *is* does not logically imply *ought*).

---

[1] This tradition includes, among others, pre-Socratic philosophers of nature, Spinoza, Leibniz, Hegel, Wittgenstein's *Tractatus*, and Heidegger's *Sein und Zeit*.

Michael Devitt's *Realism and Truth* (1991) starts with a clear formulation of five 'maxims'. They imply that the ontological issue of realism (OR) should be settled before any epistemic (ER) or semantic (SR) issue, where the latter two should be sharply distinguished. If these maxims are taken to be premisses in arguments for realism, pragmatists may complain that the question has been begged against them—they are not 'confusing' ontology, semantics, and epistemology, but rather 'blurring' such distinctions on purpose. Moreover, other kinds of scientific realists, like Raimo Tuomela (1985), who accept the *scientia mensura* principle ('science is the measure of all things'), would claim that all questions about existence are a posteriori, and therefore they will be decided last, only after science has reached its completion.

Devitt's main thesis is that truth should be separated from ontological realism (Devitt 1991: p. x): 'No doctrine of truth is constitutive of realism: there is no entailment from the one doctrine to the other' (ibid. 5). This thesis is correct at least in the sense that an ontological realist may accept an anti-realist notion of truth, and semantical or representational realism alone does not tell which particular statements are true and which are false (ibid. 42). On the other hand, Devitt himself defines the realist correspondence theory of truth so that it presupposes (i.e. entails) the existence of a mind-independent reality (ibid. 29). Similarly, many formulations of epistemological realism would not make sense without some minimal assumptions of ontological realism.

Michael Dummett (1982) argues that we should approach OR via SR and ER. Let S be a 'disputed' class of statements (e.g. about unobservable entities or about the past). Then 'realism' about S is the thesis that the statements in S satisfy the principle of *bivalence*, i.e. they are objectively true or false in virtue of a mind-independent reality. Anti-realists about S instead reject bivalence (cf. Luntley 1988), and suggest a theory where truth and meaning depend on our actual epistemic opportunities and capabilities.

It is fair to expect that the philosophy of language will help to clarify the issues of realism and anti-realism. Ontological questions are certainly intertwined with semantical and epistemological ones. But it is very doubtful whether the study of language and meaning as such could resolve any metaphysical issues. For example, there may be statements h such that h does not have a determinate truth value. Is this an argument against realism? I think the answer is no, since h may simply be a vague statement (e.g. 'It is raining now'), while the reality which h speaks about (e.g. weather) is completely mind-independent. In other words, ontological realism need not entail the principle of bivalence.

I agree with Devitt that it is desirable, for the sake of clarity, to keep the various problems of realism conceptually separate—as far as we can. But this does not imply that we could—or should—'settle' the ontological issue 'before any epistemic or semantic issue', or that we should eventually avoid 'hybrid' doctrines (Devitt 1991: 47). Realism is a philosophical world view, a 'large-scale philosophical package' in Richard Boyd's (1990) sense, and its successful defence requires that we try to find the most plausible combinations of ontological, semantical, epistemological, axiological, methodological, and ethical positions. In other words, it does not seem promising to expect that OR could be convincingly solved without considering SR, ER, AR, MR, and VR—and the interconnections between these theses—as well.

In particular, critical scientific realism in the form in which it will be defended in this book is a wholesale 'research programme' within the philosophy of science, and its merits have to be evaluated by its contributions to all the problems of realism listed above.[2]

## 1.2 Science and other belief systems

Science is a source of cognitive attitudes about the world, characterized by its reliance on the self-corrective scientific method.[3] The community of scientists is engaged in solving cognitive problems by proposing hypotheses or constructing theories and by testing them through controlled observation and experimentation. The reports of such studies are then evaluated and critically discussed by other scientists. Thus, for the most part, scientific activities do not involve belief in the sense of holding-to-be-true: rather the scientists propose hypotheses and pursue research programmes in investigating the limits of the correctness of their theories. However, such enquiry is always based upon some assumptions or 'background knowledge'. If successful, it will also have tentative results, in principle always open to further challenge by later investigations, which constitute what is usually referred to as the 'scientific knowledge' of the day.

---

[2] While I defend scientific realism in connection with OR, SR, ER, AR, and MR, I reject moral realism. Here I differ from Richard Boyd (1988), whose scientific realism includes a naturalist version of moral realism. This problem is discussed below in Section 8.2. See also Ch. 10.

[3] The characterization of science as 'self-corrective' is due to Peirce. See Peirce *Collected Papers* (*CP*), 5.575.

In this sense, science is a 'local belief system' which can be compared and contrasted with other methods that are used to acquire beliefs about the world: myths, religion, metaphysics, and common sense.

The history of Western culture has been dominated by world views which combine ingredients from different domains: religion, metaphysics, and science have coexisted, as they are taken to deal with separate problems by their own methods. On the other hand, the contents of these belief systems may also be in direct conflict with each other: for example, our current scientific knowledge about the evolution of human beings contradicts a literal interpretation of Genesis. There may also be a potential conflict in content, if religion or metaphysics makes claims about cognitive problems that science has not yet solved. But, in such a case, there is also a clash between acceptable methods in the pursuit of truth: for example, it is not acceptable by scientific standards to adopt religious beliefs on the basis of faith without any rational grounds or evidence (as the 'fideists' recommend), or on the basis of holy scriptures and personal mystic experiences.

Let us define the *scientific world view* as the position that science is the *only* legitimate source of beliefs about reality. A slightly more cautious formulation says that science, as we know it today, is the *best* method (or at least a better method than any other) for pursuing knowledge. A person advocating the scientific world view accepts only beliefs that are in principle justifiable by scientific methods (e.g. large parts of our common-sense views and beliefs obtained through reliable sources of information may be included here), and in a cognitive conflict situation prefers the results of science to opposite claims.

One form of the scientific world view is *positivism*, founded by Auguste Comte in the 1830s. Comte believed in a historical law of progress for humanity: religion is replaced by metaphysics, which in turn is overcome by 'positive science' (see Comte 1970).[4] Another form of positivism was formulated half a century later in Ernst Mach's phenomenalism: the world is a 'complex of sensations', and the task of science is to give an 'economical' description of it (see Mach 1959). Mach's views inspired the 'monistic' movement led by Wilhelm Ostwald.

In this strict empiricist tradition, the metaphysical systems of traditional philosophy are taken to be false or unjustified. But as scientific knowledge is here restricted to beliefs that are certain by empirical

---

[4] Even though Comte's 'law' has some truth in it as a very broad generalization of the trend of Enlightenment in history, he clearly underestimated the force of myths and religions in captivating the thinking of mortal humankind.

evidence, this view also cuts from science its theoretical aspects. Thus, this kind of scientific world view is anti-realistic with respect to scientific theories. However, it may nevertheless 'accept' theories in a sense which does not involve the ideas of truth and knowledge. For example, according to *instrumentalism*, theories lack truth values but still are more or less useful tools for predicting observable events.[5]

Comte's programme was continued in a more radical form by the Vienna Circle (Moritz Schlick, Rudolf Carnap, Otto Neurath). Its 1929 pamphlet on the 'scientific outlook' asserted that religion and metaphysics should be rejected, since they only treat 'pseudoproblems' and contain 'meaningless' statements. The logical empiricists proposed criteria (such as verifiability and empirical testability) which would imply that all metaphysics is without 'cognitive significance', but such criteria turned out to be either ineffective or too strong (again cutting away much of the quantitative and theoretical parts of genuine science) (cf. Hempel 1965: ch. 4). The verification criterion is still used as a weapon against general epistemological scepticism in Michael Dummett's (1978) semantical anti-realism (cf. Section 4.6).

Karl Popper's (1959) criterion of falsifiability for demarcating science and metaphysics (which for him is non-scientific but not meaningless) implied that all unrestricted existence claims are metaphysical. In spite of his support for the realist interpretation of theories against instrumental-ism (Popper 1963), and his insistence that existential statements may be parts of well-tested theories, his demarcation criterion lumps, in a problematic way, statements like 'God exists', 'Electrons exist', and 'Stones exist' into the same class of metaphysics (cf. Popper 1974).

The realist interpretation of theories was defended after 1950 by, among others, Herbert Feigl, Wilfrid Sellars, J. J. C. Smart, Mario Bunge, and Hilary Putnam. However, if the realist allows for statements which go beyond the limit of observability, the borderline with metaphysics becomes problem-atic again. Thomas Kuhn and Imre Lakatos argued in the 1960s that all scientific research programmes contain metaphysical background assump-tions, which are taken to be irrefutable as long as the programme is continued and become overthrown only when the whole programme is eventually rejected (see Lakatos and Musgrave 1970). Thus, in spite of many examples of clear cases, it is not evident that there is a sharp dividing line between science and metaphysics after all. Further, to

---

[5] Instrumentalism has a long history in astronomy: in the Platonic tradition, an astro-nomical theory was expected merely to 'save the phenomena', instead of being a realistic hypothesis with a truth value (true or false). See Duhem (1969) and the examples in Section 5.4.

support the realist view of science, perhaps some 'metaphysical' concepts and background assumptions are needed.[6]

In its earlier historical development, science was associated with belief systems and fields of study (e.g. astrology) which are non-scientific by the present standards. Today philosophers demarcate science from such *pseudo-sciences*, which often try to disguise themselves as 'scientific' disciplines (e.g. parapsychology, scientology, anthroposophy, creationism, ufology), by means of criteria which appeal to factors like critical method, intersubjective testability, progress, and autonomy.[7]

The positions discussed above can be expressed in a general form as follows. Let W be a belief system (i.e. a part of a world view). Then a *W-realist* is one who takes W seriously as a source of acceptable cognitive attitudes about the world. This means that he is at least a 'broad' (or 'Dummettian') realist who assigns a truth value to the beliefs in W, but he may also be a 'narrow' realist who accepts the beliefs in W as true or truthlike in a realist sense (cf. Bigelow 1994). A *W-anti-realist* instead may support the 'weak' thesis that W is false, or the 'strong' (or 'Dummettian') claim that the statements in W are meaningless and lack truth values. A weak or strong W-anti-realist may, nevertheless, 'accept' W in some weaker non-cognitive sense which does not imply the claim that W represents reality.

Thus, a religious realist typically claims that there are gods, angels, demons, fairies, brownies, etc. with characteristic features and behaviour. A 'narrow' religious realist is a theist, a 'weak' religious anti-realist is an atheist, while a 'strong' religious anti-realist asserts that religious statements are metaphysical and meaningless (cf. Abraham 1985). A metaphysical realist asserts the existence of some abstract entities and principles (such as Plato's ideas, Leibniz's monads, Hegel's objective spirit) which are not accessible to the scientific method. A *common-sense realist* takes our everyday beliefs about 'ordinary objects' to be correct. A *scientific realist* in the broad sense treats all scientific statements as claims with truth values; in the narrow sense, the realist tentatively endorses scientific knowledge as true or truthlike, and accepts the existence of the theoretical entities postulated by successful theories.

It is important to emphasize, as we have seen in the case of positivism, that all advocates of the scientific world view are not scientific realists. Conversely, some scientific realists are not willing to commit themselves

---

[6] In this spirit, we shall discuss some 'metaphysical' issues, especially in Ch. 2. Putnam's attack against what he calls 'metaphysical realism' is discussed in Ch. 7.

[7] For the demarcation problem between science and pseudo-science, see Popper (1959), Grim (1982), Niiniluoto (1984: ch. 1), and Laudan (1996).

to the scientific world view, but try to maintain a 'peaceful coexistence' between science and religion, both in the broad sense.

This broad sense is not the only possible way of understanding the nature of world views, however. Ernst Cassirer's (1965) neo-Kantian approach advocates relativism about world views: science, metaphysics, art, religion, and myth are 'symbolic forms' that have their own standards of truth and objectivity. Another influential trend, inspired by Ludwig Wittgenstein's later philosophy, is to accept religion and myths as language-games—without commitment to any beliefs as holding-to-be-true (see Wilson 1970). In other words, such approaches favour religion and myths in the strong anti-realist fashion without regarding them as sources of knowledge about the world. At the same time, they make their position immune to cognitive criticism and argumentation.

Science is often contrasted with the world view of *common sense* which is based upon our everyday experience (cf. Devitt 1991; Musgrave 1993). This contrast is sometimes thought to imply that common sense is a form of *naive realism* which takes the world to be precisely as it appears to us, while religion, metaphysics, and science add some interpretation over and above the 'raw' material of 'pure' perception. However, it is more plausible to admit that even our everyday perceptions are 'laden' with our practical interests, conceptual categories, and theoretical assumptions (see Kaila 1979): we tend to see what we wish, are able to detect, and expect. Hence, there is no unique common-sense framework, and 'naive realism' is itself a myth. But this does not prevent us from speaking about the common-sense view that dominates in a culture at a certain time.

The world view of a common-sense realist is called the *manifest image* by Wilfrid Sellars (1963). It differs from the 'original image' where all inanimate and animate things are still conceived as thinking and acting agents. The manifest image includes a conception of man as a person or agent, but it also assumes the existence of ordinary observable objects (stones, trees, tables, stars). Sellars allows that this image is closed under elementary scientific inference, such as inductive generalization. It thus includes what is now called 'folk physics' and 'folk psychology' (Churchland 1988). The manifest image is thus a kind of surface level of the common-sense conceptions of a typical member of our contemporary culture.

According to Sellars, the *scientific image* differs from the manifest one primarily by its reliance on the 'method of postulation': scientific theories introduce unobservable theoretical entities to explain the behaviour of the observable objects. The scientific image is not uniquely fixed, since new theories are proposed to improve the earlier ones—the true theory, Sellars (1968) urges, is reached only in the ideal 'Peirceish' limit. A scientific realist is, therefore, committed only to the existence of the entities postulated by this limit theory.

It is characteristic of Sellarsian realism that the scientific image is taken to replace the manifest image, and the 'scientific objects' eliminate those of 'folk physics' and 'folk psychology'. Sellars thus advocates a strong form of *eliminativist* realism: the objects of the manifest image are 'unreal' (cf. Pitt 1981). Weaker non-eliminativist realism instead accepts that both scientific and manifest entities may be real (see, for example, Popper 1972; Bunge 1977–9; Boyd 1984; Tuomela 1985).

Eliminativism thus applies against common sense its strong attachment to the scientific world view: the progress of critical scientific thinking supports the thesis that fairies, demons, and gods are merely figments of our imagination. Similarly, the strong Sellarsian realist suggests that the common-sense objects of the manifest image will be abolished when science uncovers the true nature of reality: of Eddington's famous two tables (table as a middle-sized ordinary artefact, and table as a bunch of atoms), only the-table-as-described-by-physics really exists.[8]

On the other hand, many philosophers see no special problems in accepting both common-sense and scientific realism; Peirce called such a view 'critical common-sensism'. For example, Devitt takes the former to be committed to the mind-independent existence of the 'tokens of most current observable common-sense and scientific physical types', and the latter to the tokens of 'most current unobservable scientific physical types' (1991: 24). However, if it is added that the latter entities '(approximately) obey the laws of science', as Devitt does (ibid. 47), the conflict between common sense and science becomes apparent: scientific theories make common-sense generalizations more precise and, at least in some respects, correct them. Then the consistency of a position which endorses both common-sense and scientific realism at the same time becomes problematic. As we shall see (Section 5.3), this issue can be resolved by means of the concepts of approximate truth and truthlikeness.

## 1.3  Critical scientific realism and its rivals

We are now in a position to summarize the kind of scientific realism that will be defended in this book. The varieties of realism and its

---

[8] Tuomela (1985) gives a detailed discussion of Sellarsian realism and its variations. This strong realism has inspired the so-called eliminative materialists—Feyerabend and Rorty in the 1960s, Patricia and Paul Churchland in the 1980s. See P. S. Churchland (1986) and P. M. Churchland (1979; 1988). See also Section 5.4.

alternatives are charted in Fig. 1 in terms of their attitudes toward truth (cf. Niiniluoto 1986*b*).[9]

*Critical scientific realism* can be distinguished from its alternatives by the following theses (cf. Niiniluoto 1987*b*):

At least part of reality is ontologically independent of human minds.                                                          (R0)

Truth is a semantical relation between language and reality. Its meaning is given by a modern (Tarskian) version of the correspondence theory, and its best indicator is given by systematic enquiry using the methods of science.          (R1)

The concepts of truth and falsity are in principle applicable to all linguistic products of scientific enquiry, including observation reports, laws, and theories. In particular, claims about the existence of theoretical entities have a truth value.                                                                          (R2)

Truth (together with some other epistemic utilities) is an essential aim of science.                                              (R3)

Truth is not easily accessible or recognizable, and even our best theories can fail to be true. Nevertheless, it is possible to approach the truth, and to make rational assessments of such cognitive progress.                                            (R4)

The best explanation for the practical success of science is the assumption that scientific theories in fact are approximately true or sufficiently close to the truth in the relevant respects. Hence, it is rational to believe that the use of the self-corrective methods of science in the long run has been, and will be, progressive in the cognitive sense.          (R5)

Thesis (R0) is the minimum assumption which distinguishes *ontological realists* from subjective idealists, solipsists, and phenomenalists. The logical positivists of the early Vienna Circle rejected (R0) as a metaphysical claim without accepting its negation, either.

---

[9] The reader should be warned that a chart like Fig. 1 is a heuristic device. Especially when names of philosophers are linked with its branches, interpretations and qualifications are needed. For example, Paul Feyerabend (1975) calls himself a 'methodological anarchist' (see Section 10.3), but he is mainly attacking the idea of scientific method, rather than truth, so that his position can be best classified as scepticism (see Section 4.1). The branch of 'anarchism', which claims that there is no coherent notion of truth at all, might include some postmodern or poststructuralist thinkers (see the criticism in Norris 1996). Note also that, among major thinkers, we have not placed Thomas Kuhn in Fig. 1. Cf. Ch. 7 for the interpretation of Kuhn as an internal realist.

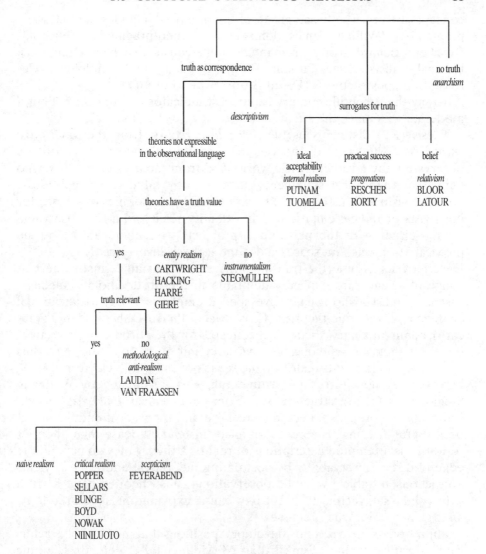

FIG. 1. Realism and its alternatives

Thesis (R1) separates the *semantical realists*, who define truth as correspondence between language and reality, from the *pragmatists*, who replace this realist concept of truth with some epistemic surrogate (such as verified, proved, coherent with our knowledge, warrantedly assertable, limit of enquiry, consensus of the scientific community), and from the epistemological *anarchists*, who deny the existence of any reasonable concept of truth. The broad group of 'pragmatists' includes here classical pragmatists (William James, John Dewey), neo-pragmatists (Nicholas Rescher, Richard Rorty), semantical anti-realists (Michael Dummett), internal realists (Hilary Putnam, Raimo Tuomela), and sociological relativists and constructivists (David Bloor, Bruno Latour).

To say that scientific enquiry is our best indicator of truth is to adopt a moderate version of the scientific world view (cf. Section 1.2).

Thesis (R2) distinguishes the *theoretical realists* from the *descriptive empiricists*, who regard theories as economical descriptions of the observationally given empirical world, and from the *instrumentalists*, who deny that theoretical statements have a truth value (cf. Nagel 1961). Descriptivism and instrumentalism are typical philosophies of science for positivists or radical empiricists who identify reality with the observable world—either with the perceptual 'p-objects' (phenomenalism) or the physical 'f-objects' in space and time (physicalism) (cf. Kaila 1979). Descriptivists assume the translatability thesis that all terms in the language of science are explicitly definable in the observational language. Instrumentalists, who usually give special emphasis to the idealizational character of scientific theories (Ernst Mach, Pierre Duhem, Henri Poincaré), admit 'auxiliary' theoretical concepts for the purpose of prediction, but treat them as symbolic tools without interpretation—they are thus 'strong' theoretical anti-realists in the sense of Section 1.2 (cf. Worrall 1989, however). A new form of instrumentalism is formulated by Wolfgang Stegmüller's (1976) 'structuralism'. Some anti-realists make the 'weak' claim that theoretical statements are false and theoretical entities are at best useful fictions. Theoretical realists instead at least take theories seriously as attempted descriptions of reality: a theory may go beyond the edge of direct observability by postulating theoretical entities, if it yields predictions testable by public observation. Thus, theories have a truth value, and a satisfactory theoretical or causal explanation is required to be an argument with true premises.

Philosophers have recently developed positions that might be characterized as critical 'half-realism'. Ernan McMullin (1984) defends scientific realism, but suggests that theoretical laws are metaphorical statements which are not 'literally true or false'. John Worrall (1989) favours *structural realism* which is realist with respect to theoretical laws but not with respect to theoretical entities. Nancy Cartwright (1983) defends *entity realism*, accepting theoretical entities which play a role in causal explanations, but denies realism about theoretical laws (see also Hacking 1983; Harré 1986; Giere 1989). As we shall see in Chapter 5, my own favourite form of critical realism goes beyond both structural and entity realism: it appeals to the idea that theoretical statements in science—both universal ones expressing laws and existential ones expressing ontological claims—may be strictly speaking false but nevertheless 'truthlike' or 'approximately true'.

Thesis (R3) separates the *axiological realists* from the *axiological and methodological non-realists* who admit that theories have a truth value, but regard it as irrelevant to the aims and procedures of science. This kind of non-realism usually regards the truth of theories as inaccessible and replaces it as an aim of science with some methodological surrogate—such as successful prediction, simplicity, or problem-solving ability (Nelson Goodman, Thomas Kuhn, Larry Laudan). Bas van Fraassen's (1980) *constructive empiricism* requires that a theory should save the phenomena by being 'empirically adequate': what the theory says about the observable should be true.

Finally, theses (R4) and (R5) distinguish the *critical realists* from the *naive realists*, who believe that certified truth is easily accessible, and from the *sceptics*, who deny the possibility of true knowledge or progress towards it. Paul Feyerabend, who started his career as a scientific realist, can be mentioned as a contemporary sceptic. Critical realism has been represented by the 'fallibilist' tradition in epistemology. In its two main variants, fallibilism claims that scientific theories are either uncertain-but-probably-true or false-but-truthlike hypotheses. It has been advocated by such diverse thinkers as Friedrich Engels, Charles Peirce, Karl Popper, Mario Bunge, and Wilfrid Sellars (cf. Niiniluoto 1987a).[10]

One cannot help admiring the skill and vigour with which these alternative philosophical positions have been developed. Their great variety is also appreciated by critical scientific realists who wish to learn from both their allies and opponents.

## 1.4 Realism and the method of philosophy

In defending critical scientific realism, I shall proceed by discussing ontological, semantical, epistemological, axiological/methodological, and

---

[10] The term 'critical realism' has been used in the history of philosophy in different senses. Kant's philosophy is often called 'critical', as he wrote three famous *Critiques*, but Kant was not a scientific realist. Peirce called himself 'a scholastic realist'. Later American pragmatism, especially John Dewey, was attacked by a group of 'critical realists' (see Morgenbesser 1977). A book on *Critical Realism* was published by the 'evolutionary naturalist' Roy Wood Sellars in 1916 (see Hooker 1987). Moritz Schlick's early work *Allgemeine Erkenntnislehre* of 1918 (see Schlick 1985), which attacked Machian positivism and neo-Kantianism, was characterized as 'empiricist critical realism' by his student Herbert Feigl in 1938 (see Schlick 1979: p. xx). Popper called his philosophy 'critical rationalism'. See also Bhaskar (1989).

ethical questions in separate chapters. In due course, the branches of
Fig. 1 will be explicated and assessed in more detail. Here it is in order to
make some additional remarks on the philosophical method that I shall
follow in my argument.

(a) *Formal vs. historical methodology*. The message of the Kuhnian
revolution was sometimes interpreted as the thesis that philosophy of
science should follow a descriptive historical method—and give up the
Carnapian quest for the logical and quantitative explication of concepts.
While we may agree with Lakatos that 'philosophy of science without
history of science is empty; history of science without philosophy of
science is blind' (Lakatos 1976: 1), a sharp contrast between formal
and historical methods in science studies is nevertheless misleading and
unnecessary. Logical and quantitative methods are by no means restricted
to the 'synchronic' study of completed scientific systems, but can be applied
as well to the 'diachronic' study of scientific change.

At least since Derek de Solla Price's *Little Science, Big Science* (1963),
it has been clear that the growth of science (measured by the volume
of the literary output of the scientists) can be studied by quantitative
methods. Science indicators, now investigated in 'scientometrics' and
widely used as a tool of science policy, are as such not measures of the
growth of knowledge, since they simply count publications and citations
by ignoring their semantic content (see Section 6.1). But this is no inherent limitation of the quantitative method. Thus, the Carnap–Hintikka
measures of semantic information or the Tichý–Oddie–Niiniluoto
measures of verisimilitude can be used for expressing, in quantitative
terms, that a new body of scientific knowledge 'tells more' and is 'closer to
the truth' than an old one (cf. Section 3.5). The latter measures also allow
us to make precise such Peircean notions of dynamic epistemology as
'approach' or 'converge towards the truth'. Further, it is by now well
established and accepted that the study of theories and scientific change
can successfully employ concepts borrowed from set theory (the 'structuralism' of Suppes, Sneed, and Stegmüller) and logical model theory
(Pearce 1987a).

As Nowak (1980) correctly observes, when philosophers of science give
descriptions of scientific activities, they usually make some idealizing
assumptions. It is then an important task to make these descriptions more
realistic by gradually removing these assumptions. Another task is to
derive, relative to a sufficiently accurate description of science and to some
philosophical (axiological) premises, methodological recommendations
for doing good science (cf. Section 6.2). Formal methods may be useful for
both of these tasks.

(*b*) *Normativism vs. naturalism.* Logical empiricism is often portrayed as an attempt to establish by logical analysis and rational reconstruction general prescriptions for sound science, or ideal models and norms expressing what science ought to be. Thus, philosophy of science is an a priori account of scientific rationality. On the other hand, the pragmatist tradition—in the broad sense exemplified by W. V. O. Quine's (1969) 'naturalized epistemology' and the historical/sociological approach to the philosophy of science—holds that scientific rationality has to be grounded in the actual practice of scientific research.[11]

In my view, philosophy has a lot to learn from empirical or factual disciplines like psychology, cognitive science, and the history and sociology of science. But this does not mean that epistemology could be reduced to empirical psychology, as Quine suggests, any more than ethics can be reduced to cultural anthropology. One obstacle for such reduction is *conceptual*: while human beliefs may be objects of 'naturalized' empirical and theoretical studies, epistemological concepts like 'truth', 'justification', 'confirmation', and 'knowledge' are not determined by 'nature', but rather their specification or definition is a matter of philosophical dispute. In the same way, the demarcation between science and non-science is a basic problem in the philosophy of science, and every attempt to study the actual history and practice of science already presupposes some answer to this problem.

Another obstacle for reduction comes from the *normative* dimension. As 'ought implies can', it may be reasonable to demand that normative epistemology does not go beyond the factual human capabilities in cognition. The descriptive question of how we actually think is thus relevant to the normative question of how we ought to think (cf. Kornblith 1985). But this does not mean that the latter could be solved simply by studying the former. I shall illustrate this by commenting on the debate between 'normativists' and 'naturalists' in the philosophy of science.

Following Lakatos in the 'naturalist' demand that methodology should be tested against the actual historical record of the sciences, Laudan (1977) required that a methodological theory should capture as rational certain intuitively clear cases of good science. Later he rejected this 'intuitionist meta-methodology' (Laudan 1986). But even if Laudan explicitly acknowledged the 'palpable implausibility' of the claim that 'most of what has gone on in science has been rational' (ibid. 117), he still insisted that theories of scientific change (Kuhn, Feyerabend, Lakatos, Laudan) should be tested by the actual history of science. The following quotation suggests

---

[11] See the discussion in Hempel (1983) and Kornblith (1985).

that Laudan in fact is willing to include all historical cases among the relevant test cases:

> In their original forms, these philosophical models are often couched in normative language. Whenever possible we have recast their claims about how science ought to behave into declarative statements about how science does behave. We have a reasonably clear conscience about such translations since all the authors whose work we have paraphrased are explicitly committed to the claim that *science, because it is rational, will normally behave in ways which those authors normatively endorse.* . . . it is plain that philosophers of the historical school draw the internal/external distinction so as to include within the range for which their normative views are accountable virtually all the widely cited and familiar historical episodes of post-16th century physical science. (Laudan *et al*. 1986: 148–9, my italics)

The programme for 'testing theories of scientific change' has already produced impressive and useful case studies (see Donovan, Laudan, and Laudan 1988). But if the cognitive aims and methods of scientists have changed throughout history, as Laudan convincingly argues in *Science and Values* (1984*a*), and if the scientists have acted on the basis of their methodological principles, it simply cannot be the case that 'virtually all' historical cases could exhibit the same shared pattern of methodological rules. Hence, there is no hope whatsoever that any non-trivial normative theory of scientific change could pass 'empirical tests'.

If a case study reveals, for example, that Galileo or Ampère did not appeal to novel predictions to support their theories, does this 'contra-indicate' Lakatos's demand that a good theory ought to be successful in making novel predictions? Instead of using Galileo's and Ampère's behaviour as 'tests' of methodological rules, we may simply conclude that they had not read Whewell's, Popper's, and Lakatos's writings. In this sense, a normative *ought* cannot be derived from, or refuted by, a historical *is*.

Similar problems arise, if the naturalist programme is applied to contemporary scientists. Ron Giere, in his book *Explaining Science* (1988), gives interesting material to show that high-energy physicists at least sometimes behave as 'satisfiers'. He also suggests that the long debate on whether 'scientists, as scientists, *should* be Bayesian information processors' is futile:

> We need not pursue this debate any further, for there is now overwhelming empirical evidence that no Bayesian model fits the thoughts or actions of real scientists. For too long philosophers have debated how scientists ought to judge hypotheses in glaring ignorance of how scientists in fact judge hypotheses. (Ibid. 149)

But this view ignores the fact that, for centuries, theory and practice have already been in a mutual interaction in the field of scientific inference. Scientists learn to do science through implicit indoctrination and explicit instruction from their masters, textbooks, and colleagues. So if a case study reveals that a group of real scientists favours 'bold hypotheses' and 'severe tests', we may judge that they, or their teachers, have read Popper. And if some scientists do not behave like Bayesian optimizers, the reason is probably that the Department of Statistics—and the introductory courses of methodology—in their university are dominated by representatives of the 'orthodox' Neyman–Pearson school (cf. Mayo 1996).

To avoid this kind of vicious circularity in the testing procedure, we should find some strange tribe of scientists who have never been contaminated by any methodological or philosophical ideas. But naturalism is certainly implausible, if it suggests that the best advice for the conduct of science can be learned from those of its practitioners who are most ignorant of methodology!

These remarks indicate, in my view, that the debate between the positions of Fig. 1 cannot be resolved by studying how scientists in fact behave. While it is important for the scientific realists to have a realistic picture of scientific activities, and therefore to pay serious attention to historical and sociological case studies, they should also maintain the possibility of criticizing the way science is actually done. In considering the ontological, semantical, epistemological, axiological, methodological, and ethical problems, we need support from scientific knowledge, but genuinely philosophical aspects of these issues remain in the agenda. These observations mean, against naturalism, that the choice between the interesting positions will at least partly be based upon philosophical premisses. This is also a motivation for discussing many traditional philosophical issues in a book on scientific realism.

I am not advocating a return to a foundationalist 'first philosophy' in the sense criticized by Quine. Today we often hear the claim that science does not at all need philosophy as its foundation. This thesis has been supported in two radically different ways. The 'positivist' view (Quine) urges that science may be a child of philosophy, but has since grown completely independent of her mother, i.e. mature science has happily got rid of metaphysics and epistemology. The 'postmodern' view (Richard Rorty) asserts against the 'Kantians' that nothing has foundations; hence, science in particular has no foundations either (cf. Rouse 1996). Both views seem to imply that there is no special task for a philosophy of science: science studies simply collapse into historical and sociological description. For the positivist, this is motivated by the belief that science, as it is, is the paradigm of human rationality. For the postmodern thinker, on the other hand, there is no interesting account of rationality to be found anywhere.

I think both of these extremes are wrong. Science as a rational cognitive enterprise is not yet complete: its tentative results are always corrigible and in need of analysis and interpretation, and its methods can still be improved in their reliability and effectiveness. The ethics of science also has to be developed as a part of the philosophical conversation about the social role of scientific practices. Philosophy of science cannot give any absolute and final foundation for science, but it cannot leave science as it is. There is a legitimate need to raise normative questions about scientific enquiry and knowledge, to set up standards, and (if necessary) also to criticize the activities of science. To be sure, such pronouncements are fallible and cannot be expounded from an armchair: philosophy of science and special sciences have to be able to engage in a mutual dialogue.

(c) *Natural ontological attitude.* The problem of realism has haunted philosophers so long that every now and then there appear attempts to 'dissolve' this query by rejecting it.

The most famous of these attempts was made by the Vienna Circle: in his programme of 'overcoming metaphysics by the logical analysis of language', Carnap announced in 1928 that the realism debate was a meaningless pseudo-problem (see Carnap 1967). Schlick's famous article in 1931 declared that both realism and anti-realism (positivism) were meaningless theses (see Schlick 1959). However, both of these claims were based upon very narrow empiricist criteria of meaning: translatability to the phenomenalistic language of elementary experiences (Carnap), and verifiability in principle by observations (Schlick). Such strict theories of meaning were soon liberalized, and the realism debate was resurrected.[12]

Arthur Fine (1984) claims that 'realism is well and truly dead'. Its death had already been announced by neo-positivists, the process was hastened by the victory of Niels Bohr's non-realist philosophy of quantum mechanics over Albert Einstein's realism, and the death was finally certified when 'the last two generations of physical scientists turned their backs on realism and have managed, nevertheless, to do science successfully without it'.

Fine—well known for his earlier sustained attempts to defend a realist interpretation of quantum theory (cf. Fine 1986b)—is not advocating anti-realism, either: anti-realism is not 'the winner in the philosophical debate that realism has lost' (cf. Fine 1986a). What he suggests instead as

---

[12] See e.g. the work of Eino Kaila in the 1930s (Kaila 1979). See also Carnap (1936–7) and Reichenbach (1951).

'a third way' is the *natural ontological attitude* (NOA): accept the results of science in the same way as the evidence of our senses, but resist the impulse to ask any questions or to propose any additions that go beyond the history and practice of science itself. Thus, NOA claims to be neither realist nor anti-realist, since it refuses to talk of 'the external world' or to propose any particular analysis of the concept of truth. Here Fine's position agrees with the 'minimalist' account of truth (see Horwich 1990) and with anti-foundationalist denials of 'a first philosophy' (cf. Pihlström 1998).

Fine's NOA can also be regarded as an expression of philosophical despair. He in effect suggests that we suspend judgement about the positions in Fig. 1—not because they are meaningless (as the Vienna Circle urged), nor because they are irrelevant for the actual practice of science,[13] but rather because there are no resources for settling such philosophical disputes. Perhaps this is a 'natural attitude' towards philosophy—but not one that we philosophers are willing to take, in spite of the fact that battles between such wholesale philosophical orientations as realism and anti-realism will never be finally settled.

What is more, it seems to me clear that NOA after all is a variant of realism (Niiniluoto 1987c), even if it wishes to avoid the customary realist jargon and its refinements (such as the concept of approximate truth). According to Fine, NOA accepts as a 'core position' the results of scientific investigations as being 'true', on a par with 'more homely truths' (Fine 1984: 86). NOA treats truth in 'the usual referential way'—that means, presumably, something like the Tarskian fashion (cf. Musgrave 1989)—and so 'commits us, via truth, to the existence of the individuals, properties, relations, processes, and so forth referred to by the scientific statements that we accept as true' (Fine 1984: 98). Unless 'existence' has a very *unnatural* meaning here, this is a realist position. For example, a statement about the existence of electrons could not be scientifically acceptable, and thus part of NOA's core position, if electrons existed only in a subjective, phenomenalist, mind-dependent way.[14]

---

[13] Fine in fact argues that a non-realist attitude has been important for the success of quantum theory. Only some years earlier, he defended the opposite claim that 'contemporary science as a whole is struggling to free itself' from the 'regressive, if still somewhat fashionable, scientific ideology', namely 'the deeply positivist legacy of Bohr and Heisenberg' (Fine 1979).

[14] Fine (1986a) argues against 'the realist picture of an objective, external world' by raising two problems. The problem of 'reciprocity' follows from the fact that 'whatever we causally interact with, is certainly not independent of us' (p. 151). But this is a confusion of causal and ontological concepts of independence (see below Section 2.3). The problem of 'contamination' claims that interaction can give only 'information about interacted-with-things'. This issue is discussed below in Ch. 7. Cf. also Musgrave (1989).

Musgrave (1989) suggests the possible interpretation that Fine's NOA is 'complete philosophical know-nothing-ism'. But if NOA, in this interpretation, leaves it completely open which statements are to be taken 'at face value', then NOA knows nothing at all—and thus is reduced to global scepticism. This is clearly in contradiction with Fine's own statements about the core position. Hence, Musgrave concludes that NOA is 'a thoroughly realist view'.

In my own evaluation, realism is undoubtedly alive. In particular, as I shall argue in the subsequent chapters, it is only recently that realists have developed adequate logical tools for defending the crucial theses (R4) and (R5), i.e. for showing in what sense even idealizational theories may be truthlike, how the truthlikeness of scientific statements can be estimated on evidence, and how the approximate truth of a theory explains its empirical success. Even though philosophical debates do not end with winners and losers, critical scientific realism has at least been able to make progress (cf. Pearce 1987b).

# 2

# Realism in Ontology

As an ontological thesis, realism is the doctrine that there exists a mind-independent reality. This simple formulation is liable to be misleading: as we shall see in this chapter, ontological realism in fact turns out to be compatible with a surprising variety of philosophical positions. There are also parts of reality that exist in a mind-dependent or mind-involving way, as Popper reminds us in his theory of World 3. After reviewing traditional metaphysical issues in Sections 2.1 and 2.2, I shall outline my own favourite version of physical ontology that I call 'tropic realism' (Section 2.3). The most basic arguments for ontological realism are also formulated (Section 2.4).

## 2.1 Materialism, dualism, and idealism

Traditionally, the three most influential metaphysical views are materialism, dualism, and idealism (see Fig. 2). As most ontological discussions are still conducted with this terminology, I shall briefly summarize these views in this section.

According to *materialism*, everything is composed of, or determined by, matter, where matter as a substance is characterized by its being 'extended' (as Descartes said), i.e. located in space and time, and thereby the object of the physical sciences. While the structure and properties of matter are gradually revealed by physics (atoms, elementary particles, quarks, fields of energy, superstrings, space-time, etc.), philosophical materialism has emphasized that matter exists 'outside' our mind and independently of it. At the same time, mind itself is material in some sense, or at least depends on matter.

Materialism has three main varieties, as distinguished by C. D. Broad (1925). *Radical* or *eliminative* materialism claims that all terms referring to the mental are 'delusive': their alleged referents are simply unreal (cf. Churchland 1988). *Reductive* materialists accept the existence of the mental, but claim that it is in fact identical with, or 'nothing but', some class of material phenomena (things or processes) (cf. Smart 1968). *Emergent*

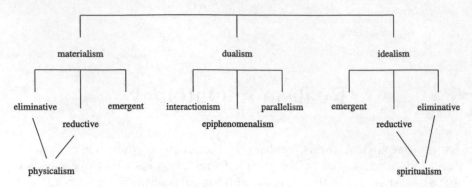

FIG. 2. Metaphysical views

materialists accept the existence of some mental phenomena which are 'emergent', causally efficient properties of sufficiently complex material wholes or systems (cf. Bunge 1977–9; Margolis 1978; Searle 1992; Niiniluoto 1994b). Such emergent properties of a system S cannot be derived by any true physical theory from information concerning the elements of S and their interrelations—in this sense, a whole may be 'non-additive', more than the sum of its parts.[1] This view does not assume any substance outside matter, but acknowledges the existence of non-physical properties— therefore, it is also called *property dualism*.[2]

According to *idealism*, everything is composed of, or determined by, mind, where mind or spirit as a substance is characterized by thinking (Descartes), consciousness, or intentionality (Brentano). This doctrine has two main versions: in *subjective idealism*, mind always refers to the mental life of individual human subjects; in *objective idealism*, there is a superhuman and all-embracing 'objective mind' outside and above the subjective finite human minds. Subjective idealism thus includes doctrines like *solipsism* ('the world equals the contents of my thought'), Bishop Berkeley's slogan *esse est percipi* ('to exist is to be perceived'), and Mach's *phenomenalism* ('the world consists of sensations and their complexes'). Objective idealism is represented by the omnipotent and spiritual God of many religions, Plato's ideas, Plotinos' One, Spinoza's substance, and Hegel's absolute spirit.

Just like materialism, the two versions of idealism may exist in three

[1] Emergence is often defined as an epistemic and theory-relative term: an emergent property of a whole (relative to theory T) is not deducible by means of T from a characterization of its parts (see Hempel 1965: 263; Nagel 1961: 368–71). I employ here an ontological or metaphysical definition which quantifies over all (not only actually known) true theories. See also the essays in Beckermann, Flohr, and Kim (1992).

[2] This term is used by Churchland (1988). For a representative collection of recent work on physicalism and materialism, see Moser and Trout (1995).

forms: eliminative, reductive, and emergent. Carnap's *Aufbau* with its 'autopsychological' basis (if interpreted 'materially' as an ontological doctrine, against Carnap's own wish) was an example of reductive subjective idealism (cf. Carnap 1967). Hegel's system, where nature and subjective minds are generated from the ultimate spiritual reality, is an example of emergent objective idealism.

Against the 'monistic' views of materialism and idealism, *dualism* claims that matter and mind are two independently existing substances. Descartes's *interactionism* assumes that matter and mind are in causal interaction; Spinoza's *parallelism* takes matter and mind to consist of 'parallel' series of events which do not causally influence each other; finally, T. H. Huxley's *epiphenomenalism* conceives the mental as a kind of shadow causally produced by the material basic events, but without constituting a genuine causal process which has independent causal powers.

## 2.2 *Popper's three worlds*

Karl Popper's three worlds ontology, introduced in 1960, gives us a convenient way of expressing the distinctions of Section 2.1.[3]

In Popper's terminology, *World 1* contains physical things and processes—from middle-sized ordinary objects (stones, tables) to small (atoms, electrons, cells), large (stars, galaxies), and process-like entities (fields of force). In brief, World 1 consists of the material—both inorganic and organic—nature.

*World 2* is the domain of consciousness, in both animals (with a central nervous system) and human beings. It consists of the mental states and processes within individual minds. For humanity, World 2 thus contains what is called 'psyche' or 'soul'.

*World 3* consists of the products of human social action. For Popper, the typical denizens of this realm are abstract entities like propositions, arguments, theories, and natural numbers. But, unlike Plato, he conceives them as human-made, often unintentional by-products of social action, especially the creation of symbolic languages. Besides such human-made abstractions, World 3 may be taken to include other artefacts—such as tools, works of art, cultural products, and social institutions. In brief, World 3 is composed of all those abstract, cultural, and social entities which are neither (merely) physical things and processes nor 'in our heads'.

Materialism can now be characterized as the doctrine that takes World 1 to be ontologically and temporally primary over Worlds 2 and 3.

[3] See Popper (1972). See also Niiniluoto (1984: ch. 9; 1992*b*) and Pihlström (1996).

Eliminative materialism claims that only World 1 exists. Reductive materialism allows talk about World 2 and 3 entities, but asserts that they are identical with, or reducible to, World 1 entities and their complexes. For both of these views, World 1 is causally closed, and physics as the science of matter is ultimately able to give an account of the whole reality. Thus, they represent the doctrine of *physicalism* (cf. Fig. 2).

Similarly, World 2 is the primary part of reality for a subjective idealist. Eliminative and reductive forms of idealism claim that everything is really mental; thus, they represent the doctrine of *spiritualism*. The so-called 'neutral monists' are usually objective idealists: they take the original and ultimate reality to be non-material and non-subjective, so that it is similar to World 3, with the difference that it is not human-made.

So far the three 'worlds' have been used only as a convenient terminology which helps us to classify different types of entities. Popper himself associates his ontology with an evolutionary picture of reality and 'objective knowledge': Worlds 2 and 3 are evolutionary products of World 1. Neither of them could exist without World 1, but they have achieved a 'relatively independent' status by being able to influence World 1 entities causally by a 'feedback mechanism'. In other words, Worlds 1 and 2 are in causal interaction, and World 3 also influences World 1 via World 2. Such causal powers are for Popper criteria of reality, so that all the entities in the three worlds belong to reality. Yet, World 3 is human-made, not the pre-existing abstract realm of the Platonist.

The assumptions about causal connections between the three worlds have been perhaps the most controversial part of Popper's doctrine. In my view, there is an even more straightforward way of defending the reality of World 3 entities: our natural and scientific languages ontologically commit us to such things as numbers, concepts, novels, symphonies, and societies, and attempts to reduce them to physical or subjective mental entities have been utterly implausible (see e.g. Bunge 1981).

It has been argued that to speak about World 3 entities is illegitimate 'reification' of material human activities and practices (O'Hear 1980). However, on this basis it is difficult to account for the uniqueness of such entities as Beethoven's 'Eroica' Symphony: a symphony has multiple instances in Worlds 1 and 2, but it is not identical with any of them. Cultural entities in World 3 are not 'things' in an ordinary sense: they have a beginning in time, and perhaps sooner or later they will be destroyed, but they are not located in space. The 'Eroica' Symphony does not exist in space, even though its various kinds of physical and mental instances are so located.

If this line of thought is right, then the most natural and coherent interpretation of the three worlds doctrine is emergent materialism. This anti-reductionist view is thus a materialistic alternative to the physicalist reduction of World 3 to World 1. Realistic interpretations of science have been based upon both of these alternatives, and for most purposes in this book it is not necessary to settle the issue here. But especially in Chapters 7–9, it will be an important question whether Worlds 1 and 3 can be conceptually distinguished from each other in a reasonable way.

Another way of interpreting the three worlds ontology is emergent idealism: it usually takes World 3 to be primary, and then accepts Worlds 1 and 2 to be real as mental creations or social constructions. In Chapters 7–9, we have to argue also against such attempts to reduce World 1 to World 3.

Dualist views in the Cartesian tradition assert the independent existence of World 1 (matter) and World 2 (mind), but find difficulties in locating God in this ontology. Another kind of dualism is represented by the 'anti-humanist' French structuralists, who have announced the 'death of the subject' (i.e. the disappearance of the individual authentic Self in World 2), but admit the reality of material (World 1) and cultural (World 3) phenomena.

## 2.3  Existence, mind-independence, and reality

Specific realist theses in ontology concern the *existence* of some entity or a class of entities:

The entities in X exist.                                                  (1)

To be a realist about tables and atoms is to claim that tables and atoms exist (cf. Section 1.2).

The weak claim (1) does not yet say anything about the mode of existence of Xs. One specification of (1) would take Xs to be *physically* existent, i.e. to have a location in physical space and time:

The entities in X exist in physical space and time.              (2)

Some philosophers restrict the concept of existence to physical existence; if they admit something spatio-temporally non-existent in their ontology, they use other words (like Russell's 'subsistence') for these other aspects of reality. Many physicalists, whose conception of reality includes only matter that is describable by means of physical theories using a framework of space-time, would equate reality and physical existence.[4]

---

[4] For the concept of existence, see Aune (1986).

As I wish to leave open the possibility of non-reductionist materialism, I shall use the term 'exist' in a broader sense which in principle allows also for the existence of non-physical entities.

Strong ontological realism about X adds to (1) that Xs exist 'objectively', independently of the mental:

The entities in X exist in a mind-independent way.                              (3)

When X is non-empty, (3) entails what Devitt calls 'fig-leaf realism' (1991: 23):

Something objectively exists independently of the mental.              (4)

Thesis (3) about mind-independence in general can be reformulated by replacing 'mind' by some mind-involving thing, such as human will, desires, perception, language, knowledge, or values. John Searle (1995: 150) formulates 'external realism' as the doctrine that 'the world exists independently of our representations of it'.

Thesis (4) is still ambiguous in several respects. As we have seen in Sections 2.1 and 2.2, 'mind' may refer to the subjective human psyche or to an objective, superindividual spirit. This gives two reformulations of (4):

Something exists independently of human minds.                          (5)

Something exists independently of subjective and objective        (6)
minds.

It is clear that (6) entails (5) as a special case, but the converse does not hold. An objective idealist may think, for example, that physical objects are human-mind-independent, but at the same time occurrent events in God's mind. In spite of being one of the most important upholders of scientific realism, Charles Peirce advocated objective idealism in his metaphysical writings: in his own words, he supported a 'Schelling-type idealism, which takes matter to be effete mind', and laws of nature to be changing 'habits' of this world-mind (*CP* 6.101–2).

If the existence of supernatural objective minds is denied, thesis (5) will imply (6). We shall argue in Section 2.4 that, while (6) is an untestable 'metaphysical' claim in a pejorative sense, (5) can be supported by science.

The concept of mind-*independence* should be understood in the sense of ontological priority or presupposition: A is *ontologically dependent* on B if A could not exist without B existing. For example, my dream last night and my toothache now are ontologically dependent on my mind, and (according to all forms of materialism) my mind is ontologically dependent on my brain. To test the independence of A on B, ask whether A could still exist in the world where B has disappeared.

Ontological independence should be clearly distinguished from *causal independence*: A is causally independent of B if B cannot causally influence A. The physical and the mental are constantly in causal interaction: for example, a tree as an object of my visual sensation causally brings about a mental event, a perception, in my mind; I can plan in my mind, and then execute with my body, an action of moving and shaping a stone. The existence of such interactions is not an argument against ontological independence: the stone is ontologically independent of me, even though I am able to interact causally with it.

As we shall see, these two concepts of independence are frequently confused with each other (cf. Section 5.4, and Chs. 7 and 9). For example, it is sometimes argued that nature and culture cannot be distinguished, because human activities can influence and transform all allegedly natural objects or attributes (such as landscapes, forests, rocks, animals, human bodies, including their sex, etc.). But the fact that nature is more and more causally transformed into artefacts does not demolish the conceptual ontological distinction between Worlds 1 and 3.

The basic form of *ontological realism* (OR) can now be formulated as the claim that at least part of reality is ontologically independent of human minds. (Recall (R0) in Section 1.3.) Sometimes *nature* is used as the name for the collection of mind-independent entities; then OR says that nature is ontologically mind-independent.[5]

OR follows from physicalist versions of materialism. For a radical or eliminativist materialist, there are no minds, so that *everything* is trivially mind-independent. For a reductive materialist, a human mind is identical with certain material entities or processes (brains, brain states), and certainly most material things in the world are ontologically independent of human brains.

OR is also entailed by emergent materialism. In Popperian terms, OR says that *World 1 is ontologically independent of World 2* (whereas World 3 is ontologically dependent on Worlds 1 and 2). Hence, OR does not entail physicalism.

Ontological realism does not entail materialism, either. By definition, dualists are also realists, since they accept, besides the mind, the existence of a material mind-independent substance.

Ontological realism in the sense (5) is incompatible with subjective idealism. The stronger formulation (6) excludes objective idealism as well.

---

[5] I usually avoid using the term 'naturalism', which is fashionable but ambiguous. In my view, emergent materialism can be appropriately called 'non-reductive naturalism', since it does not admit anything 'supernatural'. But many authors, following Quine's rejection of 'first philosophy', use 'naturalism' to mean a doctrine which is the same as, or entails, physicalism (see Section 1.4).

Rescher (1982) has argued that, in spite of ontological mind-independence, the world is 'conceptually mind-involving'. He calls this view *conceptual idealism*. More precisely, it claims that 'nature for us', 'reality-as-we-picture-it', 'our reality', is conceptualized in terms which involve an essential reference to minds and their capabilities. As an epistemological view this sounds tautological: how could 'our world' fail to be dependent on us, or how could 'reality-as-we-picture-it' be independent of our representations? Whether conceptual idealism is correct or not, it is compatible with OR. In a later book, Rescher (1988) again distinguishes ontological idealism ('to be real is to be recognized as such by a real mind') from conceptual idealism ('to be real is to be recognizable as such by a possible mind'). This time 'conceptual idealism' amounts to the weak and speculative thesis that reality is knowable by 'some physically realizable (though not necessarily actual) type of intelligent being'. This claim, which only concerns the ways in which reality can be known or recognized, is compatible not only with OR but with materialism as well. I am inclined to think that it should not be called 'idealism' at all, since it does not attribute any constitutive role to the human or superhuman mind.

## 2.4 The world and its furniture

The thesis of ontological realism does not say anything about the nature of mind-independent reality—except its existence. It is thus compatible with various theories which characterize the elements of reality as objects, events, processes, fields, or systems.

In particular, OR does not entail the world picture, the so-called *classical realism*, usually associated with classical Newtonian mechanics: the world consists of mass points, and their systems, which have a sharply defined location, mass, and momentum, and obey deterministic laws of motion. Indeed, a very different picture of the micro-world is given by (the received interpretation of) quantum mechanics, which implies that the state of atomic systems is causally dependent on their interactions with other such systems or with macroscopic measuring devices. But the possibility that we may intentionally make causal interventions into the micro-world and in a sense 'create' its properties does not imply the ontological mind-dependency of nature (cf. Section 5.4).

The hot issue of traditional metaphysics was the debate between 'nominalists' and 'realists'.[6] Both of them are (or usually are) ontological

---

[6] See Armstrong (1978), Loux (1978).

realists in our sense. According to *nominalism*, the world consists of particulars and nothing but particulars; general terms like 'brown' and 'horse' are only linguistic vehicles for classifying individuals. A Platonist or *transcendent realist* claims that there are eternally and independently existing universals, like brownness and horseness. A *moderate* (Aristotelian) realist takes universals to be immanent, always combined with individuals as their 'forms'. David Armstrong (1978) defends a type of immanent universalism: universals are peculiar kinds of physical entities (that is, belong to World 1) which can exist or be instantiated in many places at the same time.

A 'predicate nominalist' explains properties in terms of predication: a dog Skip is brown, because we apply the predicate 'brown' to it. This idea has been a source of anti-realist views in contemporary philosophy: it seems to imply that, independently of human languages, the world consists merely of 'bare' or propertyless particulars. The language-independent world is an 'amorphic mass of individuals', without any structure at all, before human beings introduce concepts for describing it (cf. Ch. 7). Such versions of nominalism fail to explain why a predicate is correctly applicable to some objects and not to others.[7]

The alternatives to nominalism have not appeared to be very plausible, either, if they require the assumption of transcendent universals. The Aristotelian view of immanent universals has gained popularity through Armstrong's work, and some philosophers believe it to be the best foundation of scientific realism (see e.g. Tooley 1987). However, some realists feel that this theory requires strange entities that are multiply and undividedly located: the same universal (e.g. brownness) is wholly present in two distinct brown particulars. A further difficulty is the problem of instantiation: if uninstantiated universals are accepted (see Tooley 1987), they seem to be Platonic entities; but if every universal must have instances in the actual world (see Armstrong 1978), then it is difficult to explain the existence of laws of nature which typically involve uninstantiated properties and counterfactual conditionals.

For an emergent materialist, the following account of physical objects and properties seems promising. I cannot pretend that the following sketch would solve all the open problems here, but I believe it is in the right direction.

Let us first note that, instead of bare particulars, physical objects have

---

[7] Armstrong (1978) gives forceful criticism against various versions of nominalism. According to 'resemblance nominalism', objects are similar in virtue of their 'natures', but here the 'nature' of an object obviously has to be understood as some sort of property— which is precisely the problem that nominalism tries to avoid.

been understood as pieces of material substance with attributes (*substance theory*) or as sets of properties (*bundle theory*). If properties are universals, the latter theory cannot explain the difference between 'numerically identical' individuals.[8] Let us, therefore, consider the possibility that physical objects are *bundles of tropes* in the sense of D. C. Williams (1953). Tropes are 'property-individuals', qualities located in space and time, such as the-brownness-of-Skip and the-softness-of-the-fur-of-Skip.[9] Tropes as quality-instances have natural relations of similarity.[10] The dog Skip is a bundle (or the mereological sum) of jointly occurring tropes; its similarity with other brown things is explained by the objective likeness of their brownish tropes. No special substance is needed, nor a universal, independently existing, and multiply located brownness. While the physical tropes exist in the mind-independent World 1, the *property* of being brown can be understood as the class of similar tropes (cf. Williams 1953). As a class is most naturally conceived as a human-made construction, created by abstraction from similar tropes, properties belong to World 3. Here it is not a problem that some of such properties may be uninstantiated in the actual world. This view might be called *tropic realism*.

Like all other ontological systems, the trope theory has its difficulties, which are now being actively investigated. Armstrong has recently become more favourable to tropes than before: he says that the trope theory (which he regards as 'moderate nominalism') is 'an important and quite plausible rival' to his earlier moderate realism, and considers it in a form (attributed to John Locke) which takes tropes to be attribute-individuals tied with pieces of independently existing material substance (see Armstrong 1989).

What has been said about properties applies more generally to *relations* between objects. Relations have been understood as transcendent or immanent universals, or nominalistically in terms of n-place predicates (n>1). Campbell (1990) favours the theory that relations do not really exist. In my view, a tropic realist should understand genuine relations between objects primarily as n-ary property-instances (e.g. the love-between-John-and-Mary). The general relation of loving is then formed by abstraction from such tropes.

Besides *intrinsic* properties, which characterize what or how a particu-

---

    [8]  See the discussion in Loux (1978).
    [9]  Tropes are also called 'Stoutian particulars', since they were discussed by G. F. Stout in 1923. Campbell (1990) calls them 'abstract particulars', in contrast to physical objects which are 'concrete particulars'. See also Armstrong (1978; 1989), Lewis (1986), Bennett (1988), and Bacon (1995).
    [10]  For the concept of similarity, see Goodman (1972) and Niiniluoto (1987a: ch. 1).

lar object is in itself (e.g. 'white', 'two-legged'), objects have also *relational properties*, which involve relations to some further objects. For example, while 'x is a father of y' expresses a two-place relation,

x is a father=$_{df}$($\exists$y)(x is a father of y)

is a relational property of x.

Locke's distinction between *primary* and *secondary qualities* is often understood in terms of the intrinsic–relational division, but this is somewhat misleading. The primary qualities (such as solidity, extension, figure, motion, rest, and number) presuppose *spatial*, *temporal*, and *causal relations*.[11] Moreover, *quantitative* properties (like 'has the length of 5.2 metres') presuppose scales of measurement that are constructed from comparisons between objects.[12] Secondary qualities (such as colour, sound, smell, and taste) can be understood in different ways: as experiences in animal and human minds, as dispositions of physical objects to produce certain types of experience in the mind of a perceiver, but also as physical dispositions to generate or reflect certain physical influences (e.g. an object is red if it is able to reflect light rays of wavelength between 647 and 700 nm). In the last alternative, they are ontologically mind-independent attributes of physical objects.

Objects with their relations constitute *complex objects* or *systems*. The most general theory of wholes, consisting of any kind of parts with any kind of relations, is mereology.[13] More specific conceptions require that the elements and parts of a complex object are spatio-temporally and causally connected.

Changes in the state of a system (e.g. sunrise, opening of a window) are *generic events* or *event types*. The occurrence of a generic event at a moment of time, or more generally, in a spatio-temporal location or zone, is a *singular event*. Causally continuous sequences of events constitute *processes*. Bertrand Russell has argued that physical objects can be constructed from events that are their successive temporal slices (e.g. 'Socrates-at-time-t'). More generally, *process ontologies* (in contrast to thing ontologies) take the dynamic concepts of event and process to be more basic than the concept of object.[14]

Many philosophers define events simply as instantiations of properties—

---

[11] See Reichenbach (1956), Sklar (1974), Salmon (1984).
[12] For the theories of measurement, see Krantz *et al.* (1971).
[13] For the basic concepts of mereology, see Bunge (1977–9).
[14] Hegel, Peirce, Whitehead, and Bohm are among the advocates of process ontology. See Aune (1986). Also the contemporary Standard Theory of elementary particles can be understood as relying on process ontology. For example, one of the hypotheses tested today in high-energy accelerators is that the mass of particles is created in interaction with the Higgs field.

without linking this concept to change. According to Kim (1973), an event is an exemplification at a time of a property by a substance or a relation by substances. Chisholm (1970) takes such properties within events to be universals, but Bennett (1988), attributing this view to Leibniz, holds that events can be understood as tropes, i.e. property-instances in a spatio-temporal zone. In this case, it also possible to think that causality is primarily a relation between tropes. Hence, tropic realism can be formulated as a version of dynamic ontology.

Tropic realism does not imply that there is a privileged conceptual framework (nature's own language as it were) for categorizing and describing reality. The general descriptive terms of our language refer to classes of tropes (e.g. 'red') or classes of physical object (e.g. 'cat'), i.e. to properties and substances, and these classes can be formed by our conceptual activity in various ways. The world does not divide itself uniquely into *natural kinds* (cf. Quine 1969), but nevertheless the 'redness' and 'cathood' of some physical objects is based upon their objectively existing features. Our way of speaking about tropes is derivative from the talk about their classes: a name for a trope is obtained by adding indexical expressions to a property term.

This means also that tropic realism does not entail *essentialism*, which claims that particular objects possess some of their properties 'essentially' or 'necessarily', some only 'accidentally'. The *identity* of an object or event is always relative to a description. It is up to us to agree on those intrinsic and relational properties that guarantee the preservation of the 'identity' of a certain kind of entity. Some changes transform an object into another kind, while 'mere Cambridge changes' preserve its identity.[15]

While idealism and dualism regard the human mind as an independent substance or process-like stream of mental events, reductive materialism identifies the mind with the brain as a physical system. Emergent materialists think that mentality or consciousness is an emergent characteristic of the complex system of the human brain with its cultural and social environment. In contrast to eliminative materialists, all these views admit that, in some sense or another, World 2—i.e. the human mind and its contents (such as thoughts, beliefs, perceptions, hallucinations, volitions, pains, feelings, and emotions)—is real (see Section 2.3).

Here it is important to recall Peirce's 'medieval' definition of reality that he attributed to Duns Scotus: what is *real* is 'independent of the vagaries

---

[15] According to Peter Geach, a 'mere Cambridge change' typically occurs when we introduce a new predicate or relational term to describe an object, and thereby a new description becomes true of it, but the object itself is not changed in any genuine or intrinsic way. See Shoemaker (1984: 208).

of me and you', i.e. its characters are 'independent of what anybody may think them to be' (*CP* 5.311, 5.405). By this criterion, my seeing a pink elephant in my room is a real mental fact about me, but the elephant, as the object or content of this hallucination, is not a part of reality.

According to tropic realism, physical properties and events as tropes are mind-independent. However, ontological realism need not deny that physical objects may also have non-physical, *mind-involving properties* which ontologically presuppose relations to consciousness or to cultural and social institutions.[16] For example, a tree is sacred if and only if there are people who worship it; a landscape is pleasant if and only if it pleases some people; a piece of gold has economic value if and only if it can be used as an object or measure of commercial exchange. Similarly, material artefacts (tables, tools, houses, works of art) have both physical properties (weight, geometric form, colour) and non-physical relational properties (designer and manufacturer, intended function, commercial value).

A physical object with its physical and non-physical properties is a *cultural entity* in World 3. Such an entity has, as it were, a material kernel in World 1, but enriched with its relations to World 2 and 3 entities it becomes a cultural object with some mind-involving relational properties.[17] In spite of their 'mixed' character, we can conceptually distinguish the World 1 and World 3 parts of cultural entities.

Besides material artefacts, World 3 also contains *abstract* constructions, such as novels, symphonies, numbers, and propositions. Such objects do not have physical properties at all, but they can be documented in World 1 (a symphony by its score, sound waves on air, or compact disc; a proposition expressed by a sentence) and manifested in World 2 (the thoughts and ideas of a composer; a mental construction of a mathematician). Without

[16] Devitt (1991: 247) says that the 'natures' of tools are 'functions that involve the purposes of agents'. Searle (1995: 10) calls mind-involving properties 'observer-relative', in contrast to features 'intrinsic to nature'. (Reference to 'observers and users' is perhaps too narrow to indicate all mind-involving intentional attitudes toward to the world.) This is not the same as the distinction between Worlds 2 and 1, however, since for Searle intrinsic features of reality include 'those that exist independently of all mental states' plus the mental states themselves (ibid. 12). On the other hand, Searle includes among 'ontologically subjective' entities mental states (like pain) and the observer-relative features, and he emphasizes (correctly, I think) that statements about such entities may be 'epistemologically objective'. However, Searle also includes within this class artefacts (like screwdrivers) and the functions assigned to them. The point of the Popperian notion of World 3 is that we can avoid using the misleading term 'subjective' in characterizing such public social entities as screwdrivers.

[17] This means that the non-physical properties of a cultural entity (e.g. the price of a commodity) are not 'supervenient' on its own physical properties. In general, I do not find the concept of supervenience very useful in ontology: for example, the supervenience of the mental on the physical is compatible with parallelist dualism.

such documentation and manifestation an abstract entity cannot survive in World 3.[18]

When an object has a property, or several objects bear relations to each other, we speak of *states of affairs* or *facts*. Traditionally, *singular* facts (e.g. a particular piece of chalk is white at a moment of time) are distinguished from *general* facts (e.g. snow is white). General facts can be understood as classes of singular facts. Singular facts may be complex in the sense that they involve many objects or properties. Simple singular states of affairs have the structure $\langle a, P, t \rangle$, $\langle a, b, R, t \rangle$, etc., where a and b are particular objects or events, P is a property, R is a dyadic relation, and t is a moment of time.[19] Depending on the ontological theory, P and R may be understood as universals (Russell, Chisholm, Armstrong) or tropes (Stout).

Facts may be positive ('John loves Mary') or negative ('Mary does not love John'). A complex fact involving a group of people A and a relation R may tell for each pair $\langle a, b \rangle \in A \times A$ whether R holds between a and b or not. Such a complex fact corresponds to *relational systems* or structures in the sense of Tarski's model theory (see Section 3.4).

The totality of all facts is the *actual world* (comprising Worlds 1, 2, and 3). In language we can also describe alternatives to the facts about the actual world. Such alternative states of affairs, when they are compossible, constitute *possible worlds*.

The so-called 'modal realists' claim that possible worlds are as real as the actual world (Lewis 1986). In my view, it is rational to accept 'Ersatz realism' (Stalnaker 1984) which takes possible worlds to exist only in the form of linguistic descriptions (cf. Hintikka 1975). In this sense, possible worlds are ontologically mind-involving.

It does not follow that an ontological realist needs to be an *actualist* who identifies the real with the actual. For example, fire has the capability of burning human skin, even if it is not actually burning anyone's skin anywhere now; a social custom of raising one's hat is preserved even at those moments of time when no one has the opportunity to follow it; the atoms of transuranic substances belong to reality, even if they may fail to be actualized at a given moment. Following Aristotle, the domain of reality can thus be taken to consist of actual and potential things and properties: against Hume, dispositions, causal powers, objective physical probabilities or propensities, and laws endowed with nomic necessity could

[18] This was observed by Carnap in *Aufbau* (see Carnap 1967).
[19] Barwise and Etchemendy (1987) make a distinction between Fregean and Russellian propositions (and facts). The former contain as constituents individual names, the latter individual objects.

be included among *real potencies*.[20] This seems also to be the content of what Peirce called 'scholastic realism': his category of 'thirdness' expresses the idea of 'real generals' in the world. Unlike Aristotelian universals, Peirce's 'generals' are relational, and their existence means that the world is governed by lawful regularities.

The real potencies or possibilities should be distinguished from *conceptual possibilities*. Some 'realist' (read: Platonist) philosophers have wished to populate reality with anything that can be conceived or imagined in a logically consistent way. This 'Meinongian jungle' contains all the strange creatures of human imagination.[21] A reasonable ontology should distinguish the real things from the fictional figments of our imagination: for example, Donald Duck is a fictional entity, while reality contains pictures of Donald Duck (in World 1), love for Donald Duck (in World 2), and the cult of Disneyland (in World 3).

To conclude this section, we should say something about the relation of the ontological views to the project of scientific realism. If scientific realists are committed to the scientific world view (cf. Section 1.2), perhaps they should apply the principle of ontological parsimony (the so-called *Occam's razor*), restrict their attention only to scientifically accepted or acceptable statements, and exclude metaphysics from their system? If one yields to the horror of metaphysics (with the logical positivists and Dummett), this recommendation seems to be warranted. But that would presuppose a sharp semantic dichotomy between meaningful science and meaningless metaphysics (see Section 1.2). In my view, it is more plausible to take science and metaphysics to be in mutual interaction with each other without a fixed borderline.

The *scientia mensura* doctrine argues that science should be allowed to decide ontological questions (see Sellars 1963; Tuomela 1985). I agree that science is the best source for beliefs about reality. This suggests the viability of science-based metaphysics, however. For example, current developments in science (especially in quantum mechanics) point to the direction that the universe is a dynamically developing causal system which is at least partly governed by probabilistic laws. This gives support to an anti-reductionist evolutionary and indeterminist process ontology, even though as a statement about the entire world this is a metaphysical claim. Of course, this tentative generalization from current science is fallible and may be mistaken. Further, we have no a priori guarantee that science will decide, even in the ideal 'Peircean' limit (cf. Section 4.6),

[20] For defences of propensities, see Popper (1982), Fetzer (1981), and Niiniluoto (1988*a*). For real potencies, see Harré and Madden (1975) and Bhaskar (1975; 1989).
[21] Meinong's ontology is discussed in Bergman (1967).

such issues as the existence of God, determinism vs. indeterminism, or universals vs. tropes.

Conversely, ontological concepts and theses are relevant to the scientific realist in several ways. First, scientific research programmes cannot help using general ontological terms like 'object' and 'fact'. Such terms are needed in the interpretation of the content of our best theories in science, and (*pace* Fine 1984) some philosophical content has to be given to them. Secondly, ontological terms are needed in order to formulate the philosophical programme of scientific realism, and attempts to defend or to denounce this programme usually appeal to specific (often tacit) ontological assumptions. For example, even though one cannot claim that tropic realism could be justified by scientific evidence, or that scientific realism necessarily presupposes this ontological doctrine, I find it occasionally useful to articulate and to defend scientific realism by referring to it. The opponents of 'metaphysical realism' (cf. Ch. 7) in turn usually rely in their criticism on some metaphysical doctrine like nominalism.

Pihlström (1996) argues against metaphysical forms of realism that ontological issues, even though important, are always 'pragmatically' relative to our 'practices' and 'interests'. But it might be the case that the best way of accounting for the pervasive features of the institutional practice we call science is to assume some metaphysical view like the trope theory, so that in this case such metaphysics would have a pragmatic justification.

## 2.5 Arguments for ontological realism

Ontological realism is sometimes taken to be such a weak thesis that it is not really 'worth fighting for'. However, it is useful to consider here some arguments in favour of OR, since they usually give grounds for something stronger than (4)—for common-sense or scientific realism. We shall also see later that arguments against subjective idealism can be repeated, in different variations, in connection with many anti-realist positions.

A further proof that OR should be found interesting comes from the attempt of the Vienna Circle to reject it (and its negation) as meaningless metaphysics (Section 1.4). The basis for this claim was that no finite amount of observations could resolve the debate whether there is an 'external' mind-independent reality or not—whatever we perceive could be interpreted or accommodated in the light of both alternatives.[22]

[22] Schlick (1959) suggests, however, that a form of 'empirical realism' can be defended. In the same way, Kant presented a 'refutation of idealism' (see Kant 1930). This distinction between empirical and metaphysical realism seems to presuppose a Kantian distinction

   Edmund Husserl's phenomenology, on the other hand, starts from the idea that OR is part of our non-reflective 'natural attitude' toward the world. The phenomenological project of studying our mental acts and their contents starts only after a reduction, where the external world is 'bracketed', i.e. in *epoche* we suspend judgement about the truth of OR. Neo-pragmatists like Rorty recommend such a suspension in a categorical way: 'the whole project of distinguishing between what exists in itself and what exists in relation to human minds . . . is no longer worth pursuing' (Rorty 1998: 75).

   We are not here considering the problem of whether entities like tables and electrons exist at all. Rather, both realists and idealists usually agree about the existence of such things, but they clash in the question of their mind-independence. For the idealist, such entities are assumed to be in some sense 'inside' the mind or 'constituted' by the mind. It is easy to understand that this question cannot be solved, if objective idealism is allowed: any attempt to defend (6), e.g. by introducing an entity which can be plausibly claimed to be independent of all human minds, can be countered by arguing that after all this entity (like all of us) is just a figment in God's mind. What on earth could ever refute such a metaphysical conviction?

   On the other hand, if our aim is to defend (5), the prospects seem more promising. In Section 4.2, we shall argue that there are epistemic criteria for helping to distinguishing the real world from my dreams. However, some metaphysical formulations of solipsism, which locate a 'transcendental ego' outside the empirical realm, may turn out to be just as unfalsifiable as objective idealism.

   Some philosophers have attempted to construct proofs for the existence of the external world. Sometimes they are only indirect, i.e. attempts to refute all the known idealistic arguments against realism. The strongest efforts in this direction try to show that subjective idealism is internally incoherent. Putnam's (1981) 'brains in a vat' argument is a recent variant of them. Another is given by Roger Trigg in his *Reality at Risk* (1989). If successful, such arguments would show that OR as a factual statement is an example of a necessary truth. But at least for a scientific realist, it is very doubtful whether metaphysics could have the power to prove a priori such principles.

   The most famous a posteriori proof of the external world is due to G. E. Moore who held up his two arms in front of an audience (see Moore

between phenomena and noumena (see Section 4.3). Schlick's claim is also similar to Fine's NOA, and again it is difficult to see why his 'empirical' realism would not be realism in the ordinary ontological sense (see Section 1.4).

1959). As the two hands are external objects in space, thesis (5) seems to be proved via (2). The most famous reply to Moore is by Ludwig Wittgenstein in *On Certainty* (1969). Wittgenstein suggests that OR is not a statement to be proved at all, but rather a fundamental principle of our world view which makes it possible to evaluate the certainty of other statements, i.e. it is the 'inherited background against which I distinguish between true and false' (p. 94). Hence, it would be misleading to say that I 'know' OR. Searle (1995) formulates this idea by saying that external realism is a 'background condition of intelligibility'. OR is not an empirical hypothesis, and the only 'proof' of it is a Kantian 'transcendental argument': whenever 'we attempt to communicate to achieve normal understanding' we 'must presuppose external realism'.

I think transcendental philosophy gives a useful perspective on OR. There are numerous situations of speaking and acting where the truth of OR is presupposed as a necessary condition. Indeed, most participants in the realism vs. anti-realism debates make assumptions (e.g. normal communication, the existence of human bodies, human activities and practices, artefacts, books, written languages, laboratories) which presuppose some mind-independent entities. As these assumptions may be mistaken, the transcendental argument does not conclusively prove the truth of OR, as Searle rightly points out. But still it is very forceful, since a person who tries to argue against OR, but at the same time presupposes it, is driven into incoherence.

Searle suggests that transcendental arguments are the *only* arguments for external realism. However, it seems to be possible to conceive situations where we have suspended judgement about the correctness of OR and consider possible evidence for its truth. I think it is clear that OR cannot be *proved* in this way. However, if we do not quest for certainty, the situation may look different. For example, Eino Kaila (1926) claimed that the *Aussenwelt-Hypothese* is confirmed or made *probable* by observations in everyday life.

Let us consider the Berkeleyan form of subjective idealism and its claim that the table in front of me is ontologically dependent on its being perceived. This claim means that the table does not (cannot) exist if it is not perceived. So I close my eyes, but still I can feel the table, hear a knock on it, perhaps smell it. The idealist thus can insist that I still perceive the table (without seeing it, but by other senses). So next I go out of the room, but my friend looking in at the window notices no change: the table continues to exist as before. Alas, says the idealist, now it is the friend's perception which sustains the table's existence. (This is the difference between solipsism and phenomenalism.) But the test can be repeated by replacing my friend with a camera, which records the events in the room. Now this recording seems to take place, even when the camera is left alone in the room with the table. The camera certainly does not have a mind of its own, yet it appears to register the continuing (or at least twenty-four times per second) existence of the table in the room. The idealist cannot seriously contend that my mind, when seeing later the table-pictures on the film, somehow retrospectively causes or guarantees the existence of the camera and the table in the room and their interaction. But then he is left with the hopeless task of explaining why the table-pictures appear on the film even when the table did not exist (by his lights) in the room.

The *Camera Argument* can be extended by asking the idealist to explain why I seem to be able to perceive the same table at different moments of time, and how several persons can simultaneously see the table at the same place. The *Principle of Common Cause* suggests in this case that there is some entity which causes all these mutually agreeing perceptions.[23] This hypothesis is further confirmed by successful predictions: I shall see the table in the room tomorrow, a new person brought to the room will see it as well.

The inference from agreeing perceptions to physical objects is *abductive* in Peirce's sense, i.e. it makes an inference from effects to causes, from observations to their best explanation.[24] The same kind of abductive inference is used not only in common sense but in science as well: the best explanation of an observed curved path in Wilson's cloud chamber is the existence of an electrically charged particle emitted by a radioactive substance.

An abductive argument is not deductive, and it cannot guarantee certainty to its conclusion. It is an ampliative inference, which at best gives some credibility (or epistemic probability) to the conclusion.

Perception is a special case of causal interaction between a human mind and external reality. The possibility of hallucinations shows, however, that we may be mistaken in our belief that a perception is the result of an external cause. Karl Marx concluded, in his 1845 'Theses on Feuerbach', that 'the dispute over the reality or non-reality of thinking that is isolated from practice is a purely *scholastic* question' (Marx 1975: 422). In other words, the issue of ontological realism should be considered in connection with human action: the proof of external realities comes only through our success in interacting with them or manipulating them. The 'proof' of pudding is in eating.

---

[23] See Reichenbach (1956), Salmon (1984).
[24] For abduction, see Peirce *CP* 6.522–8. Cf. Section 6.4 below.

This *Argument from Successful Action* is repeated by Ian Hacking (1983) in the context of scientific experimentation. According to Hacking, electrons are real if you can spray them, i.e. if you can use the causal properties of electrons to interfere in other parts of nature. Thus, the best case for realism does not come from observation or representation, but rather from our success in 'intervening'.

Perhaps the most devastating argument against subjective idealism comes from science. Let us call it the *Argument from the Past*. We have very strong scientific evidence—from cosmology, astronomy, physics, chemistry, biology, botany, zoology, and anthropology—that the universe has existed for more than 15,000 million years, the earth for 4,500 million years, fish for 500 million years, mammals for 200 million years, and the first hominids for about 5 million years. Again this is not a deductive proof, but rather an inductive argument, a retroduction in Hempel's (1965) sense. But it is important that this empirical evidence is compelling also for those who attempt to avoid 'theoretical entities' and to stay within the limits of phenomenalist science: fish and horses are 'respectable' observable things for an empiricist. The same is true of an advocate of Fine's NOA (cf. Section 1.4) and even a 'solipisism of the present moment'. Hence, there are good reasons to claim that there was a time in the history of our planet when no human minds (nor any mind-involving things like human perceptions, languages, etc.) had yet appeared through evolution. Let's say this moment of time is $t_0=5$ million years BC. This knowledge gives us a powerful test of mind-independence: whatever existed before $t_0$ must be ontologically independent of the human mentality.[25]

A phenomenalist may resist inferences to unobservable entities, like atoms, but, by the above argument, he will be committed by scientific evidence to the reality of the past. Thus, science gives us strong evidence that, for example, stones and trees existed before $t_0$. Moreover, contemporary science also tells us that these material objects are now composed of atoms—and were so composed already 5 million years ago. Hence, science inductively warrants the thesis that stones, trees, and atoms are

[25] This is V. I. Lenin's 1909 argument against Mach's phenomenalism (see Lenin 1927; cf. Niiniluoto 1986*a*). (Following Engels and Lenin, 'dialectical materialism' advocated a sort of evolutionary ontology and critical realist epistemology, where absolute truth is approached as an asymptotic limit by relative truths (see Niiniluoto 1987*a*: ch. 5), while many trends in Western Marxism were instead influenced by views opposing realism.) Mach himself denied that he was an idealist in Berkeley's fashion. His 'elements' are sensations only relative to an ego, which itself is a collection of sensations. When Mach was asked what happens to the elements when the ego disappears, he replied that they will then continue to exist in different combinations (see Mach 1959). This suggests that Mach could be interpreted as a tropic realist whose 'elements' are observable tropes. A similar interpretation could be suggested of the elements of Wittgenstein's *Tractatus* (1922).

ontologically mind-independent; ontological, common-sense, and scientific realisms are correct, and subjective idealism is wrong. In other words, if someone takes contemporary science seriously, he or she cannot advocate subjective idealism.[26]

An eliminativist realist takes only atoms to be real, but stones as bunches of atoms to be unreal (cf. Section 1.2). It is sufficient for the above argument that atoms existed before time $t_0$. A common-sense realist may, instead, drop the reference to atoms and stay on the level of common-sense objects existing before $t_0$. Both alternatives are fatal to ontological anti-realism. The point is that there is overwhelmingly strong scientific empirical evidence for at least disconfirming the metaphysical doctrine of subjective idealism.

---

[26] According to Rorty (1998: 72), 'given that it pays to talk about mountains, as it certainly does, one of the obvious truths about mountains is that they were here before we talked about them'. Rorty denies, however, that the 'utility' of such language games implies the existence of mountains in 'Reality as It Is in Itself'. In my view, if Rorty accepts that mountains existed before we talked about them, he should accept OR at least in the same sense—instead of claiming that OR is 'a dead end' serving no purpose (ibid. 73).

# 3

# Realism in Semantics

Twentieth-century philosophy is famous for its 'linguistic turn'. The philosophy of language has gained a central place in both the analytic and hermeneutic traditions. Preoccupation with problems concerning language has become an important source of anti-realism in contemporary thinking: some philosophers deny that there is any extralinguistic reality inseparable from language, others deny that language could have any objective relation of representation to such a reality (Section 3.1).

In this chapter, I defend realism in semantics by understanding Tarski's model-theoretic definition (Section 3.3) as an adequate explication of the classical correspondence theory of truth (Section 3.4). According to this theory, truth is a non-redundant concept which establishes, via a non-physical notion of reference or interpretation, a non-epistemic language–world relation. Epistemic definitions of truth are discussed and rejected in Section 4.6. I also show how the realist account of truth and falsity can be extended, via the concept of similarity, to notions like truthlikeness and approximate truth which indicate how a statement can be false but still 'close to the truth' (Section 3.5).

## 3.1 Language as representation

Realism in semantics—thesis (R1) in Section 1.3—asserts that *truth is a semantical relation between language and reality*. We have already discussed reality in Chapter 2; now it is time to speak about languages and their relations to the world.

In the general sense, *language* is a system of signs (Eco 1986). The tokens of such signs are usually material things or events in World 1 (e.g. spoken or written letters, symbols, pictures, electric pulses, waves, gestures), but they can also be mental ideas or thoughts in World 2. However, language is not simply a set or collection of signs, but also the realization of signs in actual speech and writing (*parole* in Saussure's sense), i.e. a class of human activities (cf. Davidson 1990). Further, language is a system of linguistic norms (*la langue* in Saussure's sense) which regulate the structural interconnections of signs and their relations to extralinguistic reality. In this sense, whether languages use natural or artificial signs, they are human social constructions in World 3 (Niiniluoto 1981).

Animals and human beings use signs for various purposes. Mimes, gestures, and cries express emotions and attitudes. A bird's singing may be a signal of warning. Karl Bühler distinguished these *expressive* and *signal* functions of language from its *representative* function: language allows us to refer to external reality, to describe things and states of affairs. Ernst Cassirer (1944) took this aspect of language to be the characteristic feature of man as *animal symbolicum*. Later philosophers (with Austin and Searle) have studied the various ways in which language can be used to make 'speech acts' (such as assertion, argument, explanation, command, persuasion, baptizing, wedding).

Representation is thus only one of many functions of language. But the existence and importance of the other purposes does not make this one insignificant.

Language as representation belongs to the domain of semantics. Following the terminology of Charles Morris (1938), the *syntactics* of a language L is concerned with the intralinguistic relations between the signs of L. For natural languages (e.g. English), the syntax or 'grammar' tells what expressions belong to L and what composite expressions are grammatical sentences of L. The *semantics* of L studies the relations of linguistic expressions to extralinguistic reality. It tries to account for the representational function of language by analysing how the terms and sentences of L are associated with meaning (sense, intension) and reference (denotation, extension). The *pragmatics* of L studies the origin, uses, and effects of signs in relation to the users of L.

While the early stage of logical positivism was primarily occupied with syntactics, the work of Tarski and Carnap in the mid-1930s started a new era of logical semantics (see Carnap 1942). In the 1950s, this approach culminated in model theory and possible world semantics (cf. Hintikka 1988a). Later it was extended to the study of natural language within 'logical pragmatics' (Davidson, Montague semantics, Hintikka's game-theoretical semantics). This programme usually takes truth to be the fundamental concept of semantics, and defines meaning (and related notions) in terms of truth-conditions.

Another approach, linked with American pragmatism, behaviouristic psychology, and Wittgenstein's later philosophy, analyses meaning in terms of use—i.e. as a pragmatic notion (cf. Quine 1960; Sellars 1963). While Quine (1990) opts for the view of truth as 'disquotation', the treatment of meaning as use often leads to a definition of truth in epistemic terms (such

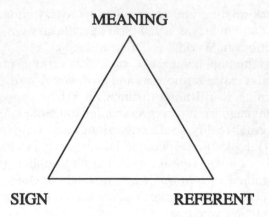

FIG. 3. The semiotic triangle

as assertability), and thereby at least the direct connection of truth with a realist notion of representation is lost (cf. Rosenberg 1974, however). There are also other approaches, like the old and new rhetoric, which study the ways of human argumentation on the level of pragmatics, independently of semantic questions about truth.

A kind of reconciliation of these approaches is expressed in Jaakko Hintikka's (1975) slogan: *semantics is based on pragmatics*. In contrast to the claims of Field (1972), language–world relations are no more physical facts in World 1 than languages themselves: these relations are also human-made social constructions in World 3, created by linguistic communities within activities that Wittgenstein called 'language games'. In this interpretation, language games are not only intralinguistic 'indoor' games, as some Wittgensteinian philosophers think, but also 'outdoor' games for establishing connections between language and reality. Through such activities there exist in World 3 institutional 'semantical facts' which are not reducible to purely physical facts.

This view is implied already by Peirce's celebrated definition of a *sign* or *representamen* as 'something which stands to somebody for something in some respect or capacity' (*CP* 2.228). Peirce is here reformulating, for the purposes of his 'semeiotic', the traditional Stoic doctrine of signs (Gr. *semeion*) (see Fig. 3). According to Peirce, in order for a sign to refer to an object, there must be 'somebody', a person using the sign, who interprets the sign. The first sign will create another sign, the 'interpretant', in the mind of that person—and thereby an endless *semiosis*, process or play of signs, is started. However, the study of signs cannot be reduced to these semiotic sign–sign relations (as the poststructuralists think) or to any two-dimensional relation between an acoustic signifier and ideal signified (as Saussure's semiology does). The structure of a sign is triadic, and a sign will also 'stand for something, its object'.

Peirce differentiated between two ways of understanding the object of a sign: the *dynamic* object is its 'object in itself' and the *immediate* object is 'the object as it is represented' (see Peirce 1966: 390).

Peirce also distinguished three kinds of sign in terms of the grounds of their relation to their objects (*CP* 2.247–9). An *index* is 'a sign which refers to the Object that it denotes by virtue of being really affected by that Object'. Thus, s is an index of w, if w causally affects or produces s (e.g. smoke is a sign of fire, a footprint is a sign of a foot). An *icon* refers to an object by virtue of likeness or similarity (e.g. the picture of a cat is an icon of the cat). A *symbol* is a conventional sign that refers to its object by a rule or law (e.g. the word 'cat' is a symbol of a cat).

Most words in natural language are symbols in Peirce's sense. Peirce himself classified proper names (and demonstrative pronouns) among indices, but equally well one might understand them as symbols, since they (e.g. 'Julius Caesar') denote their objects by a convention introduced at the moment of baptizing. General words ('cat') are typically introduced by conventions adopted within linguistic communities.

In the light of these distinctions, it seems that an attempt to reduce all reference relations to some physical relations (such as causality), as physicalists and naturalists try to do, must fail.[1] Icons and symbols are usually not indices. Similarly, even though sentences and scientific theories may give 'pictures' of facts, as Wittgenstein argued in *Tractatus* (1922) and Sellars (1963) suggested in his notion of 'picturing', it is a mistake to think that all representation must be pictorial. Some symbols may have an iconic element, but iconicity is not a necessary aspect of representation. Representation, truth, and knowledge should be possible even if language (or human mind) is not a 'mirror of nature'.

This point suggests that Rorty's (1980; 1991) anti-representational view of language, which he attributes partly to Davidson, is based on too narrow a notion of representation.

Generalizing Jean van Heijenoort's distinction for logic, Jaakko Hintikka (1997) has drawn attention to the opposition of two conceptions of language (see also Hintikka and Hintikka 1989). One of them is 'language as the

---

[1] Conventions concerning reference relations may of course employ, among other things, the concept of causality (cf. Section 5.2). It has become one of the dogmas of physicalism to understand reference as a purely physical and causal relation—as if all linguistic signs were indices in Peirce's sense. See, for example, Field (1972), Fodor (1987), Davidson (1990), Rorty (1991), Stich (1990).

universal medium'; with some variations, it is represented by Frege, Russell, Wittgenstein, Neurath, Heidegger, Gadamer, Derrida, Quine, and Martin-Löf. The other is 'language as calculus', supported by Peirce, Hilbert, Löwenheim, Husserl, the later Carnap, Tarski, and Hintikka.

Following the summary of Martin Kusch,[2] the *universal medium* conception is characterized as follows:

Semantics is inaccessible.                                              (UM-1)

We cannot conceive of a different system of semantical        (UM-2)
relations.

Model theory and the conception of possible worlds are        (UM-3)
to be rejected.

Linguistic relativism is to be accepted.                          (UM-4)

Metalanguage is a misuse of language.                             (UM-5)

Truth as correspondence is at best inexplicable and          (UM-6)
perhaps even unintelligible.

The countertheses of the *calculus* conception of language are then:

Semantics is accessible.                                              (C-1)

It is possible to conceive of a different system of seman-        (C-2)
tical relations.

Model theory and the notion of possible worlds are            (C-3)
intelligible.

Linguistic relativism can be opposed.                             (C-4)

Metalanguage is possible and legitimate.                          (C-5)

The idea of truth as correspondence is intelligible.              (C-6)

The basic assumption of the universal medium account is well illustrated by Wittgenstein's *Tractatus*: there is one and only one world, and one language which pictures this fixed universe. The meaning relations between the language and the world are thus fixed. Since the language is universal, we cannot go and look at it from outside. Any attempt to do this turns out to be meaningless. Hence, semantics is inaccessible, and a correspondence notion of truth is ineffable or inexpressible in language.

The calculus conception instead acknowledges the existence of several languages or sign systems which can be reinterpreted in several ways in

---

[2] See Kusch (1989: 6–7). Kusch's work is a careful study of Husserl, Heidegger, and Gadamer in the light of this distinction.

different domains. We shall see in Section 3.3 below how this idea can be formulated in model theory by using a suitable metalanguage ML for a given object language L.

## 3.2  Logical, analytic, and factual truth

It is natural to ask whether truth is a syntactic, semantic, or pragmatic concept. It is helpful to consider first the notions of logical truth and analytic truth, and then proceed to 'factual' or 'material' truth.

For the formal languages of logic and mathematics, the syntax specifies the concept of well-formed formula (wff) or sentence as an expression built from the alphabet by rules of formation. Axioms and rules of inference define the concepts of deduction (from a set of premises). Systems of natural deduction employ only rules of inference without logical axioms. Thus, *proof theory* allows us to define syntactically concepts like logical deduction, provability, and consistency.

An alternative approach follows Leibniz in defining logical truth as truth in all possible worlds. A variant of this idea is the definition of tautologies by truth-tables in Wittgenstein's *Tractatus*. More generally, *model theory* allows us to define semantically concepts like logical consequence (as necessarily truth-preserving inference), logical truth, and consistency.

Kurt Gödel proved the Completeness Theorem for first-order predicate logic in 1930. This remarkable achievement of modern logic shows that syntactical (proof-theoretic) and semantical (model-theoretic) concepts are coextensive in elementary logic. Thus,

> A sentence B of predicate logic is provable ($\vdash$ B) iff B is          (1)
> logically true ($\vDash$ B).

The result (1) means that the concept of *logical truth* can be defined syntactically as provability (within a suitable system). This is obviously connected with the traditional idea that logical truth is truth in virtue of the logical form of a sentence. For example,

> All unmarried men are men                                                  (2)

is true in virtue of its form

> $\forall x(Ux\&Mx\rightarrow Mx)$.                                          (3)

Whatever interpretation is given to the predicates 'U' and 'M', the truth of (3) follows from the meanings of the logical constants $\forall$, $\&$, $\rightarrow$;

besides the semantical treatment in terms of truth-tables and models, this meaning can be specified in terms of inference rules.

Logical truth is traditionally regarded as a special case of the wider notion of analytic truth. A sentence expresses an *analytic truth* (falsity) if it is true (false) in virtue of the meanings of its constituent terms; otherwise it is *synthetic*. For example,

All bachelors are men                                                                    (4)

is analytically true, since English language includes a meaning postulate to the effect that

'Bachelor' means 'unmarried man'.                                                        (5)

Substitution of 'unmarried men' in (4) for 'bachelors' reduces (4) to the logical truth (2).

Analytic truth is clearly a semantic concept, since it appeals to meanings. Again a syntactical characterization is possible: an analytic truth is derivable from general logical laws and definitions (Frege 1950: 4). More precisely, let MP be the set of all *meaning postulates* associated with language L. Meaning postulates are sentences of L that express metalinguistic meaning statements of type (5) as explicit definitions in L:

($\forall$x)(x is a bachelor iff x is unmarried and x is a man).                           (6)

Then a sentence is *analytic-for-L* if it is derivable from the meaning postulates MP of L (Carnap 1966). The semantic import of this definition is expressed by Stenius (1972): a sentence of L is analytic-for-L iff according to the linguistic conventions for L it is true whatever be the case.

Quine's (1953) famous criticism of the analytic–synthetic distinction is based on the claim that concepts like synonymy, definition, interchangeability *salva veritate*, semantic rule, or meaning postulate are no less in need of clarification than analyticity itself.

It is no doubt true that we do not understand the syntactic concept of meaning postulate, unless we appeal to semantic principles like (5). Such an appeal is not circular, however, since (5) itself is not claimed to be analytic-for-L. To answer Quine's challenge, the concept of meaning has to be given an independent definition. One way of doing this is the following. With Carnap and Montague, a *concept* (or intension) can be defined as a function from possible worlds to extensions (e.g. the concept of cat picks out from each possible world the class of cats in that world) (cf. Hintikka 1988*a*). Then the meaning of a linguistic term in language is *semantically determinate*, if it designates a concept; otherwise it is to some extent *vague*. If two terms designate the same concept, they have the same meaning. Two languages of the same type are *intertranslatable* if their (primitive and defined) terms designate the same class of concepts. Equivalence classes of intertranslatable languages constitute *conceptual systems*.[3]

Quine complains that the concept 'analytic-for-L' for some particular language does not generally characterize analyticity for a variable language L (1953: 34). But the above approach makes it clear that analytic truth is always relative to language in a semantic sense, i.e. a syntactical entity associated with meanings or meaning postulates. Meaning change implies conceptual change: when the meaning postulates for L are changed, we get a different language with different analytic truths, and thereby the conceptual system designated by L is changed as well.

The gist of Quine's argument comes in his final section:

it becomes folly to seek a boundary between synthetic statements, which hold contingently in experience, and analytic statements, which hold come what may. Any statement can be held true come what may, if we make drastic enough adjustments elsewhere in the system ... Conversely, by the some token, no statement is immune to revision. (Ibid. 43)

Here we see that the dogma Quine is really attacking is the assumption that some statements are immune to revision (and, for him, such revisions always arise from sensory stimulation). But we have seen that *this dogma can be rejected without denying the analytic–synthetic division within a language*. Statements like (4) are irrefutable only as long as the definition (5) of 'bachelor' is accepted; if (5) is revised, (4) need not be the case any more. Similarly, even logical truths like (2) are revisable, if we are willing to change the meanings of the logical constants.

The truth value of a synthetic sentence in L depends on what is the case—in spite of the meaning postulates of L. A synthetic truth is therefore said to express a *factual* or *material* truth.

According to the classical *correspondence theory*, going back to Aristotle and the 'adequacy' theory of the scholastics, material truth is a relation between a belief and reality. The bearers of truth may be taken to be sentences, statements, judgements, propositions, or beliefs. A statement is true if it describes an actually existing state of affairs, i.e. if it expresses a fact; otherwise it is false.

I shall argue in the next sections that Tarski's semantic definition suc-

---

[3] Cf. Niiniluoto and Tuomela (1973), Pearce (1987*a*). Davidson's famous thesis that there are no alternative conceptual schemes (see Davidson 1984: ch. 13) leads him to a sort of universalist view that there is essentially only one language. In my view, there are lots of examples of rival conceptual systems (e.g. colour terms in different languages).

ceeds in making precise this classical account of truth. Here I comment on the attempts to make truth a syntactic notion. Epistemic definitions of truth are discussed in Section 4.6.

The *coherence theory* of truth was supported by some Hegelian idealists (Bradley, Blanshard), who associated it with a metaphysical view about the world as a whole or a totality. Coherence in this tradition is a strong holistic notion, but attempts to define it in terms of mutual entailments have not been successful (Rescher 1973).

Another version was advocated in the early 1930s by some logical empiricists (Neurath, Hempel), who claimed that a sentence cannot 'correspond' to any extralinguistic reality. In this view, truth has to be defined in terms of relations between sentences: a judgement is true if it forms a coherent system with other judgements. If coherence here means consistency, it appears that truth has been defined by purely syntactical means. This hope is not warranted, however.

First, to be plausible at all, a coherent class of sentences should be maximally large. But if T is a complete consistent theory, then the 'coherence' of a sentence A with T simply means that A belongs to T. Theory T is then only a list of all true statements, and such an enumeration of truths does not amount to a definition of the concept of truth.

Secondly, Neurath and Hempel knew that in fact there are a number of mutually incompatible but internally coherent bodies of propositions. Therefore, to pick out a unique system of truths they had to appeal to a non-logical (and non-syntactical) idea, such as 'the system which is actually adopted by mankind, and especially by the scientists of our cultural circle' (Hempel 1935). Russell made the devastating objection that, according to the Neurath–Hempel doctrine, 'empirical truth can be determined by the police' (Russell 1940: 140). A more charitable interpretation would be to treat this theory as a naturalist account of accepted beliefs in science (Hempel 1965).

Another way of giving a syntactic characterization of truth could be based on the model of (1) which guarantees that (at least in simple cases) logical truth equals *provability*.[4] However, when we go to substantial or factual truth, this equation breaks down. Already in the case of arithmetic,

---

[4] There is a debate over whether the meaning of sentential connectives should be given by truth-tables or by rules of inference (see Prawitz 1977). I think both of these approaches are useful and illuminating. The latter alternative is favoured by the advocates of intuitionistic logic. However, in general semantics seems to me more basic: the concept of provability is always relative to a deductive system, and the choice of the axioms and inference rules is guided by the wish to capture as theorems a class of truths relative to some frame of interpretations or models. For an alternative approach, proceeding from inference rules to truth, see Brandom (1994).

Gödel's Incompleteness Theorem (proved in 1931) implies that, for any recursive axiom system, there are true statements about natural numbers that are not derivable from the axioms. Moreover, as provability is always relative to a deductive system (its axioms and rules of inference), the attempted identification of truth and provability would presuppose that we are already in possession of a unique and right system.

It seems that the only way of rescuing the equation between truth and provability is to interpret the latter notion in an *epistemic* way. Michael Dummett's 'Truth' (in 1959) proposed 'to transfer to ordinary statements what the intuitionists say about mathematical statements' (Dummett 1978: 17): we are entitled to call a statement A either true or false only if 'we could in finite time bring ourselves into a position in which we were justified either in asserting or in denying A' (ibid. 16). This means that truth and falsity are made to depend on epistemic concepts like justified assertion.

In the same way, the coherence theory has been interpreted as an epistemic (rather than merely syntactic) theory: a proposition is true if it coheres 'with a certain system of beliefs' (Walker 1989: 2).

From now on, the main rivals in my discussion are the accounts of truth as a semantic notion (correspondence theory) or as an epistemic notion (pragmatism in its many variations).

### 3.3  How semantics is effable: model theory

Alfred Tarski's 1933 paper is the most important classical study in the concept of truth.[5] It divides the history of the theory of truth into pre-Tarskian and post-Tarskian periods. It was greeted with great enthusiasm by Rudolf Carnap and Karl Popper as early as 1935.[6] But Tarski's own English article in 1944, later the standard reference to his ideas among philosophers, applies his insights to natural language in an informal and potentially misleading way.[7]

In my view, Tarski's real achievement is expressed in the model-theoretic concept of truth. A mature formulation was given in the 1950s, especially in joint papers with Robert Vaught in 1957, and it has later become the standard definition of truth in textbooks of logic.[8] This

---

[5] The German translation appeared in 1936. For the English translation, see Tarski (1956: ch. VIII).

[6] See Carnap (1963: 61) and Popper (1974: 78).

[7] See Tarski (1944). This article has been reprinted several times; see, for example, Feigl and Sellars (1949: 52–94).

[8] Cf. Bell and Slomson (1969), Monk (1976). For the history of model theory, see Henkin *et al.* (1974), Hintikka (1988*a*), and Hodges (1986).

conception makes explicit those ingredients of Tarski's approach which clearly distinguish it from the disquotational account of truth. The model-theoretic treatment of semantics is successfully applicable not only to artificial formal languages but also to fragments of scientific and natural languages.[9]

Let us first recall the model-theoretic definition of truth for a simple first-order language L.[10] Assume that the non-logical vocabulary of L contains individual constants $a_1, a_2, \ldots$ and predicates P, Q, ... Then an *L-structure* $M=(X, I)$ is a pair where X is a *domain* of individuals and I is an *interpretation function* from L to X such that $I(a_i) \in X$ for individual constants $a_i$, $I(P) \subseteq X$ for one-place predicates P, $I(Q) \subseteq X^2$ for two-place predicates Q, etc. Another formulation is to treat the pair (L, I) as an interpreted language, and define a structure for this language as a *relational system* of the form $(X, s_1, \ldots, A_1, \ldots, R_1, \ldots)$ with designated elements (s), subsets (A), and relations (R) that are the I-images of the vocabulary of L in the domain X.

For atomic sentences of L, truth in structure $M=(X, I)$ is defined by conditions of the form

$$M \vDash P(a_1) \text{ iff } I(a_1) \in I(P) \tag{7}$$
$$M \vDash Q(a_1, a_2) \text{ iff } \langle I(a_1), I(a_2) \rangle \in I(Q).$$

An open formula A of L with a free variable $x_i$ does not have a truth value in a structure M until some element of X is assigned to $x_i$. Let $s = \langle s_1, s_2, \ldots \rangle$ be an infinite sequence of objects from X. Then the relation $M \vDash_s A$, i.e. sequence s *satisfies* formula A in structure M, is defined by recursion on the complexity of A. For example,

$$M \vDash_s A \vee B \text{ iff } M \vDash_s A \text{ or } M \vDash_s B \tag{8}$$
$$M \vDash_s \forall x_i A \text{ iff } M \vDash_{s(i/b)} A \text{ for all } b \in X$$

where s(i/b) is the sequence obtained from s by replacing $s_i$ with b. The basic clauses for atomic formulas have the form

[9] Pioneering work on the applications of model theory to the languages of scientific theories was done by Przełecki (1969). See also Tuomela (1973) and Pearce (1987a). In my own work on truthlikeness, I have always relied on the Tarskian model-theoretic concept of truth (see Niiniluoto 1987a).

[10] Tarski's programme of course can be, and has been, generalized to more complex cases (see Davidson 1984). In the possible worlds semantics, truth is defined for intensional languages, with nomic and causal modalities (see Lewis 1973; Stalnaker 1984; Fetzer 1981) and propositional attitudes (Hintikka 1975). For sufficiently rich formal languages and fragments of natural language, the game-theoretical definition of truth has turned out to be useful. See Hintikka (1996). Game-theoretic semantics gives a realist or objectual treatment of atomic sentences and quantifiers. What is said below about Tarski's approach as a form of correspondence theory applies to the game-theoretical definition as well.

$$M \vDash_s P(x_i) \text{ iff } s_i \in I(P) \tag{9}$$

$$M \vDash_s Q(a_i, x_j) \text{ iff } \langle I(a_i), s_j \rangle \in I(Q).$$

When A is a sentence of L, i.e. A does not contain occurrences of free variables, it is satisfied in M by one sequence s if and only if it is satisfied by all sequences. Thus, the relation $M \vDash A$, i.e. A is *true in* M, or M is a *model of* A, can be defined by

$$M \vDash A \text{ iff } M \vDash_s A \text{ for every s.} \tag{10}$$

The key ideas of this definition include the following:

(i) Language L has a definite syntactical structure.
(ii) Truth is defined for sentences (well-formed closed formulas) of L.
(iii) Truth is defined relative to a structure M.
(iv) The definition of truth presupposes that the syntactical elements of L are mapped to the structure M by an interpretation function I.
(v) The recursive definition of truth for quantified sentences presupposes the relation of satisfaction between open formulas and sequences of objects.

All of these ideas, except (iii) and (iv), were made clear already in Tarski's original 1933 paper.

As Wolenski (1993) observes, condition (i) does not mean that L has to be a formal language in the logician's sense. Rather, L has to be syntactically well determined so that its sentences have a unique compositional structure. As Tarski (1944) points out, this requirement may be at least approximately satisfied by portions of a natural language. It is thus misleading to say that Tarski was 'thoroughly sceptical about the applicability of his theory to natural languages' (Haack 1978: 120).

According to (iii), the model-theoretic concept of truth in a model is relative to an L-structure M. The same language L can be interpreted in different domains X, X', . . . , or by different interpretation functions I, I', . . . on the same domain X. In the Leibnizian terminology, the L-structures M are (or represent) the possible worlds that can be distinguished within the vocabulary of L.

The model-theoretic notion of truth is a flexible tool for expressing relations between sentences of formal languages L and set-theoretical L-structures. When a branch of mathematics (e.g. group theory, arithmetic) is expressed in a formal language, Tarski's definition allows us to study the various structures that are models of such axiomatic theories. If the theory has a *standard model* M*, i.e. a unique intended interpretation (like

the structure of natural numbers N for arithmetic), then truth-in-M*
captures the standard or intended notion of truth for language L.

More generally, as the actual world is one among the possible worlds,
truth in the actual world should be a special case of truth in possible worlds.
Let L be a fragment of natural language which speaks about ordinary
objects (such as atoms, cells, stones, trees, animals, human beings, nations).
Then among the L-structures M there is a unique L-structure M* which
represents the actual world.[11] This structure M*=(X*, I*) contains a class
X* of actual objects and an interpretation function I* which maps the
syntactical elements of L to their actual extensions in X* (cf. LePore 1983).
Sentences of L that are true in M* are then *actually true*. Sentences that
are actually but not logically true express *factual* or *material truths* about
the actual world.

Tarski's 1933 paper operates with an 'absolute' concept of truth which
is not relativized to a model. But, with reference to 'the Göttingen school
grouped around Hilbert', he noted that there is also a relative concept of
'correct or true sentence in an individual domain $a$', where 'we restrict the
extension of the individuals considered to a given class $a$' (Tarski 1956:
199). Truth in the absolute sense then means the same as correctness in
'the class of all individuals' (ibid. 207).

For his explication of truth, Tarski thus assumed that the class X* of
all actual objects is given. His relative concept applies to classes that are
*subdomains* of X*.[12] This interpretation is confirmed by Tarski's remark
that such specific individual domains are relevant in connection with
various special sciences (ibid. 239).

Hence, in 1933 Tarski did not yet have the general model-theoretic

---

[11] This statement needs two qualifications. First, in order that the notion of actual truth
is captured, the domain of M* has to be maximal in the sense that it includes all of the relevant types of actual objects (cf. Cox 1997). Secondly, the uniqueness of M* presupposes
that the language L is semantically determinate: if L contains vague expressions, M* is
replaced by a class of L-structures (see Przełecki 1969; Niiniluoto 1987a: 146). Sundholm
(1994) claims that the application of model theory to the semantics of natural language
presupposes an absolute conception of THE REAL WORLD, 'fixed and ready, sharply
delineated in all its aspects and where the answer to every possible question is already
decided'. This thesis seems to presuppose the assumption that natural language is a
universal language. However, model theory links a language L only to a L-structure M*
which is a fragment of the actual world, without assuming a 'ready-made world' (cf. Ch. 7).
This structure decides answers only to those questions that may be asked within L. I do not
think it makes sense to speak about 'all possible questions'.

[12] These subdomains of the actual world are comparable to the 'situations' of Barwise
and Etchemendy (1987). Their approach makes it explicit that a sentence need not be
interpreted as speaking about the whole actual world, but may be correlated with some part
of the world only. The same idea was emphasized in J. L. Austin's formulation of the
correspondence theory of truth (cf. Johnson 1992). Hintikka's (1975) 'small worlds' are
subdomains of full possible worlds. Cf. n. 11.

concept which defines truth relative to any possible domain. But this general notion was not introduced as late as 1957, as Hodges (1986) claims, since it was needed and explicated already in Tarski's 1936 paper on logical consequence (see Niiniluoto 1999*a*). Here Tarski talked about models which interpret the non-logical vocabulary of a sentence by 'arbitrary sequences of objects' (Tarski 1956: 417).

## 3.4 Truth as correspondence: Tarski's definition

Tarski's position with respect to the universal medium–calculus distinction is interesting (cf. Section 3.1). He noted the 'universality' of our everyday 'colloquial' language. If the semantics of this universal language is expressed within itself, the liar paradox leads to inconsistency (Tarski 1956: 164). Formally adequate semantics for the colloquial language is possible only by splitting it into a series of languages which correspond to a hierarchy of metalanguages (ibid. 267).

Tarski's early work on truth, before the mature model theory, seems to exemplify a middle position between the universal medium (one language—one world) and calculus (many languages—many worlds) views. For Tarski, there is *only one world but many languages*. In his 1935 address on 'scientific semantics', Tarski blamed earlier attemps for proceeding 'as though there was only one language in the world' (ibid. 402). Moreover, from the viewpoint of a metalanguage ML, an object language L itself is part of the world, and ML must contain both expressions of the original language L and expressions of the morphology (structural description) of language (ibid. 403). Therefore, the language ML has the power to speak about the relations between L and the rest of the world.

Let us use quotation marks to form metalinguistic names of object language expressions. Thus, 'cat' is a name for the English word composed of the letters 'c', 'a', and 't'. Then the Tarskian picture of language can be illustrated by Fig. 4. The denotation or reference relations between object language (English or Finnish) and entities in the world are indicated by arrows, and reference relations between metalanguage and object language by dotted arrows. The words of the object language (or, more precisely, their tokens) reappear as parts of the world. The relations of all entities in the world can be discussed in a sufficiently rich metalanguage, which makes 'scientific semantics' possible.

Although Tarski himself used the concept of fact only in his presystematic statement of the correspondence theory, a similar picture (see Fig. 5)

SEMANTICS

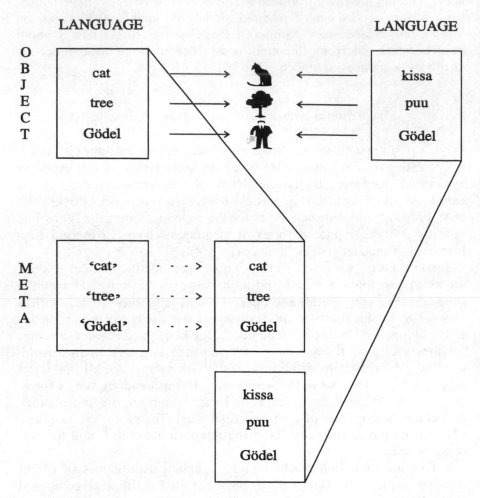

Fɪɢ. 4. Tarski's semantics

can be drawn for complex expressions: sentences designate facts in the world (arrows), quotation mark names in the metalanguage refer to object language sentences (dotted arrows).

In these pictures, there is a fixed interpretation of language, which is compatible with conditions (UM-2)–(UM-3) of the universal medium view, but nevertheless semantics is accessible (C-1), metalanguage is possible (C-5), and truth is a language–world correspondence relation (C-6). The step to the model-theoretic calculus conception would require that

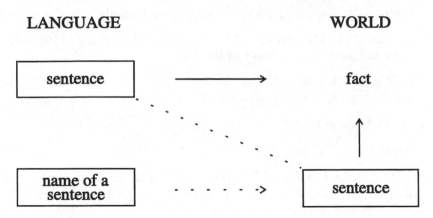

FIG. 5. Semantics for sentences

alternative reference relations (interpretations) and alternative worlds are also considered.

How can a metalanguage ML express semantical relations between an object language L and the other parts of the world? Simply by stating them. For example, the denotation relations, or arrows in Fig. 4, can be expressed by

'Cat' denotes cats (11)
'Cat' refers to cats
'Cat' means cat
'Kissa' (in Finnish) denotes cats. (12)

Statements of this form express contingent semantical facts about English and Finnish. They should not be confused with tautologies like

'Cat' means (the same as) 'cat'. (13)

It might have happened that the English linguistic community used some other word than 'cat' to refer to the animal in question (cf. Niiniluoto 1981). It is also important to realize that, in terms of Fig. 4, (11) expresses a language–world arrow, not the dotted arrow between a name of a word and the word (which is simply established by our convention about the use of quotation marks).

Statements like (11) describe particular language–world relations, but they do not define what denotation is or when it holds between two entities. Tarski's 1944 paper does not pay attention to this problem, but in 1933 he points out (in a footnote) a connection between denotation and satisfaction:

Name 'a' denotes object b iff b satisfies the formula 'x is a'.          (14)

(Tarski 1956: 194). The concept of satisfaction is characterized for simple sentential functions by examples of the form

b satisfies 'x is white' iff b is white                                    (15)
a and b satisfy 'x sees y' iff a sees b

(ibid. 190). More generally,

b satisfies 'x is P' iff b is P$^\wedge$,                                   (16)

where P$^\wedge$ is the translation of P into the metalanguage (ibid. 192).

Combination of these two accounts gives us the unsurprising result that 'a' denotes b iff b is a, i.e.

'a' denotes a.                                                             (17)

We are thus back to statements of the form (11). Field (1972) concludes that Tarski's theory of denotation for proper names amounts to a mere list: name N denotes object a iff either a is France and N is 'France' or ... or a is Germany and N is 'Germany' (cf. Horwich 1990). In model theory, however, the denotation relation is conceptualized by the interpretation function I. The condition (16) for satisfaction is replaced by clauses of the form (9).

Tarski never developed an account of how such language–world relations are established. For artificial formal languages, the interpretation function I is fixed by stipulation, but for natural languages usually the terms have historically received meanings created and sustained by the consensus and the language games of the linguistic communities (cf. Section 3.1). In Peirce's terms, most words in natural language are symbols, i.e. their relations to their objects are based upon conventions.

The full meaning of a term (in Montague's sense) is a function which gives its extension in all possible worlds. Meaning or intension in this sense also contains the interpretation function I* which gives the extension of a term in the actual world M*. It should be noted that this function I* is not normally specified extensionally by enumerating ordered pairs. I* is rather specified by giving definitions or partial rules and 'recipes' for 'calculating' its values in the world M* (cf. Hintikka 1975: p. xiv). In this sense, we can know the meaning of a term without yet knowing its actual extension.

Tarski's model-theoretic account of truth presupposes that the object language is interpreted, but it is compatible with various methods of fixing reference. In other words, Tarski shows how the actual truth of sentences of L depends on their interpretations (by function I*) in the actual world

M\*. In this sense, Field (1972) is right in pointing out that Tarski in a sense reduces the concept of truth to the concept of reference. But his account leaves open the question whether reference itself is defined, e.g. by descriptive or causal methods.[13]

Figs. 4 and 5 lead directly to Tarski's famous condition of *material adequacy*: the definition of truth for language L should entail all T-equivalences of the form

$$x \text{ is true iff } p \tag{T}$$

where x is a name of a sentence in L and p is the translation of this sentence in the metalanguage ML (Tarski 1956: 188). In Tarski (1944), it is always assumed that L is contained in ML, so that p in (T) is a sentence in L and x is its name 'p':

$$\text{'p' is true iff p.} \tag{18}$$

Tarski's own illustration of condition (T) in his 1933 paper comes from the case where L is the formal calculus of classes:

$$n_1n_2(1_{1,2}+1_{2,1})_{1,2}(1_{2,1}) \text{ is true iff} \tag{19}$$

for any classes a and b we have $a \subseteq b$ or $b \subseteq a$

(Tarski 1956: 189). If L is formal arithmetic, and the metalanguage ML includes the usual mathematical notations, we may have

$$Q(k_1, k_2) \text{ is true in N iff } 1<2. \tag{20}$$

It is clear from the spirit of Tarski's discussion that these conditions presuppose an interpretation function in the model-theoretic sense. For example, the term $k_1$ is interpreted as the natural number 1 in N, the predicate Q as the smaller-than relation < in N, etc.

Condition (20) is analogous to the case where L is German and ML is English:

$$\text{'Schnee ist weiss' is true iff snow is white.} \tag{21}$$

As Davidson (1984) correctly points out, Tarski does not define the concept of translation between L and ML for his T-equivalences of this type. However, the point of (21) is not that there is an antecedently given translation between German and English, but rather that such a translation is induced by the fact that the terms 'Schnee' and 'weiss' are interpreted in the actual world to denote entities that we in English denote by 'snow' and 'white' (see Fig. 6).

---

[13] For theories of reference, see Haack (1978), Devitt and Sterelny (1987). Cf. Section 5.2.

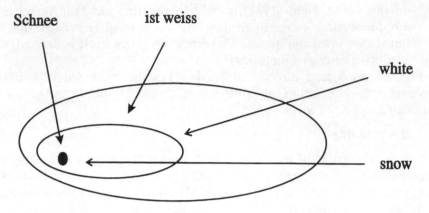

FIG. 6. Tarski's T-equivalence

If the object language L is included in the metalanguage ML, we get Tarski's (1944) standard example:

'Snow is white' is true iff snow is white.                          (22)

Here we do not have the problem about translation, but now there is a threat of triviality: many philosophers, among them Putnam, Soames, and Etchemendy, claim that T-equivalences of the type (22) are trivial tautologies.[14]

This charge against (22) is not convincing, however. We have already observed that statements of the form (11) and (12) express contingent facts about natural languages. Similarly, (21) and (22) express in Fig. 5 the arrow (designation relation) between a sentence and a fact, not a translation between object language and metalanguage.

Tarski emphasizes that the T-equivalence is not a definition of truth, but rather an adequacy condition for a definition. However, his claim that the definition would be the infinite conjunction of all T-equivalences (for the sentences of L) is misleading (Tarski 1956: 188). In the same way, a conjunction of conditions (16) would not be a definition of denotation. A T-equivalence has to be derived from, and explained by, a definition which links linguistic expressions to their interpretations in the world.

Jennings (1987) observes that Tarski's (T) has been understood in two different ways. He concludes, correctly I think, that (T) is *expressed* in terms of the object language L and the metalanguage ML, but *states* something about the relation between language L and the world (cf. Fig. 4).

---

[14] See Etchemendy (1988) and the critical remarks in Davidson (1990).

Hence, Tarski's semantic definition of truth is not merely *disquotational* (cf. Quine 1990).

Jennings holds, however, the thesis that this reading of Tarski leads to 'ontological relativism': ML refers to (and only to) the same world referred to by L. I do not see that this leads to any kind of relativism (cf. (C-4) above). The only argument that Jennings gives is mistaken: he assumes that a true biconditional of the form

'Phlogiston is given off during combustion' is true iff    (23)
phlogiston is given off during combustion

commits us to the existence of phlogiston, but certainly an equivalence statement can be true even when its both sides are false.

Putnam (1983a) claims that (21) holds in all possible worlds, even in those counterfactual cases where 'Schnee ist weiss' means that water is liquid. Therefore, Putnam argues, the property of truth has not been conceptually analysed at all: Tarski's definition takes into account only the spelling of a string of letters in L and facts about the world describable by sentences of L, but there is no reference to speakers or uses of words. What Putnam ignores here is the fact that Tarski is always speaking about an interpreted language: truth is relative to an interpretation function. If the interpretation of the terms 'Schnee' and 'weiss' is changed by the users of the language (cf. Fig. 6 again), the equivalence (21) does not hold any more.

Stich (1990) correctly notes that our beliefs can be correlated with the world by many reference relations REF, REF', REF'', . . . (corresponding to the choice of the interpretation function I above). Each of these defines a truth-relation TRUE', TRUE'', . . . Why should we, Stich then asks, be interested in TRUTH at all—rather than TRUTH', TRUTH'', etc.? This argument again ignores the fact that by changing I we get different interpreted languages. Creating new languages is certainly an interesting project, but it does not require that we give up our present language—or that we are 'conservative' in still using the old language.

Rorty (1998: 6) suggests that we would be 'more sensitive to the marvelous diversity of human languages' if we ceased to ask whether they correspond to some 'nonhuman, eternal entity'. But the question about correspondence can be asked relative to each different language which human beings have cared to create.

The existence of many truth-relations is not a problem for Tarski, but a natural feature of his model-theoretic approach to formal languages. In the natural language, the terms have historically received an interpretation I* through the convention or consensus of the linguistic community ('cat' in English and 'kissa' in Finnish are names of the same animal). This interpretation I* may very well be changed in the future, but as long as it remains accepted we are interested in it—at least if we wish to analyse the concept of actual truth relative to our own natural language.

Johnson (1992) argues that Tarski's approach is not adequate, since it 'seems to make every meaningful sentence true or false by definition'. In a 'full-bodied' correspondence theory, Johnson says, 'true statements are true *because* things are the way they are', but in Tarski's semantic conception 'true sentences are true because they are specified to be so' (see also Peregrin 1995: 214). This is, indeed, the case, when we fix by stipulation an interpretation of a formal language relative to a structure. But the terms of natural language ('Schnee', 'snow', 'white', etc.) have antecedently meanings through the conventions of linguistic communities—and we do not decide the colour of snow, nor its expression in English or Finnish. We give names to colours, but it is up to nature to decide what the colour of snow in fact is (cf. Section 9.2).

It has been objected that Tarski does not tell what the predicates true-in-L for a variable L have in common, and therefore he is not giving a proper theory or definition of truth (Davidson 1990; Putnam 1994). However, Tarski is giving an *explication* of the concept of truth: such an explication does not proceed by an explicit definition (of the form 'truth is . . .'), but rather by progressing step by step from simpler cases to more complex cases. The paradigmatic applications are extended to new similar cases so that certain stipulated adequacy conditions are satisfied (cf. Carnap 1962). Tarski's approach to truth should be understood to be a research programme: truth is first defined for set theory and first-order logic, and then extended to fragments of natural language, scientific languages, indexical expressions, vague statements, intensional languages, etc. (cf. Davidson 1984).

Further, there is a general schema underlying Tarski's approach, as Carnap showed in his semantical works in the late 1930s. Carnap's (1942) presentation has the virtue that it makes explicit the *designation* function des in a semantical system S, where S is an interpreted language corresponding to the pair (L, I). For Carnap, designation is a language–world relation: individual constants designate individual objects and predicates designate properties. A recursive definition parallel to Tarski's conditions shows how sentences designate propositions. For example, if b designates London and P designates the property of being large, then P(b) designates the proposition that London is large. Composite sentences are treated by clauses of the type (8). Then the truth of a sentence in a semantical system S is defined by condition

> Sentence s is true in S if and only if there is a proposition p (C)
> such that s designates p in S and p.

Condition C resembles Tarski's T, but it is clearly stronger than T, since here the semantical connection between the sentence s and its truth-condition p is made explicit by the relation of designation (meaning, saying)—and no undefined notion of translation is involved. As the designation relation for sentences is given by Tarski's recursive definition using the designation function for terms, it is not here an undefined semantic notion. Carnap also noted that this formulation refutes the objection that the semantical definition 'is not general but is given by an enumeration of single cases' (see Schilpp 1953: 901). Variants of schema (C) have been given by Kirkham (1992: 130–2) as expressing the 'essence' of the correspondence theory of truth.

Tarski (1944) makes it clear that his semantic conception gives a 'precise form' of the classical Aristotelian or correspondence view of truth. He also dissociates his approach from the redundancy theory of truth.

When Tarski stresses the epistemological neutrality of his definition, he is not referring to the debate on correspondence vs. its rivals, but rather to issues like realism and idealism. Haack's claim that 'Tarski did not regard himself as giving a version of the correspondence theory' (Haack 1978: 114) is not warranted.

If Tarski's condition (T) would exhaust his account of truth, his view could be understood to be disquotational or minimalist (Horwich 1990)— and could not be claimed to give an explication of the correspondence theory. But we have already found reason to reject this interpretation of Tarski.

Haack accepts that Tarski's concept of satisfaction, as a relation between open sentences and sequences of objects, 'bears some analogy to correspondence theories', but instead 'Tarski's definition of *truth* makes no appeal to specific sequences of objects, for true sentences are satisfied by all sequences' (1978: 113). Davidson (1984) has also interpreted Tarski as a correspondence theorist because of his notion of satisfaction. But recently he has given up this view for similar reasons to Haack (Davidson 1990).

I think it is correct to regard satisfaction as a realist language–world relation. Tarski's treatment of quantifiers is thereby objectual rather than substitutional: quantified sentences are made true by objects in the world, not by their substitution instances in the language. But this is not the basic or only reason for understanding Tarski's approach as a correspondence theory (see Niiniluoto 1987a: 138, 479). It is the interpretation function I* which links terms and sentences to the actual world. The truth-conditions for sentences without quantifiers ('John loves Mary') could be defined without the concept of satisfaction (see formula (7)), and they depend via I* on a correspondence relation between language and reality.

Davidson's main objection to correspondence theories is that 'there is nothing interesting or instructive to which true sentences might correspond' (Davidson 1990: 303). It is correct that Tarski's definition avoids the use of phrases like 'fact'. But I think here Davidson overlooks the Tarskian idea that sentences correspond to structures or models that are fragments of the actual world, i.e. Tarskian relational systems serve as *truth-makers* in his account. The sentence 'John loves Mary' is interpreted by I* to assert the state of affairs that John loves Mary, i.e. <I*(John), I*(Mary)> belongs to the relation I*(love). It is this fact—consisting of the couple and their loving relation—to which this sentence corresponds if it is true.

Tarski's recursive approach shows how the truth of complex sentences can be reduced to the truth or satisfaction of atomic statements; in this view, the truth-maker is a relational structure.[15] Hintikka's (1996) game-theoretical semantics is an even more flexible account of this process of interpretation. To understand these definitions of truth as correspondence theories, we need not assume that each complex statement is made true by an equally complex fact (cf. Searle 1995). In Hintikka's treatment, such a complex fact is replaced by a game which has the structure of a tree, where branches represent the various ways in which the sentences may be verified or falsified, and truth means the existence of a winning stategy for the verifier.

## 3.5 Truthlikeness

Besides the classical *bivalent* logic with two truth values (truth, falsity), logicians have developed systems of three-valued and *many-valued* logic.

---

[15] Pendlebury (1986) makes a similar suggestion that sets of atomic facts are sufficient as truth-makers, and no disjunctive and general facts are needed. Cox (1997) objects that this makes truth relative to worlds, but this is beside the point, since—as we have seen—truth in a structure is the basic concept of semantics.

Their generalizations include semantic theories (such as *fuzzy logic*) which operate with continuous degrees of truth in the interval [0, 1].

For example, the *degree of truth* of the statement 'It is raining now' equals one if and only if it is clearly raining, and zero if and only if it is clearly not raining. Indefinite borderline cases (such as drizzle and mist) receive degrees of truth between 0 and 1. This treatment is useful, since many terms of ordinary and even scientific languages are semantically vague.[16]

Semantic vagueness should be distinguished from epistemic uncertainty. Degree of truth is, therefore, different from *epistemic probability*, which has its maximum value one for certainty (certain truth) and its minimum value zero for certain falsity. Values between 0 and 1 indicate cases of insufficient evidence, lack of knowledge (see Section 4.5).

In many languages, the concept of probability is derived from the Latin *verisimilitudo*, likeness-to-the-truth or similarity-to-the-truth. This term was introduced by ancient sceptics (Carneades, Cicero) as a reply to the Stoic *apraxia* argument: he who does not know the truth, cannot act. The idea was that it may be rational to act on what-is-like-truth. This has been expressed by the slogan 'probability is the guide of life', which clearly refers to epistemic probability: we need not be fully certain of the truth of a hypothesis in order to act upon it.[17]

Another interpretation—discussed and criticized by Augustine in *Contra Academicos* (AD 384)—is that verisimilitude indicates falsity which is nevertheless 'close to the truth'. This idea became important in the fallibilist epistemology which claims that our knowledge at best 'approximates' and 'approaches' the truth without ever reaching it (Cusanus, Peirce, Engels). It was not until 1960 that the first serious attempt to define this notion of truthlikeness for scientific theories was made by Karl Popper.[18]

Popper's great insight was that truthlikeness as a logical concept, and fallible indicators of truthlikeness (like 'corroboration'), have to be distinguished from probability. His qualitative definition applies to theories, understood as sets of sentences closed under deduction (see Popper 1963; 1972). A theory B is defined to be *more truthlike* than theory A if and only if

$$\text{either } A \cap T \subseteq B \cap T \text{ and } B \cap F \subset A \cap F \qquad (24)$$
$$\text{or } A \cap T \subset B \cap T \text{ and } B \cap F \subseteq A \cap F,$$

---

[16] For the concept of vagueness, see Fine (1975).
[17] See Burnyeat (1983) on the early sceptical tradition.
[18] For the history of verisimilitude, see Niiniluoto (1987*a*: ch. 5). Cf. Niiniluoto (1999*b*).

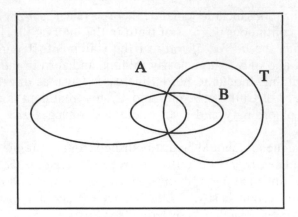

FIG. 7. Popper's definition of truthlikeness

where T and F are the sets of true and false sentences, respectively, and $\subset$ is the proper subset relation (see Fig. 7). Unfortunately this definition does not fulfil its intended application, since it does not make false theories comparable: as Pavel Tichý and David Miller proved in 1973, if B is more truthlike than A in the sense (24), then B must be true (see Miller 1974).

Popper's intuitive idea was simple and natural: a theory is truthlike if it has a large *overlap* with the set T of all truths (in the given language). Another way of expressing this requirement is the following: the symmetric difference

$$A \Delta T = (A-T) \cup (T-A) \tag{25}$$

should be as small as possible. Here A–T is the *falsity content* of A, whereas T∩A is the *truth content* of A. In the limit, A∆T is empty if and only if A=T, i.e. a theory is maximally truthlike iff it coincides with the whole truth of T.

As an admirer of Tarski, Popper defines the theory T to be true in the Tarskian sense, which he also takes to be a version of the correspondence theory of truth. But this does not prevent us from seeing that Popper's approach can be understood as a generalization and modification of classical coherence theories of truth: overlap of sets is one way of making the elusive notion of coherence precise. For Popper, the truthlikeness of a theory depends on its 'coherence' with the set of all truths, and maximum coherence means that the theory becomes indistinguishable from the total system of true propositions.

The connection between Popper's definition and the coherence theories is not merely an accident: the latter were generally in trouble when

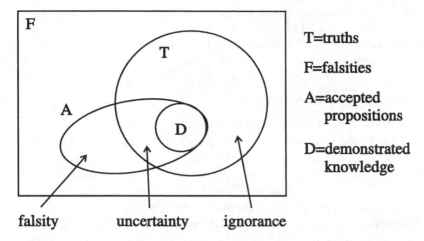

falsity        uncertainty     ignorance

T=truths

F=falsities

A=accepted
    propositions

D=demonstrated
    knowledge

FIG. 8. Types of error

distinguishing between different types of *errors* that should be avoided (see Fig. 8). The scepticist strategy was to avoid errors of *falsity* by refusing to accept any propositions, but they thereby committed errors of *ignorance* by failing to accept true propositions. Spinoza's version of coherence theory could not allow errors of falsity, since he took human minds to be parts of God's mind (Walker 1989).

Bradley's thesis that all propositions are false was based, among other Hegelian peculiarities, upon the confusion between errors of falsity and ignorance. For example, the proposition 'This rose is red' is said to have some degree of truth, but also some degree of falsity, since it does not tell all about the flower. The same mistake ('our theories are not true, hence false, since they do not tell the whole truth') has been repeated many times in the history of philosophy. In the subsequent chapters, we shall refer to its versions as the *All-or-Nothing Fallacy*.

Popper avoids the confusions of the coherence theories by making a clear distinction between the truth content and falsity content of a theory (cf. Figs. 7 and 8). It is an irony of history that the Tichý–Miller refutation of definition (24) is based upon the fact that after all there is a subtle relation between errors of falsity and errors of ignorance: when the former are decreased, the latter are by implication increased.

In spite of some attempts to rescue Popper's definition, it seems to me that Popper's mistake was the assumption that truthlikeness could be defined merely by means of truth value (truth/falsity) and logical deduction. The failure of his definition casts doubt on any related attempt to develop a coherence theory of truth.

What was missing from Popper's approach was the concept of *similarity* or *likeness*. Quine's (1960) famous objection against Peirce was that the relation 'nearer than' is defined for numbers but not for theories. The similarity approach, to be outlined below, takes seriously the equation

$$\text{truthlikeness} = \text{truth} + \text{similarity}. \tag{26}$$

The concept of truth itself is not modified here, as in fuzzy logic, but rather similarity is used for measuring distances from the truth. This approach was first proposed in 1974 by Risto Hilpinen and Pavel Tichý, and soon followed by Ilkka Niiniluoto, Raimo Tuomela, and Graham Oddie.[19] The main results of this programme were published in Oddie's *Likeness to Truth* (1986) and Niiniluoto's *Truthlikeness* (1987*a*).

To outline my favourite formulation of the similarity approach, let us represent *cognitive problems* by finite or infinite sets of statements $B = \{h_i \mid i \in I\}$, where the elements of B are mutually exclusive and jointly exhaustive, i.e.

$$\vdash \sim (h_i \And h_j) \text{ for all } i \neq j, \; i, j \in I \tag{27}$$

$$\vdash \bigvee_{i \in I} h_i .$$

The simplest example of a cognitive problem in the sense of (27) is a yes-or-no question $\{h, \sim h\}$ consisting of a hypothesis and its negation. For each cognitive problem B there is an associated language L where the statements $h_i$ are expressed. If L is an interpreted and semantically determinate language, it describes a unique fragment $W_L$ of the actual world (cf. Section 3.3). Conditions (27) guarantee that there is one and only one element $h^*$ of B which is true (in the sense of the Tarskian model theory) in the structure $W_L$ (see Fig. 9).

If $h^*$ is unknown, we face a cognitive problem B with the *target* $h^*$: which of the elements of B is true? The statements $h_i$ in B are the *complete potential answers* to this problem. The *partial* potential answers are non-empty disjunctions of complete answers, i.e. they belong to the disjunctive closure D(B) of B:

$$D(B) = \left\{ \bigvee_{i \in J} h_i \mid \varnothing \neq J \subseteq I \right\}.$$

The crucial step is now the introduction of a real-valued function $\Delta : B \times B \rightarrow R$ which expresses the *distance* $\Delta(h_i, h_j) = \Delta_{ij}$ between the elements

---

[19] See Miller (1974; 1994), Oddie (1986), Niiniluoto (1977; 1985*a*; 1987*a*), Kuipers (1987; 1992), Kieseppä (1996), Zwart (1998). A survey of the recent literature is given in Niiniluoto (1998).

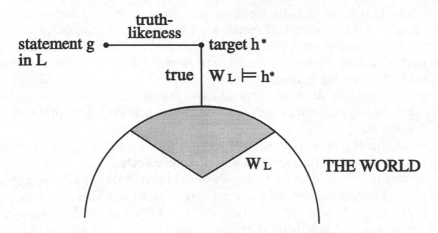

FIG. 9. Definition of truthlikeness

of B. Here $0 \leq \Delta_{ij} \leq 1$, and $\Delta_{ij}=0$ if and only if i=j. This distance function $\Delta$ has to be specified for each cognitive problem B separately, but there are 'canonical' ways of doing this for special types of problems. Examples of such distances and metrics can be found in many scientific disciplines: mathematics, statistics, computer science, information theory, biology, psychology, and anthropology (see Niiniluoto 1987a: ch. 1).

First, $\Delta$ may be directly definable by a natural metric underlying the structure of B, which is usually a part of the mathematical representation of the problem situation (e.g. the state space of a physical theory). For example, if the elements of B are point estimates of an unknown real-valued parameter, their distance is given simply by the geometric metric on real numbers R, i.e. the distance between two real numbers x, y$\in$ R is |x−y|. The Euclidean distance between two points x=$(x_1, \ldots, x_n)$ and y=$(y_1, \ldots, y_n)$ in $R^n$ is

$$\sqrt{\sum_{i=1}^{n}(x_i-y_i)^2}. \tag{28}$$

If the elements of B are quantitative laws, then their distance is given by the Minkowskian metrics between functions. Thus, if f: [a, b]$\rightarrow$R and g: [a, b]$\rightarrow$R are continuous real-valued functions of one variable, their Minkowskian distances are defined by

$$\Delta^p(f,g)=\left(\int_a^b |f(x)-g(x)|^p \, dx\right)^{1/p}. \tag{29}$$

Formula (29) gives the city-block metric for p=1, the Euclidian metric for p=2, and the Tchebycheff metric max |f(x)−g(x)|, a≤x≤b, for p=∞. For example, two functions are $\Delta^\infty$-close to each other if their values are close to each other for all the arguments, and $\Delta^2$-close if their values are close to each other on the average.[20]

If the elements of B are probabilistic statements, then the relevant distance is the information-theoretic divergence between probability distributions.

Secondly, let L be a first-order language with a finite non-logical vocabulary. For a monadic language with one-place predicates $M_1, \ldots, M_k$, the *Q-predicates* are defined by conjunctions of the form $(\pm)M_1(x)\& \ldots \&(\pm)M_k$, where (±) is replaced by the negation sign ~ or by nothing. The distance between Q-predicates can be simply defined by the number of different claims they make about the primitive predicates $M_1, \ldots, M_k$, divided by k. (Thus, when k=3, the distance between $M_1(x)\&M_2(x)\&M_3(x)$ and $M_1(x)\&M_2(x)\&\sim M_3(x)$ is 1/3.) As Carnap suggested, the primitive predicates can sometimes be organized into families of mutually exclusive and jointly exhaustive attributes (e.g. the space of colour terms, the number of children in a family). Q-predicates are then defined by conjunctions taking one element from each family. Each family may have its own natural distance function (e.g. yellow is closer to red than green), which generates a Euclidean distance between Q-predicates. In this way, the class **Q** of the Q-predicates constitutes a metric conceptual space, i.e. a classification system which is a qualitative or discrete counterpart to state spaces defined by quantities (cf. Niiniluoto 1987a: ch. 4).

When **Q** is given, we can define in the Carnap–Hintikka style the set of *state descriptions* (location of a finite number of individuals in the cells of **Q**), the set of *structure descriptions* (the proportion of individuals in the cells of **Q**), and the set of *constituents* of language L (which cells are empty and which non-empty). Each of them defines a cognitive problem in the sense of (27): all statements in the monadic language L can be expressed as a disjunction of state descriptions, and all generalizations (i.e. quantificational statements without individual constants) as a disjunction of constituents. These normal forms, when relativized to the

---

[20] Note that here we are primarily defining the distance between two functions in terms of the distances between their corresponding values. The attempt to do this purely syntactically would lead to the difficulty, well known in catastrophe theory, that sometimes the courses-of-values of two functions may be very far from each other even though their formulas differ only very slightly in one parameter value (e.g. f(x)=a/x and g(x)=b/x, when a is a small negative and b a small positive constant).

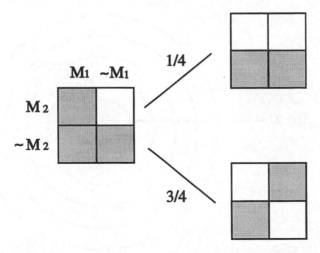

FIG. 10. The Clifford distance between monadic constituents

quantificational depth of a generalization, can be extended to full first-order language with relations. The distance $\Delta$ for these problems can be defined by counting the differences in the standard syntactical form of the elements of B.

For example, a monadic constituent tells us that certain kinds of individuals (given by Q-predicates) exist and others do not exist; the simplest distance (the so-called Clifford distance) between monadic constituents is the number of their diverging claims about the Q-predicates divided by the total number of Q-predicates (see Fig. 10).[21] If a constituent has a small Clifford distance from the true constituent, it will also imply a large number of true existential or universal generalizations (Niiniluoto 1977). For some purposes, however, it is useful to refine the Clifford measure by letting the penalty of a mistaken claim depend on the distance between the Q-predicates. For example, if $C_1$ locates all ravens in the brown cell and $C_2$ locates them in the yellow cell, and in fact all ravens are black, then $C_1$ and $C_2$ have the same Clifford distance from the truth; but if brown is closer to black than yellow, then $C_1$ should be closer to the truth than $C_2$.

Distance between depth-d constituents (for finite d) leads in the limit to a distance measure between complete theories in a first-order language L, as they correspond to infinite sequences of deeper and deeper constituents.

[21] For disputes about the distance between constituents, see Oddie (1986) and Niiniluoto (1987a: ch. 9.3).

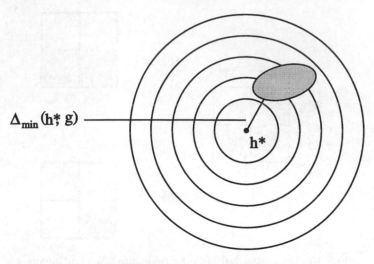

$$\Delta_{\min}(h_*^*, g)$$

FIG. 11. Closeness to the truth

If B contains complete theories in L, then D(B) includes arbitrary first-order theories in L.

The next step is the extension of $\Delta$ to a function $B\times D(B)\rightarrow R$, so that $\Delta(h_i, g)$ expresses the distance of partial answer $g\in D(B)$ from $h_i\in B$. Let $g\in D(B)$ be a potential answer with

$$\vdash g = \bigvee_{i\in I_g} h_i,$$

where $I_g\subseteq I$. This statement g allows all the potential answers in $I_g$ and excludes those outside $I_g$. Hence, g is true if and only if its normal form includes h*. Define

$$\Delta_{\min}(h_i, g)=\min_{j\in I_g}\Delta_{ij}$$

$$\Delta_{\sum}(h_i, g)=\sum_{j\in I_g}\Delta_{ij}\bigg/\sum_{j\in I}\Delta_{ij} \tag{30}$$

$$\Delta_{ms}^{\gamma\gamma'}(h_i, g)=\gamma\Delta_{\min}(h_i, g)+\gamma'\Delta_{\sum}(h_i, g) \quad (\gamma>0,\ \gamma'>0).$$

(If B is infinite, the sums have to be replaced by integrals.) Here $\Delta_{\min}$ is the minimum distance from the allowed answers to the given answer, $\Delta_{\sum}$ is the normalized sum of these distances, and $\Delta_{ms}$ is the weighted average of the min- and sum-factors (see Fig. 11).

Then g is *approximately true* if $\Delta_{\min}(h^*, g)$ is sufficiently small; if the degree of approximate truth of g is measured by

$$AT(g, h^*)=1-\Delta_{min}(h^*, g), \tag{31}$$

this definition guarantees that the following condition is satisfied:

g is approximately true to the degree 1 iff g is true. (32)

For example, if the true value of a parameter $\theta$ is 5.0, then the statement $\theta \in [3.0, 4.9]$ is approximately true.

Truthlikeness in the Popperian sense is not simply closeness to being true, but it combines the ideas of truth and information. For example, the short interval estimate [4.8, 4.9] is more truthlike than the longer (and informationally weaker) interval estimate [3.0, 4.9], even though their degree of approximate truth is the same.

Hence, truthlikeness has to be defined through a 'game of excluding falsity and preserving truth'. These two goals are to some extent opposite to each other, so that we need a method of balancing between them. This is achieved by the *min-sum*-measure $\Delta_{ms}^{\gamma\gamma'}$, where the weights $\gamma$ and $\gamma'$ indicate our cognitive desire of finding truth and avoiding error, respectively. Note that if we favoured only truth ($\gamma'=0$), then nothing would be better than a trivial tautology, and if we favoured only information content ($\gamma=0$), then nothing would be better than a logical contradiction. Thus, the *degree of truthlikeness* $Tr(g, h^*)$ of $g \in D(B)$ (relative to the target $h^*$ in B) is defined by

$$Tr(g, h^*)=1-\Delta_{ms}^{\gamma\gamma'}(h^*, g). \tag{33}$$

The properties of the measure Tr include the following nice features:

$0 \leq Tr(g, h^*) \leq 1.$ (34)

$Tr(g, h^*)=1$ iff $g=h^*$. (35)

Among true statements, but not among false statements, (36)
truthlikeness covaries with logical strength.

$Tr(g, h^*)=1-\gamma'$ if g is a tautology. (37)

Assume $j \notin I_g$. Then $Tr(g \vee h_j, h^*)>Tr(g, h^*)$ iff $\Delta_{*j}<\Delta_{min}(h^*, g)$. (38)

If g is false, then $Tr(h^* \vee g, h^*)>Tr(g, h^*)$. (39)

Here (35) expresses the idea that maximum truthlikeness is achieved only by the complete truth $h^*$. By (36), logically stronger true statements are more truthlike than weaker truths. This condition is not satisfied by Tichý's and Oddie's average distance measure.[22] On the other hand, it is

---

[22] For the dispute about the average measure, see Oddie (1986) and Niiniluoto (1987a: ch. 6.6). Kieseppä (1996) reconsiders this issue in the context of continuous quantities, where subsets of the state space with measure zero create problems for the min-sum-measure.

important that the same does not hold generally for false statements, since logically stronger falsities may lead us further away from the truth. (Many attempts to save Popper's original approach have stumbled on Tichý's 'child's play objection': Newton's theory cannot be improved by adding an arbitrary falsity to it.) (38) expresses Popper's truth content principle, since h*∨g entails precisely the true deductive consequences of g.

The weakest true statement is a tautology. In our formulation of cognitive problems, tautology is the disjunction of all complete answers, and thus it represents the suspension of judgement (cf. Levi 1967). In other words, tautology is the answer 'I don't know'. By (37), false answers may be better than a tautology, if they are sufficiently close to the truth—therefore, some false statements may be more truthlike than some true ones.[23] More precisely, a complete answer $h_i$ is more truthlike than a tautology if and only if $\Delta_{i*}$ is smaller than an upper bound which is approximately equal to $\gamma'/\gamma$. False complete answers $h_i$ which do not satisfy this condition are misleading in the sense that they are worse than ignorance. This also gives an operational device for choosing the appropriate values of $\gamma$ and $\gamma'$ for a cognitive problem: in typical cases, $\gamma'/\gamma$ should be approximately equal to 1/2.

If the distance function $\Delta$ on B is trivial, i.e. $\Delta_{ij}=1$ for all $i \neq j$, then Tr(g, h*) reduces to a special case of Levi's (1967) definition of epistemic utility. In this case, the min-factor simply expresses the truth value of g, and the sum-factor reduces to a measure of information content (i.e. the number of false disjuncts in the normal form of g).

The motivation for the definition of truthlikeness originally arose from the fallibilist recognition that many of our everyday beliefs and perhaps most of our current scientific theories are strictly speaking false. Therefore, it is important that the treatment given above can be extended to cases where the cognitive problem B does not contain any true alternatives. This happens if B is defined relative to a false presupposition b (e.g. an idealizing assumption). Then the relevant target can be defined as the most informative statement in B that would be true if b were true (see Niiniluoto 1987a: 262). Instead of hitting the complete truth, the problem is then to find the 'least false' among the available alternatives (cf. Section 5.3).

---

[23] This is, indeed, one of the adequacy conditions of Oddie (1986) and Niiniluoto (1987a). Aronson, Harré, and Way (1994) assume, instead, that no false statement can have more verisimilitude than a true one (p. 118). They also suggest that 'truth is a limiting case of verisimilitude' (p. 124). These differences from my min-sum definition (which they mistake for the min-max definition) is explained by the fact that Aronson *et al.* seem to confuse truthlikeness with approximate truth (which has just the property (32) they desire). Aronson's own definition explicates distances by type-hierarchies of concepts.

Another extension concerns vagueness, i.e. the case with an indefinite target. For example, if truth is represented by an interval $[\theta_0, \theta_1]$, then a point estimate $\theta$ may fail to have a definite truth value, but still its distance from the truth can be defined as the average distance between $\theta$ and the points in $[\theta_0, \theta_1]$.

The given definition of truthlikeness is syntactic in the sense that distances are taken to reflect differences in the form of sentences. However, state descriptions, structure descriptions, and constituents are linguistic representations of complete states of affairs or possible worlds (relative to the expressive power of the given language L). Hence, a distance function between such sentences induces a distance between states of affairs or possible worlds (see Niiniluoto 1987a: ch. 10.3). Such distances are called measures of *structure-likeness* by Theo Kuipers (1992). The structuralist school conceptualizes distances between set-theoretic structures by Bourbaki's notion of uniformity.[24]

With the concept of structure-likeness, the definition of approximate truth can be reformulated by the equivalent condition: g is approximately true in structure M if and only if g is true in a structure M' which is sufficiently close to M (cf. Weston 1992).

L. J. Cohen (1980) suggested that *legisimilitude*, i.e. closeness to laws or lawlike truth, is a more interesting concept for philosophers of science than verisimilitude. The point is clear: science is not interested in just any accidentally true features of the world, but its lawlike or nomic features. It is argued in Niiniluoto (1987a: ch. 11) that legisimilitude can be explicated as a special case of the similarity approach by choosing the cognitive problem in the appropriate way (so that the associated language includes the modal concepts of necessity and possibility). This illustrates again the flexibility of the target approach. Moreover, it can be claimed that Kuipers's (1987) notion of 'theoretical verisimilitude' is a special case of legisimilitude (cf. also Zwart 1998).

To avoid misunderstanding, it should be emphasized that the actual degrees of truthlikeness of various statements are not the main point of the formal construction; that is rather our aim to make sense of statements of the form '$g_1$ is more truthlike than $g_2$'. This comparative judgement is explicated by the condition that $\mathrm{Tr}(g_1, h^*) > \mathrm{Tr}(g_2, h^*)$.

Truthlikeness comparisons are 'robust', i.e. independent of the choice of the relevant quantitative parameters in the similarity judgements, if $g_1$ is uniformly better than $g_2$ in all relevant respects. Kuipers (1992) studies such 'non-arbitrary' situations with a qualitative concept of betweenness,

[24] See Balzer, Moulines, and Sneed (1987: ch. VII), Moulines and Straub (1994). For criticism, see Kieseppä (1996).

but I do not think this covers the most typical cases of rival hypotheses in science. The concentration on the 'safe' cases leads only to partial orderings, while my quantitative treatment gives a linear ordering of all the relevant hypotheses.

The definition of truthlikeness by the min-sum-measure avoids the Tichý–Miller trivialization theorem against Popper's account. At least it shows that the idea of being 'close to the truth' makes perfect sense—against the charges of many anti-realist critics (e.g. Laudan 1984a).

But there is another important objection to the similarity approach: Miller's (1974) famous example with 'Arizonan' (hot if and only if windy) and 'Minnesotan' (hot if and only if rainy) weather shows that comparative judgements of verisimilitude are not invariant with respect to one-to-one translations between languages. An attempt to fix a unique privileged language, relative to which truthlikeness is to be determined, has to rely on 'essentialist' metaphysics, Miller adds. Some philosophers have concluded that the basis of truthlikeness is 'shaky', too subjective and arbitrary (Urbach 1983), and have sought other related concepts (such as knowledge and approximate causal explanation) that, they argue, are not in the same way sensitive to linguistic variance (Barnes 1991; 1995).

To understand Miller's argument, it should be emphasized that degrees of truthlikeness are invariant under logical equivalence within one language: if $\vdash g \equiv g'$ in L, then $Tr(g, h^*) = Tr(g', h^*)$. Degrees of truthlikeness would indeed be 'arbirtary' if this condition were violated. But Miller's invariance condition involves two languages. In my view, it is too strong, since metric relations (distances, uniformities, etc.) in general are not preserved under one-to-one mappings. Such mappings may, therefore, change the cognitive problem in a crucial way (cf. Zwart 1998). Miller's examples also involve coordinate transformations with very odd predicates which no scientist would take seriously (Niiniluoto 1987a: ch. 13). This suggests a possible, as such quite effective, reply to Miller's argument: consider degrees of truthlikeness only relative to languages and cognitive interests that are in fact used within the scientific community (cf. Weston 1992; Kieseppä 1996).

But this is not all that can be presented as a reply to Miller. While the restriction to a unique privileged language would indeed involve questionable metaphysics, the idea that languages can be chosen arbitrarily, just as we happen to wish, is based on extreme nominalism. (Reasons for avoiding nominalism were discussed in Section 2.4.) It is more plausible to think that reality sets constraints on the rational choice of languages. As William Whewell expressed in a forceful way, a scientific language should enable us to formulate informative true general statements (see

Whewell 1840: 509). In particular, a language should be chosen so that it is adequate for the given cognitive problem. For example, if our problem is to explain the variations of a quantity F, our language should include at least the most important factors that actually have a lawful connection to F. In this sense, it may be possible to find, for each cognitive problem, a practically ideal language (or a sequence of more and more adequate languages) (cf. Niiniluoto 1984: 90).

An even more general point can be expressed by saying that truthlikeness is not a purely semantic notion, but it has also a pragmatic or methodological dimension. This is due to the fact that the concept of *similarity* is pragmatically ambiguous: similarity between two objects a and b presupposes a given class of relevant characters and weights for these characters (Niiniluoto 1987a: ch. 1). In other words, in speaking about the (degrees of) similarity between a and b we have to assume that a and b are compared relative to a description (Niiniluoto 1988b). In our analysis of verisimilitude, this is shown in three ways by the relativization of truthlikeness to cognitive problems. First, distances from 'the whole truth' are not relative to the whole world, whatever that might mean, but only relative to a target h*, i.e. the most informative statement of a certain complexity in a given language (cf. Fig. 9).[25] Thus, truthlikeness depends on what we want to know in a given situation. For example, when genuinely new concepts are introduced to the language, the target (and the cognitive problem) will be changed. Secondly, the choice of the underlying distance function $\Delta$ usually involves several dimensions of a qualitative or quantitative conceptual space, and such dimensions have to be weighted by their cognitive importance.[26] Thirdly, the min-sum-measure $\Delta_{ms}$ contains two parameters $\gamma$ and $\gamma'$ that express our cognitive interests in finding truth (relief from agnosticism) and in avoiding error (relief from error). These two factors point in opposite directions (cf. Levi 1967), and the balance between them is a context-sensitive methodological decision which depends on our values, and cannot be effected on purely logical grounds.

[25] For the target approach, see Niiniluoto (1977; 1987a; 1994a).
[26] One way of defending my project is to say that it aims at a theory with many kinds of philosophical applications and methodological recommendations. If one constructs such a theory as a description of the behaviour of scientific communities (cf. Section 1.4), then one may add that the relevant weights of similarity judgements are implicitly or explicitly parts of normal scientific practice. For example, in cladistic studies of taxonomy, plants are described by a large number of their characters, and distances are then obtained by counting the common features (i.e. the characters have equal weights). Whenever a physicist represents his theory by equations in an Euclidean state space, the dimensions of the space are taken to have equal importance.

There is thus an important difference between the notions of truth and truthlikeness. Apart from its dependence on the interpretation of language (cf. Section 3.3), truth is a purely semantic concept. This is seen also in the fact that truth is invariant in translations which preserve semantic properties. It is normal to require that if h is true in language L, and if t is a one-to-one translation of L to another language L', then the translation of h in L' is true in L'.[27] Concepts like similarity, information content, and truthlikeness are not invariant in the same sense, but rather pragmatically ambiguous. But this feature, which associates them with other important methodological concepts like confirmation and explanation, does not make them useless for the purposes of the philosophy of science.

[27] For the concept of translation, see Pearce (1983; 1987a; 1987b), Schröder-Heister and Schäfer (1989). Note that truthlikeness is not usually variant with respect to translations between natural languages, like English and German, as Resnik (1992) mistakenly thinks.

# 4

# Realism in Epistemology

As an epistemological thesis, realism claims that it is possible to obtain knowledge about mind-independent reality. But, of course, not only World 1, but the mind-dependent Worlds 2 and 3 as well, should be objects of our cognition. In this chapter, I defend critical epistemological realism, which accepts fallibilism as a *via media* between scepticism and infallibilism (Section 4.1), distinguishes reality from dreams by the invariance criterion (Section 4.2), and rejects the Kantian idea of unknowable things-in-themselves (Section 4.3). For a realist, our knowledge is uncertain, incomplete, and truthlike, but it is 'directly' about reality (Section 4.4). Further, epistemic probability and expected verisimilitude serve as indicators of truth and truthlikeness (Section 4.5). On this basis, I consider and reject theories which attempt to define truth in epistemic terms (coherence, pragmatist, and consensus theories) (Section 4.6).

## 4.1 Certainty, scepticism, and fallibilism

Ever since Plato and Aristotle, the main tradition of epistemology has been *infallibilism*—the view of genuine knowledge (Greek *episteme*) as 'justified true belief', which is distinguished from error by its truth and from mere 'opinion' (Greek *doxa*) by its certainty and incorrigibility. For Plato, the paradigmatic form of knowledge is provided by geometry, whose theorems can be certified by rigorous proofs from the axioms.[1] For Aristotle, the first principles of science are necessary and general truths about the immutable essences of things, and science gives demonstrative knowledge ('know why') by the syllogistic derivation of phenomena from their causes. Modern rationalists, like Descartes, claimed that we can obtain a priori

---

[1] Plato's conception of propositional and theoretical knowledge ('know that') was still closely linked with practical 'know-how': a shoemaker, who knows the idea of a shoe, is able to make, prepare, or produce shoes. This view about the special significance of maker's knowledge has been important in the history of epistemology. For the tradition of maker's knowledge from Plato to Hobbes, Vico, and Kant, see Hintikka (1974). Cf. also the Kantian views in Section 4.3 and the constructivist views in Ch. 9.

knowledge by 'clear and distinct' ideas. Some modern empiricists, like Francis Bacon, still maintained the view that inductive inference could produce certainty. When David Hume challenged the idea that inductive inferences could ever prove their conclusions to be true or even probable, the empiricists still upheld their quest for certainty by claiming that our knowledge in fact is always based upon, and even extends only to, the immediate certainties of 'the given'.

According to the *classical definition* of propositional knowledge,

> X knows that h iff                                            (1)
> (*a*) X believes that h
> (*b*) h is true
> (*c*) X has justification for h.[2]

An infallibilist interprets condition (*c*) in the strong sense where justification implies certainty:

> ($c_1$) X is certain that h.

Here ($c_1$) not only says that X is subjectively certain, or fully convinced, that h, but that in some objective sense X is absolutely certain about the truth of h, i.e. X is in a situation where he cannot be wrong about h.

Absolute or dogmatic knowledge claims can be challenged in all areas, however. Perhaps closest to condition ($c_1$) comes our knowledge of logical and analytic truth (see Section 3.2). Propositional logic and some axiomatic theories in mathematics are decidable, i.e. there are effective methods of identifying their axioms, rules of inference, valid deductions, and theorems. Such knowledge is thus based on mechanical mental reasoning or calculation, and hence is a priori, i.e. independent of sense perceptions about external facts.[3] But even in these cases it is logically conceivable that some error of reasoning, or a misapplication of mechanical rules, has been made without our noticing it. First-order predicate logic with relations is undecidable, so that there is no effective finite test of logical truth or falsity.

*Perceptual* knowledge can be mistaken in many ways. The reliability of my senses depends on, or varies with, my condition and external circumstances. Information gained by observation may be non-veridical, dis-

---

[2] For discussion of the classical definition of knowledge, including Gettier's famous objections to it, see Pappas and Swain (1978). For the debates between foundationalist and coherentist approaches, see Dancy and Sosa (1992) and Haack (1993).

[3] I have discussed the recent quasi-empiricist views of mathematics (cf. Tymoczko 1986) in Niiniluoto (1992*b*).

torted, misleading, or illusory—and my act of perceiving may be merely a hallucination. Also my *memory* may deceive me.

*Introspective* knowledge about our own mental states is also liable to error. My subjective certainty that I am now happy, love my friends, or disbelieve in ghosts may be due to illusion and self-deception.

These sceptical doubts can be reconfirmed by noting that both our common-sense views and even the surest conclusions of science have repeatedly turned out to be mistaken. Other putative sources of human knowledge—such as intuition, divine revelation, clairvoyance—usually lead to widely disparate conclusions, and thus have no legitimate grounds for leading to certainty of any degree.

Hence, the other side of the epistemological coin defined by infallibilism is *scepticism*: as knowledge in the strong sense $(1)(a)(b)(c_1)$ turns out to be impossible, the sceptic concludes that knowledge exists in no sense. This strategy is operative also in some of the best contemporary defences of scepticism, such as Peter Unger's *Ignorance* (1975). Thus, a typical 'dogmatic' sceptic is not a philosopher who denies the absolutist conception of knowledge. Instead, he assumes this strong conception, and then proceeds to argue that knowledge (in this sense) is impossible.

This mode of thinking could be called *All-or-Nothing Fallacy*. Its different forms propose a strong or absolute standard for some category (e.g. truth, knowledge, conceptual distinction), and interpret the failure or impossibility of satisfying this standard as a proof that the category is empty and should be rejected. (In Section 3.5 we saw an example of this fallacy in Bradley's doctrine of truth and falsity.)

As Plato observed, radical forms of global scepticism also face the problem of incoherence: if the sceptic claims that

No knowledge is possible,                                                      (S)

then there cannot be any knowledge about thesis (S) itself.

A Pyrrhonian sceptic, like Sextus Empiricus, suspends judgement (Greek *epoche*) on all questions—even on the thesis that knowledge is impossible (see Sextus Empiricus 1985). Such scepticism tries to avoid problems of self-refutation and dogmatism with the principle that 'To every argument an equal argument is opposed'. This Pyrrhonian view is supported by Paul Feyerabend: 'For every statement, theory, point of view believed (to be true) with good reasons *there exist* arguments showing a conflicting alternative to be at least as good, or even better' (Feyerabend 1987: 76).[4]

---

[4] For the history of scepticism, see Burnyeat (1983) and Popkin (1979). See also Sextus Empiricus (1985).

As a global theoretical stance, *epoche* about everything, Pyrrhonian scepticism is irrefutable in the same vicious way as the metaphysical positions of solipsism and objective idealism (cf. Section 2.5). But, as we have already seen in Section 3.5, the basic problem of ancient scepticism is that the suspension of judgement, while relieving us from making false assertions, also leads to 'errors of ignorance'. Suspension of judgement may be a rational 'local' position for some open scientific questions and unsolvable non-scientific ones (e.g. the existence of God).[5] On the other hand, a thesis to the effect that *no* statement is better supported by evidence than its rivals (or its negation) is too implausible to be interesting (cf. conditions $(c_2)$ and $(2)(c')$ below). There are members of the Flat Earth Society, but anyone who claims that flat and round earth are equally well supported by the existing arguments fails or refuses to take serious consideration of the weight of evidence.

Therefore, the best answer to the sceptic challenge is to find a *via media* between the two extremes of infallibilism and scepticism: according to the view that Charles Peirce aptly called *fallibilism* (from the Latin word for 'error'), all human knowledge is liable to error.

If we take seriously the fact that there is always a risk of error in knowledge claims, then it is reasonable to modify the strong conception $(1)(a)(b)(c_1)$. At best we may say with Kant that true and completely certain knowledge is a 'regulative idea' in our epistemic endeavours. But in real life—both in everyday affairs and in science—we are dealing with 'knowledge' in a weaker sense.

This strategy leads to two forms of fallibilism.[6] According to *weak fallibilism*, condition $(c)$ has to be interpreted so that it allows for varying degrees of certainty and uncertainty. One important formulation of weak fallibilism is the *Bayesian* approach, where all factual claims h are treated as hypotheses that have a numerical epistemic probability P(h/e) on the basis of accepted or available evidence e. Here P(h/e) is understood as the rational *degree of belief* in the truth of h in the light of e (see Section 4.5). Various theories of 'probable knowledge' and 'probabilistic induction'— from Laplace and Jevons in the nineteenth century to de Finetti, Carnap, and Hintikka in the twentieth century—have tried to answer the sceptical challenge by showing how the degrees of belief of scientific hypotheses can be determined. Some Bayesians (like Levi and Hintikka) have also for-

---

[5] Global and local forms of scepticism are distinguished in Pappas and Swain (1978).

[6] The distinction between weak and strong forms of fallibilism is made in Niiniluoto (1984). It should be noted that many philosophers, including Peirce, have given support to both of these forms of fallibilism. Cf. Popper (1963; 1972). Recent defences of fallibilism include Haack (1993) and Musgrave (1993).

mulated *acceptance rules* which tell when it is rational tentatively to add a hypothesis to the evolving body of knowledge.[7]

The weak fallibilist thus retains conditions ($a$) and ($b$), but replaces ($c_1$) by something like

($c_2$) h is more probable or more acceptable than its rivals on the available evidence.

Another formulation of weak fallibilism is based on Peirce's idea of inductive probabilities as *truth-frequencies*: probability is the ratio of true conclusions among all conclusions when a mode of argument is repeated indefinitely (*CP* 2.647–58). Frequentist approaches in statistics (such as Neyman–Pearson tests and estimation methods) follow the same idea. Frank Ramsey reformulated the justification condition ($c$) as

($c_3$) h is obtained by a reliable process.

(Sometimes this is added as a fourth condition to the definition of knowledge.) Alvin Goldman's (1986) epistemological *reliabilism* also analyses scientific knowledge in terms of the truth-producing power of the processes leading to it. For example, colour perception in normal conditions is a reliable source of beliefs in this sense, since it gives the right result in almost all cases.

Reliabilism covers cases where a belief is obtained from a source which is usually right (e.g. TV news). Another non-statistical way of interpreting condition ($c_3$) is suggested by Israel Scheffler (1965):

($c_4$) X has the right to be sure that h.

Scheffler's example is education, i.e. knowledge obtained from a teacher. Another example would be a witness in court. What is common to these cases is this: I have the *right* to be sure about h if my source of information has the *duty* to tell the truth about h. In this form ($c_4$) is compatible with fallibilism. Lay knowledge about scientific matters is normally based upon such information from scientific 'authorities' or experts.

Alan Musgrave (1993) has formulated a conception of *conjectural knowledge* by accepting 1($a$) and ($b$), but by replacing ($c$) with

($c_5$) X is justified in believing that h.

This condition is similar to Scheffler's ($c_4$). It should be distinguished from the classical ($c$) which demands a justification for h itself, not for a belief

---

[7] For the Bayesian treatment of scientific inference, see Levi (1967), Niiniluoto and Tuomela (1973), Niiniluoto (1987a), Howson and Urbach (1989), Cohen (1989), Earman (1992), Festa (1993).

that h. Musgrave interprets $(c_5)$ so that it does not entail that h is certain or even probable for X (in the Bayesian or Peircean sense). Instead, Musgrave's 'fallibilist realism' follows Popper's 'critical rationalism' in understanding $(c_5)$ to mean that h has 'withstood serious criticism'. In other words, the scientists have done their duty by putting h through severe tests and h has been 'corroborated' by passing these tests (see also Miller 1994).

While the weak fallibilist retains the condition $(1)(b)$, or at least allows that many uncertain conjectures are in fact true or at least possibly true (Watkins 1984), a *strong fallibilist* recognizes that even the best claims of science are normally inexact, approximate, or idealized, i.e. they are not true in a strict sense. Therefore, $(b)$ should be replaced by a condition that requires h to be truthlike or approximately true (see Section 3.5). Then the first condition can also be changed, since the strong fallibilist does not believe that even his best hypotheses are strictly true. Thus, the strong fallibilist suggests that the classical definition (1) is replaced by

> X knows that h iff $\qquad\qquad\qquad\qquad\qquad\qquad\qquad$ (2)
> $(a')$ X believes that h is truthlike
> $(b')$ h is truthlike
> $(c')$ X has reason to claim that h is more truthlike than its rivals on available evidence.

Condition $(c')$ guarantees here that X cannot at the same time know two mutually contradictory hypotheses.

For example, if I estimate that Finland has 5 million inhabitants, conditions $(a')$ and $(b')$ are satisfied. To transform this into knowledge in the classical sense (1), my point estimate should be replaced by a sufficiently wide interval estimate which covers the true value with a high degree of certainty (cf. Levi 1986; Kieseppä 1996). However, point estimates are in fact used both in everyday knowledge and in statistical inference. As Maher (1993: 219) observes, this is also the case with scientists who formulate theories and laws without broad margins of error.

As truth alone does not guarantee high truthlikeness (recall that truthlikeness involves an information factor), (2) is in a sense more demanding than (1). A weaker variant of (2) would replace 'truthlikeness' with 'approximate truth'; this wide notion would contain the classical definition (1) as a special case. A mixed or intermediate definition might combine $(a)$ with $(b')$ and $(c')$. This would characterize the epistemic state of the eighteenth-century scientists with respect to Newton's theory: they believed in the truth of a theory which is at best approximately true.

Condition $(c')$ may be correct even in cases where Musgrave's $(c_5)$ fails, since even falsified hypotheses may be close to the truth (cf. also Section 4.5). The converse relation depends on whether the Popperian notion of corroboration is an indicator of truthlikeness, as Popper himself claimed (Popper 1972) without being able to sustain it (Niiniluoto 1989) (cf. Section 4.5).

A reliabilist version of strong fallibilism should replace ordinary truth-frequencies by the ability of a process to produce results that are close to the truth. For example, the measurement of some quantity (e.g. length, electric current) is not reliable in the strict sense that it would often (or ever) produce exactly true results. But still its results are reliable in the sense that they tend to be close to the true value.

To summarize, realism in epistemology should employ the fallibilist conceptions of probable, conjectural, and truthlike knowledge—and thereby avoid the Scylla of infallibilism and the Charybdis of scepticism.[8]

But before we are ready to develop the fallibilist position, it is still necessary to consider the Cartesian challenge of scepticism concerning the external world (Section 4.2) and Kant's reformulation of the epistemological question (Section 4.3).

## 4.2 Knowledge of the external world

Modern philosophy has been dominated by Descartes's formulation of the problem of knowledge. Descartes was a dualist (see Section 2.1). He urged that the thinking subject (or 'I') can have 'clear and distinct' knowledge only of its own states, so that knowledge about the 'external world' (matter and other minds) becomes problematic. To answer this sceptical challenge, Descartes built his own metaphysical edifice.

Among the empiricists, John Locke made it clear that our immediate knowledge concerns only 'ideas' which are caused by external things, so that the certainty of our knowledge about external reality would need a guarantee that mental ideas resemble their causes. This assumption was denied by Bishop Berkeley.

In their quest for certainty, the Cartesian challenge drove many

---

[8] It is interesting to note that the revival of Pyrrhonism in the 16th century led to a position, called 'constructive scepticism' by Popkin (1979), which allows for probable truths about appearances. This weakly fallibilistic view (Marin Mersenne, Pierre Gassendi) was a precursor of later empiricism, pragmatism, and positivism. But there was also another trend of strong fallibilism (Robert Boyle), which was ready to extend the scope of truthlike knowledge to theoretical hypotheses about the reality beyond immediate observations (see Laudan 1973; 1981b).

philosophers to positions which are far from common sense. The rationalist school developed from Cartesian dualism into ontological idealism in the nineteenth century, so that no external world remained as an object of knowledge (see Section 4.3 below). Radical empiricists tried to save the certainty of knowledge by first restricting its objects to specific phenomenal entities (like impressions, sensations, or sense data), and then arguing that anything beyond these objects (like physical objects and other minds) is a 'logical construction' from phenomena. By this move, phenomenalists attempted to show that the world need not be reached by uncertain inference, since it is in fact reducible to, or definable by, the phenomena.

Perhaps the most radical form of Cartesian scepticism concerns our ability to distinguish dreams and reality. This issue was raised already in Plato's dialogue *Theaetetus* (see also Descartes 1968: 96–7). The thesis that merely illusory, imagined, or dreamed experiences do not contain any characteristic that would distinguish them from 'real' presentations was called the *Theaetetus theorem* by Eino Kaila in 1958 (see Kaila 1979).

The Theaetetus theorem does not deny that sometimes in dreaming I may have a strongly felt conviction that 'this is only a dream'. What Plato and Descartes were after is a general criterion which would exclude all doubt about my state. But if F is proposed as a property of my experience which serves as a criterion of waking, it is always possible to claim that I only dream that my experience has the property F. For example, the familiar everyday rule 'Pinch yourself!' is not conclusive, since I could dream that I pinch myself and feel pain.

Kaila concluded that the almost universally accepted Theaetetus theorem is valid. However, he argued that Descartes failed to distinguish *logical doubt* from *empirical uncertainty*: even if it is always logically possible to doubt the reality of our impressions, this does not imply that we ought to be in fact empirically uncertain about the reality of our perceptions. Another way of expressing this conclusion would be to say that we may have knowledge of the external world by fallibilistic standards (see Section 4.1).

Many philosophers who accept the Theaetetus theorem for momentary experiences have sought criteria of reality in the interrelations of longer sequences of experiences. In his *New Essays on Human Understanding* (written in 1704), G. W. Leibniz admitted that 'it is not impossible, metaphysically speaking, for a dream to be as coherent and prolonged as a man's life', but this is highly improbable.

Consequently I believe that where objects of the sense are concerned the true criterion is the linking together of phenomena, i.e. the connectedness of what happens at different times and places and in the experience of different men. (Leibniz 1982: 374)

In monographs published in the 1930s, Eino Kaila accepted and elaborated Leibniz's discussion: the defining character of reality is *invariance*, regularity, lawlikeness, and the possibility of prognosis. But these features are matters of degree. Kaila proposed that different types of things can be placed on a scale of levels according to their *degree of reality* defined by their degree of invariance: first, elusive perceptual experiences (after images, mirror images), then more constant perceptual objects (the experience of pain), next everyday physical objects (stones, tables), and finally objects postulated by scientific theories (atoms) (Kaila 1979; Niiniluoto 1992*a*). It is clear that dream experiences have a low degree of invariance, as they are highly irregular and unpredictable, and should be placed on the first levels of Kaila's hierarchy.

Kaila's argument seems to lack a crucial premiss: why should invariance indicate reality? In other words, if one possible or potential world exhibits more invariance or regularity than another, why should it have a greater chance of being real? I think at least one argument could be based on the theory of evolution: the present state of the universe is the result of chemical, biological, and cultural evolution, and this evolution would not have been possible in a lawless world. The evolution of the human species would not be possible either in an irregular dream world. The facts of evolution themselves might be only a part of our dream (as Sami Pihlström has pointed out to me), but by the Leibnizian standard this is highly improbable.

Even though the evolutionary argument supports the reality of our waking world, one has to be careful not to stretch this conclusion too much. Our actual world is not the completely ordered utopia of many evolutionary metaphysicians; it includes chance and irregularity as well.[9] Even if we have reason to believe that we are not dreaming, the amount and nature of invariances are still an open question that has to be studied by scientific enquiry.[10]

---

[9] Peirce argued in his 'tychism' that the world is indeterministic. See also Popper (1982), Fetzer (1981), Salmon (1984), Earman (1986), Niiniluoto (1988*a*), and Suppes (1993).

[10] It is interesting to note that modern art and technology have given new flavour to the classical problem of reality. Susanne Langer presented in *Feeling and Form* (1953) her famous thesis that film as such, as a poetic art, uses 'the dream mode'. Visual arts like painting create an artificial or 'virtual space', which can be seen but not touched. Cinema, having learned to use a moving camera, is like a dream: it creates an illusion of reality, a virtual present, where the camera takes the place of the dreamer. In the history of poetics, ever since the time of Cicero, such an illusion of reality has been called 'verisimilitude'—which has thus a quite distinct meaning from the use of the same concept in the philosophy of

## 4.3 Kant's 'Copernican revolution'

Immanuel Kant's famous 'Copernican revolution' solves the Cartesian epistemological problem by making a distinction between the 'noumenal' realm of things-in-themselves (*Dinge an sich*) and the 'phenomenal' realm of things-for-us. Of the things-in-themselves we cognize only that they exist and 'affect our senses' (see Kant 1930: 1), but otherwise they 'must ever remain unknown to us' (ibid. 188). The proper object of our knowledge is the world of phenomena—this world is cognizable for us, since it is partly mind-dependent, constituted by the specifically human mental faculty (space and time as forms of our sensible intuition, causality as one of the categories of our understanding). But the epistemological or transcendental subject is for Kant a free *Ding an sich*, not bound by causality, and it has to be distinguished from the 'empirical self' in the world of phenomena. Thus, Kant combines 'transcendental idealism' with 'empirical realism', which 'refutes idealism' in the special sense that the world of phenomena is not mind-dependent relative to the empirical self.

Kant's strategy is essentially based upon the tradition of maker's knowledge: 'we only cognize in things *a priori* that which we ourselves place in them' (ibid., p. xxix). A priori knowledge of objects is possible, if 'the object conforms to the nature of our faculty of intuition' (ibid., p. xxix). Indeed, we cannot perceive any object without placing it in space and time, and we cannot think of objects without imposing causal relations between them. According to Kant, this spatio-temporal-causal structure supplied by our mind follows the laws of Euclidean geometry and Newtonian mechanics.

It seems incontestable that our visual images do have some sort of geo-

science (see Section 3.5). The question 'Am I dreaming or seeing a film?' has gained new significance in the 'postmodern' communication society, where we live in the middle of signs, neon lights, information channels, networks, TV screens, movies, and videos—and reality is more and more transformed into a 'web' of representations of reality. As these representations (e.g. photographs, TV news) can easily be manipulated and distorted by 'image processing', we may begin to lose our sense of reality. The most radical philosophers of this postmodern culture are claiming that reality itself ceases to exist and is transformed to a *hyperreality* or a *simulacrum*, an apparent copy intended to deceive us (see Baudrillard 1984). Another successor problem to the dream vs. reality issue is created by the new computer technologies that allow us, using data gloves and helmets, to enter a three-dimensional *virtual reality* (cf. Rheingold 1991). Here we are no longer external observers, but also actors or participants immersed in a synthetic 'cyberspace' created by our interaction with a programme in the memory of a digital computer. In spite of this attempt to create a perfect illusion of reality, I think that the Leibniz–Kaila invariance criterion is still applicable at least in the present stage of technology.

metrical structure. Also the spaces of other sensuous qualities have a topological or metric structure.[11] This can be granted to Kant. (Today we would explain such features of human cognition by the theory of evolution.) But it does not follow that our visual space is Euclidean (cf. Suppes 1993: ch. 26)—its geometry could be one of the non-Euclidean systems developed in the nineteenth century.

The discovery of non-Euclidean geometries is fatal to Kant's system in an even stronger sense. It led to a systematic distinction between *pure* and *applied* geometry; the former is a priori and analytic, the latter is a posteriori and synthetic. In pure geometry, we can construct alternative systems of axioms and derive theorems from them. Which system of pure geometry then applies to a given object depends on the object: the sphere as two-dimensional is elliptic, the saddle surface is hyperbolic, etc. These observations suggest that, *contra* Kant, we have to distinguish between the mind-involving *visual space* and the mind-independent *physical space*. Similarly, we have to distinguish our time-consciousness, our experience of time, from the objectively existing temporal relations.[12] The structure of physical space and time does not depend on our sensuous or perceptual faculties, but can be studied by means of testable theories in physics. According to Einstein's theory of relativity, four-dimensional space-time has a Minkowskian metric, and its geometric structure is non-Euclidean.

Kant's conception of causality as mind-involving is also problematic. If causality is limited to the domain of 'possible experience', how can the unknown thing-in-itself 'affect our senses', i.e. 'cause' our sensations or 'appearances'? (See also Kant 1950: 36.) This seems to be a straightforward contradiction in Kant's system. And is there any interaction between the things-in-themselves, and what keeps them together, if there are no mind-independent causal laws governing their realm? Kant was much preoccupied in explaining the 'synthetic' unity of our perceptions and mental events, but he failed to appreciate the need of causality and physical laws

---

[11] For treatments of conceptual spaces, see Carnap (1967), Goodman (1951), Niiniluoto (1987*a*: ch. 1), Gärdenfors (1990).

[12] Problems of space and time are analysed in Reichenbach (1951), Grünbaum (1973), Sklar (1974), and Suppes (1993). Geometric conventionalism claims that the principles of physical geometry can be chosen in alternative ways, if we are willing to make adjustments elsewhere in our theoretical framework in physics. Following Poincaré, this thesis has been taken as a ground of anti-realism or instrumentalism about physical geometry. It seems to me that the invariance criterion (see Section 4.2) works here quite well: the physical reality is again constituted by invariances or regularities which constrain our freedom in giving them mathematical representations in geometric terms.

as an external and mind-independent 'cement of the universe' (see Mackie 1974).

On this interpretation, Kant's 'Copernican revolution' thus explains the possibility of a priori knowledge about partly mind-dependent phenomenal objects, but only at the expense of declaring us for ever ignorant or agnostic about the things-in-themselves.

Kant's influence on later philosophy is enormous. His *critical* or *transcendental idealism* is still realistic in the ontological sense, since it accepts the mind-independent existence of things-in-themselves. This assumption was a headache for most of his followers. The neo-Kantian schools still had a dominant position in the German universities at the beginning of this century, but they were challenged by other variants of the Kantian view.

German *idealism*, in its subjective and objective forms, expelled *Dinge an sich* from the Kantian system (cf. Section 2.1). Mach's *phenomenalism* took the further step of eliminating the epistemological subject, the transcendental ego, leaving only the phenomenal world, including a phenomenal ego as a bundle of sensations. The *neo-Kantians* emphasized the idea that a-thing-in-itself is a *Grenz-Begriff* or a 'limit of thought' (Cassirer 1965; Hintikka 1974). Husserl's *phenomenology* puts the objective world into 'brackets', i.e. suspends judgement about its existence, and concentrates on the analysis of the ways in which our theoretical and practical interests constitute our 'life-world'. For Heidegger, human existence is always being-in-the-world, and the world is always the world as conceived and cognized by humans (cf. Section 7.1). Similarly, *pragmatism* (at least in its radical forms) excludes all talk about the world-in-itself as meaningless or pointless (cf. Rorty 1998): it is senseless to speak of reality as divorced from the conceptual and cognitive practices of the (temporally unlimited) scientific community. Hence, the objective concept of truth (correspondence with the world-in-itself) also has to be replaced with truth-for-us (coherence, verifiability, or assertability relative to the world-for-us) (see Section 4.6).

The *logical positivism* of the Vienna Circle in the late 1920s can be regarded as a sophisticated form of anti-metaphysical pragmatism. Both Moritz Schlick and Rudolf Carnap argued that ontological realism and its negation (i.e. the 'old positivism' of Mach) are meaningless: 'The denial of the existence of a transcendent external world would be just as much a metaphysical statement as its affirmation' (Schlick 1959: 107). (Cf. Ch. 2.) This is clearly different from Kant's view: 'while we surrender the power of *cognizing*, we still reserve the power of *thinking* objects, as things in themselves' (Kant 1930: p. xxxiii). A new influential version of the verificationist doctrine emerged in the 1970s in Michael Dummett's semantical anti-realism (cf. Section 4.6). Nicholas Rescher's (1982) conceptual idealism and Hilary Putnam's (1981) internal realism instead return to a Kantian position (cf. Ch. 7).

## 4.4 Critical epistemological realism

*Critical realism*, as a form of epistemological thought, can also be motivated in Kantian terms: Kant's phenomena could be interpreted as expressions of our *partial knowledge* of the things as they are 'in themselves' in mind-independent reality (Niiniluoto 1984). This idea accepts 'direct' realism and the correspondence theory of truth, but it is not 'naive', since our knowledge of reality is always laden with some conceptual framework and is not assumed to be completely and exactly true. Still, this view rejects relativism and scepticism. If we recognize that Kant's categories are not fixed, but rather historically changing (Hegel) and bound to human-made languages (Peirce), then each conceptual framework provides us with a perspective on objective reality. By employing and enriching such frameworks, and by empirically testing scientific theories formulated in these frameworks, we have a rational method of approaching nearer to the truth, i.e. finding deeper and deeper partial descriptions of the world.

While an idealist abolishes the Kantian things-in-themselves, a critical realist eliminates the phenomena: an epistemological subject is *directly*, without a veil, in contact with reality (cf. Section 5.4). Thereby the Kantian idea of unknowable *Dinge an sich* is rejected. However, what is rejected is not the idea of such things, but rather their *unknowability*. This is the common argument of such different realists as Peirce (*CP* 5.310–11) and Lenin (1927). It is a mistake to speak with Kant about 'the necessary limitation of our theoretical cognition to mere phenomena' (Kant 1930: p. xxxv), since the object of our knowledge is the noumenal world.

In the case of perception, this means that, for instance, in seeing a tree the object of my perception is the tree as a physical object—not a phenomenon or a sense datum somewhere between me and the tree (Hintikka 1975). In hallucinations, the observed object is merely a figment of imagination, but in other cases perceptions are directed at external objects and situations. This 'direct realism' is compatible with the Wittgensteinian view that all seeing is *seeing as* (cf. Hanson 1958). The logic of perception allows us to formalize statements of the form 'A sees b as an F' (e.g. 'I see a bush as a bear'), where b is the external object that A is looking at (through a causal influence from b to his sense organs) and 'this is an F' is the content of his perceptual experience (Niiniluoto 1982). Perception is illusory if b is not an F, and veridical if b is an F. It is generally true that our perception does not disclose the whole object b in all its aspects. Even veridical perception reveals only a part of its object, which is *inexhaustible* by any finite number of observations.

More generally, according to critical scientific realism, scientific knowledge with its empirical and theoretical ingredients—obtained by systematic observation, controlled experiments, and the testing of theoretical hypotheses—is an attempt to give a truthlike description of mind-independent reality.

Several Kant scholars have favoured—instead of the 'two worlds' account given in Section 4.3—a 'double aspect' or 'one-world interpretation' of Kant's doctrine.[13] According to them, things-in-themselves and phenomena do not constitute two ontologically distinct domains of entities, but rather two ways of conceiving the same objects. On this interpretation, Kant would agree with the realists that there is really only the domain of objects: a phenomenon as an 'appearance' is an object-as-we-experience-it or object-as-we-conceive-it.[14]

I think there are many difficulties in the attempt to reconcile Kant's own statements with the one-world interpretation. If this view is accepted, it is misleading to say that a phenomenon is the *object* of our knowledge, since it is rather the *content* of our act of cognition. Kant has also no ground for urging that 'we can have no cognition of an object, as a thing in itself' (1930: p. xxxiii), since our cognition may be veridical depending on whether its propositional content corresponds to the way the things-in-themselves are.

It is important to remember that for Kant a phenomenon contains something more than a noumenon—namely, spatio-temporal and categorial properties and relations supplied by our mind. Therefore, Kant is right in saying that things-in-themselves lie 'beyond the sphere' of a priori cognition. But the further claim that all cognition is limited to mere phenomena presupposes that all a posteriori knowledge is restricted to phenomena.

---

[13] The one-world interpretation of Kant has been defended by Allison (1983). For discussion, see Walker (1989), van Cleve (1992), and Pihlström (1996). Hintikka (1975; 1984) defends the inexhaustibility of the things-in-themselves, but more as a formulation of his own position than as an interpretation of Kant. A very clear presentation of the inexhaustibility of reality, taken as an argument against the neo-Kantian doctrine of reality, is given by Schlick (1985). It is not essential for my purposes to decide this deep problem in Kant exegesis. If Kant really meant to endorse the one-world interpretation, he was a critical realist who failed to express his view properly. In any case, the position discussed in Section 4.3 is the one that has influenced the history of philosophy as the doctrine of 'Kantianism', and deserves to be discussed as an interesting and important challenge to realism.

[14] Phenomena in this sense correspond to Husserl's *noemata*, or correlates of our intentional actions, in the so-called 'object-theory' of the notion of *noema* (see Drummond 1990).

Here Kant makes a double mistake from a realist's viewpoint. First, he asserts that a posteriori knowledge does not concern things-in-themselves. This is similar to the claim that we do not see trees but sense data. A realist instead thinks that the observable properties and relations belong to the objects, i.e. a 'phenomenon' is an observable part of an external object, and observational knowledge is about this object. Secondly, Kant has to assume that 'our faculty of cognition is unable to transcend the limits of possible experience' (ibid., p. xxx). This is similar to the claim that *all* knowledge is about the observable. A scientific realist instead argues that scientific theories typically make empirically testable assertions about theoretical (non-observational) entities and properties. Kant's difficulties arise thus from the fact that his view of human cognition is too narrowly empiricist (cf. Hintikka 1974; 1984).

To illustrate the difference between Kant and realism, consider the case of an oar which seems to bend in water. Here the visual phenomenon is the-oar-as-bent-in-water. However, we have good reason to believe that the oar-in-itself is not bent in water. This is confirmed by other senses (touch) and various experiments, and (more conclusively) by an optical theory which explains, by laws of refraction, why the oar seems to us to bend. Here we have theoretical knowledge about physical reality; it goes beyond the object taken as a phenomenon, and corrects our visual perception (cf. Sellars 1963).[15]

Hence, on my reading, Kant's attitude towards the things-in-themselves seems to be again an instance of the All-or-Nothing Fallacy (cf. Section 4.1). From the premiss that they cannot be completely known, i.e. that they are *inexhaustible*, he concludes that they are *inaccessible*, not knowable at all (see also Schlick 1985). Alternatively, from the premiss that we do not cognize objects *purely* as they are in themselves, he concludes that we have no knowledge of them. Unlike Kant, a critical realist acknowledges 'dirty' (partial, incomplete, inexact, conceptually relative, etc. but truthlike) forms of knowledge.

To make critical epistemological realism plausible, two important aspects of knowledge formation should be emphasized. Both of them were recognized by Peirce.

---

[15] Following Heikki Kannisto, Pihlström suggests that Kant could accept empirically testable theoretical postulations (in particular, physical space) in his 'empirical' world. One might add that such 'scientific objects' are mind-involving, since they are objects-as-described-by-scientific-theories, but it is difficult to see how they could be 'phenomenal' in any interesting sense. I think this kind of one-world interpretation might lead us toward an ontology which resembles the Sellarsian eliminative materialism (cf. Ch. 2). For an attempt toward a Kantian realism, see Rosenberg (1980).

The first point is that knowledge about mind-independent reality pre-supposes *causal influence* and *interaction* between the object and subject of cognition. Information about an external fact can reach our mind only through a causal process—such as perception by our sense organs, meas-urement by instruments, manipulation of nature in experiments. Peirce expressed this idea by saying that the 'fundamental hypothesis' of the method of science is this:

There are Real things, whose characters are entirely independent of our opinions about them; those Reals affect our senses according to regular laws, and, though our sensations are as different as are our relations to the objects, yet, by taking advantage of the laws of perception, we can ascertain how things really and truly are; and any man, if he have sufficient experience and he reason enough about it, will be led to the one True conclusion. (*CP* 5.384)

This view is developed in recent causal theories of knowledge, which are generalizations of the causal theories of perception (Goldman 1967). Even though happy guesses may happen to be true, their justification requires causal interaction. To justify the hypothesis that an object a is F the fact that a-is-an-F must somehow causally affect our beliefs. Fallibilist versions of such an account accept that the sources of knowledge (e.g. our senses, measurements) are *reliable* only in some degree.

Secondly, knowledge is a *social* product of a community of investigators. Peirce argued that 'logic is rooted in the social principle' (*CP* 2.654): our interests should be identified 'with those of an unlimited community', since it is to be hoped that truth can be reached by a process of investigation that carries different minds 'by a force outside of themselves to one and the same conclusion' (*CP* 5.407). Thus, the proper subject of knowledge is the *scientific community*. Popper (1963) expressed this idea by arguing that no conclusion of an individual scientist can be a result of science before it has gone through and passed a process of critical discussion within the scientific community.

The social character of science is thus a consequence of the fallibility of individual scientists. But also any finite group of scientists can present only more or less conjectural knowledge claims (cf. Section 4.1). To attribute a collective belief to a community C, it seems to me that it is not quite ade-quate to apply the concept of 'mutual belief', requiring that each member of C has the belief and believes that other members have the belief. Rather, the scientific community C believes that p if the best experts in the relevant problem area in C believe that p (cf. Section 10.3). This account, which resembles Putnam's (1975) principle of 'division of linguistic labour', would require an analysis of the structure of authority relations within the scientific community (cf. Kitcher 1993).

Critical realism argues against Kant (and against the tradition of maker's knowledge) that fallible knowledge about mind-independent reality is possible in spite of the fact that this world is not a human construction (Niiniluoto 1984: 216). The fallibilist account can be extended from World 1 to Worlds 2 and 3 as well, even though maker's knowledge has a limited validity in these domains.[16] We do not possess any incorrigible direct access to the events and states of our own mind, or to the products and institutions of our own culture and society. Still, there are scientific methods of gaining fallible knowledge about these domains, too.

## 4.5 Epistemic probability and verisimilitude

A dogmatic epistemological realist claims that we may gain absolutely certain and strictly true knowledge about reality. A *critical* realist admits that both truth and certainty are matters of degree. Thereby a critical realist avoids the All-or-Nothing Fallacy typical of the sceptical doctrines favoured by disappointed absolutists.

The Bayesian school defines the *epistemic probability* $P(g/e)$ of a hypothesis g given evidence e as the rational degree of belief in the truth of g on the basis of e. This function P satisfies the characteristic conditions of probability measures:

$0 \leq P(g/e) \leq 1$           (3)

$P(g/e)=1$ if $e \vdash h$

$P(\sim g/e)=1-P(g/e)$

$P(h \lor g/e)=P(h/e)+P(g/e)-P(h \& g/e)$

$P(h \lor g/e)=P(h/e)+P(g/e)$ if $\vdash \sim(h \& g)$.

If t is a tautology, then $P(g/t)=P(g)$ is the *prior* probability of g. Bayes's Theorem says now that the *posterior* probability $P(g/e)$ is proportional to $P(g)$ and the likelihood $P(e/g)$:

$P(g/e)=P(g)P(e/g)/P(e)$.          (4)

Epistemic probabilities covary with logical weakness, in the sense that weaker statements are more probable than stronger ones:

[16] The problem of knowledge concerning Worlds 2 and 3 cannot be discussed in any detail in this book. See, however, Section 5.4 below, and Niiniluoto (1981; 1984; 1985b; 1992b; 1994b).

If $h \vdash g$, then $P(h/e) \leq P(g/e)$.                                      (5)

For this reason, Karl Popper (1959; 1963) required that science should strive for *im*probable hypotheses. Such propositions have a high *information content*, measured by

$$\text{cont}(g) = 1 - P(g).$$                                        (6)

However, it is possible that the prior probability $P(g)$ is low and the posterior probability $P(g/e)$ is high at the same time. In such cases measures of the form

$$P(g/e) - P(g)$$                                              (7)

and

$$P(g/e)/P(g)$$                                               (8)

have high values. The logarithm of (8), which is equal to $\log P(e/g) - \log P(e)$, has been proposed by I. J. Good as a measure of the 'weight of evidence'. Following Carnap (1962), the Bayesians have analysed inductive inference by measuring the *degree of confirmation* of g on e by measures (7), (8), or their normalizations (cf. Hintikka 1968). One variant of these measures is Popper's own probabilistic definition of the *degree of corroboration* of a theory g relative to tests e (see Popper 1959; Niiniluoto and Tuomela 1973).

Such quantitative measures of confirmation also define corresponding qualitative and comparative notions. Both (7) and (8) imply the *positive relevance* criterion: e confirms g iff $P(g/e) > P(g)$. Further, (8) implies the *likelihood principle*: e confirms h more than g iff $P(e/h) > P(e/g)$.

These Bayesian measures are tools for a weak fallibilist, since they treat probability as an indicator of truth. If g is known to be false, its epistemic probability is zero (and its degree of confirmation or corroboration is minimal):

$$P(g/e) = 0 \text{ if } e \vdash \sim g.$$                                 (9)

Popper's measure of corroboration has the same property. A strong fallibilist is not happy with this result, since a false hypothesis may nevertheless have cognitive and practical virtues by being close to the truth.

To find tools for strong fallibilists, let us return to the account of truthlikeness in Section 3.5. There we defined the degree of truthlikeliness $\text{Tr}(g, h^*)$ of a partial answer g to a cognitive problem B relative to the most informative true element $h^*$ of B.

As in genuine cognitive problems the target $h^*$ is unknown, the value of Tr(g, h*) cannot be directly calculated.[17] But it would be disappointing if truthlikeness could not be used at all to make any actual comparisons of the cognitive value of rival theories. At least we should like to understand the structural properties of such comparative assessments. For this purpose, I have proposed a method of *estimating* degrees of truthlikeness on the basis of available (observational and theoretical) evidence e.[18] My suggestion is to view science as an attempt to maximize *expected truthlikeness*. This idea presupposes a concept of epistemic probability, and thus combines the idea of verisimilitude with a central tool from the programme of weak fallibilism. The true Popperians, who reject inductive or personal probabilities, cannot follow me in this direction.

To estimate the degree $Tr(g, h*)$, where h* is unknown, assume that there is an epistemic probability measure P defined on $B=\{h_i | i \in I\}$. Thus, $P(h_i/e)$ is the rational degree of belief in the truth of $h_i$ given evidence e, and $Tr(g, h_i)$ is what the degree of truthlikeness of g would be in case $h_i$ were true. The *expected degree of verisimilitude* of $g \in D(B)$ given evidence e is then defined by summing up over $i \in I$ the values $Tr(g, h_i)$ multiplied by the corresponding probability of $h_i$ on e:

$$ver(g/e)=\sum_{i \in I} P(h_i/e)Tr(g, h_1). \tag{10}$$

If B is a continuous space, P is replaced by a probabilistic density function p on B, and

$$ver(g/e)=\int_B p(x/e)Tr(g, x)dx. \tag{11}$$

This measure allows us to say that g' *seems more truthlike* than g on evidence e if and only if $ver(g/e)<ver(g'/e)$.

For example, let $\theta_* \in R$ be the unknown value of a real-valued parameter. Then maximizing the expected verisimilitude of a point estimate $\theta_o$ is equivalent to the 'Bayes rule' of the Bayesian statisticians: minimize the posterior loss

$$\int_R p(\theta/e)|\theta - \theta_o|d\theta.$$

The solution $\theta_o$ is given by the median of the posterior distribution $p(\theta/e)$; if the loss function is the quadratic $(\theta - \theta_o)^2$, then the solution is the mean

---

[17] This is in fact one of Augustine's objections to the concept of verisimilitude. See Niiniluoto (1987a: 161; 1999b).
[18] For the measure ver and its properties, see Niiniluoto (1977; 1979; 1987a). Cf. also Maher (1993).

of $p(\theta/e)$. This is an example of a standard scientific method which has a direct interpretation in terms of verisimilitude. A similar account can be given of Bayesian interval estimation, where the loss of accepting an interval is defined by the distance of this interval from the truth (see Niiniluoto 1986c; Festa 1993).

The relation between the functions Tr and ver is analogous to the relation between truth value tv and probability P, i.e.

$$Tr{:}ver{=}tv{:}P. \tag{12}$$

This can be seen from the fact that the posterior probability $P(g/e)$ equals the *expected truth value* of g on e:

$$\sum_{i\in I} P(h_i/e)tv(g, h_i) = \sum_{i\in I} P(h_i/e) = P(g/e).$$

The properties of function ver include the following:

If $P(h_i/e)=1/|I|$ for all $i \in I$, then $ver(h_i/e)$ is a constant for all $i \in I$. \hfill (13)

If $P(h_j/e) \approx 1$ for some $j \in I$, so that $P(h_i/e) \approx 0$ for $i \neq j$, $i \in I$ \hfill (14) then $ver(g/e) \approx Tr(g,h_j)$.

$ver(g/e)=1$ iff, for some $j \in I$, $g=h_j$ and $P(h_j/e)=1$. \hfill (15)

High probability is not generally sufficient for high estimated \hfill (16) verisimilitude. For example, if g is a tautology, $P(g/e)=1$ but $ver(g/e)=1-\gamma'$.

It is possible that $ver(g/e) \approx 1$ but $P(g/e)=0$. \hfill (17)

Assume that $P(h_j/e)=1$, $j \in I_{g_1}$, and $j \in I_{g_2}$. Then $ver(g_1/e) >$ \hfill (18) $ver(g_2/e)$ if $g_1 \vdash g_2$, not $g_2 \vdash g_1$.

Here (13) says that the complete answers $h_i$ are estimated to be equally truthlike if our epistemic probability distribution over them is even. By (14) and (15), if we know by e that $h_j$ is the true answer, $ver(h_j/e)$ has its maximum value one.

The next results highlight the differences between estimated verisimilitude and probability. Tautologies are maximally probable but not highly truthlike. The estimated verisimilitude of a statement g may be very high, even if its probability on e is zero, i.e. evidence e refutes g (cf. (9)). This is natural, since a refuted hypothesis may nevertheless be close to the truth. Bayesian degrees of confirmation and Popper's degrees of corroboration (even though he claimed that they are indicators of verisimilitude) fail to satisfy (17). Result (18) shows that in some cases ver, unlike posterior probability, may favour logical strength.

It is also possible to combine the concepts of truthlikeness Tr and epistemic probability P in other ways (see Niiniluoto 1987a; 1989). *Probable verisimilitude* $PT_{1-\varepsilon}(g, h*/e)$ expresses the probability given e that g is truthlike at least to the given degree $1-\varepsilon$. *Probable approximate truth* $PAT_{1-\varepsilon}(g, h*/e)$ expresses in turn the probability given e that g is approximately true within the given degree $1-\varepsilon$. The main difference between ver and PAT is that the latter satisfies a principle like (5) for probability P.

These concepts allow us to say, for example, that a sharp point estimate, which has the probability zero, is nevertheless probably approximately true (since a small interval around this value may be highly probable). For example, assume that $x$ is a random variable with a Gaussian error curve: $x$ is $N(\theta, \sigma^2)$, i.e. $x$ is normally distributed with the mean $\theta$ and variance $\sigma^2 > 0$. If $x_1, \ldots, x_n$ are n independent repetitions of this measurement, and if $y$ is their mean value, then $y$ is $N(\theta, \sigma^2/n)$. If now the prior probability $p(\theta)$ of $\theta$ is sufficiently flat, then by Bayes's Theorem the posterior distribution $p(\theta/y)$ of $\theta$ given an observed mean y is approximately $N(y, \sigma^2/n)$. The probability of a sharp point hypothesis $\theta = \theta_o$ is zero, but the posterior probability that this hypothesis is approximately true to the degree $1-\varepsilon$ (where $\varepsilon > 0$) is $\Phi((\theta_o + \varepsilon - y)/(\sigma/\sqrt{n})) - \Phi((\theta_o - \varepsilon - y)/(\sigma/\sqrt{n}))$, where $\Phi$ is the cumulative distribution function of the standardized normal distribution. If $\theta_o$ is chosen as y, i.e. our hypothesis states that the unknown parameter $\theta$ equals the observed mean y, then this value reduces to $2\Phi(\varepsilon\sqrt{n}/\sigma) - 1$, which approaches 1 when n grows without limit. More generally, for any point hypothesis which differs from y less than $\varepsilon$, its probable approximate truth approaches 1 when the measurements are indefinitely repeated. Similar results hold for expected verisimilitude ver: if distance is measured by $|\theta - y|$, then its expected value relative to $p(\theta/y)$ equals $2\sigma/\sqrt{2\pi n}$, which approaches 0 when n grows without limit (see Niiniluoto 1987a: 283); if distance is measured by $(\theta - y)^2$, then its expected value is simply the variance $\sigma^2/n$ of $p(\theta/y)$, so that it too approaches 0 when n grows without limit.

Still another kind of idea is to estimate the truthlikeness of a statement g by measuring its distance $D(g, e)$ from an evidence statement e, which by itself is assumed to be a reliable indicator of truth (cf. Section 6.3). Zamora Bonilla (1992) has discussed this idea in the case where e is the conjunction of all accepted empirical laws (instead of containing singular observation statements).

## 4.6 Epistemic theories of truth

In Section 3.4 we defended Tarski's semantic definition of truth as an adequate formulation of the classical correspondence theory. The theory of truthlikeness in Section 3.5 relies on the Tarskian model-theoretic approach, and the definition of function ver in Section 4.5 shows how truthlikeness can be estimated on evidence, if epistemic probabilities are available.

We are now ready to evaluate rival accounts which claim truth to be an 'epistemic concept'.[19] My attitude towards such views can be well expressed by a quotation from Tarski (1944):

It seems to me that none of these conceptions have been put so far in an intelligible and unequivocal form. This may change, however; a time may come when we find ourselves confronted with several incompatible, but equally clear and precise, conceptions of truth. It will then become necessary to abandon the ambiguous usage of the word 'true', and to introduce several terms instead, each to denote a different notion. Personally, I should not feel hurt if a future congress of the 'theoreticians of truth' should decide—by a majority of votes—to reserve the word 'true' for one of the non-classical conceptions, and should suggest another word, say, 'frue', for the conception considered here. But I cannot imagine that anybody could present cogent arguments to the effect that the semantic conception is 'wrong' and should be entirely abandoned.

The various non-classical proposals, if made precise, may define highly interesting and valuable epistemic or methodological concepts. But why should they be called conceptions of 'truth'?

To justify the talk about 'epistemological theories of truth', such theories should be self-sufficient so that they do not explicitly or implicitly rely on the semantic or realist concept. Further, if such an account defines, in epistemic terms, a property $\phi(h)$ of sentences h, it should satisfy the analogue of Tarski's T-equivalence:

$\phi(h)$ iff h.                                                                (T′)

I shall argue that these conditions are not satisfied by the currently existing epistemic accounts of 'truth'.

Most versions of these accounts are variants of Peirce's 1878 pragmatist definition of truth as the limit towards which the opinion of the scientific community is gravitating:

[19] Tuomela (1990) says that truth is 'epistemic' in the sense that the existence of truth presupposes languages which are human constructions. This weak sense is certainly acceptable: languages and semantical facts belong to World 3 (cf. Ch. 3). But internal realism has typically denied the distinction between objective truth and its epistemic indicators, and I disagree with the strong claim that truth should be defined or characterized in epistemic terms.

The opinion which is fated to be ultimately agreed to by all who investigate, is what we mean by the truth, and the object represented in this opinion is the real. (*CP* 5.407)

What Peirce is here attempting is a methodological characterization of truth, as this concept appertains to 'the experiential method of settling opinion' (*CP* 5.406). Peirce applies here his 'pragmatist maxim' to the concept of 'truth', in order to clarify this idea or to find out its real content for us. Such a characterization, if successful, would imply the condition (T′), since Peirce also claims that the limit of enquiry represents, i.e. corresponds to, real things which causally influence the belief formation in the scientific community. In other words,

'h' belongs to the ultimate opinion of the scientific commu-     (19)
nity iff h.

Later pragmatist accounts try to characterize truth by epistemological and methodological concepts: verification (James), proof or provability (Dummett, Prawitz, Martin-Löf), warranted assertability (Dewey, Sellars), the ultimate consensus of a discourse community (Habermas), ideal acceptability (Putnam, Rorty), best-explaining theories (Tuomela).[20]

It is not always clear whether the epistemic accounts are really intended as *definitions* of truth. In my interpretation, Peirce accepted the basic idea of the correspondence theory, but wanted to find a coextensive characterization of this concept (Niiniluoto 1980; 1984). In the same way, James and Dewey occasionally claimed that they were only trying to express the 'cash value' or an 'operational definition' of correspondence (see R. A. Putnam 1997). Hilary Putnam (1990; 1994) has recently expressed reservations about the claim that truth is 'ideal acceptability' (see Putnam 1981). It is possible to understand the pragmatist tradition so that it denies the possibility of giving definitions or theories about truth (see Davidson 1996; Rorty 1998; cf. Pihlström 1996). On the other hand, many followers and opponents of this philosophical school have taken the epistemic doctrines of truth literally. As my aims are systematic, I continue to discuss them in this spirit as rivals to the realist correspondence theory.

The motivation for such epistemic accounts can be seen by a comparison with the classical conception of knowledge (1). The point of the

---

[20] See James (1907), Dewey (1938; 1941), Sellars (1968), Dummett (1978), Martin-Löf (1987), Putnam (1981; 1990), Tuomela (1985), and Habermas (1983). Also Harré (1986) appeals to epistemic ideas in his notion of truth. For criticism, see Russell (1940), Haack (1978), Niiniluoto (1984), Devitt (1991).

pragmatist is that our best, or only, access to truth is via justified beliefs within enquiry. If we are successful in defining conditions (*a*) and (*c*), we have *a fortiori* characterized condition (*b*) as well—to the extent it is possible for human beings to do so (cf. Dewey 1941).

As our system of justified beliefs is evolving, not yet completed, it would be preposterous—and highly relativistic—to identify truth with beliefs that are *up to now* or *here* justified, verified, or proved. Some pragmatists have nevertheless taken this line: William James (1907) said that truth emerges from our acts of verification. Dummett (1978) is worried that the definition of truth by 'possible verification' might commit him to the realist principle of bivalence. However, as Carnap argued in 1936 after having read Tarski (Carnap 1949), while the evidence-related concepts like verification and confirmation are tensed, the notion of truth is timeless (at least for indicative, temporally definite statements). (See also Russell 1940.)

Therefore, the pragmatists usually follow Peirce in characterizing truth by verifiability, provability, or assertability under timeless *ideal* conditions.

The problem then is to give an intelligible definition of the ideal state which does not presuppose the realist notion of truth and implies (T'). It seems to me that attempts in this direction have led to fictional idealized states of communities and their knowledge that are much more difficult to understand than the realist's conception of the actual world (*pace* Sundholm 1994). Sometimes the reference is ultimately the system of knowledge in God's mind (Walker 1989). Sometimes appeal is made to counterfactual possibilities of verification (which requires that counterfactuals could be understood without the notion of truth). Sometimes the ideal theory is simply described as one which 'survives all possible objections' (Rorty 1982), has 'every property that we like' except 'objective truth' (Putnam 1978: 125), or belongs to the ideal 'Peirceish' conceptual framework (Sellars 1968).

Putnam (1990) makes the important point that there is no single ideal state implying all truths, but rather for each cognitive problem there is an ideal state for that problem. Yet several questions remain. First, there is the problem of *recognition*: how do we know which ideal epistemic state is really the right one? How could we identify the Peirceish framework? How do we choose between alternative coherent systems of belief? How do we know that a final consensus has been reached by the right kind of discourse free from domination? The realist would try to answer these questions by relying on the concept of truth (e.g. pick up that coherent system which has the right kind of correspondence to our world, accept a consensus based on truth-preserving arguments from true premisses). But, due to the threat of circularity, these answers are not available to those who try to defend an epistemic account of truth.

Secondly, condition (T') may fail, because even the ideal limiting opinion may be *false*. Most pragmatists are fallibilists, but their definition of truth assumes that *in the limit* the scientific community has incorrigible knowledge. This is a very strong assumption, especially if the scientific method is understood in a broad sense that allows the scientific community to settle its ultimate opinion by appealing to such 'non-veric' criteria as simplicity (cf. Section 6.3). What is even more important, arguments for the claim that an ideal theory 'could not be false' have not been successful.[21] For us it is interesting to note that the concepts of truthlikeness Tr and expected verisimilitude ver (cf. Sections 3.5 and 4.5) give us precise tools for characterizing ideal conditions: for example, a theory T may be a limit of a sequence of our best theories $T_1, T_2, \ldots$ (*pace* Quine 1960), or its expected verisimilitude $ver(T/e_n)$ may approach the maximum value 1 when evidence $e_n$, $n \rightarrow \infty$, is increasing.[22] But even these conditions do not entail that T is a true or correct description of reality.

It is remarkable that Peirce saw this difficulty: he remarked that science is 'destined' to converge toward the truth only *with probability one*.[23] For example, in a real-life methodological situation a real-valued parameter may be estimated by successive averages of unbiased, normally distributed measurements (cf. Section 4.5); then the limit equals the right value *with probability one*—or 'almost always', as the mathematicians say. This means that after all presupposition (19) of Peirce's characterization of truth does not hold. This lesson has not been understood by those of Peirce's followers who still attempt to *define* truth by 'Peircean limits'.

Thirdly, if truth were *defined* by the limit of scientific enquiry, then we would get the undesirable result that the thesis

Scientific knowledge approaches to the truth (20)

[21] One of them is Putnam's model-theoretic argument, which attempts to show that the ideal theory could not be false. For criticism, see Tuomela (1985) and Niiniluoto (1987a: 142).

[22] For the definition of such convergence conditions, see Niiniluoto (1980; 1984; 1987a). See also Rosenberg's (1980) and Tuomela's (1985) use of them in the characterization of truth. Laudan's (1973; 1981a; 1984a) 'confutation of convergent realism' is misleading in giving the impression that all forms of scientific realism depend on the assumption that truth coincides with the limit of enquiry. For a distinction between 'myopic' and 'messianic' realism, see Levi (1985).

[23] See *CP* 4.547 n. This is a generalization of a criticism that can be made against the frequentist theory of physical probability: probability should not be defined as the limit of relative frequency, since, by the Strong Law of Large Numbers, these values are identical only with probability one. Cf. Niiniluoto (1980; 1984; 1988a).

becomes an analytic truth. The epistemological success of science is guaranteed by a verbal trick. The thesis of the self-corrective nature of science is trivialized (cf. Laudan 1973). For a realist, (20) is instead a factual statement whose truth (if it is true) depends on the methods of science (Niiniluoto 1984).

Fourthly, condition (T′), or (19), presupposes that the scientific community is able to reach at least in the ideal limit *all truths* about the world.[24] If we are ontological realists, this is highly questionable: why should human epistemic capabilities cover the whole of reality in all of its aspects? At least we cannot know this a priori, and we should not base our definition of truth upon such an assumption. Again we meet an instance of the All-or-Nothing Fallacy: if all truths are not knowable to us, then the concept of truth is taken to collapse.

The knowability of the world is not any inherent property of reality, but always relative to the available methods. A scientific realist is convinced that science makes cognitive progress also by improving its methods (see Boyd 1984). The borderline between the knowable and the unknowable is not fixed, but is moving with the invention of new methods. But we do not know yet what the ultimate forms or standards of the scientific method are. For example, we are only beginning to understand the computational limitations of the thinking of humans and computers (cf. Thagard 1988). This is, I think, a strong argument for the realist concept of truth which should in principle allow for the possibility that some truths about the world are for us 'recognition transcendent'.

The difficulties of epistemic definitions of truth are illustrated by statements about the past. There are lots of temporary facts about nature and society which leave no records or traces for posterity. Russell's (1940) example is the fact about the number of sneezes by Winston Churchill in 1949. For the realist, a statement about this number is objectively true or false, where this truth value depends on the actual state of affairs during the year 1949. (I am assuming here that the concept of sneezing is semantically well defined.) But no evidence is available for us today which would help us to know this truth value. Some anti-realists have tried to avoid the conclusion that such currently undecidable statements about the past lack truth values. Usually appeal is made to the idea of 'verifiability in principle', which seems to be the liberal notion that any fact in the world could

---

[24] Almeder (1983) defends the thesis that there is only a finite number of scientific problems, and they will all eventually be solved. For criticism, see Niiniluoto (1980; 1984). A more plausible view, where problems proliferate in the progress of science, is given in Rescher (1984).

'in principle' be known—and there the distinction between realist and epistemic notions of truth disappears. Jardine (1986) has made the more specific suggestion that statements about the past would be decided by travelling backwards with a time machine—thus making the notion of truth depend on science fiction (cf. the criticism in Newton-Smith 1989). Putnam (1992), in his 'realism with a human face', has allowed that undecidable statements about Caesar do have truth values, since there was a time when at least Caesar knew or had access to their truth value, but this admission seems to involve a kind of epistemological anthropocentrism or speciesism: why cannot we accept as real those facts that were witnessed by Caesar's horse? And what is wrong with facts about nature which no conscious being has witnessed? (Cf. Ch. 7.)

In his most recent work, Putnam (1994) has acknowledged that there can be completely recognition-transcendent truths, such as 'There are no intelligent extraterrestrials'. This seems to mean that he has given up the thesis of the epistemic nature of truth—a former cornerstone of his internal realism.

A possible counter-argument to realism comes from the Kantian 'Copernican revolution': let the reality (or at least humanly-meaningful-reality) conform to our cognitive capabilities! In modern discussion, this view is known as *semantical anti-realism*. It gains its plausibility from the constructivist or intuitionist philosophies of mathematics: the domain of mathematical objects is not a ready-made Platonic world, but it comes into existence only through the activities of the mathematicians. Proving theorems is a central part of these constructive activities. Therefore, reality and truth in mathematics is conceptually connected with provability.

Even in mathematics the equation of truth and provability faces difficulties. In his very sophisticated and powerful system of intuitionistic type-theory, Per Martin-Löf (1987) identifies a proposition with the set of its proofs, but these proofs are understood as 'proof-objects' rather than 'proof-acts'. Then he defines a proposition A to be 'actually true', if a proof-object for A has actual existence, 'potentially true', if a proof-object for A is 'really possible', and 'true *simpliciter*', if a proof-object is 'logically possible'. However, a constructivist may with good reason suspect that this talk about timeless proof-objects not yet constructed by anyone may involve some sort of Platonist or Aristotelian metaphysics.[25]

Moreover, the attempt to extend the basic idea of intuitionism to factual

---

[25] See the discussion between Dummett and Göran Sundholm in McGuinness and Oliveri (1994).

truth, as Dummett (1978) suggests, leads to problems. In mathematics, we have a relatively solid understanding of the concept of proof—even the existing disagreements can be located quite sharply in certain types of disputed principles of inference (such as indirect existence proofs on infinite domains). In the field of empirical science, there are no good counterparts to mathematical proofs: factual statements cannot be conclusively 'proved'; only some of them can be empirically verified; most interesting scientific statements are hypotheses which can be indirectly tested and thereby confirmed only to some degree.[26] When Crispin Wright (1993) appeals here to empirical assertability-conditions, which are probabilistic or inductive, he enters the interesting domain of inductive acceptance rules; but even though work has been done in this area (cf. Levi 1967), these notions are hardly better understood than the realist conceptions of world and truth. Indeed, to define factual truth by our methods of verification and assertion would presuppose an impossible task: all problems of epistemology should be solved before we can understand the concept of truth. What is more, it is not plausible to suppose that physical reality is 'constructed' by our epistemic activities—in any sense resembling the constructions of mathematical entities (cf. Chs. 7 and 9).

Semantical anti-realists can formulate their argument also by putting reality in brackets and staying on the level of meaningful discourse in language. This move can guarantee condition (T') by a trick: the *verification-ist theory of meaning* restricts the range of meaningful sentences h to those whose truth value can be decided by finite means. Then there cannot be any 'recognition-transcendent' meaningful truths, and the possible counter-instances to (19) are excluded.

This anti-realist move is usually formulated as an argument against truth-conditional semantics. For Dummett, realism with respect to some subject matter is the question whether the Principle of Bivalence holds for that domain: when truth is understood classically as correspondence, the statements are true or false in virtue of reality existing independently of us. But this classical conception leads to the conclusion that undecidable

---

[26] Aarne Ranta (1994), who skilfully applies Martin-Löf's type-theory to the analysis of natural language, suggests that railways from Moscow to Hong Kong are proof-objects for the proposition that there is a railway from Moscow to Hong Kong. This is in fact very much like Russell's early formulation of the correspondence theory of truth. Ranta mentions also the idea that tropes could serve as truth-makers for propositions; this is again a case of a realist conception of truth. To make objects, events, and tropes 'proof-objects' in an epistemic account of the truth of judgements, we should add, for example, a proof that the given object is a railway from Moscow to Hong Kong. But then we have to face the problem of telling what such 'proofs' are.

statements are also meaningful. Such statements are not meaningful, and the Principle of Bivalence fails, if meaning is defined by assertability-conditions (instead of truth-conditions).

In my view, this is not an argument against the classical correspondence theory of truth, but rather against a special theory of *understanding* language. Dummett clearly assumes that

> Person X understands statement h if and only if X knows the     (21)
> meaning of h.

If meaning is now defined by truth-conditions, then the meaning of undecidable statements could not be 'manifestable' in the right way in the use of language. (Recall Wittgenstein's principle that meaning is use.) But if truth is defined non-classically as warranted assertability, an alternative account of meaning is obtained:

> X knows the meaning of h if and only if X knows the     (22)
> assertability-conditions of h.

These two principles together imply:

> X understands h if and only if X knows the assertability-     (23)
> conditions of h.

We have already noted how difficult it would be to specify the conditions of assertability for empirical statements—and likewise for theoretical scientific statements. But what is even more problematic for verificationism, (23) seems to fail for mathematical statements as well. I certainly admit that, in learning mathematics, we gain *deeper* understanding when we come to know proofs of theorems. But it is equally clear that most of us have no difficulty in understanding the Four Colour Theorem (cf. Tymoczko 1986) and Fermat's Last Theorem, i.e. understanding in truth-conditional terms what these theorems express, even though we do not have the faintest idea of their proofs (and would not understand the proof if presented to us).

Among the many motivations for semantical anti-realism (in addition to inspiration from constructive mathematics and the later Wittgenstein's philosophy of language) is the problem of scepticism. The anti-realist seems to establish the interesting result that all 'reality' or all 'truth' is accessible to scientific enquiry. However, this is achieved by a verbal stipulation: reality or meaningful discourse is simply cut down or limited so that it perfectly fits scientific knowledge. I think this reply to scepticism is what the jurists call 'exaggerated caution', since there are other ways of responding to the scepticist challenge. A scientific realist finds that the success of science is offered here at too cheap a price: it should be achieved by improving the methods and results of science, not by limiting a priori its potential domain.

# 5

# Realism in Theory Construction

Concept and theory formation is a fundamental task of science. The traditional realism vs. instrumentalism dispute concerns the status of scientific theories (Section 5.1). According to the usual formulation of scientific realism, the theoretical terms of successful theories refer to real entities in the world, and the theoretical laws and principles are true. This view has to be qualified, however, since many theories contain approximations and idealizations—therefore, their existential and general claims are at best truthlike (Section 5.3). The similarity account of approximate truth and truthlikeness helps to make precise the idea of charitable theoretical reference, and thus to show how reference invariance is possible in spite of meaning variance (Section 5.2). Examples of the realism debate in connection with astronomy, quantum mechanics, psychology, and economics are discussed in Section 5.4.

## 5.1 Descriptivism, instrumentalism, and realism

It is a central task of the philosophy of science to give an account of scientific concept and theory formation. Following the successful work in metamathematics (Gottlob Frege, David Hilbert), philosophers at the turn of the twentieth century started to apply the tools of modern logic to the study of the language of science and the structure of scientific laws and theories.[1]

The positivist school accepted the empiricist view that concepts are learned from experience. They attempted to show that science uses an 'empirical' or 'observational' language, and all meaningful concepts are reducible to this language. More precisely, the *observational language* $L_0$ contains, besides logical vocabulary, only observational terms (individual constants, one-place and many-place predicates $O_1, \ldots, O_m$). These terms are directly connected to the empirical world through sense perception, measurement, or 'operational definitions'. All other terms are explicitly

[1] See Suppe (1977), Nagel (1961), Hempel (1965), Tuomela (1973), Niiniluoto (1984).

definable by the observational language. The full language of science L, which contains also *theoretical terms* $M_1, \ldots, M_k$ (like 'electron', 'force', 'energy', 'temperature', 'gene'), is in this sense reducible or translatable to the observational language $L_0$.

On this *descriptive view* of theories, a scientific theory is simply a set of sentences T in the language L. As advanced theories are formulated in axiomatic form, T is the set of logical consequences of a set of axioms A. Thus, T itself is closed under deduction. As Ernst Mach put it, the main task of a theory is to give an 'economical' description of the phenomena (see Fig. 12).

The logical empiricists of the Vienna Circle developed two formulations of descriptivism. The *phenomenalists* took the empirical world to consist of sensations and their complexes; hence, the observational language $L_0$ contains phenomenal terms referring to subjective experiences. For the *physicalists*, the world consists of publicly observable things and properties; the observational language in this case is an empirically interpreted physical language. Both views can accommodate the descriptive conception of theories, as Rudolf Carnap's work in 1926–35 shows.

The rationalist and Kantian traditions regard concepts either as innate elements or as free creations of the human mind. Concepts are like nets that we throw out to the world. As Mach himself and the French conventionalists (Henri Poincaré, Pierre Duhem) noted, such concepts are often idealized and do not as such correspond to anything in the world. If this

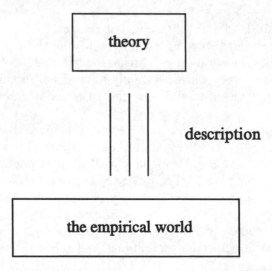

FIG. 12. Descriptive view of theories

view is combined with the assumption that reality (or at least the reality accessible to science) equals the empirical world, the position known as *instrumentalism* is obtained (cf. Section 1.3).

The instrumentalists typically assume with the descriptivists that the language of science contains the observational part $L_0$, but they also admit the use of 'auxiliary' theoretical terms which are not reducible to $L_0$ via definitions. These auxiliary terms are understood as tools or instruments for the purpose of systematizing observational statements (thereby making theories more simple or economical) or for making observable predictions (see Fig. 13). These linguistic or symbolic tools are given no interpretation, i.e. they are not taken to be referring to anything, and the statements including them lack a truth value. This semantical claim as such leaves open the ontological question of whether anything beyond the observable exists. An instrumentalist may be agnostic concerning the existence of theoretical entities (like atoms, electrons, forces, black holes, neuroses), but usually they are treated as at best useful fictions.

Besides systematic natural sciences, instrumentalism has been defended also in the case of history. For example, Franklin Ankersmit (1989) claims that historical concepts like 'the Renaissance' do not 'refer to historical reality itself' but to narrative interpretations of the past. As the past 'can no longer be observed', it 'cannot be the proper object of investigation'. The historian's task is to construct a narratio or a coherent historical story on the basis of the traces that the past has left, but it is not 'meaningful'

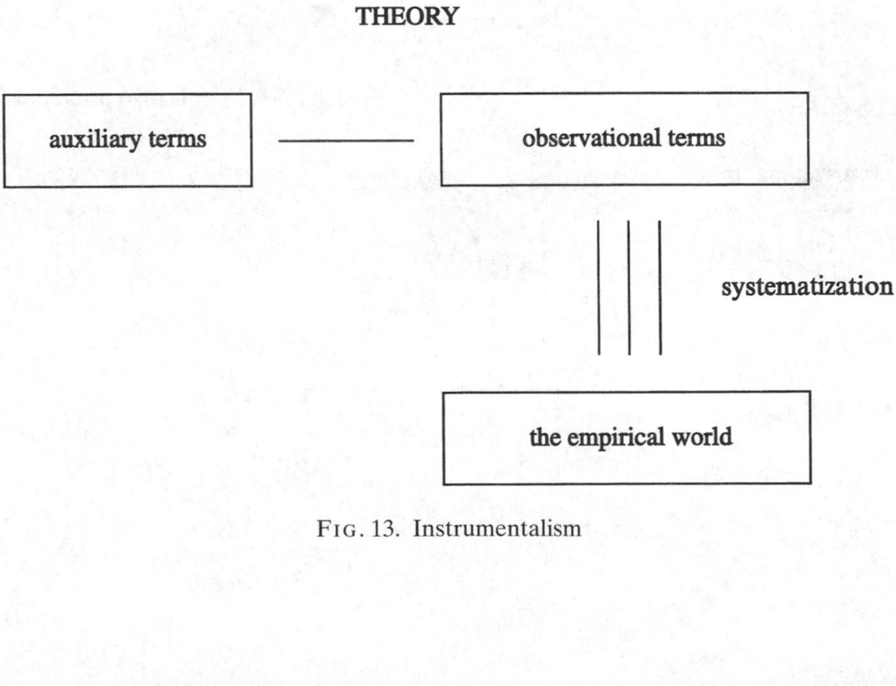

**THEORY**

FIG. 13. Instrumentalism

to speak about a correspondence of the narratio and the actual past. In other words, Ankersmit has the same attitude towards events in the past as an instrumentalist has to unobservable theoretical entities.

Carnap's seminal article 'Testability and Meaning' (1936–7) proved convincingly that dispositional terms (like 'magnetic', 'fragile', 'jealous') are not explicitly definable by observational terms. Within the analytic philosophy of science, this argument led to the Received View of theories as 'partially interpreted' sets of statements. According to the two-layer account, the uninterpreted 'pure theory' is connected to the observational part via 'bridge principles' or 'correspondence rules', which may have any logical form (instead of explicit definitions), and the observational terms are then linked with the empirical reality (see Fig. 14). Here the observational terms are taken to be completely interpreted, i.e. their extension in the world is fixed, but this does not uniquely fix the extensions of the theoretical terms, which thus remain only partially interpreted.

The Received View is still open to the instrumentalist interpretation, since the bridge principles need not guarantee that theoretical statements have a truth value. Carnap hesitated about this question, while Herbert Feigl (1950) defended the realist view that theoretical terms are meaningful by their reference to unobservable entities.

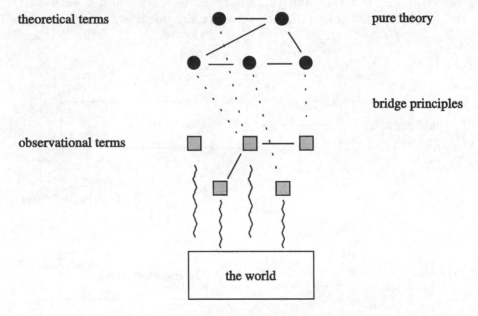

FIG. 14. The received view

Carl G. Hempel (1958) raised this issue in his *Theoretician's Dilemma*: if the theoretical terms of a theory T achieve deductive systematization among observational statements, then the same systematization is achieved by an observational subtheory $T_c$ of T in the observational language $L_0$ (as shown by a logical result of Craig). If the theoretical terms are dispensable in this sense, the argument continues, there can hardly be any reason to assume that they are cognitively significant referring terms.

One way of constructing the theory $T_c$, which has the same deductive consequences as T itself in $L_0$, was discovered by Frank Ramsey in 1929. Replace the theoretical predicates '$M_1$', '$M_2$', . . . , '$M_k$' of T by predicate variables '$w_1$', '$w_2$', . . . , '$w_k$', and quantify them existentially. The resulting second-order statement $T^R$

$$(\exists w_1)(\exists w_2) \ldots (\exists w_k)T(w_1, w_2, \ldots, w_k, O_1, O_2, \ldots, O_m) \tag{1}$$

is known as the *Ramsey sentence* of theory T. However, it is not clear that Ramsey's approach really supports instrumentalism or fictionalism, since $T^R$ asserts the existence of some entities corresponding to the original theoretical terms $M_1, \ldots, M_k$, and there is no guarantee that these entities are observable. Carnap was willing to allow them to be purely mathematical constructions (cf. Carnap 1966), but Feigl (1950) argued that the entities satisfying (1) should be restricted to classes defined by physical properties (cf. Hempel 1965).

Later discussion about the Theoretician's Dilemma has not given support to instrumentalism. It has been shown in detail that the introduction of new theoretical terms gives important methodological gains in deductive systematization (Tuomela 1973). As Hempel himself expected, theoretical terms are logically indispensable to inductive systematization: there are theories T and observational statements e and h such that h is inducible from e and T (or from e relative to T) but h is not inducible from e and the Craigian reduction of T (see Niiniluoto and Tuomela 1973).

As an alternative to descriptivism and instrumentalism, the thesis of *theoretical realism* asserts that all scientific statements in scientific theories have a truth value (see thesis (R2) in Section 1.3). A scientific realist takes theories seriously as attempted descriptions and explanations of reality. A theory may go beyond the edge of direct observability by postulating theoretical entities, if it yields predictions testable by public observation. For this conception, as Sellars (1963) argues convincingly, it is crucial to distinguish between the *semantic* relations of the theory to the reality it tries to describe and the *methodological* relations of the theory to the observational processes used for testing the theory (see Fig. 15). For example, quantum mechanics is a theory about the micro-world of

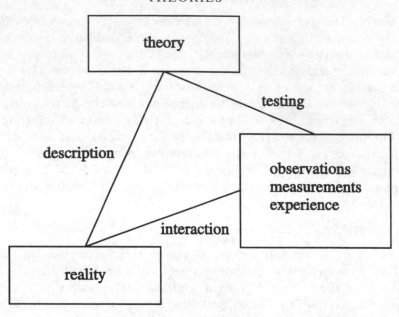

FIG. 15. Scientific realism

elementary particles, not about observations and measurements in laboratories (cf. Section 5.4). A psychological theory of consciousness is about
mental processes, not about their manifestation in behaviour (cf. Section
5.4). A historical narrative is about events in the past, not about their traces
and documents existing today.

Fig. 15 does not yet say anything about the question whether the theory
is good as a description or representation, i.e. successful in terms of reference or truth. These questions have to be studied separately (see Section
5.2 and Ch. 6).

We have already prepared the ground for this realist interpretation of
theories. It makes sense to speak about mind-independent reality (Ch. 2)
and about semantic non-epistemic relations between statements and
reality (Ch. 3). The truth value of a theory is independent of epistemic
issues—the testing process does not influence this truth value, but only our
rational estimates of this truth value (Section 4.5).

I have here construed instrumentalism as a position which accepts the
correspondence theory of truth, but claims that this concept is not applicable to theoretical statements (cf. Section 1.3). Semantical anti-realists,
who advocate an epistemic concept of truth and a restricted notion of
reality, are not instrumentalists in this sense, but they could be 'instru-

mentalists' in John Dewey's (1938) sense: theories (like language in general) are a tool of prediction, so that this view of theories would resemble Fig. 13 rather than Fig. 15. Related views are supported, for instance, by Chalmers (1976) and some 'practical materialists' in the Marxist school. But there are also philosophers who wish to combine theoretical realism with an epistemic notion of truth. These *epistemic scientific realists* basically accept the picture in Fig. 15, but analyse the theory–world relation by some other concept than truth—e.g. by Sellars's notion of 'picturing' (see Sellars 1968; Tuomela 1985; cf. Brandom 1994, however).

Scientific realism is also in conflict with the *anti-representationalist* view of language that Richard Rorty defends by appealing to Donald Davidson. Rorty urges that the realism vs. anti-realism issue arises only for those representationalists who take language to be a better or worse representation of the world (Rorty 1991: 2). He admits that the use of the word 'atom' in physics is 'useful for coping with the environment', but this utility should not be explained by notions like representation (ibid. 5; cf. Rorty 1998). Here we can see that Rorty's anti-representationalism in fact combines ideas of instrumentalism in both senses discussed above.

It is essential to theoretical realism that it is meaningful to speak about ontologically mind-independent reality—this minimum assumption is the 'fig-leaf realism' of Devitt (1991). When Ernest Nagel (1961) suggested that, given the ambiguity in the term 'reality', the whole opposition between realism and instrumentalism is merely 'a conflict over preferred modes of speech' (p. 152), he was relying on the idea that reality could be defined as 'that which is invariant under some stipulated set of transformations' (p. 149) (see also Carnap 1966). This argument is not convincing. The conception of reality as a hierarchy of more and more general and deep phenomenal invariances was developed by Kaila in the 1930s (cf. Section 4.2 and Kaila 1979), but he combined it with the translatability thesis from theoretical to observational language. This approach leads neither to instrumentalism nor to realism but rather to the descriptive view of theories. When Kaila eventually gave up the translatability thesis in the late 1940s, his position became clearly a realist one: the physical reality described by theories is different from the phenomenal domain in Fig. 15 (see Niiniluoto 1992*a*).

The realist view of theories gained indirect support from the collapse of the observational–theoretical dichotomy, which is a common premiss of descriptivism and instrumentalism. Following Wittgenstein, N. R. Hanson (1958) argued that all seeing is *seeing as*. Thomas Kuhn (1962) and Paul Feyerabend (1962*a*) argued that observations are *theory-laden*, relative to variable conceptual-theoretical frameworks. (At this stage of his career, Feyerabend was still a scientific realist.) This basically Kantian epistemological viewpoint undermines strict or naive versions of empiricism, and it was used by sophisticated critical realists to support the picture of Fig. 15 (cf. Tuomela 1973).

There are various pragmatic, context-dependent ways of dividing scientific terms into two classes: old vs. new, antecedently understood vs. not yet understood, measurable vs. non-measurable by available instruments, measurable-relative-to-theory-T vs. not-T-measurable, etc. But there do not seem to be any convincing grounds for a *semantic* division such that on one side the statements have a truth value and on the other side they lack a truth value. If this is the case, then the basic premiss of instrumentalism fails.

The theory-ladenness of observations leads, however, to other arguments which challenge scientific realism. These issues will be discussed in the next section.

I conclude this section by remarks on three important views that have been regarded as contemporary heirs of instrumentalism.

Bas van Fraassen's (1980; 1989) *constructive empiricism* differs from instrumentalism, since he admits that theories have a truth value.[2] His emphasis on the importance of explanation also differs from the descriptivist Mach–Duhem tradition. However, van Fraassen urges that the truth value of a theory is irrelevant to the aims of science. Using a slogan which links him to the ancient instrumentalist programme, he demands that a theory should 'save the appearances'. Constructive empiricism requires, instead of truth, that a theory is 'empirically adequate': what the theory says about 'the observable' is true. The acceptance of a theory involves only the claim that it is empirically adequate, not its truth. This requirement is illustrated in Fig. 16: theory is true in a model, and the observable is isomorphically embeddable in this model. (Such partial truth about observational substructure is called 'pragmatic truth' by Mikenberg, da Costa, and Chuaqui 1986.)

A realist of course agrees that empirical adequacy is a desirable property: the observational consequences of a theory should be true—or at least approximately true. But as soon as van Fraassen admits that theories have a truth value, it becomes problematic to claim that the truth 'about the observable' is the only relevant feature of acceptable theories. If a theory saves the phenomena by making false theoretical postulations or

---

[2] Discussion on van Fraassen's philosophy of science is contained in Churchland and Hooker (1985). See also Hooker (1987), Devitt (1991), and Psillos (1994a). For further comments, see Sections 6.4–5.

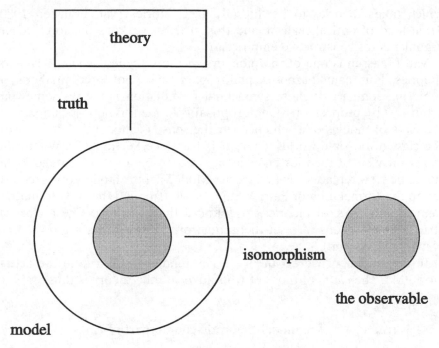

FIG. 16. Constructive empiricism

constructions (in the white area of the model in Fig. 16), is this as good as saving the same phenomena by a true or truthlike theory?

Van Fraassen would regard the realist's intervention as question-begging. His reply is theoretical scepticism: the truth of theories should not be required, since we do not have any knowledge about the unobservable. He supports this view with the thesis that theory is underdetermined by evidence (cf. Section 6.3) and with an attack on abduction or inference to the best explanation (van Fraassen 1989) (cf. Section 6.4).

As many realist critics have pointed out, van Fraassen's position pre-supposes here that there is an important observational–theoretical dis-tinction. Van Fraassen himself admits that this distinction is not unique, but depends on our theories. For his epistemological purposes, he requires that the former category includes only observability by unaided human senses, but for a fallibilist this seems clearly unsatisfactory: even naked observation reports are uncertain to some degree, and their epistemic status does not sharply differ from measurement results by scientific instru-ments (or from indirectly testable theoretical hypotheses). It should also be noted that van Fraassen construes his opposition to the form of realism which takes theories to be 'literally true' stories (van Fraassen 1980: 8), instead of critical realism, and this at least weakens the force of his arguments for constructive empiricism.

Van Fraassen is one of the pioneers of the so-called *semantic view* of theories. For many purposes, philosophers have invented methods of replacing sentences (whose syntactical formulation is always somewhat arbitrary) by propositions. One proposal is to identify a proposition with the class of models of a sentence (in the sense of model theory) or with the class of possible worlds where it is true (see Section 3.3). Where the *statement view* of theories takes a theory T to be a set of sentences, the semantic view replaces T with the class Mod(T) of the models of T. According to the formulation of Patrick Suppes, who applied this idea to mathematical and physical theories, to define a theory is to define a class of structures by means of a set-theoretical predicate (e.g. 'is a group', 'is a Newtonian system').[3]

In the statement view, a theory T is intended to be true in the actual world M*. The *claim* of those of who advocate the theory is thus

$$M^* \vDash T, \qquad\qquad\qquad (2)$$

i.e. T is true in M*. The model-theoretic counterpart of (2) is

$$M^* \in \text{Mod}(T), \qquad\qquad\qquad (3)$$

i.e. M* is a model of T.

The *structuralist school* (Joseph Sneed, Wolfgang Stegmüller, Carlos Ulises Moulines, Wolfgang Balzer) develops this basic idea by defining a theory directly as a set of structures **M**, and thereby eliminating (talk about) the language of the theory.[4] Further, they define the set **I** of the *intended applications* of the theory: **I** is the historically changing domain of situations where the supporters of the theory think the theory to be applicable. For example, the initial set **I** for Newton's theory included planets, freely falling bodies, projectiles, and pendulums—and later, when the theory developed, rigid bodies, temperature, etc. In other words, instead of thinking the theory to have one global application (i.e. the actual world), the theory is taken to have several, possibly overlapping applications. The claim of the theory is then, instead of (3),

$$\mathbf{I} \subseteq \mathbf{M}. \qquad\qquad\qquad (4)$$

---

[3] For the semantic view, see Suppe (1989) and Giere (1988).

[4] I give here only a simplified account of the structuralist approach. For more details, see Stegmüller (1976), Balzer, Moulines, and Sneed (1987). Cf. also Balzer, Pearce, and Schmidt (1984), Pearce and Rantala (1984), Niiniluoto (1984), Kieseppä (1996).

I think these ideas are important and useful. They are not incompatible with the statement view, since at least in most typical cases a class of structures **M** can be defined by sets of sentences in languages with sufficiently rich vocabulary and logic, i.e. **M**=Mod(T) for some T (cf. Niiniluoto 1984: ch. 6; Pearce 1987a). They can be understood in the realist sense, since (4) then requires the theory T to be *true* in all intended applications in set **I**. This also suggests that the truthlikeness of a theory T should primarily be evaluated relative to each intended application M in **I**. For example, instead of asking what the degree of truthlikeness of Einstein's Special Relativity Theory is, we should study separately its accuracy for cosmological models, planets, satellites, etc. (cf. Gähde 1997). If a global measure of the truthlikeness of a theory T is needed, it should be a weighted sum of the degrees Tr(T, M) for the intended applications M in **I** (cf. Niiniluoto 1987a: 370–1).

However, the structuralist approach has received an instrumentalist flavour from Sneed's theory-relative distinction between T-theoretical and T-non-theoretical terms, and the Ramseyan reformulation of the claim (4). According to Sneed, the intended applications **I** of a theory T are T-non-theoretical, and the 'empirical claim' of T asserts that

> Each T-non-theoretical structure $M_0$ in **I** can be extended     (5)
> by T-theoretical functions so that the extended structure M is
> a model of T

(cf. (1)). In the case where the T-non-theoretical vs. T-theoretical distinction agrees with van Fraassen's observational vs. theoretical distinction, and the extension of $M_0$ may be undertaken by any suitable theoretical functions, the Sneedian empirical claim (5) amounts to van Fraassen's empirical adequacy (cf. Fig. 16). For a scientific realist this is not a sufficient guarantee that the empirical claim (5) 'saves' the phenomena in class **I** in the right way. A scientific realist is interested in the truth of the full theory, not only its observational consequences, and therefore he would require that the theoretical functions are chosen so that they correspond to real things in the world (cf. Feigl 1950).

Larry Laudan (1977) argues, following Kuhn, that science is a *problem-solving* rather than truth-seeking activity. However, he is not an instrumentalist, since (like van Fraassen) he admits that theories have a truth value. But, according to Laudan (1984a), truth is a utopian aim of science, and should be replaced by the demand of success in problem-solving, especially prediction. When Laudan in his recent work speaks about the 'confirmation' of theories (cf. Laudan 1996), he cannot mean that success in problem-solving indicates the truth of the theory itself: he clearly must understand such confirmation as a warrant for the next empirical predictions from the theory. This is in harmony with Laudan's (1990*b*) self-portrait as a 'pragmatist'. While Laudan may thereby seem to avoid the problems of the semantic interpretation of theoretical languages, we shall see that he is forced to make problematic assumptions about reference and truth in his attempt to refute scientific realism (see Section 6.4). The realist can accept the idea of science as problem-solving, if success in solving cognitive problems is linked with the notion of truth (see Section 6.1).

## 5.2  *Meaning variance, reference, and theoretical terms*

The Received View, or two-layer conception of theories, takes the meaning of theoretical terms and statements to be parasitic upon their relation to the observational language (see Fig. 14). Against this principle of *semantic empiricism*, the scientific realists separate questions of testability (methodological relations between theory and observation) and meaning (semantic relations between theory and reality). (See Fig. 15.) The realist thus owes an explanation of the ways in which such theory–world relations are established.

If semantic empiricism is given up, it is natural to suggest that the meaning of a scientific term somehow depends on the whole theory where this term occurs. This is the principle of theory-ladenness of meanings: the theoretical framework gives an 'implicit definition' of its basic concepts. The most sophisticated empiricists had convincingly argued for 'holism' in theory–observation relations: according to the *Duhem–Quine Thesis*, a theory meets experience only as a whole.[5] In a similar way, a scientific realist may adopt a principle of *meaning holism*: the meaning of a term is 'its position within the network of propositions of a theory'.[6] This definition—which resembles the basic idea of Saussure's semiology—implies the thesis of *Radical Meaning Variance*:

> Every change in theory T changes the meaning of each       (RMV)
> non-logical term occurring in T.

Applied to the observational terms occurring in T, this means that their meaning also varies with theoretical changes. Hence, RMV entails the thesis of the *theory-ladenness of observations*:

---

[5] See Duhem (1954) and Quine (1953).
[6] This formulation is given in H. I. Brown (1977: 120). See also Kordig (1971).

> Observations are theory-laden; there is no neutral     (TLO)
> language of experience.

Another important principle, apparently a consequence of RMV, is the *thesis of incommensurability*:

> The meanings of terms in two different theories are     (IC)
> different; the theories carve up the world in different
> ways, and cannot be translated to each other.

These results, which seem inevitably to follow from the realist principle of theoretical meaning holism, give a serious challenge to scientific realism—as Kuhn and Feyerabend in particular argued in the 1960s.

The source of the trouble is obviously the strong meaning holism which leads to RMV: it implies meaning variance in *all* changes, even in the most trivial or insignificant ones, of a theory (cf. Suppe 1977; Papineau 1996*b*). The idea of a term's position in a theoretical net is syntactical, and it is by no means clear that it has some definite connection to semantic meaning.

Philosophers seeking a more plausible formulation of the theory-dependence of meaning have proposed various accounts which still satisfy *Weak Meaning Variance*:

> Some changes in theory T may change the meanings of     (WMV)
> some terms in T.

The task of the theory of meaning is to specify the content WMV.

An immediate advantage of WMV over RMV is that it allows for a sharper version of TLO: it need not be the case that each observation term occurring in theory T is laden-with-the-assumptions-of-T. Even though *every* term is laden with *some* theory, so that there is no neutral observation language, a term in T may be laden with some other theories than T. For example, terms describing visual observations by means of optical instruments (human eyes, telescopes, microscopes, etc.) are laden with optical theories, but not with electric or thermodynamic theories. Thus, it may happen that a term occurring in two rival theories $T_1$ and $T_2$ is neither $T_1$-laden nor $T_2$-laden—and in this sense is neutral between them. For example, telescope recordings (in spite of their optics-ladenness) may provide a basis for comparing astronomical theories.

One proposal for establishing WMV is to divide a theory T into its *analytic component* $T_A$ and *synthetic component* $T_S$, so that $\vdash T \equiv T_A \& T_S$, and changes in $T_A$ (and only those) create meaning variance. Many philosophers have taken Quine's (1953) objections to be fatal to any attempt in this direction, but we have defended in Section 3.2 the possibility of making the analytic–synthetic distinction within a language. More specifically, Carnap (1966) suggested that $T_S$ could be the Ramsey sentence $T^R$ of theory T, and $T_A$ its so-called Carnap sentence $T^R \rightarrow T$. It is possible to understand Carnap's division so that the original axioms of theory T are synthetic (see Winnie 1975). The significance of this proposal depends on the interpretation of the Ramsey sentence: if the factual content of the theory is restricted to its observational claims, the questionable idea of semantic empiricism is presupposed (cf. Tuomela 1973).

Another approach, due to Ajdukiewicz and Carnap, is to express the conceptual presuppositions of a theory syntactically as meaning postulates MP, and to treat the theory as a conjunction of axioms A and meaning postulates, i.e. $T \equiv A\&MP$. The change from theory $T \equiv A\&MP$ to another theory $T' \equiv A'\&MP'$ exhibits conceptual change or meaning variance to the extent that sets MP and MP′ differ from each other (Giedymin 1971).[7]

The third approach is based on the concept of translation. Language $L_1$ is *translatable* to language $L_2$ if every sentence of $L_1$ is correlated with a sentence of $L_2$ with the same meaning (e.g. the same truth-conditions). $L_1$ is *strongly translatable* to $L_2$ if all non-logical terms of $L_1$ are explicitly definable by terms of $L_2$. Languages $L_1$ and $L_2$ are *incommensurable* if neither of the two is translatable to the other. If two incommensurable languages contain common terms, the change from one to the other exhibits meaning variance.[8]

Kazimierz Ajdukiewicz advocated in the 1930s *radical conventionalism*, which asserts the existence of 'incompatible' languages without a common, meaning-preserving extension (see Ajdukiewicz 1978). *Radical incommensurability* between $L_1$ and $L_2$ in this sense can be expressed as follows:

> There is no language L to which both $L_1$ and $L_2$ are    (IC1)
> translatable.

IC1 entails incommensurability in the ordinary sense:

> The languages $L_1$ and $L_2$ cannot be translated to each    (IC2)
> other (in one or two ways).

(Namely, if $L_1$ were translatable to $L_2$, $L_2$ would be the language L in condition $IC_1$.) On the other hand, IC2 does not entail IC1: meaning variance

---

[7] I have used meaning postulates to explicate meaning variance in Niiniluoto (1987*a*). In order to compare two rival theories T and T′ for truthlikeness, we may have to include among their statements the conflicting meaning postulates.

[8] Stegmüller suggested that the structuralist concept of reduction between structures (cf. Balzer, Pearce, and Schmidt 1984) helps to avoid the problem of incommensurability between languages. Pearce (1987*a*) showed, however, that under certain assumptions relations between structures induces a translation between languages.

does not exclude the possibility of considering rival theories in a richer conceptual framework.

Hence, in spite of weak incommensurability IC2, two theories $T_1$ and $T_2$ in languages $L_1$ and $L_2$ may be compared for their truthlikeness by considering them as rival answers to a cognitive problem within a language L to which $L_1$ and $L_2$ are translatable, i.e. by comparing the truthlikeness of the translations of these theories in L (see Pearce 1987b).

A good example is provided by the step from Ptolemy's geocentric system to Copernicus' heliocentric system. These theories contain a common term 'planet' (i.e. a heavenly body orbiting around the centre of the system). Its meaning changes in the referential sense, since the extension of 'planet' in Ptolemy's theory includes (among other things) the sun and the moon but not the earth.[9] But even though this is the case, both theories can be expressed in a richer conceptual framework which contains proper names for known heavenly bodies and allows the definition of Ptolemian planets and Copernican planets.

A radical incommensurabilist could still argue—relying on Quine's (1960) thesis about the indeterminacy of translation—that all languages are incommensurable: any attempt to translate sentences or terms from one language to another remains incomplete or indeterminate in some respect. This appears to be Kuhn's view. According to Kuhn (1983), incommensurability between two theories means that 'there is no language, neutral or otherwise, into which both theories, conceived as sets of sentences, can be translated without loss'. This is condition IC1, when complete translation is meant. As Kuhn (1993) emphasized in his later work, such incommensurability does not preclude the possibility of a historian of science becoming 'bilingual' and *learning* other languages (like Aristotelian physics) without being able to translate them into his own vocabulary.

As Kuokkanen (1990) claims, Kuhnian incommensurability is also compatible with the existence of *incomplete* translations. But still incommensurability denies complete translatability, so that complete translation entails commensurability (cf. Pearce 1987a; Schröder-Heister and Schäfer 1989).

A complete reversal of this view is Davidson's (1984) thesis, which claims that there are no alternative conceptual frameworks that differ from our own. The problem of incommensurability would be thereby dissolved. He considers separately the cases of total and partial failures of

[9] This is Brown's (1977: 116) example against Scheffler's (1967) idea of reference invariance. Thagard (1992) gives an elegant treatment of conceptual change in terms of type-hierarchies.

translation, and argues that no solid meaning can be given to the idea of conceptual schemes which 'organize' sense experience or reality in different ways. According to Davidson, when we know what sentences a speaker asserts or holds true, we cannot even make the first steps of interpretation without assuming a great deal about the speaker's beliefs. If we want to understand others, and to identify their beliefs, the principle of charity has to be applied by counting 'them right in most matters'. This common stock of true beliefs has been called a 'bridgehead' by Martin Hollis (see Hollis and Lukes 1982). This bridgehead then guarantees the translatability of the other speaker's language to our own. For Davidson, such a translatability then becomes a 'criterion of languagehood'—and, as a consequence, gives reason to reject conceptual relativism and the scheme–content distinction.

Davidson's argument leads in a peculiar way to the universal medium view of language (cf. Section 3.1)—according to some critics, even to solipsism and conceptual imperialism (cf. Pihlström 1996: 163–74). Rescher (1980) argues that there are pragmatic criteria for identifying and comparing different languages. Further, Davidson's principle of charity, which implies that most of our own beliefs are true, seems to be too strong: if we grant that our common-sense beliefs and scientific hypotheses are typically at best approximately true, the case of partial failures of translation is put into new perspective. Perhaps it is a typical case that there are different conceptual systems with incomplete or partial translations between them?

In my view, the truth lies between the extreme positions. Natural languages may contain parts that are incommensurable in the sense IC2. Incommensurability in the stronger sense IC1 may be found among theories existing in the history of science, and among belief systems in other cultures (cf. Wang 1988) and in pseudo-sciences. But, nevertheless, there are many ways of comparing the content and truthlikeness of rival scientific theories (cf. Pearce 1987a).

To make this claim plausible, the realist has to admit moderate versions of WMV and TLO, to deny the naive cumulative model of scientific change (see Pera 1985, however), but still show the possibility of some sort of continuity within theory-change. I shall concentrate here on the idea of reference invariance (cf. Section 5.3, too). For the purposes of this book this is an important possibility: if two theories speak about the same things, then they can be construed as rival answers to the same cognitive problem, and the machinery of Section 3.5 is in principle applicable to their comparison.

Israel Scheffler (1967) argued, against Kuhn and Feyerabend, that *reference invariance* is compatible with meaning variance. Two terms with different meanings (e.g. 'the Morning Star' and 'the Evening Star') may refer to the same object. Thus, it should be possible for two rival theories to speak about the same entities in the world and make different claims about them (see Fig. 17). (Cf. Musgrave 1979.) Here T and T′ might be classical and relativistic mechanics, respectively, which both refer to the same quantity *mass*, although the former mistakenly asserts mass to be independent of the movement of a physical body.

Is there a theory of reference which allows for reference stability in the sense of Fig. 17? The theories developed by philosophers of language seem to run into difficulties with this question.

There are two main types of theories of reference for proper names (see Haack 1978; Devitt and Sterelny 1987). John Stuart Mill argued that proper names have a 'denotation', but no 'connotation', i.e. they simply refer to objects without giving any description of them. Frege opposed such *direct* theories by claiming that proper names also have a meaning (*Sinn*). *Descriptive* theories of reference have attached to proper names definite descriptions, such as 'Plato's teacher' for 'Socrates' (Russell) or 'a thing which pegasizes' for 'Pegasus' (Quine), or clusters of descriptions (Searle, Strawson). *Causal* theory of reference (see Kripke 1980; Putnam 1975) is a new form of direct theory: reference is fixed by a causal chain backward to the original event of baptizing or a dubbing ceremony; hence, a person may succeed in referring by a proper name to an object, even though he does not know any true descriptions about it. (In the simplest case of demonstrative reference, two persons point to the same object in front of them and may make conflicting statements about it. See Quine (1960), however.)

When applied to general terms occurring in scientific theories, a direct or causal account seems problematic. What could be the original event of

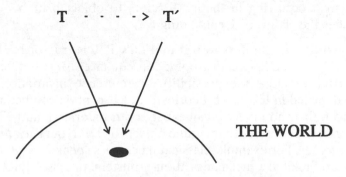

FIG. 17. Reference invariance

giving a name to an unobservable elementary particle or mental event? As ostension to such entities is not possible ('I baptize this thing as electron . . .') (see Leplin 1979), the original name-giving already has to rely on some descriptive phrases (Nola 1980). Kripke, Putnam, Lewis, and Devitt have proposed indirect causal descriptions, such as 'Electron is the object which causes this trace in Wilson chambers', 'Light is whatever, in our world, affects our eyes in a certain way' (see also Hardin and Rosenberg 1982). More generally, a theoretical term refers 'to those aspects of reality that prompted its use'. This proposal allows reference invariance, but it can be claimed to allow too much: as the use of all terms is presumably 'prompted' by some aspect of reality, and as no constraints are put to our possible mistakes about the nature of these aspects or objects, the causal account fails to account for reference failure (e.g. 'phlogiston', 'ether', and 'demon' are not referring theoretical terms) (cf. Laudan 1984c; Cummiskey 1992).

Dissatisfaction with purely causal theories of reference has led many philosophers to claim that reference fixing needs some descriptive elements (e.g. Nola 1980; Kroon 1988). In fact, even in the causal account, a phrase like 'whatever causes observable events of type O' picks out a unique kind only if it is a part of a framework of laws or theoretical assumptions. This leads us towards an account of theoretical terms as 'implicitly defined' or 'cluster concepts' (Putnam 1975), where the referent of a term in theory T is defined as the object that satisfies T or most of the assumptions of T.

Let us now formulate a Fregean descriptive account of reference for general terms: term t may be correctly applied to object b in linguistic community C if and only if b satisfies all of the descriptions attached to term t by the beliefs in community C. Applied to theoretical terms, this idea could be formulated as follows:

> A term t occurring in theory T refers to object b iff b      (DR1)
> satisfies the claims of T containing t.

In other words, t in T refers to b if and only if T is true of b. However, principle DR1 would have catastrophic consequences for scientific realism.

First, DR1 excludes the possibility of reference invariance, i.e. the situation depicted in Fig. 17. If theories T and T' contain conflicting claims relative to t, then no object b can satisfy both theories T and T'. Hence, rival theories cannot refer to the same objects by DR1, but *each theory has its own ontology*. For example, classical mechanics speaks about 'Newtonian mass' and relativist mechanics about 'Einsteinian mass'. DR1 thereby supports Kuhn's criticism of realist views about theory change: theoretical transitions in science have no ontological continuity, since reference is not preserved.

Secondly, it is not only that reference is not preserved, but for most theories reference fails altogether. The history of science teaches us that many scientific theories are false. Thus, no objects in the actual world can satisfy their claims. According to DR1, they can at best speak about 'idealized' or 'imaginary' objects that cannot be found in the real world. The theory of ideal gases 'refers' to ideal gases rather than real gases; rival theories of electrons 'referred' to such strange creatures as Lorenz-electron, Bohr-electron-1911, and Bohr-electron-1925.

This consequence might lead some philosophers to claim that such non-referring theories fail to be meaningful at all. Strawson argued that, for instance, the sentence 'The present king of the France is bald' presupposes the existence of the French king, and if this presupposition is not satisfied the whole sentence is meaningless. Russell instead analysed non-referring definite descriptions so that sentences containing them are false (i.e. they make a false existential claim).

Definition DR1 thus leads to *theoretical anti-realism*: each theory speaks about entities that it itself defines. Theories are trivially true about these entities, but in typical cases these entities have nothing to do with reality.

It is obvious that the realists have to reject the definition DR1, but in a way that preserves its correct core. The first attempt in this direction was N. L. Wilson's *Principle of Charity* in 1959: the referent of a term is the object which makes true most of the beliefs of the speaker. Peter Smith's (1981) formulation is the following: term t may be correctly applied to object b in linguistic community C if and only if b satisfies a suitable *majority* of the descriptions attached to term t by the beliefs in community C. Applied to scientific terms, and letting a theory T express the beliefs of the scientific community, this idea gives an alternative to DR1:

> A term t occurring in theory T refers to object b iff b          (DR2)
> satisfies the majority of the claims of T containing t.

However, it is doubtful whether DR2 covers typical cases where a theory is false but 'close to the truth'. In many such cases, when the theory is approximate or idealized, it need not be the case that most, or even any, of the statements of the theory are strictly speaking true. For example, a quantitative law may deviate from the true law at each point, but still be truthlike.

One attempt to avoid anti-realism has been made by Psillos (1994b) in his 'functional conception', which allows that the 'introductory description' of a putative entity (i.e. its causal role and some of its properties) can be later extended by further investigation. However, it is still the case that the term does not refer at all if no entity satisfies this introductory description. Thus, Psillos in effect applies DR1 by replacing theory T with the introductory description, or DR2 by replacing the 'suitable majority' by the introductory description.

It seems to me, however, that in many real cases the initial descriptions of causally identified theoretical entities are to some extent mistaken. For example, when the syndrome called AIDS was identified, the hunt for its cause, the HI-virus, was started in medical laboratories. Later studies revealed that initial assumptions about the causal processes were simplistic: the HI-virus exists in many variants, and the causal mechanisms and conditions producing AIDS are still unknown to a large extent.

Putnam's (1975) formulation of the Principle of Charity, i.e. his *Principle of Benefit of Doubt*, allows that the person proposing a term may make reasonable changes in the original description. Even though there are no objects satisfying Bohr's description completely, some do it approximately. According to a 'charitable interpretation', Bohr referred precisely to those entities by his term 'electron' (cf. Fig. 17).

Another form of this idea is sketched by David Lewis (1970): if a theory T is not realized by any entity, it may still have a 'near-realization' which realizes another theory T′ obtained from the original theory T 'by a slight weakening or a slight correction' (p. 432). Then the theoretical term in T denotes the entity which is 'the nearest near-realization' of the theory, if it 'comes near enough'.

When applied to singular reference, this treatment could be called the *caricature* theory of reference. A good caricature of a person b distorts the outlook of b by an amusing exaggeration of the features of b, but still it must bear sufficient similarity to its model so that we easily see the reference to b.

A weakness of the so far proposed accounts of charity is their reliance on an intuitive notion of approximate truth or nearness. A more precise formulation can be given by employing the concepts of approximate truth AT and truthlikeness Tr (Niiniluoto 1987*a*). Usually these concepts have been applied by assuming that the interpretation of the given language L is fixed, and the best theory T in L is looked for (see Section 3.5). Here, instead, theory T in language L is given, and we look for the interpretation of L that makes T most truthlike. More precisely, we assume a dynamic situation where one term t in theory T is still uninterpreted, while other terms are antecedently understood.

Let AT(T, b) be the degree of approximate truth of theory T relative to the 'system' consisting of the object b, and Tr(T, b) the corresponding

degree of truthlikeness of T relative to b. Here b may be a singular object
(e.g. a black hole in a certain region of space), or a kind of object (e.g. neu-
trino, Oedipus complex) which serves as a candidate for the interpretation
of term t. Two new definitions of reference are thereby obtained:

> Term t occurring in theory T refers to the actual object b          (DR3)
> which maximizes AT(T, b).

> Term t occurring in theory T refers to the actual object b          (DR4)
> which maximizes Tr(T, b).

DR4 is more demanding than DR3, since a high degree of truthlikeness
guarantees also a high degree of approximate truth. DR3 can be understood as a precise version of Putnam's Principle of Benefit of Doubt and
Lewis's account of near-realizations. DR4 was proposed in my lecture in
January 1992 (published in Finnish in 1994).[10] For singular reference, a formulation of DR4 was given independently by David Martens in his 1990
doctoral dissertation: Martens (1993) says that a mental thought t 'comes
close enough to reference' to individual b, or has 'reference-likeness' to b,
if it is adequately truthlike to think that t refers (in the sense of DR1)
to b.

The interpretation of the antecedently understood terms in T limits the
choice of b. If needed, additional restrictions may be placed on the choice
of b: for physical theories, b should be an object or system in the physical
World 1; for psychological theories, b should belong to the mental World
2; for social theories, b is a cultural entity in the man-made World 3.
Otherwise we might have cases of unintended reference which resemble
categorial mistakes.

Lewis (1984) argues that only an 'elite minority' of entities are eligible
to serve as referents: they are not 'miscellaneous, gerrymandered,
ill-demarcated', but rather 'carved at the joints' in a natural way (see also
O'Leary-Hawthorne 1994). This formulation seems to presuppose metaphysical realism, i.e. that there is a uniquely best way of carving the world
into entities. Another view allows that such carvings can be done in different ways within alternative ontological frameworks (cf. Ch. 7). Then
rules like DR3 and DR4, which seem to contain quantification over all
eligible entities, should be relativized to an ontological framework of
acceptable kinds of entities.

Both DR3 and DR4 include the special case where a theory refers to
an object by giving a perfectly true description of it. But in general

---

[10] See also Niiniluoto (1997a; 1997b). In developing this account, I have benefited from
critical remarks by Mr Panu Raatikainen.

successful reference to actual objects does not presuppose the strict truth of the theory. Both definitions allow that Lorenz and Bohr in 1911 and in 1925 referred to the same electron—which, moreover, is still studied by contemporary physicists. Putnam's famous 'meta-induction', namely 'just as no term used in the science of more than fifty (or whatever) years ago referred, so it will turn out that no term used now refers' (Putnam 1978: 25), is blocked, since its premiss is not valid (see also Section 7.4).

DR3 and DR4 are formulated as very liberal criteria, since they allow almost any old theory to be 'referring'. For example, the phlogiston theory failed, since its existential claim about phlogiston was false. While for some purposes it may be useful to think that this theory referred to oxygen (even though, of course, it gives a mistaken description of oxygen), there is clearly also a need for a less liberal conception. This is achieved by placing a suitable lower bound to the values of AT(T, b) and Tr(T, b), and giving credit for successful reference to b only if this *threshold* is exceeded.[11] Such a threshold is not determined by logic; rather I think it depends on the pragmatic context.

This does not mean that the concept of being a referring term becomes arbitrary: successful reference still depends on what kinds of entities exist in the real world. But, in order to fix the threshold in some particular case, the scientific community has to decide how charitable it wants to be. If a very high threshold is chosen, then reference is achieved only by true (DR3) or completely true (DR4) theories. For the purposes of historical comparisons, it might be fair to choose a low threshold and grant, for instance, that the ancient atomists referred to something like our molecules. The physicist in the early twentieth century did interpret the rival theories of the electron as speaking about the same entity.

Definitions DR3 and DR4 allow for cases where the reference of a term t is so to say 'overdetermined': it may be the case that already a part of the assumptions of T is sufficient to fix uniquely the interpretation of t. Papineau (1996*b*) suggests that such cases help to solve the problem with Weak Meaning Variance (WMV) without assuming that there is a precise way of dividing the theory T into two parts, one determining the meaning of t and the other not.

Definitions DR3 and DR4 do not exclude the case of a 'tie': it may happen that AT(T, x) or Tr(T, x) is maximized by two different kinds of objects b and c. In such situations, we may say that the term t refers to both b and c. This is comparable to Hartry Field's (1973) suggestion that the

---

[11] We shall see in Section 6.4 that this account of reference has important consequences in the debates concerning the so-called 'pessimistic meta-induction' from the history of science.

Newtonian 'mass' is indeterminate between two references, the rest mass and the relativistic mass.

It has been proposed that the reference of 'mass' is ambiguous, sometimes referring to rest mass, sometimes to relativistic mass, in a context-dependent way. An elegant defence of this view is given by Philip Kitcher. We should give up, he argues, 'the presupposition that there should be a uniform mode of reference for all tokens of a single type' (Kitcher 1993: 101). In other words, a scientific term may have 'a heterogeneous reference potential'. Here he allows that reference may be fixed either by causal or by descriptive means. Kitcher illustrates this view by arguing that Priestley referred to oxygen by the description of his first experience of breathing 'dephlogisticated air' (ibid. 100). Cavendish was also referring to oxygen when he described the process of producing 'dephlogisticated air' by heating the red calx of mercury. But on other occasions they misdescribed this new gas as something obtained by the removal of phlogiston from the air—and failed to refer.

This kind of context-sensitivity can be explicated by principles like DR4. It may happen that $Tr(T, x)$ is maximized by a, but $Tr(T_0, x)$ by b, where $T_0$ is a subtheory T. A token of a term t, when it occurs in statements $T_0$, refers to oxygen, but in another context T it may fail to refer, since the truthlikeness of T remains below the threshold.

Still, the idea of heterogeneous reference potential seems problematic. It is one thing to say that the advocates of the phlogiston theory were *mistaken*, and another to imply that they were *confused*. To construe the achievements of Priestley so that the tokens of his basic term sometimes referred to phlogiston, sometimes to oxygen, and sometimes to nothing seems like saying that Priestley's theory was incoherent, without a uniquely fixed subject matter.

These remarks illustrate the fact that there need not be any unique answer to the question about *the* referent of a term. If a historically accurate conception of something like the speaker's intended reference is meant, then it seems appropriate to interpret Priestley's language as homogeneously as possible in the context of the whole of the phlogiston theory. Contrary to Kitcher's claim, an account that attributes reference failure to Priestley does not preclude the fact that his theory implied many important new truths. However, *we* are not prevented from presenting a historical reinterpretation from the standpoint of Lavoisier's later theory, where Priestley's terms refer to oxygen (see Section 6.4).

These distinctions are difficult to make by principles DR3 and DR4 which employ the objective, non-epistemic concepts of approximate truth and truthlikeness. But these conditions can also be reformulated by using concepts that are relative to available evidence (statement e expressing observational and theoretical evidence) and beliefs (represented by an epistemic probability function P). Then we may define concepts like *probable approximate truth* and *expected verisimilitude* (see Section 4.4). Let PAT(T, b/e) be the probability given evidence e that theory T as applied to object b is approximately true (to a given degree), and let ver(T, b/e) be the expected degree of truthlikeness (given evidence e and probabilities P) of the theory T as applied to object b. Let A be the person whose degrees of belief are expressed by measure P. Then two new definitions for reference are obtained:

> Person A refers by term t occurring in theory T to the          (DR5)
> actual object b which maximizes PAT(T, b/e).

> Person A refers by term t occurring in theory T to the          (DR6)
> actual object b which maximizes ver(T, b/e).

Here DR5 and DR6 allow us to define the reference of a term relative to the beliefs of a scientific community at some stage in the history of science (e.g. chemistry in Priestley's time) by considering their available evidence and accepted beliefs, and distinguish this from our reference relation relative to the evidence and beliefs that we now have.

In fact, the caricature model of reference as such is not quite appropriate for science, since theories are not pictures of already known objects (such as the drawings of Charles de Gaulle and Elvis Presley). Rather they are attempts to describe some so far *unknown* theoretical entities on the basis of incomplete, partial, uncertain, and indirect information. In this sense, they can be compared to the pictures of unknown murderers sometimes published by the police, drawn by an artist or by a computer relying on the evidence provided by eyewitnesses. (The picture of the still unidentified assassin of Prime Minister Olof Palme is a case in point.) If the picture itself is bad, it may mislead us to accuse an innocent bystander who best fits the description. But if such a picture is good enough, it refers to the true murderer by DR3 and DR4. Principles DR5 and DR6 help to explain why we, in our incomplete evidential situation, may be misled into thinking that the sufficiently correct picture refers to some in fact innocent person: relative to our beliefs, the picture refers to the wrong person.

## 5.3  Laws, truthlikeness, and idealization

The thesis (R2) of Section 1.3 says that the concepts of *truth and falsity* are in principle applicable to all linguistic products of scientific enquiry, including *observation reports, laws, and theories*. This thesis gives two important problems for the realist's agenda: lawlikeness and idealization.

*Laws of nature*, as parts of scientific theories, are expressed by statements which are essentially universal (i.e. not logically equivalent to singular statements about a finite number of instances) (see Nagel 1961; Hempel 1965). As direct observational evidence concerns singular instances, this already creates the classical problem of induction. The impossibility of verifying genuinely universal generalizations has sometimes motivated instrumentalist interpretations of their nature as 'inference tickets' without a truth value (Schlick, Ryle). It was thought that this was sufficient to account for their role in systematizing observational statements.

For a theoretical realist, laws of nature are linguistic expressions of *regularities* or *invariances* which exist 'out there' in nature. Laws as statements are human constructions, but causal and other regularities are mind-independent aspects of reality (*pace* Kant; Rescher 1982).

Some philosophers go so far as to claim that mind-independent lawlikeness is the ultimate reality, more basic than historically changing material objects. Peirce's thirdness and Kaila's invariances (cf. Section 4.2) could be mentioned in this connection. For example, it is a contingent fact how matter is spread out within the universe, and the state of the world is continuously changing in this respect; but, as a matter of natural necessity, the law of gravitation continues to hold in the universe. Especially when such laws are assumed to have a mathematical character, there is a whiff of Platonism in this view (see Brown 1994).

A methodological defence of the view that laws are the only realistically interpreted elements of theories has been put forward by John Worrall (1989), who calls his position *structural realism* (following Jerzy Giedymin). Worrall refers to Henri Poincaré's statement that Nature for ever hides 'the real objects' from our eyes, so that 'the true relations between these real objects are the only reality we can attain'. A similar view was defended by Schlick on the philosophical ground that language can express only the 'form' of facts, not their 'content' or intrinsic quality (see Schlick 1985). This idea receives some support also from model theory: even the strongest mathematical theories are able to specify their intended interpretation only up to isomorphism (cf. Bell and Slomson 1969). Another defence might come from the modern theories of measurement (Krantz *et al.* 1971) which construe all quantities from comparative (hence relational) concepts. In my view, however, it seems too strong to claim that scientific knowledge could not involve genuinely one-place predicates (in addition to many-place predicates and relational one-place predicates) (see Section 2.4).

Worrall's motivation comes from the pessimistic meta-induction, as he seeks an alternative to the ontological idea of reference invariance (see Section 5.2). He illustrates the thesis by showing that Fresnel's optical laws were retained in Maxwell's theory, even though they understood the nature of light in different ways: for Fresnel, light waves are disturbances in a mechanical medium or ether, while for Maxwell they are vibrations in an electromagnetic field.

I think it is correct that in some examples there is more continuity on the level of theoretical laws than on the level of theoretical ontologies. But Worrall's own example presupposes that there was some continuity on the level of ontology after all: both Fresnel and Maxwell were speaking about light. Moreover, as Worrall himself admits (and as we shall see later in this section), it is quite typical as well that laws are modified by 'concretization'. Hettema and Kuipers (1995) show that the early theories of electrons, while referring to the same target entity, systematically corrected the proposed laws.

More generally, we have also seen in Section 5.2 that the determination of theoretical reference involves the laws of the theory. Structural realism contains an important insight, but I do not think that theoretical laws and ontologies can be separated as sharply as it assumes.

There are many rival views about the nature of laws. The *Humean* regularity theory takes laws to be simply extensional generalizations about the actual world. The law 'All ravens are black' specifies the colour of all actual ravens in the past, present, and future: the class of ravens is a subset of the class of black things. Similarly, probabilistic laws are analysed in terms of the relative frequencies of attributes in reference classes (see Salmon 1984; van Fraassen 1989). This treatment is in harmony with philosophical empiricism.

The critics of the Humean view argue that the extensional account is not sufficient to distinguish merely accidental generalizations and genuine laws. In many methodological applications (explanation, prediction, causal inference, confirmation), it seems that laws have *counterfactual* force. In spite of Hume's empiricist criticism, there is an element of 'nomic' or 'causal' *necessity* in universal laws, and its counterpart in probabilistic laws is the notion of *propensity* and *probabilistic causality* (see Fetzer 1981; Niiniluoto 1988*b*; Suppes 1993). This view has been defended by constructing semantic treatments of counterfactuals and nomic statements by using the techniques of the possible worlds semantics for intensional logic.[12] Some philosophers assume underlying mechanisms and 'causal powers' to explain laws (Bhaskar 1975; Harré 1986), and some assume laws to be relations between universals (Armstrong 1978; Tooley 1987), but it may be possible to construe a realist view of laws also from a trope ontology of events.

A survey of these metaphysical issues and logical technicalities is beyond the scope of this work. But it is important to note here that the concept of truthlikeness is equally well applicable to extensional statements about the actual world and (as 'legisimilitude' in L. J. Cohen's sense) to nomically necessary or probable laws (see Niiniluoto 1987a: ch. 11). Therefore, I shall concentrate in this section on another challenge to the realist view of laws and theories.

The problem of *idealization* has been grist to an instrumentalist's mill. However, I argue in this section that the concept of truthlikeness helps to give an adequate realist account of the role of idealization in theory construction.

An instrumentalist is typically a believer in the empirical world, describable by our language of everyday experience (be it phenomenalist or physicalist). The mathematical description, employing classical analysis with real numbers, goes beyond this world. Against Galileo's mathematical realism, which takes the Book of Nature to be written in mathematical language, many instrumentalists regard mathematical entities as fictions which may help to achieve the aims of a physical theory, but which are too sharp to give true descriptions of reality.[13] A classical formulation of this view was given by Duhem (1954), who restricted truth to unsharp empirical reality and denied the truth values of mathematical theoretical descriptions.

This problem of idealization should be solved by a theory of measurement (metrization) which shows precisely under what conditions empirical relations (e.g. is heavier than, is longer than) can be represented isomorphically by means of relations between real numbers. Such

[12] Roughly speaking, a counterfactual 'If p then q' is true if and only if q is true in those p-worlds that are closest to the actual world. A nomic statement 'Necessarily all Fs are G' is true if and only if the generalization $\forall x(Fx \rightarrow Gx)$ is true in all physically possible worlds. A physical probability statement $P(G/F)=r$ is true if and only if in each trial of kind F there is a dispositional tendency of strength r to produce an outcome of kind G.

[13] Hartry Field (1980) defends a nominalistic position where only space-time points are real, and mathematical entities used in physical theories are fictional. Husserl's (1970) remarks on the idealizational nature of 'Galilean physics' have inspired an instrumentalist view, where the 'resulting' mathematical universe is a human construction and 'reality itself' is the life-world (see Gurwitsch 1967).

representation theorems give a licence to a realist to explain how and why mathematics is applicable to the representation of reality.[14]

The Duhemian is right in pointing out that exact mathematical representation is often based upon counterfactual assumptions. If L is a quantitative language that is too sharp in this sense, the real world relative to L is not simply one L-structure $M^*$ (cf. Section 4.4), but rather a class $\mathbf{M}^*$ of L-structures. In this case, a sentence of L is true (false) iff it is true (false) in all structures in $\mathbf{M}^*$; otherwise its truth value is indeterminate (cf. Przełecki 1969). But even for these indeterminate cases it is possible to assign degrees of truthlikeness (see Section 3.5; cf. Niiniluoto 1987a; Kieseppä 1996). In this way, a semantic treatment of the 'idealized' language L becomes possible.

Another important type of idealization is the key to Galileo's method: to formulate and demonstrate his law of free fall, Galileo assumed that the fall was taking place in a vacuum, without the disturbing effect of the resistance of air. Bodies condensed to geometric points, perfect spheres, and frictionless planes are other standard imaginary creatures that allow the scientist to study physical phenomena in their pure form. Similar idealizational methods, where some factors are counterfactually excluded from consideration, have been used in all fields of science—in particular, in economics and other social sciences.[15]

The most comprehensive treatment of the method of idealization has been given by the Poznań School (Krajewski 1977; Nowak 1980). The starting point is typically an equation that expresses, for all objects x of a certain kind, the functional dependency of a quantity $F(x)$ on a finite number of other quantities $q_1(x), \ldots, q_n(x)$:

$$F(x)=f_0(q_1(x), \ldots, q_n(x)). \tag{T}$$

However, it is known in advance, or discovered later, that T excludes the influence of some other factors $w_1, \ldots, w_k$, which are secondary relative to the primary or 'essential' ones $q_1, \ldots, q_n$. The factual law T is then expressed as an *idealizational law*, which is conditional on the counterfactual assumptions that the factors $w_1(x), \ldots, w_k(x)$ have the value zero:

$$w_1(x)=0 \& \ldots \& w_k(x)=0 \rightarrow F(x)=f_0(q_1(x), \ldots, q_n(x)). \tag{$T_0$}$$

---

[14] In fact, there is no 'mystery' here. See Niiniluoto (1992b) and theories of measurement (Krantz *et al.* 1971) and Suppes (1993).

[15] Nowak (1980) indeed argues that Marx, who was 'the Galileo of the social sciences', used the method of idealization and concretization in his *Capital*.

In the next phase, the idealizing assumptions are removed one by one by *concretization* (factualization), i.e. by adding the factors $w_k(x), \ldots, w_1(x)$ to the law and by modifying the function $f_0$ at each step:

$$w_1(x){=}0\& \ldots \& w_{k-1}{=}0 \to F(x){=}f_1(q_1(x), \ldots, q_n(x), w_k(x)) \qquad (T_1)$$

$$w_1(x){=}0 \to F(x){=}f_{k-1}(q_1(x), \ldots, q_n(x), w_2(x), \ldots, w_k(x)) \qquad (T_{k-1})$$

$$F(x){=}f_k(q_1(x), \ldots, q_n(x), w_1(x), \ldots, w_k(x)). \qquad (T_k)$$

The last law $T_k$ is again factual (even though it may be based on hidden idealization relative to even further factors).

Bohr's *Correspondence Principle* says that the old theory should be obtained as a special case of the new theory, when some factors have a limiting value zero (e.g. some laws of classical mechanics are obtained from relativistic ones by letting the velocity of light c grow to infinity or $1/c \to 0$; or from quantum mechanics by letting Planck's constant $h \to 0$). For the sequence $T_0, \ldots, T_k$ this means that, for $j=1, \ldots, k$,

$$f_{j+1}(q_1(x), \ldots, q_n(x), z, w_{k-j+1}(x), \ldots, w_k(x)) \to \qquad (CP_j)$$
$$f_j(q_1(x), \ldots, q_n(x), w_{k-j+1}(x), \ldots, w_k(x)), \text{ when } z \to 0.$$

Condition $CP_j$ guarantees that $T_{j+1}$ entails $T_j$. Therefore, when the *Correspondence Principle* holds for each step of concretization, we have

$$T_k \vdash T_{k-1} \vdash \ldots \vdash T_1 \vdash T_0. \qquad (6)$$

Nowak's (1980) treatment is purely syntactical. He uses material implication in the idealizational laws; this makes them trivially true, since the antecedent conditions are false. In his attempt to give a realist interpretation, where idealization and concretization are a method of approaching to the truth, he has to postulate *ad hoc* a new conception of truth for such statements. For this reason, I think it is more natural and promising to take $\to$ in idealizational laws to be the counterfactual conditional (e.g. in the sense of Lewis 1973) (see Niiniluoto 1986b).

This treatment gives us, by theorem (35) of Chapter 3, immediately the result: if $T_k$ is true, then the sequence (6) of theories $T_0, T_1, \ldots, T_k$ increases in truthlikeness. In this case, concretization is a method of approaching nearer to the truth.[16] The same holds if the still unknown true theory is a concretization of $T_k$ and the Correspondence Principle holds.

---

[16] See Niiniluoto (1986b). Semantically speaking, the models of the theories in (6) constitute a sequence where the earlier structures are approximately reducible to the latter ones. For other work on concretization and truth-approximation, see Brzezinski *et al.* (1990), Kuipers (1992), Hettema and Kuipers (1995), Nowakowa (1994), Kuokkanen (1994).

On the other hand, each step in concretization can be made in an infinite number of mistaken ways—even when the Correspondence Principle holds.

For example, in classical mechanics the mass $m_v$ of a body moving with velocity v is assumed to be a constant m independently of v:

$m_v=m.$            (7)

Einstein's theory replaces (7) with

$$m_v=m\big/\sqrt{1-v^2\big/c^2}\,.$$            (8)

While (8) entails

$1/c=0\rightarrow m_v=m,$            (9)

there is an infinite number of functions (of m, v, and c) that satisfy the same condition.

Comparison of (7) and (8) shows that $m_v$ is approximately m ($m_v\approx m$) if v is sufficiently small:

$v\approx0\rightarrow m_v\approx m.$            (10)

The classical law $m_v=m$ is thus approximately deducible from Einstein's law for small velocities v, i.e. deducible by the approximation $v\approx0$. More generally, a statement E is *approximately deducible* from theory T if and only if T logically entails statement E′ which is approximately the same as E (see Fig. 18) (cf. Tuomela 1985; Niiniluoto 1987*a*).

Nancy Cartwright (1983) has argued that generally 'approximations take us away from theory and each step away from theory moves closer towards the truth' (p. 107). This is illustrated by an example where inaccurate predictions are improved by adding an empirical 'correlation factor' that is

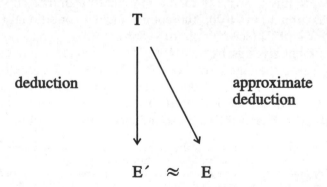

FIG. 18. Approximate deduction

'not dictated by fundamental law' (p. 111). In terms of Fig. 18, Cartwright claims that E (e.g. the 'phenomenological laws' of applied physics) is 'highly accurate' (p. 127) or true, while the strict prediction E' from fundamental theories is less accurate or further from the truth. But then the fact that approximations lead us closer to the truth argues for the falsehood theories (p. 15).

Cartwright (1983) defends a position called *entity realism* (cf. Hacking 1983), which is in a sense halfway between realism and instrumentalism. This view is diametrically opposite to Worrall's structural realism, but both can be criticized by pointing out that facts and theories are 'interpenetrated', as Putnam (1995: 60) says. Cartwright accepts the existence of theoretical entities that figure in causal explanations, but declares that the fundamental laws of physics are not true. It is not quite clear whether she wants to say here with instrumentalists that theories lack a truth value or merely that theoretical laws are false.[17]

As we have repeatedly emphasized, it is not a surprise to critical scientific realists that scientific theories are typically strictly speaking false. However, this does not exclude the possibility that such false theories are nevertheless highly truthlike. This observation allows us to formulate a realist reply to the issues raised by Cartwright.

Cartwright (1991) defends her view in a form which claims that theories are 'true only of what we make'. In other words, theoretical laws 'lie' about the nature of existing things, and the relation of truth holds only between laws and human-made constructs or models. In the same spirit, Kitcher (1993: 125) says that idealizational theories are 'true by convention' about referents 'fixed by stipulation'.

Ron Giere (1988) presents a similar view by saying that a theory is *trivially true* in a model it defines, and the model is *similar* to 'the real system' in specified respects and to specified degrees (see Fig. 19). In this way, Giere tries to avoid using the tricky or 'bastard' concepts of truthlikeness and approximate truth.

However, Giere fails to notice here that

truth+similarity=verisimilitude.

(Cf. (26) in Section 3.5.) Indeed, the basic definitions in Section 3.5 can be reformulated in terms of Fig. 19 by speaking about similarity between

---

[17] In her later work, Cartwright (1994) has acknowledged that she was 'deluded about the enemy' in her *How the Laws of Physics Lie* (1983): what should be resisted is not realism but 'fundamentalism' (i.e. the view that fundamental laws are true and universally in force everywhere). It seems to me that the concept of truthlikeness is a useful tool in an attack against such fundamentalism.

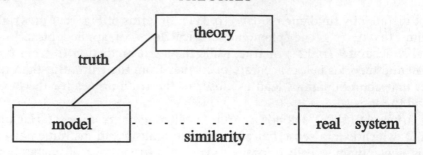

FIG. 19. Giere's constructive realism

structures. Precise definitions for such similarity relations, in a variety of methodological cases, have been explored since 1974 by the supporters of the 'similarity approach' to truthlikeness. Thus, when models vary over all structures satisfying the theory, Fig. 19 leads to the concept of approximate truth: a theory is approximately true if it is true in a model which is similar to the real system (i.e. to the fragment of the actual world in which we are interested in our enquiry) (see also Weston 1992). (Hence, what Aronson, Harré, and Way (1994) call 'verisimilitude' is approximate truth in my sense.) A theory is truthlike if the whole class of its models is similar to the real system. If the theory contains counterfactual idealizational assumptions, then it has to be compared to factual statements through 'concretization', where idealizations are removed. (See Fig. 20.)

Hence, instead of avoiding the issues of verisimilitude, Giere's 'modest constructive realism' turns out to be representable within the framework of critical realism based upon the concepts of approximate truth and truthlikeness.[18]

Boyd's (1979) account of reference by 'theory constitutive metaphors' is also based upon the concept of similarity (cf. Cummiskey 1992): a theory introduces a 'primary subject' (e.g. optical ether) which is supposed to be 'similar' or 'analogous' to a 'secondary subject' (e.g. liquid as a medium of

[18] In formulating his 'perspectival realism', Giere (1996) says that theories represent the world by using non-linguistic models as their vehicles. The basic picture is still the same as Fig. 19. Giere compares theories to maps: it depends on the interests of the intended users of maps which features of the terrain are mapped and to what degree of accuracy. All this is well in harmony with my emphasis on how the notion of truthlikeness depends on the formulation of the cognitive problem (see Section 3.5). However, I cannot agree with Giere when he then claims that it does not 'make sense to question whether a map is true or false' (p. 13). Certainly a map of restaurants in Manhattan, in the service of the interests of culinarists, can be true or truthlike, depending on its completeness and accuracy in locating the restaurants in the area—a claim to the opposite seems to involve the All-or-Nothing Fallacy again.

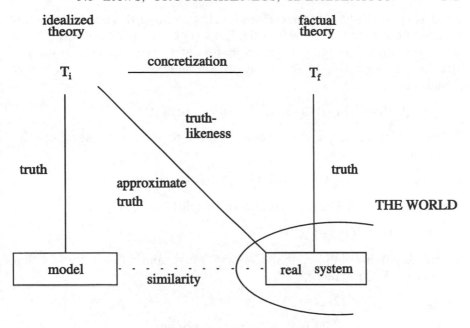

FIG. 20. Truthlikeness and idealization

waves). The demand of similarity here restricts the scope of acceptable error. The success in articulating such similarities is then taken to be a warrant for a realist interpretation of the theory's ontology.

From this perspective, a realist can argue that in many cases our theoretical predictions are closer to the truth than the empirically established 'phenomenological' laws (cf. McMullin 1985). In Fig. 18, this means that (*contra* Cartwright's examples) E′ is more accurate than E, i.e. E′ *corrects* E. The derivation of E′ from T gives then an approximate and corrective explanation of the initial statement E. Cartwright doubts the existence of such situations, where corrections come from 'the top down' rather than from 'the ground up' (1983: 111). But both theoretical and applied science abound in examples where theory T helps to improve an empirical statement E by entailing another statement E′ which is more concrete and more accurate than E.

Let us take a simple classical example, where the process of concretization is guided by Newton's theory. If the earth is a sphere with radius R and mass M, and G is the gravitational constant, Newton's Law of gravitation and the force law (force=mass×acceleration) entail that the acceleration of a freely falling body at the height h above the surface of the earth is $-GM/(R+h)^2$. On the surface level, where $h=0$, this acceleration has a constant absolute value $g=GM/R^2$. Let $s_y(t)$ be the position of the body at time t, when the body starts from rest at $s_y(0)=0$. As acceleration is the second derivative of the position, we should solve the differential equation

$$d^2s_y(t)/dt^2=-GM/(R+h-|s_y(t)|)^2=-gR^2/(R+h+s_y(t))^2.$$

When h (and, hence, $s_y(t)$) is small relative to R, this equation can be approximated by

$$d^2s_y(t)/dt^2\approx-(1-2(h+s_y(t))/R)g=-(1-2h/R)g+r^2s_y(t),$$

where $r^2=2g/R$. The general solution of this differential equation is

$$s_y(t)=(1-2h/R)g/r^2+C_1e^{rt}+C_2e^{-rt},$$

where $ds_y(0)/dt=0$ implies that $C_1=C_2=C$ (say), and $s_y(0)=0$ implies that $2C=-(1-2h/R)g/r^2$. Hence,

$$s_y(t)=(1-2h/R)(2-e^{rt}-e^{-rt})g/r^2.$$

If $e^x$ is approximated by $1+x+x^2/2$, then we obtain

$$s_y(t)\approx-(1-2h/R)gt^2/2. \tag{11}$$

By making the approximation $h\approx0$, equation (11) reduces to Galileo's law of free fall

$$s_y(t)=-gt^2/2. \tag{12}$$

Here it is important that (11) is empirically more accurate than (12). Moreover, (11) is a concretization of Galileo's law (12), and the Correspondence Principle holds, since (11) entails

$$h=0\to s_y(t)=-gt^2/2. \tag{13}$$

Another illustration is provided by exterior ballistics (see Niiniluoto 1994$d$). The simplest mathematical model, the Parabolic Theory, is based on the idealizing assumptions that the shot is a mass point with constant mass m, the medium is vacuum, and the shot is affected only by gravity. Further, the validity of Newton's laws is assumed. If the initial position is $(0, 0)$, the initial velocity is $v_0$, and the angle with the x-axis is $\alpha$, then the assumptions imply that the position $(s_x(t), s_y(t))$ at time t is given by

$$s_x(t)=tv_0\cos\alpha \tag{14}$$
$$s_y(t)=tv_0\sin\alpha-gt^2/2.$$

The Classical Theory, developed by Jean Bernoulli in the early eighteenth century, adds the resistance of air as a linear or quadratic function of velocity. For the linear case, where this resistance is $-\beta v$ for a constant $\beta > 0$, the equations (14) are replaced by the approximate equations

$$s_x(t) \approx t v_0 \cos\alpha \ (1 - \beta t/2m) \tag{15}$$
$$s_y(t) \approx -gt^2 + t v_0 \sin\alpha \ (1 - \beta t/2m).$$

The Principle of Correspondence is satisfied: if $\beta \to 0$, the equations (15) approach (14).

The concretization (15) of (14) gives three types of advances. First, the curve defined by (15) is closer to the empirical observed path than the curve defined by (14). To show this improvement in accuracy or truthlikeness, we may use Minkowskian distances defined between curves (see (29) in Section 3.5). Secondly, singular predictions are improved. For example, (15) gives a more accurate prediction than (14) for the distance before the shot hits the ground. Thirdly, ballistics as an applied design science is likewise improved, since (15) allows us to derive more truthlike rules of action than (14).[19] For example, the parabolic curve implies Tartaglia's rule: to obtain maximum distance, use the initial angle $\alpha = 45$ degrees. The corrected equation implies that an angle smaller than 45 degrees should be used. More precisely, $\alpha$ should satisfy the condition

$$\sin\alpha = \left( \sqrt{\beta^2 v_0^2 + 8m^2 g^2} - \beta v_0 \right) \big/ 4mg,$$

which reduces to Tartaglia's condition when $\beta \to 0$.

These examples illustrate how Newton's theory may serve as a useful guide in the process of concretization, in spite of the fact that it is known to be false. It is plausible to suggest that such a practical success is an indicator of the truthlikeness of Newton's theory (cf. Niiniluoto 1994d). This is one way of interpreting Ron Laymon's (1982) thesis that a theory is 'confirmed' if the use of more realistic initial conditions leads to more accurate predictions.

Let us finally note that the account of truthlike idealizations may apply also to common-sense views. There is a lively debate over whether specific common-sense frameworks are structured like scientific theories—for example, Paul Churchland (1989) defends this 'theory theory' with respect to 'folk psychology' (see Section 5.4). Without taking any general standpoint on this issue, it seems to me that there are systems of educated common-sense beliefs that could serve as the theories in Fig. 20. For

---

[19] In Section 6.1 we follow von Wright (1963a) in calling such conditional rules of action 'technical norms'.

example, a common-sense realist typically believes in 'folk physics', claiming that material objects exist as rigid bodies in a Euclidean space. This model is similar to the real system of physical objects and physical space, and the degree of similarity is remarkably high in relatively small neighbourhoods. This means that the common-sense view is, at least in domains relevant to everyday life, approximately true. As suggested in Section 2.2, this account also helps us to show in what way one can be (at least in some areas) a common-sense realist and a scientific realist at the same time: in spite of the falsity of common-sense views, and their incompatibility with more accurate scientific theories, these views may nevertheless be 'close to the truth', and one may appreciate their cognitive value without commitment to their strict truth.

## 5.4  *Examples of the realism debate*

We have seen that there are general philosophical reasons for regarding realism as an attractive position in ontology, epistemology, and philosophy of science. But the applicability of the ideas presented so far should be tested also in relation to theories in various scientific disciplines. Today there is much specialized and highly advanced professional work in the history and philosophy of science about such foundational questions. In this work, I can only give brief and non-technical illustrations of how the issues of realism have arisen in some selected cases: astronomy, quantum mechanics, psychology, and economics.

(*a*) *Astronomy*. Pierre Duhem published in 1908 a book on the idea of physical theory from Plato to Galileo (Duhem 1969). Its title, ΣΩΖΕΙΝ ΤΑ ΦΑΙΝΟΜΕΝΑ, was taken from Simplicius' famous description of the task of astronomy in the Platonic tradition:

What circular motions, uniform and perfectly regular, are to be admitted as hypotheses so that it might be possible to save the appearances presented by the planets?

An astronomical theory, like Eudoxus' system of homocentric spheres or Ptolemy's system of eccentrics and epicycles, has attained its goal when it has 'saved the phenomena'. If there are several such accounts, the simplest hypothesis should be selected. But speculations about the nature of heavenly bodies, or about their true causes and essences, are beyond the tasks of astronomy.

Geminus (1st century BC) stated clearly the distinction between a hypothesis introduced merely to save the phenomena and a hypothesis which is true or false. In later terminology, this is the distinction between *instrumentalist* and *realist* interpretations of scientific hypotheses and theories. Geminus also suggested that the ancient Greeks generally interpreted theories in physics in the realist way (following the ideas of Aristotle) and theories in astronomy in the instrumentalist way. But, as Duhem illustrated, this consensus was later broken: some Aristotelians (e.g. Averroës) extended realism to astronomy as well, while some early Renaissance philosophers treated all science on the model of saving the appearances.

The contrast between realism and instrumentalism was highlighted by the Copernican Revolution.[20] Copernicus himself was convinced that his heliocentric theory not only saved the appearances, but was also true—conformed to the real nature of things and to the principles of physics. Joachim Rheticus urged in 1540 that the Copernican hypotheses were 'most true' (*verissimae*), since he arrived at them by the physicist's method, i.e. from effects to causes. But when Copernicus' *De revolutionibus* finally appeared in 1543, the preface by Andreas Osiander claimed that the author's novel proposal was merely a device for 'calculation' and 'correct computation'—it did not tell 'how things really were', and was neither true, likely (*verisimile*), nor certain.

The later partisans of the Copernican theory (Giordano Bruno, Johannes Kepler, Galileo Galilei) adopted the realist interpretation. As Cardinal Bellarmine advised Galileo in 1615, the Catholic Church approved the use of the Copernican system for the calculation of the calendar, but one should not claim 'absolutely' that the earth really moves and the sun is the fixed centre of the universe. In 1616 the Holy Office of the Church found the Copernican theory to be incompatible with sound (Aristotelian) physics and with holy scripture. In 1633, a year after Galileo's *Dialogue*, the doctrine was condemned: Cardinal Barberini (later Pope Urban VIII) had tried in vain to convince Galileo that the heliocentric system could not be proved. According to his argument, it is not 'beyond God's power and wisdom' to arrange alternative ways which would 'save all the phenomena displayed in the heavens'.

Galileo is usually treated as the hero of modern science. Duhem's view was quite different. He granted Galileo only the insight that all the phenomena of the inanimate universe should be saved together. But in their understanding of the scientific method 'the Copernicans stubbornly stuck

---

[20] See Duhem (1969); Blake, Ducasse, and Madden (1960: ch. 2); Brophy and Paloucci (1962). Feyerabend's *Against Method* (1975) argues that Galileo 'cheated' his opponents.

to an illogical realism': 'logic sides with Osiander, Bellarmine, and Urban VIII, not with Kepler and Galileo' (1954: 113).

Duhem's *To Save the Phenomena* was a part of his own campaign for instrumentalism, advocated in his 1906 book on the aim and structure of physical theories (Duhem 1954). His historical interpretations have not been unchallenged. Thus, Lehti (1986) argues against the standard view of Ptolemy's *Almagest* as an instrumentalist work. Musgrave (1991) attacks Duhem by claiming that astronomical instrumentalism—from Plato, Eudoxus, Apollonius, and Hipparcus to Ptolemy—is a myth. Musgrave points out that there is an important difference between conceding the conjectural or hypothetical character of some scientific theory and taking the theory to be an uninterpreted symbolic device. Agreeing with Jardine (1979), he suggests that what Duhem described as debates between realists and instrumentalists were in fact disputes between dogmatic and critical realists.

(*b*) *Quantum theory*. The status of scientific theories had become a hot issue in physics already by the late nineteenth century. Robert Kirchhoff and Ernst Mach argued that physical theories should describe, in the most 'economical' way, observable phenomena and their functional interconnections. On this basis, Mach criticized the concepts of absolute time and space in Newton's mechanics (Mach 1960)—paving the way for the special theory of relativity of Albert Einstein. Mach rejected the existence of atoms: for him atoms were mere fictions without physical reality. Mach's programme was supported by Heinrich Hertz's reformulation of mechanics which eliminated the theoretical concept of force (Hertz 1956). Duhem's instrumentalism (and Mach's own practice in science) allowed the use of auxiliary terms and theoretical hypotheses to save the phenomena, but such hypotheses should not be understood as explanations with a truth value. Also Henri Poincaré's conventionalism regarded the axioms of geometry and mechanics to be 'definitions in disguise'—they are not true or false, but more or less 'convenient'. The defenders of realism against Machian positivism and instrumentalism included Ludwig Boltzmann, Max Planck, and Albert Einstein (after his work on Brownian motion). What seemed to be the decisive argument for the theory of atoms, and thereby for Planck's realism, came from experimental work in physics, especially Wilson's cloud chamber which almost allowed the physicist 'to see' the atoms. Conflicting philosophical interpretations of this problem situation were given by the neo-Kantians of the Marburg school and by the logical empiricists in Vienna (Moritz Schlick, Rudolf Carnap) and Berlin (Hans Reichenbach).

This was the lively historical background of the new quantum theory created in the 1920s by the generation of such great physicists as Albert Einstein, Niels Bohr, Werner Heisenberg, Erwin Schrödinger, and Wolfgang Pauli.[21] It also helps us to locate some well-known and important positions on the nature of quantum theory in the conceptual net developed in earlier chapters (cf. Niiniluoto 1987c). This approach has its limitations: the philosophical views of real-life physicists are usually 'mixed' cases of different influences and doctrines, and they cannot be reduced to the 'pure' states defined by the abstract distinctions of the philosophers. But this fact also makes the continuing re-evaluation of the foundational discussions of physics philosophically rewarding. I believe that, in particular, the elaboration of various kinds of realist and non-realist approaches in recent philosophy of science gives us tools for understanding better the positions taken by the creators of quantum theory.[22]

A good starting point for the discussion is Niels Bohr's philosophy of complementarity which continues to be an important object of various interpretations.[23] According to Henry J. Folse (1985; 1987), Bohr is a physicist who wishes to avoid ontological discussion—and thus favours a position similar to Fine's NOA (cf. Section 1.4). However, Folse argues, Bohr is committed to a form of realism, i.e. to 'upholding the view that it is the task of science to understand the nature of physical reality as it exists independently of the phenomena through which we experience it'. More precisely, Bohr must accept that the same 'atomic object' causes, via physical interactions, different complementary 'phenomenal objects'. The classical description—with the wave and particle pictures—refers to properties belonging only to a phenomenal object. Indeed, no pictorial description of the atomic object is available. While the complementary phenomena are not representations of the physical object that produces them, still the combination of these complementary descriptions exhausts all that can be known about this independent reality.

As Folse's Bohr accepts the existence of quantum-mechanical objects behind the phenomena, he is at least an entity realist. Hence, he cannot be a phenomenalist. While there is a strong Kantian flavour in the

---

[21] An excellent survey on the early history of the interpretation problem of quantum mechanics is given by Jammer (1974).

[22] Fine (1986b) has argued that, apart from a weak 'motivational' commitment to realism, Einstein's philosophical position could be understood as representing constructive empiricism. I find this implausible: Einstein gave a strong 'Platonist' emphasis to man's ability to grasp the mathematical structure of the universe by inventing physical theories, which distinguishes him from van Fraassen's demand that theories should only 'save the appearances'.

[23] For recent, very active studies on Bohr, see Folse (1985; 1987), Faye and Folse (1994). See also Feyerabend (1962b), Hooker (1972), and Teller (1981).

distinction between atomic and phenomenal objects, where the former are causes of the latter, Bohr is not an epistemological anti-realist: quantum theory in the framework of complementarity gives us knowledge about the atomic objects in terms of their potential for causal interaction.

How could Bohr defend the idea that his atomic objects are not merely unknowable Kantian *Dinge an sich*, that it is possible to have some knowledge of them, in spite of the fact that he did not interpret the ψ-function as describing the state of quantum-mechanical objects? According to Teller (1981), Bohr treated the state function in an instrumentalist way as 'a purely symbolic device for calculating the statistics of classically or commonly described experimental outcomes in collections of phenomena grouped by shared specifications of experimental conditions'. If this is the case, laws involving the state function do not have truth values, which also excludes the possibility that Bohr is a constructive empiricist. Folse (1987) suggests that Bohr not only rejected classical realism (or the substance/property ontology) but the spectator account of knowledge and the correspondence theory of truth as well. Thus, Bohr would turn out to be a sort of pragmatist, epistemic realist, or semantical anti-realist.[24]

While Bohr rejected classical realism, he also insisted against Einstein that quantum mechanics provides a 'complete' framework for describing nature. This means that quantum theory does not assign any non-relational *intrinsic properties* to atomic objects, but only what might be called relational or *interactive properties*, i.e. properties which the object possesses or fails to possess only consequent upon the occurrence of a suitable interaction (cf. Healey 1981). Moreover, for Bohr these interactions are *observational* interactions, i.e. they involve 'preparation' or 'measurement' by macroscopic devices.

If the claim of completeness were an epistemic thesis, then atomic objects might have intrinsic properties, but they would remain unknown or it would be meaningless to speak about them. This kind of position might be attractive to some logical empiricists with a physicalist outlook or to pragmatists with a verificationist theory of meaning. However, it would be compatible with local hidden variable theories—and thus vulnerable to the objections from Bell's Theorem (cf. Readhead 1987). I do not believe that this is the view of Folse's Bohr. Rather, his claim of completeness is an ontological thesis: there are no 'pictures' of atomic objects as they exist in isolation from any observation, since such objects do not

---

[24] Also Jan Faye interprets Bohr as an 'objective anti-realist', who accepts ontological realism but whose notion of truth is epistemic or anti-realistic, as truth is taken to be conceptually connected with our ability to know it (see Faye and Folse 1994).

have any properties at all. It is only after observational interaction that we can attribute to an atomic object x the relational property 'x caused this particle-type phenomenon' or 'x caused this wave-type phenomenon'.

This conclusion suggests that Folse's Bohr is virtually identical with Feyerabend's Bohr, who maintains that 'all state descriptions of quantum-mechanical systems are *relations* between the systems and measuring devices in action' (Feyerabend 1962b). On this view, a micro-system isolated from measuring devices is a 'naked individual', a bare particular without properties. As Hooker (1972) remarks, it is doubtful whether the idea of such 'propertyless ghosts' is coherent (cf. Section 2.4).

If this interpretation is correct, Bohr is a radical nominalist with respect to the micro-world. He is also a representative of a special kind of internal realism: the independently existing naked individuals will be dressed with relational properties only through observational interactions (cf. Ch. 7).

Bohr's complementarity, as interpreted by Folse, is a weak form of realism: only naked atomic objects exist independently of observations, and our knowledge of such objects concerns their phenomenal manifestations.

This view rejects the claims that atomic objects are fictions, mere potentialities (Heisenberg[25]), exist only during observational interactions (microphenomenalism), or are created in observational interactions. It also gives up attempts to restore classical realism within deterministic (Bohm 1980) or indeterministic (Popper 1985) frameworks.

However, there are objections to Folse's Bohr which suggest that it is reasonable to search for a version of quantum realism which is stronger than Bohr's but weaker than classical realism. First, it is not plausible that an atomic object does not have any permanent intrinsic properties. It is true that the state of a quantum-mechanical system need not be independent of our measurements: such a system does not have a definite or sharply defined position and momentum, but our measurement may have the effect that the system is 'localized'. But while position and momentum are 'non-classical' interactive properties (cf. Piron 1985), the same does not hold of mass and electric charge. Without such properties, we could not

[25] 'In the experiments about atomic events we have to do with things and facts, with phenomena that are just as real as any phenomena in daily life. But the atoms or the elementary particles themselves are not as real; they form a world of potentialities or possibilities rather than one of things or facts' (Heisenberg 1962: 186). Heisenberg adds that the transition from the 'possible' to the 'actual' takes place during the act of observation (ibid. 54). Even if Heisenberg says that atoms as potentialities are not 'real', he also speaks of 'objective' tendencies and possibilities (ibid. 53, 180). Thus, it is not clear whether his position about atoms is anti-realist or not.

identify atomic objects—it would hardly make sense to say with Bohr that the *same* object produced two different phenomenal objects.

Secondly, if it is true to say that an atomic object x caused a particular phenomenon y, then it is likewise true that x has a causal power or potency to produce phenomena of type y. The object x can then be said to possess a dispositional property—and such a disposition is real even when x is isolated from measuring devices or from observations (cf. Tuomela 1978). The idea that the isolated x is propertyless, and cannot be described by true statements, seems to be incoherent.

Hence, it is possible to give quantum mechanics such a realist interpretation that atomic objects and some of their properties exist independently of observations. If this is correct, we may also have descriptions of atomic objects—of their properties, relations, and structure—which are true in the correspondence-theoretical sense. We can thus resist the pragmatist move suggested by Folse (1987). With non-classical properties we need a non-standard logic, and perhaps an idea of unsharp reality as well,[26] but not a non-realist theory of truth.

Thirdly, we may accept the existence of interactive properties without restricting our attention on observational interactions, as Bohr without warrant does. For example, an electron may fail to have a sharply defined location in a box; it may become localized by our manipulating activity with measuring devices, but equally well by interactions with other macroscopic or microscopic entities. As Simon Kochen (1985) remarks, there is no reason to give a 'privileged role to the measurement process among all interactions': quantum theory can be interpreted as 'describing an objective world of individual interacting systems'.

Thus, for an *interactive realist* (see Healey 1981; 1989), the main content of quantum mechanics is expressible by *interaction conditionals* of the form

> If a system x is in a particular state, and if a certain inter-    (16)
> action occurs for x, then x will subsequently possess a
> specified property with a certain probability.

The conditionals need not have anything to do with observations or measurements—but they are true in the quantum world, i.e. in the independent

---

[26] This conception refers to the idea that reality itself may be unsharp or indefinite relative to some quantities. Schrödinger understood clearly the distinction between blurred reality and blurred knowledge (see Rorlich 1985). Unsharp observables are discussed by P. Mittelstaedt, P. Busch, and E. Prugovecki in Lahti and Mittelstaedt (1985). For the application of the concept of truthlikeness to unsharp reality, see Niiniluoto (1987a) and Kieseppä (1996).

reality which quantum theory is primarily about. (For example, they hold of all unobserved micro-processes inside the table in front of me at this moment.) Such probabilistic laws express invariances that serve to constitute the reality of the micro-world (cf. Section 5.2).

On the other hand, quantum mechanics also entails manipulative *measurement conditionals* of the form

> If a system x is prepared in a particular state, and if a certain          (17)
> measurement occurs, then the measurement gives a specified
> value with a certain probability.

(Cf. Heisenberg 1962: 46.) It is typical of descriptivism and instrumentalism to think that such statements as (17) exhaust the content of a scientific theory; for a realist, they are test statements which can be used in the empirical appraisal of the theory (see Fig. 14). (Cf. Bunge 1973.) In brief, (16) explains (17), and (17) gives observational evidence for (16).

In this view, Bohr's philosophy of complementarity is a valuable and interesting contribution to discussions about the peculiar subject–object relations within the experimental testing of quantum mechanics. But this philosophy does not imply that we (or our minds) are somehow involved in the unobserved object–object relations described by interactive conditionals of type (16).

Bohr made the well-known remark, in the spirit of Dewey's pragmatism, that we are not only spectators but also actors in the drama of life. It is natural that quantum-theorists are impressed by our ability to manipulate the micro-world—by influencing, transforming, and even 'creating' atomic objects and some of their properties. But then they start to speak as if our use of this ability, which could be understood as a proof of realism (see Hacking 1983, and the Argument from Successful Action in Section 2.5), would somehow be responsible for all the novel exciting features of the world that quantum theory has revealed—such as wave–particle dualism, transition from potentiality to actuality, and indeterminism. For a realist, this confuses the directions of explanation and evidence: quantum measurements and observations, as described by (17), are indeterministic because the ontologically mind-independent quantum world, as described by (16), is indeterministic.[27]

---

[27] For quantum-mechanical indeterminism, where the square of the $\psi$-function is taken to express an objective probability or propensity, see Popper (1982). On this interpretation, the single case satisfies an objective probabilistic law. Hence, indeterminism in quantum mechanics does not have any anti-realist conclusions, as K. V. Laurikainen (1985) has tried to argue on Wolfgang Pauli's authority. It is true that Pauli considered 'the impredictable change of the state by a single observation' to be 'an abandonment of the idea of the isolation (detachment) of the observer from the course of physical events outside himself'. But

So is critical scientific realism able to survive the challenge of quantum theory? I have here only briefly indicated why I fail to be impressed by the frequently voiced claim that the 'paradoxes' in the interpretation of quantum mechanics inevitably lead to anti-realist conclusions. But I have not discussed all the important aspects of this broad and deep question. Its answer will depend on further work on such topics as the EPR paradox, Bell inequalities, Bohm's version of quantum mechanics, and quantum field theories.[28]

I conclude with remarks on Bernard d'Espagnat's (1983) concept of 'veiled reality'—to illustrate how critical realism is more 'sober' than some speculations inspired by quantum theory.

D'Espagnat starts from a critical discussion of the problems that 'forced' quantum mechanics to give up the idea that atoms and their constituents 'possess a reality that is completely independent of our means of observing it'. Less critically he then asserts that 'consciousness exists' and 'cannot be reduced to the notions of physics'. In the next step, he postulates the existence of 'independent' or 'nonphysical reality' which is 'beyond the frames of space and time and cannot be described by our current concepts'. This independent reality is 'veiled', since it is 'intrinsically impossible' to describe it 'as it really is'. Still, 'empirical reality' (the set of all phenomena extended in space and time) and 'consciousness' are two complementary 'reflections' of this independent reality.

There is again a strong Kantian flavour in d'Espagnat's distinction between an unknowable independent reality and its reflection as a mind-dependent empirical reality.[29] There is also a clear influence from object-

---

he compared the role of the observer in quantum theory with that of 'a person, who by its freely chosen experimental arrangements and recordings brings forth a considerable "trouble" in nature, *without being able to influence its unpredictable outcome* and results which afterwards can be objectively checked by everyone' (my italics) (see Laurikainen 1985: 282). The italicized part of the quotation shows, however, that the observer is 'detached' even from those changes which he himself has initiated (in addition to being detached from those changes that no one observes). Note also that, if we reject the idealizing assumption that the quantities in classical mechanics have sharp values, then a person who tosses a coin is in the same situation as the observer in quantum theory according to Pauli. See Ford (1983) and Earman (1986).

[28] Questions concerning Bell's inequalities and realism are discussed in Readhead (1987). In Bohm's (1980) realist interpretation, each particle has a definite position and determinate trajectory, but its behaviour is governed by an associated wave which makes the system holistic. See Cushing (1994).

[29] Laurikainen (1987) also accepts the idea of 'veiled reality'. He suggests, as an interpretation of Pauli (who was in cooperation with Carl Jung), that the veil between empirical and 'irrational' reality arises from the unconscious functioning of the human psyche. However, if unconsciousness is somehow connected with irrationality, then certainly the mind-dependent empirical reality (rather than the world behind the veil) should be the 'irrational' one.

ive idealism, since the 'nonphysical' reality is referred to by such concepts as Spinoza's substance and 'God'.

Apart from the other traditional difficulties in Spinozistic and Kantian ontologies, d'Espagnat's theory faces the problem that he seems to multiply domains of reality beyond necessity. His need for saving the possibility of objective knowledge by postulating an unknowable non-physical reality arises from the fact that he accepts a too mind-dependent account of empirical reality. For example, he claims that 'our eyes contribute to the creation of atoms' (ibid. 97). The critical realist will, therefore, reply to d'Espagnat that the concept of empirical reality is unnecessary in the ontological sense: it refers only to our partial knowledge about objective reality.[30]

With this conclusion, the idea of a veil in front of intrinsically unknowable reality becomes unnecessary. Science is a search for reality—according to realism, the aim of science is informative truth about the world. The Greek word for truth, *aletheia*, means literally 'to uncover' or 'to unveil'. There is only a veil between the known and so far unknown parts of reality. The task of science is to increase the former part and reduce the latter by moving this veil. Our aim as scientists and philosophers is not to veil reality but to unveil it.

(*c*) *Psychology*. While physics studies the material World 1, the mental World 2 is the object domain of psychology. Discussions about the possibility of psychology as a science have always been involved with classical metaphysical problems which concern the relations between Worlds 1 and 2.

Given the perplexing variety of positions in the mind–body problem (cf. Section 2.1), many philosophers and scientists have followed Emil Du Bois-Reymond's agnosticist *ignoramus* doctrine: the relation of mind and matter is a riddle that will remain unsolvable forever. As it cannot be solved (cf. McGinn 1991), some philosophers further conclude that it is a pseudo-problem to be dissolved (cf. Rorty 1980).

In this situation, the programme of scientific realism recommends that better understanding of the nature of the human consciousness can be sought by the collaboration of empirical and theoretical researchers (psychologists and cognitive scientists) and philosophers (see Kamppinen and Revonsuo 1994): the science of the human mind should be taken seriously

---

[30] See Section 4.4. Laurikainen (1987) claims that 'scientism', as 'a kind of modern religion in the academic world', 'does not acknowledge any conception of reality independent of empirical reality'. Critical realism, as I define it, is not a form of 'scientism' in this sense: nothing 'depends' on empirical reality, since that reality does not even exist in an ontological sense.

as a source of knowledge, but its results should be placed under a critical philosophical scrutiny (cf. Niiniluoto 1994*b*).

Scientific psychology, i.e. the study of the human mind by means of the experimental method borrowed from natural science, was born with the establishment of the first psychological laboratories in Germany in the 1870s (Wilhelm Wundt). This new trend was not so much directed against the common-sense view of human beings, but rather against the religious and metaphysical speculation that was regularly combined with thinking about the human soul. Indeed, psychology was at that time still a part of philosophy (cf. Kusch 1995).

Darwinian evolutionism gave an important impetus to human psychology. It was often used as an argument against parallelism, as it seems to presuppose that consciousness has causal powers: how could it otherwise have had a favourable influence on human adaptation to environment? This old argument has recently been repeated by Karl Popper and John Eccles (1977) in their defence of mental causation from the psychical World 2 to the physical World 1 (cf. Section 2.2). This idea can be understood in terms of dualistic interactionism, as Eccles does, but it can also be interpreted as supporting emergent materialism. It claims that the human mind is an evolutionary product of material nature, not capable of existing without a material basis (such as the brain), but still it has acquired a relatively independent status in the sense that there are causal influences in both directions between body and mind.

The simplest form of empiricism in psychology, John Watson's *psychological behaviourism*, does not allow any terms to refer 'inside' to the 'black-box' of human mind. This is a typical expression of positivist operationalism: scientific psychology should study only human behaviour, since that is accessible to external observation. Introspection, as a form of non-public internal perception, was rejected as a source of psychological knowledge. Theories like Sigmund Freud's psychoanalysis, which refer to the structure and contents of the human psyche (cf. Freud 1973), were also rejected on this basis. (Popper (1959), on the other hand, rejected Freud's theory on the basis of his falsificationist demarcation criterion.) The neobehaviourist school allowed the use of 'intervening variables' in the stimulus–response models of behaviour, but they were understood in the instrumentalist sense, not as terms referring to unobservable mental reality.

In 1931 Carnap accepted Otto Neurath's physicalism. All meaningful terms and statements are required to be translatable, via explicit definitions, to the universal and intersubjective 'physical' language. In the case of psychology, Carnap's *logical behaviourism* tried to show that all psychological sentences—about other minds, about some past or present condition of one's own mind, or general sentences—'refer to physical occurrences in the body of the person in question'. A typical translation of a term like 'is excited' links it with the 'disposition to react to certain stimuli with overt behavior of certain kinds' (see Ayer 1959: 197). This idea was further developed by Gilbert Ryle's *The Concept of Mind* (1949), which gives an instrumentalist interpretation to the language of behavioural dispositions.

The rise of scientific realism in the 1950s gave a new impetus to the study of human consciousness. In 1965, Hilary Putnam gave a strikingly effective 'short answer' to the question: why theoretical terms? 'Because without such terms we could not speak of radio stars, viruses, and elementary particles, for example—and we *wish* to speak of them, to learn more about them, to explain their behavior and properties better' (Putnam 1975: 234). It is clear that this 'short answer' should be applicable also to our wish to learn more about the human mind.

In 1956, Wilfrid Sellars explained in his 'myth of Jones' how mental terms could be introduced to a Rylean physical-behavioural language as new theoretical terms with public criteria of use (Sellars 1963). In 1959, Noam Chomsky's famous criticism of B. F. Skinner's behaviourism started a new era of linguistics, where the competence behind a speaker's performance became the central object of study. A parallel development took place in the new cognitive psychology, where it became permissible again—in the footsteps of Jean Piaget and L. S. Vygotski—to construct theories that refer to real processes going on within the human consciousness. This realist talk about beliefs and wants is also used by philosophers who endorse causalist theories of human intentional behaviour.[31]

The first attempt by scientific realism to develop a materialist theory of mind was a reductionist *type identity theory* (H. Feigl, J. Smart, David Armstrong): mental states are type-identical to brain states, just as water has turned out to be identical to $H_2O$ (see Rosenthal 1971). This is a version of physicalism which allows (unlike Carnap in the early 1930s) a reference to theoretical physical entities (i.e. states of the central nervous system). Later *functionalist* theories define mental events by their causal roles, or lawlike connections to other mental and bodily states: in spite of being token-identical with brain states, talk about mental events is not reducible to a physical language.[32] Anti-reductionism between psychology and physics is also characteristic of *emergent materialism*, which takes mental

[31] See Davidson (1980) and Tuomela (1977).
[32] This view was developed by Putnam, Davidson, and Fodor. See Haugeland (1981).

states to be 'emergent', higher-level, causally efficient properties of sufficiently complex material systems.[33]

After being a minority view (Paul Feyerabend, Richard Rorty) in the 1960s (cf. Rosenthal 1971), eliminative materialism has become an important research programme in the 1980s with the work of Stephen Stich and Patricia and Paul Churchland.[34] Influenced by the strong Sellarsian scientific realism, the Churchlands claim that mental terms like 'belief', 'desire', 'fear', 'sensation', 'pain', 'joy', etc. belong to the radically false 'folk psychology' and are destined to disappear (like 'phlogiston' or 'caloric' in physics) when the common-sense framework is replaced by a matured neuroscience.[35]

Daniel Dennett's theory of the mind in *Brainstorms* (1978) appears to be a sophisticated version of instrumentalism. For Dennett, a person believes that snow is white if and only if he 'can be predictively attributed the belief that snow is white' (p. xvii). In ordinary cases such mental attributions (thoughts, desires, beliefs, pains, emotions, dreams) from a third-person perspective do not pick out 'good theoretical things' (p. xx). In particular, when a 'theory of behaviour' takes the 'intentional stance', i.e. explains and predicts the behaviour of an 'intentional system' (man or machine) by ascribing beliefs and desires to it, the claim is not that such systems 'really' have beliefs and desires (p. 7).

Human mentality has some important characteristics which every theory of consciousness has to explain—or else explain away as misconceptions. They at least give difficulties to any attempt to reduce psychology to

---

[33] See Popper and Eccles (1977), Bunge (1977–9; 1981), Margolis (1978), Nagel (1986), and Searle (1992). See also Kamppinen and Revonsuo (1994), Haaparanta and Heinämaa (1995).

[34] See P. S. Churchland (1986), P. M. Churchland (1979; 1988; 1989). In my view, the much-discussed contrast between folk psychology and neuroscience is misleading. It is inspired by the Sellarsian distinction between the manifest image and the scientific image: the radical eliminativism urges that we should substitute 'scientific objects' for the ordinary things of common-sense experience. Thereby the entities of folk physics and folk psychology will be eliminated. However, to be successful, the matured neuroscience of an eliminative materialist should not only replace beliefs, desires, pains, etc. as they are ordinarily understood, but it should eliminate also their successor concepts as they are presented in our best theory of cognitive psychology. The step from behaviourism to cognitive psychology was already a revolution (cf. Thagard 1992). It is not enough for neuroscience to supersede common sense; it should compete with the advanced theories of cognitive psychology as well. On the evidence of the present state of cognitive studies, it seems plausible to guess that even future theories will contain some theoretical concepts that are correlated to what we now call emotions, volitions, and beliefs.

[35] In his more recent work, Paul Churchland (1989) has expressed some doubts about the realist notion of truth and suggested a move toward some kind of pragmatism or constructivism.

neurophysiology—in addition to the general difficulty of expressing necessary and sufficient conditions for mental states in terms of physical language. In my view, they give support to emergent materialism.

First, our mental life has a *subjective* nature: it appears to be centred or united by a unique individual inner perspective (cf. Broad 1925). Secondly, our experiences seem to have a special *quality* which is not captured by an external physical description (cf. Nagel 1986). Thirdly, mental acts are *intentional*, directed towards objects, and thereby our thoughts have a content or semantics (cf. Fetzer 1991).

As Searle (1992) correctly points out, these features are not incompatible with an attitude respecting the principles of scientific realism. Following Sellars's (1963) treatment of 'qualia', such features can be understood as theoretical constructs which are introduced to the scientific image of man by psychological theories.

To summarize, the ontological positions of contemporary scientific realists range from eliminative materialism (P. S. and P. M. Churchland), reductive materialism (Smart), and emergent materialism (Popper, Bunge) to dualism (Eccles, Swinburne) and perhaps even objective idealism (Bohm). Some of them want to eliminate consciousness, others accept its existence for various reasons.

Our relations to the social and cultural environment give one further argument against physicalist and neuroscientific reductionism. A child does not learn a language, and does not grow into a human person, unless he or she interacts with other members of a human culture. The philosophical schools of Marxism and structuralism have emphasized—even overemphasized to the extent that the subjectivity of human mind has become a problem for them—the nature of man as a cultural and social being. Again the role of the environment is not only generative but also constitutive: as Tyler Burge (1986) has argued against the principle of methodological solipsism, the identification of mental states (e.g. a mother's grief for the death of her son in war, a banker's fear of the loss of his money) may presuppose reference to other social agents and institutional facts (cf. Searle 1995).

In Popperian terms, we may say that much of the contents of the World 2 processes in individual minds is derived or learned from the cultural World 3. But it is even more interesting to note that a unique human Ego or Self is in fact constructed during a process, sometimes called the 'psychological birth', where a child is in active interaction with the social environment. According to the social theories of mind, a human Self is not ready-made, but a social construction. In this sense, a human Self is an entity in World 3.

(*d*) *Economics*. The cultural and social sciences study the human-made domain of World 3. Again, there have been progammes which attempt to reduce World 3 to World 1 (e.g. physicalism, sociobiology) or to World 2 (e.g. methodological individualism), while others have defended the reality of social facts and institutions.[36]

Among the social sciences, economics with its mathematical methods resembles most the natural sciences. Thus, the issue of realism and instrumentalism has been focused in a clear way in this field. Among philosophers of economics, Uskali Mäki has defended critical realism, while D. McCloskey draws anti-realist conclusions from a rhetorical approach to economical discourse.

Neoclassical economic theories describe business firms as rational calculating agents which maximize their profits on the basis of complete information about the quantities, costs, prices, and demand of their products. However, it is clear that such theories employ unrealistic idealizations in several respects, among them the assumptions about perfect rationality and complete information. The internal structure of the firms and most aspects of their external relations are ignored in these theories. Even the core assumption that firms (or businessmen) pursue maximum expected returns is problematic in two ways. First, the theory suggests that the maximization of profit is the only motive of the producers and ignores other relevant motives. Secondly, it involves at least a false exaggeration, since in real life firms are satisfied with less than maximum returns.

The use of idealizations has inspired anti-realist interpretations of economic theories.[37] For example, Fritz Machlup advocates ontological antirealism about neoclassical firms (fictionalism), and takes the theory of the firm to be a device for observational systematization without a truth value (instrumentalism). Milton Friedman regards such theories as false statements, but the theory may still be useful and accepted for prediction (methodological anti-realism). In other words, economic theories are nothing but 'predictive models'.

However, in spite of the unrealistic assumptions of neoclassical theories of the firm, these theories may be truthlike—and by the theory of reference given in Section 5.3, they may be taken to refer to real business firms. Similarly, in spite of idealized rationality assumptions, theories about the behaviour of the 'economic man' may refer to ordinary human beings.

---

[36] For the possibility of realism in the social sciences, see Bhaskar (1979) and Searle (1995).
[37] For debates on realism and instrumentalism in economics, see Mäki (1988; 1989; 1990). For idealizations in economics, see Hamminga and de Marchi (1994).

It is a subtle question whether idealized decision theories refer to anything like really existing utility functions of human agents. The necessary and sufficient conditions for the relevant representation theorems are satisfied only in possible worlds that are close to the actual world (cf. Niiniluoto 1986b). In this sense, quantitative real-valued utility functions do not exist in our world, but they are mathematical constructions that allow truthlike descriptions of rational human preferences and decision-making. One candidate for their actual reference might be money, which is a real quantity in the actual world, but the point of departure of classical utility theory was the observation that personal utilities differ from sums of money. An alternative suggestion is that theoretical utility functions refer to personal degrees of satisfaction (which have some kind of psychological reality) or to degrees of usefulness (which have some kind of technical reality) (see Hansson 1988), where the actual quantitative structure of such degrees is unsharp to some extent.

# 6

# Realism in Methodology

Methodology studies the best ways and procedures for advancing the aims of science. For a realist, truth (or truthlikeness as a combination of truth and information) is an important or essential goal of science, as the axiological thesis (R3) in Section 1.3 says. Hence, this aim is also reflected in the methodological norms for scientific enquiry (Section 6.2). Truth and truthlikeness also play a crucial role in the rational explanation of the success of science (Section 6.5), and in the analysis of rationality and progress in science (Section 6.6).

After some remarks about institutional and pragmatic measures of success, I concentrate on rival ways of defining cognitive success (Section 6.1). Realist measures of epistemic credit include epistemic probability, confirmation (corroboration), expected verisimilitude, and probable verisimilitude. The relation of truth and simplicity is discussed in the context of curve-fitting problems (Section 6.3). Laudan's non-realist concept of the problem-solving effectiveness of a theory is compared to Hempel's notion of systematic power. I argue that such truth-independent concepts alone are insufficient to characterize scientific advance. But if they are used as truth-dependent epistemic utilities, they serve as fallible indicators of the truth or truthlikeness of a theory (Section 6.4). This is a special case of abductive inference to the best explanation. More generally, empirical success of scientific theories, in explaining and predicting phenomena and in making the manipulation of nature possible, is an indicator of their truthlikeness. These considerations allow us to give a precise formulation of what is sometimes called the ultimate argument for scientific realism (Section 6.5).

## 6.1 Measuring the success of science

Since the 1970s a great variety of *science indicators* have been proposed for measuring scientific activities. Such measures have been developed within science studies (quantitative historiography and sociology of science, foundations of science policy), with the emergence of a new discipline, *sciento-*

*metrics*, devoted to the use of bibliometric methods in the study of the literary output of the scientists (Elkana *et al.* 1978). Depending on the indicator, the object of measurement may be an individual scientist, a research group, a research institute, a department, a university, a national system of higher education, an individual scientific publication, a journal, a scientific speciality, etc. Some indicators are straightforward measures of performance and productivity: research expenditure, number of researchers, doctoral dissertations, articles, monographs, lectures in conferences, visiting scholars, etc. When such measures of scientific output (effectiveness) are divided by inputs (costs, amount of work, etc.), we obtain relative cost–effect-type measures of efficiency—such as university degrees or publications per unit cost (Irvine and Martin 1984).

If the aim of science were simply to be productive, the measures of effectiveness and efficiency would give a good account of success in science. But science does not aim at just any results: research should have good or high *quality*, and its results should be *new* and *important*. It is, indeed, generally recognized that publication counts (or other output measures based upon simple counting) do not as such inform us about quality, novelty, and importance (cf. Chotkowski 1982).

The best method of 'quality control' in science is still *peer review* in its different variants (referees of journals, expert assessment in academic appointments, evaluation groups, etc.) (see Niiniluoto 1987*d*). The existence of institutionalized mechanisms of evaluation within the scientific community makes it also possible to define indirect indicators of scientific quality which reflect the favourable attention that a scientist or a publication has received: for example, the number of articles in refereed journals, or in journals with a high impact factor, the number of citations of an article, the number of invitations, grants, awards, and prizes.

Indicators of this sort may be called *institutional* measures of success: they give an account of the recognition, impact, and visibility of research within the scientific community. For the social and political studies of science such indicators may be very useful. If the aim of science were victory in the international competition for fame and public praise, indicators of recognition would be direct measures of success. But in spite of the popularity of the sports or competition model of research, it is more natural to regard recognition as a consequence of successful work, not an end in itself.

The indirect connection of institutional measures to high quality or importance is based on the sociological assumption that good work and only good work in science tends to be acknowledged and praised among one's peers. As this assumption is in many ways problematic (e.g. negative citations, 'the Matthew effect' or the tendency to give recognition to those who are already well established in the field, invisibility of work ahead of its time, bias arising from sectarianism and nationalism), these indicators are in general not very reliable guides to scientific quality.

The weakness of institutional indicators does not arise from their quantitative character: the quality–quantity distinction is not very relevant here, since (as we shall see) there are reasonable quantitative measures of success. The main problem of the institutional measures is their black-boxism or purely externalist perspective. These measures are designed so that bureaucrats in state administration or sociologists of science, who do not have any expertise in the field of science they wish to control or to investigate, are able to determine the values of these measures in an 'objective' way. However, if science is regarded as a cognitive enterprise striving for new knowledge, it is clear that the success of a scientific work W depends on the semantic content of W. To determine the contribution of W to the progress of science, we need to know what W says and to relate this content to the relevant problem situation—in particular, to the state of knowledge that science had reached by the time of the publication of W.

Especially since the nineteenth century, science has been very effective 'in practice', i.e. in helping to produce practical knowledge and to develop new tools and artefacts which are useful in human interaction with nature and in the rational planning of society. We may say that science has *pragmatic success* (Greek *pragma*=action), when it serves as an effective guide of our action. This aspect of science has been emphasized among others by Francis Bacon ('knowledge is power'), Marxism-Leninism ('practice as the criterion of theory'), and pragmatism ('the instrumental value of science in the manipulation of natural and social reality'). If pragmatic success is taken to be the defining goal of scientific enquiry, we may speak of an *instrumental*, *technological*, or (if the practical utilities are expressed in money) *economical* conception of science.

There are two ways of measuring the pragmatic success of science. First, a scientific theory T is potentially pragmatically successful if it helps us to derive conditional imperatives or recommendations—'technical norms' in G. H. von Wright's (1963*a*) sense—of the following form:

> If you want A, and you believe you are in situation B, then     (1)
> you ought to do X.

In order that (1) has actual practical significance in a situation s, the following conditions are required:

> Doing X in B is a necessary (or necessary and sufficient)     (2)
> condition for A.

B is true or sufficiently close to the truth in s.        (3)

Some agent a in situation s has the goal A.        (4)

Doing X (or letting X to be done) is possible for agent a in        (5)
situation s.

Here (2) expresses a causal regularity that makes (1) true. Condition (3) requires that beliefs about the situation are at least approximately correct; (4) says that the goal A is relevant for someone; and (5) says that the cause factor X should be manipulable by the agent.

For example, Newton's theory may entail true technical norms which are useful and relevant for an engineer building a bridge. A theory in medicine may entail technical norms which give effective means for healing a certain disease. A meteorological theory may fail to be actually pragmatically successful, since we are (at least under present technological conditions) unable to manipulate the relevant causes (e.g. 'To get rain in Finland, arrange a low pressure area over the North Sea').

It can be argued that typical results of *applied research* are technical norms of the form (1) which express relations between means and ends (see Niiniluoto 1984; 1993) (cf. Section 8.4). More precisely, applied research exists in two main variants: in *predictive science*, the aim is successful foresight or prediction of future events; in *design science*, the aim is to make some technological activity more effective by rules of action. Theories in design science (e.g. engineering sciences, agricultural sciences, applied medicine, nursing science, social policy studies) are collections of such norms, tied together with a common goal (e.g. productivity of fields, health, social security) (cf. Niiniluoto 1994*d*). For such theories, conditions (2)–(5) combine the idea that their results should be true, useful in practice, and relevant in society.

A theory in *basic research*, containing descriptive information about the world, may become pragmatically useful if it is possible to derive technical norms from it. But our analysis shows that actual pragmatic success is not an intrinsic property of such a theory: conditions (3)–(5) are highly context-specific extra-theoretical assumptions. It also suggests that a rough measure of the 'amount' of pragmatic success of a theory T could be the number of true technical norms derivable from T, weighted by the importance of the relevant goal A in the norm.[1]

---

[1] A more direct way of measuring the practical gain due to theory T is to relativize this concept to a decision problem. Let $a_1, \ldots, a_k$ be the available actions or decisions, let $s_1, \ldots, s_n$ be the alternative states of nature, and let $u_{ij}$ be the utility of (the consequence of) action $a_i$ when $s_j$ is the true state of nature. Let e be the available evidence, and $P(s_j/e)$ the epistemic probability of $s_j$ given e. Then, according to the Bayesian decision principle, we should choose action $a_i$ which maximizes the expected utility

The supporter of the technological conception of science thinks that the ultimate aim of enquiry is the effective manipulation of natural and social reality in order to attain human goals (cf. Rescher 1977). In this view, science is always for human *action*. But there is also a broader way of viewing theories as 'economical' *tools* of effective human *thinking*. This tradition emphasizes such virtues of theories as their *simplicity*, *intellectual economy*, and *manageability*.

There is no general agreement on the definition of simplicity. This is not surprising, since this concept has several aspects and different potential applications.[2] *Ontological* simplicity or *parsimony*, as expressed in Occam's razor, concerns the number of entities (such as objects, properties, laws, principles, and so on) postulated by a theory. *Syntactical* simplicity, as a function of syntactical form, includes notational simplicity, the number and degrees of basic predicates of a conceptual scheme,[3] the number of independent axioms of a theory, the quantificational depth of a generalization, and the number of parameters in an equation defining a curve.[4] *Structural* simplicity of an object depends on the shortest way of describing or generating it. This is the basic idea of Kolmogorov's measure of complexity. *Methodological* accounts of simplicity identify the simplicity of a scientific hypothesis with some feature related to its role in science. For example, simplicity has been defined as falsifiability (Popper 1959), testability (Friedman 1972), informativeness (Sober 1975), and economy (Rescher 1990). (See also Section 6.3.)

Let us move to measures which take into account the semantic content of science. A statement is *empirical*, if it is contingent (i.e. not logically or analytically true or false) and its truth value can in principle be decided by means of observation or experimentation. An empiricist typically thinks that the goal of science is to increase our stock of true empirical statements in the observational language $L_0$ (cf. Section 5.1). These may be obtained

$$\sum_{i=1}^{k} P(s_j/e)u_{ij}.$$

Let the maximum of this sum over $i=1, \ldots, k$ be $u(e)$. Now if theory T is accepted, probabilities $P(s_j/e)$ are changed by conditionalization to $P(s_j/e\&T)$ and the expected utility of action $a_i$ is

$$\sum_{i=1}^{k} P(s_j/e\&T)u_{ij}.$$

Let the maximum of this sum over i be $u(e\&T)$. Then the difference $u(e\&T)-u(e)$ expresses (in terms of utilities) the expected gain of accepting theory T.

[2] For discussions of simplicity, see Bunge (1961), Foster and Martin (1966), Hesse (1974), Rescher (1990), Niiniluoto (1994*e*).

[3] This was Nelson Goodman's project in defining simplicity. See Foster and Martin (1966) and Goodman (1972).

[4] For the simplicity of curves, see Popper (1959), Hesse (1974), and Gillies (1989).

directly by means of systematic observation and experimentation or indirectly by deriving them from a theory.

A theory T is *potentially empirically successful*, if T logically entails contingent statements in the observational language. Technically speaking, this means that T has non-empty empirical content $EC(T)=\{h$ in $L_0 \mid T \vdash h$ and not $\vdash h\}$. Theory T has *actual* empirical success, if it entails true empirical statements. Theory T is known to have actual empirical success, if it entails empirical statements which are known to be true. The actual empirical *failures* of a theory may be of two kinds: T may fail to entail a true empirical statement, and T may entail a false empirical statement (cf. Fig. 9 in Ch. 3).

Usually theories entail observational consequences only in conjunction with some initial conditions, so that their consequences will have a conditional form: if T with empirical assumption $e_0$ entails another empirical statement e (i.e. $T \& e_0 \vdash e$), then $T \vdash (e_0 \rightarrow e)$. This means that pragmatic success (i.e. deriving from T the conditional statement 'if I see to it that . . . , then it will be the case that . . .', which justifies a technical norm of the form (1)) is generally a special case of empirical success.

Potential empirical success may be *explanatory*: T with initial conditions entails a statement e which is known to be true, and thereby answers the question 'Why e?' It may also be *predictive* (or *postdictive*): T entails a statement e about the future (or about the past), and thereby answers the question 'e or not -e?' (cf. Hempel 1965).

If theory T has a non-empty empirical content, the cardinality of $EC(T)$ is infinite.[5] Therefore, the overall empirical success of a theory T cannot be compared to that of theory $T'$ simply by counting the number of elements in their empirical contents. If $T'$ is logically stronger than T, i.e. $T' \vdash T$, then $EC(T) \subseteq EC(T')$, i.e. the empirical content of T is set-theoretically contained in that of $T'$, but this comparison of potential success does not yet give us any method for balancing the actual empirical successes and failures of the two theories.

The criteria of empirical progress in Imre Lakatos's methodology of research programmes are based on the following idea.[6] Let $EC^t_*(T)$ be the verified empirical content of theory T up to time t, i.e. the successful or true empirical explanations and predictions from T up to time t. A new theory $T'$, which is intended to supersede T at time t+1, should retain all the known successes of T but also have 'excess corroboration' by

---

[5] This is true even in simple languages which have the logical resources of sentential connectives and quantifiers.

[6] See Lakatos and Musgrave (1970), Howson (1976). It is important for Lakatos that the concept of progress is defined for research programmes, i.e. sequences of successive theories sharing some kernel assumptions (cf. Section 6.4).

novel predictions that will be verified. In other words, $EC^t_*(T) \subset EC^{t+1}_*(T')$. Lakatos concentrates only on the empirical success of theories—without giving attention to their possible failures. And he does not give a method of comparing rival theories whose actual success does not satisfy the condition of set-theoretic inclusion, i.e. the later theory does not preserve all the successes of the former one.

A solution to the latter problem was given already in 1948 by Carl G. Hempel (see Hempel 1965: 278–88). He considered a finite class K of empirical statements with mutually exclusive information content, and defined the systematic (explanatory and predictive) power of theory T as the number of elements of K entailed by T divided by the number of all elements of K. In Hempel's example, the elements of K are the negations of the Carnapian state descriptions of a finite monadic first-order language (see Section 3.5). He generalized this definition by introducing an epistemic probability measure P for the empirical language, and by defining the information content of a sentence h by $\text{cont}(h) = 1 - P(h)$ (see Section 4.5). Let E be the conjunction of all elements of K. Now the *systematic power* of a theory T relative to E is defined by the ratio of the common content of T and E to the content of E:

$$\text{syst}(T, E) = \text{cont}(T \vee E)/\text{cont}(E) = [1 - P(T \vee E)]/[1 - P(E)] = P(\sim T/\sim E). \quad (6)$$

Hence, if T entails E (i.e. T entails all elements of K), then $\sim E$ entails $\sim T$, and $\text{syst}(T, E)$ receives its maximum value 1.[7]

Larry Laudan's (1977) concept of the problem-solving effectiveness of a theory (relative to empirical problems) is—perhaps surprisingly—essentially the same as Hempel's notion of systematic power (Niiniluoto 1990a). According to Laudan's syntactic characterization, a theory T solves an empirical problem by entailing the statement of the problem. The *problem-solving ability* of T is proportional to the weighted number of the empirical problems solved by T.[8] Laudan's difference from Hempel here is that he is less explicit in defining the relevant set of empirical statements and more flexible in the choice of the weights of these problems. Laudan also allows approximate problem solutions. Laudan further proposes that the weighted number of 'conceptual problems' generated by T should be subtracted from the solved empirical problems. For example, an inconsistent theory entails all statements and thus 'solves' all empirical problems, but

[7] For other measures of systematic power, see Hintikka (1968), Pietarinen (1970), Niiniluoto and Tuomela (1973).

[8] In his recent work, Laudan (1990a) argues that a theory is not confirmed by all of its empirical consequences.

still it fails to be a good theory, since contradiction is a severe conceptual problem.

Laudan's account of progress is similar to the idea of Eino Kaila (1939), who defined the *relative simplicity* of a theory T by the 'multitude of the experiential data derivable from' T divided by the syntactic complexity of T. Thus, relative simplicity=explanatory power/complexity (cf. Section 6.3). However, Kaila did not have available any general methods of actually counting the explanatory power and complexity of a theory.

An instrumentalist regards scientific theories merely as conceptual tools for systematizing experience (cf. Section 5.1): theories do not have truth values, so that their ultimate goal is to be simple (or 'economical') and empirically successful. Laudan's problem-solving account and Bas van Fraassen's (1980) 'constructive empiricism' in practice agree with instrumentalism in this respect: even though they admit that theories have truth values, they find this irrelevant in the analysis of the aims of science. Van Fraassen requires that a theory should be *empirically adequate*: what the theory says about the observable should be true.

In contrast, a scientific realist sees theories as attempts to reveal the true nature of reality even beyond the limits of empirical observation. A theory should be *cognitively successful* in the sense that the theoretical entities it postulates really exist and the lawlike descriptions of these entities are true. Thus, the basic aim of science for a realist is *true information about reality*. The realist of course appreciates empirical success like the empiricist. But for the realist, the truth of a theory is a precondition for the adequacy of scientific explanations.[9] Furthermore, the truth of a theory T explains its actual empirical success: the empirical content of a true theory must likewise be true (cf. Section 6.5). In particular, the solutions to predictive problems given by a true theory are true as well. But while realists may admit that empirical success as such is important for practical reasons, they will also value empirical content as a means for testing the truth of a theory (see Fig. 15 in Ch. 5).

Assume now that the cognitive aim of science includes truth (in the realist sense of correspondence with reality). As truth is not a manifest, directly detectable, or measurable property of theoretical statements, but can only be estimated or evaluated by means of the available evidence, a

[9] Here it is important to distinguish *potential* and *actual* explanations (cf. Hempel 1965). Potential explanation is defined independently of the truth value of the explanans; van Fraassen's (1980) pragmatic account of explanation does not require that the explanatory theory is true. In this sense, we may speak of the potential explanatory power of hypothetical theories. Hempel required that actual explanations satisfy the condition of truth. This is a very strong demand. For a fallibilist theoretical realist, it is appropriate to aim at explanations by truthlike theories (cf. also Sintonen 1984).

realist needs a distinction between *real* and *estimated* success: the former is unknown, the latter is known and serves as an indicator of the former.[10] Against naive empiricism, the realist may also acknowledge that our observational evidence is often false or at best approximately true, and the assessment of cognitive success should be generalized to such situations (cf. Section 6.3).

If real success is defined simply by truth value, estimated success is measured by indicators of truth. Traditionally the most important of such indicators has been *epistemic* (inductive, logical, personal) *probability*: if h is a hypothesis and e the available evidence, then P(h/e) is the rational degree of belief in the truth of h given e (cf. Section 4.5). More formally, this idea can be presented in decision-theoretical terms: let u(h, t) be the epistemic utility of accepting h when h is true, and u(h, f) the utility of accepting h when h is false. The *expected epistemic utility* of accepting h, given evidence e, is then

$$U(h/e)=P(h/e)u(h, t)+P(\sim h/e)u(h, f). \tag{7}$$

If now epistemic utility is determined by truth value (1 for truth, 0 for falsity), i.e. u(h, t)=1 and u(h, f)=0, then

$$U(h/e)=P(h/e)\cdot1+P(\sim h/e)\cdot0=P(h/e). \tag{8}$$

As Karl Popper was first to point out in his *Logik der Forschung* (1934), probability alone is not a good measure for cognitive success, since it can be maximized trivially by choosing logically weak theories: P(h/e)=1 if h is a tautology (Popper 1959). As (8) can thus be maximized by trivial truths (tautologies and deductive consequences of evidence e), the aim of science cannot be 'truth and nothing but the truth'. Therefore, Popper emphasized bold conjectures and severe refutations as the proper method of science.[11] Isaac Levi's suggestion in *Gambling with Truth* (1967) was to define epistemic utility as a weighted combination of truth value tv(h) and information content: $tv(h)+q\cdot cont(h)$ $(0<q\leq1)$, where q is an 'index of boldness'. This leads to expected utility

$$P(h/e)+q\cdot cont(h). \tag{9}$$

[10] A similar distinction has to be made in Laudan's account of progress: the actual success is measured by the number of empirical problems *solved* so far, while the problem-solving ability concerns the unknown number of problems *solvable* by a theory.

[11] In fact, these two requirements are not combined by Popper in the right way. See Niiniluoto (1984: 41). If we falsify a bold (improbable, informative) hypothesis h, we gain the information of ~h, which is low, as $cont(\sim h)=1-(1-P(h))=P(h)$. I think this is a serious argument against Popper's falsificationism, which endorses a purely negative attitude to testing hypotheses. As Levi (1967) made clear, if we wish to gain much information, we must be ready to 'gamble with truth' and be ready tentatively to accept bold hypotheses.

If cont(h) is defined by $1-P(h)$,[12] and if q=1, then (9) reduces to

$$P(h/e)-P(h). \tag{10}$$

This formula, with different normalizations, has been proposed by several philosophers as a measure for the *degree of confirmation, corroboration, factual support, weight of evidence*, etc. for h on e (see Foster and Martin 1966; Niiniluoto and Tuomela 1973). As Jaakko Hintikka (1968) showed, this measure in its variants can also be justified as an expression of the amount of information that evidence e transmits about h.

The difference (10) is greater than zero if and only if e is *positively relevant* to h, i.e. e increases the probability of h. An alternative to (10) is the ratio measure

$$P(h/e)/P(h)=P(e/h)/P(e). \tag{11}$$

This measure has the same value $1/P(e)$ for all h which entail e, whereas (8) and (10) are proportional to $P(h)$ in this case.[13]

The famous Carnap–Popper controversy did not lead to a satisfactory analysis of cognitive success. Carnap (1962) gave up realism and interpreted the epistemic probability of general laws instrumentalistically as 'instance confirmation', i.e. as support for the next empirical prediction from the law. Popper (1972) suggested that his degrees of corroboration (i.e. his measure of how well a theory has stood up in severe tests) are indicators of verisimilitude, but he failed to find adequate definitions for these concepts.

Here the degree of truthlikeness $Tr(T, h^*)$ for a theory T suggests itself as a measure of the cognitive success of T (relative to the cognitive problem with target $h^*$). (See Section 3.5.) Truthlikeness in Popper's sense combines truth and information as the two main goals of science. The min-sum-measure of truthlikeness Tr, which is relative to a chosen balance between our cognitive interests of finding truth (relief of agnosticism) and avoiding error, is a generalization of Levi's measure to situations where distance from the truth matters (cf. Levi 1986, however). The

[12] Note that Levi (1967) does not accept this cont-measure for information content.

[13] The probabilistic measures of success face the problem of 'old evidence'. Sometimes a theory T may get credit when it is shown that T entails a statement $e_0$ which is already a part of the accepted evidence e. For example, it was a major achievement of the Copernican theory that it could give an (approximate) account of the known astronomical data. However, if evidence e entails $e_0$, then $e_0$ does not confirm T at all relative to e, since $P(T/e_0\&e)=P(T/e)$. This result is due to the unrealistic assumption that epistemic probabilities are invariant under logical equivalence, i.e. they are degrees of belief for a logically omniscient agent. Therefore, I think the most plausible way out of the problem of 'old evidence' is to allow that the discovery of new deductive relation may influence epistemic probabilities. For evaluations of this idea, see Howson and Urbach (1989) and Earman (1992).

corresponding estimated success, relative to evidence e, is then measured by the function ver(T/e) of expected verisimilitude (cf. Section 4.5). This means in effect that truthlikeness is treated as the basic epistemic utility of science which is assessed relative to the empirical success of a theory (cf. Niiniluoto 1987a: ch. 12). As a variant of expected verisimilitude ver(T/e), we have also seen how the cognitive value of a theory could be measured by its probable approximate truth $PA_{1-\epsilon}(T/e)$. These definitions attempt to combine the best ingredients of the Bayesian and Popperian approaches to scientific inference.

For a theoretical realist it is important to observe that all the definitions in this section can be generalized to situations where, in addition to observational evidence e, there are accepted background theories b. For example, the relevant probabilities will then be of the form P(h/e&b) (see Niiniluoto and Tuomela 1973), and estimated verisimilitude has the form ver(T/e&b).

In the later sections, we study the relations of these measures of success and the use of them as criteria of theory-choice in science.

## 6.2  Axiology and methodological rules

We have seen in the preceding section that different ways of measuring the success of science ultimately reduce to different views about the aim of science. The task of studying this aim belongs to the *axiology* of science.

Historical and sociological naturalism (cf. Section 1.4) suggests that axiological issues about science should be resolved by studying the actual behaviour and opinions of the scientists: the aim of science is what the so-called scientists really aim at. This proposal does not work unless we already have a criterion for picking out 'the scientists' from the world. Are medicine men, engineers, priests, artists, or astrologists scientists? Answers to such questions depend partly on the characteristic activities of these professions, but also on their aims. Any workable definition of science and scientist makes some reference to axiological concepts. Therefore, the axiology of science cannot be entirely 'naturalized', but it remains a genuine part of philosophy.

Larry Laudan's important article 'Progress or Rationality? The Prospects for Normative Naturalism' (1987a) helps a lot to clarify the debate about naturalism. Laudan suggests that *methodological rules* can be understood as conditional norms of the form

If your central cognitive goal is x, then you ought to do y.          (12)

Such statements, which express connections between ends and means, are true (or warranted) if y really promotes the goal x, i.e. if

$$\text{Doing } y \text{ is more likely than its alternatives to produce } x \qquad (13)$$

is true. As (13) is a contingent empirical statement, Laudan argues, it follows that the 'naturalist meta-methodologist' will rely—instead of on pre-analytic intuitions or choices of the scientific elite—on historical data concerning means–ends relationships.[14]

One may point out that the scientist's own 'methodological norms', like social norms in general, are unconditional ('Avoid *ad hoc* explanations!', 'Make sure that your experiments are repeatable!'). Laudan's point is that methodology, as a systematic study of such norms, should construe them as conditional rules (see Kaiser 1991).

Statements of the form (12) are called technical norms by G. H. von Wright (1963*a*). I have earlier suggested that technical norms define the typical form of knowledge that is sought in applied research (see (1) above). Laudan's thesis can thus be expressed by saying that methodology is an applied science.

While I agree with this thesis, it seems to me that conditional norms of the form (12) are not typically justified inductively by historical data, but rather by studying theoretical *models of knowledge acquisition*. Such models study the effectiveness of cognitive strategies relative to epistemic goals and factual assumptions about the world. Examples can be found from disciplines like applied mathematics, mathematical statistics, game theory, decision theory, and operations research:

> If you wish to guarantee that a false hypothesis is rejected    (14)
> with high probability, perform a likelihood ratio test with a
> high level of significance.

> If your goal is convergence to the true value of parameter    (15)
> $\theta$, and if the error of measurement is normally distributed
> with the mean $\theta$, use the average of repeated measure-
> ments as your estimate of $\theta$.

> Given these beliefs and preferences, if your aim is to    (16)
> maximize your expected gain, you ought to choose this act.

An important feature of conditionally normative results of this type is the possibility of proving them a priori by mathematical demonstration

[14] An empirical study of the reliability of methodological rules obviously has to employ some methodological rules. There is a threat of a vicious circle. See the Symposium on Normative Naturalism in the *Philosophy of Science* 57/1 (1990), 1–59. See also Siegel (1996).

(for (15), see Section 4.6). At the same time, their application in some particular situation—i.e. deriving from them non-conditional norms or recommendations—requires factual, hypothetical, or empirically warranted knowledge (about the antecedents of the conditionals and the situation of their application).

Some methodological rules may be based upon conceptual connections between precisely explicated notions, so that again they can be justified a priori. For example, a scientific realist may formulate methodological rules of type (12) by means of the following results (Niiniluoto 1987*a*) which are analytically true (given Hintikka's measure of corroboration and my measure of truthlikeness):

> If a generalization has a high degree of corroboration, its     (17)
> degree of estimated verisimilitude is also high.

> If a theory is highly truthlike, its deductive consequences are     (18)
> approximately true.

(Cf. Section 6.5 for a more precise account.)

We may thus conclude that Laudan's conception of methodology as consisting of conditional norms legitimizes, besides a role for historical data as empirical evidence, also the possibility of a formal philosophy of science, so that the approach of logical empiricism is partially rehabilitated (cf. Section 1.4; Niiniluoto 1991*b*).

Laudan's conception of methodology is limited to *strategic rules* which express means–ends relationships. They are comparable to principles which state how one plays chess effectively—how to attack, defend, build strong positions, and eventually beat the opponent. However, an institutionalized activity also has *constitutive rules* (to use Searle's term) which characterize its legitimate 'moves'. In the case of chess, such constitutive rules state how the different chessmen may be moved on the table. Violation of these rules does not lead to ineffective playing, but to not playing chess at all.

Many debates in the philosophy of science concern the constitutive rules of science—rules about both the characteristic methods and aims of science. As such rules define what science is, they have a 'conventional' element, as Popper (1959) says. But a demarcation between science and non-science, or the explication of the concept of science, should also be 'close' to the accepted use of the terms 'science' and 'scientific' (cf. Kuhn 1983). The method of justifying constitutive rules cannot be purely logical or empirical, but consists in an attempt to reach a 'reflective equilibrium' (to use Rawls's term) between our normative demands for science and its actual practice (cf. Thagard 1988; Kaiser 1991).

Laudan (1983) rejects the demarcation problem: creationism is for him bad science rather than non-science. Therefore, it can be understood that he does not formulate constitutive rules for science. But how could one propose strategic rules for any game without knowing its constitutive rules?

However, Laudan (1987a) makes the important addition that 'methodology gets nowhere without axiology'. He acknowledges the 'need to supplement methodology with an investigation into the legitimate or permissible ends of inquiry'. And in *Science and Values* (1984a) he has proposed a 'reticulational model' for showing how questions about scientific values can be resolved by appeal to (temporarily) shared theories and methods.

One might object to Laudan's model that it is too restricted: disputes about scientific values may refer or appeal not only to scientific practices, theories, and methods but also to philosophical principles from fields like logic, epistemology, aesthetics, and ethics (cf. Niiniluoto 1987b). This would not be quite fair, however, since Laudan may include naturalized versions of such principles among 'theories' in his model. But still it seems problematic how a network of descriptive statements and conditional norms could ever give a *positive* justification for pursuing some value in science. In this respect, Laudan's assessment of values remains within the framework of instrumental means–ends rationality (i.e. Max Weber's *Zweckrationalitet*), and resembles Giere (1988), whose version of naturalism admits only instrumental rationality: goals are evaluated in terms of their accessibility relative to the available means, not by their having intrinsic value or being 'reasonable' (cf. Aarnio 1987; Putnam 1981; Siegel 1996).

Laudan's reticulational model thus proposes a *negative* way of eliminating *utopian* or unrealizable goals: 'the rational adoption of a goal or an aim requires the prior specification of grounds for belief that the goal state can possibly be achieved' (Laudan 1984a: 51). In my view, it would be too strong to understand this as requiring that any rational goal can actually be *reached*. But it is a serious matter, if a goal cannot be *approached*. For example, epistemological arguments against the infallibility of factual knowledge have led philosophers to reject the traditional quest for complete certainty as a general value in science. But these arguments gain their strongest support from the observation that in many (though not in all) situations even the gradual approach to certainty is excluded, since the relevant hypotheses contain counterfactual or idealizing assumptions and, therefore, are known to be false.

Thus, scientific values should be regarded as respectable if there are reasonable criteria for claiming that we have made *progress* in realizing them.

(Similarly, it is a reasonable goal to be an excellent, and even perfect, piano player, even if this goal will not be reached.) For this reason, it seems to me, Laudan's (1984a) argument that truth is a utopian aim for science is not convincing (cf. also Rorty 1998: 3). Peirce's fallibilism (cf. Section 4.1) admits that, even if there are no infallible criteria for recognizing whether truth has been realized, it is probable that this goal has been realized in many particular cases. And even in cases where truth is at best the asymptotic limit of enquiry, the measures of verisimilitude help us to assert with a fallible empirical warrant that this goal has been approached. For example, given the problem described above in (15), it can be shown that the infinite sequence of point estimates converges with probability one to the true value of the unknown parameter (see Section 4.6).

The axiology of chess is dominated by a single supreme rule: the aim of the game is to beat the opponent. A secondary rule states that, if you have lost your chance of winning, you should try to save a tie. It is only when chess becomes an art that the style of playing becomes an end in itself: we try to win with a new, short, and beautiful combination of moves.

In my view, the axiology of science should likewise be governed by a primary rule: try to find the complete true answer to your cognitive problem, i.e. try to reach or approach this goal. Truthlikeness measures how close we come to this goal. As secondary rules, we may then require that our answer is justified, simple, consilient, etc. Further, if it is known that the available answers do not include a true one, then our rule is to search for the least false among them.

## 6.3  Theory-choice, underdetermination, and simplicity

*Inductivism* is the doctrine that scientific theories are obtained by inductive inference from experience, i.e. inductive generalization is a method of both discovering and justifying theories. A different conception of inference was imposed in the nineteenth century by the introduction of explanatory theories that go beyond the surface layers of phenomena: Dalton's theory of atoms, Young's wave theory of light, Maxwell's electromagnetic field theory, Boltzmann's statistical mechanics, Schleiden's cell theory, Darwin's theory of evolution (see Laudan 1981b). The *hypothetico-deductive* or HD model, as masterfully formulated by William Whewell (1840), takes theories to be bold and 'happy guesses' or hypotheses which are tested by checking the truth of their observable predictions (cf. Popper 1959; Hempel 1965; Niiniluoto 1984). A good theoretical hypothesis should explain the old evidence and entail novel predictions. Induction is then the 'converse' of deduction: successful explanation and prediction confirms or corroborates the hypothesis, while a negative test result refutes the theory by *modus tollens* (see Fig. 21).

Even though the HD model has to be complemented in many directions—it does not say enough about scientific discovery (cf. Whewell 1840; Kleiner 1993), confirmation, and refutation (cf. Lakatos and Musgrave 1970)—it still gives us a good basic framework for discussing rival philosophical views about the problem of *theory-choice*.

The empiricists typically formulate the problem of theory-choice by assuming that the available total evidence e includes a finite number of actual observations and measurements. Then it is clear that hypothetical laws and theories in science transcend evidence at least in three ways. First, they are universal or statistical generalizations about potentially infinite populations (hence, Hume's problem of induction). Secondly, they are lawlike rather than accidental generalizations (hence, the problem of counterfactuality). Thirdly, they contain theoretical terms not reducible to the observational language (hence, the problem of theoreticity).

In historical sciences, such as cosmology, geology, zoology, palaeontology, and most of the humanities, the hypotheses typically concern some singular event in the past. Such hypotheses also transcend the evidence, consisting of the present traces and causal influences of the past, but they can be indirectly tested by the HD model.

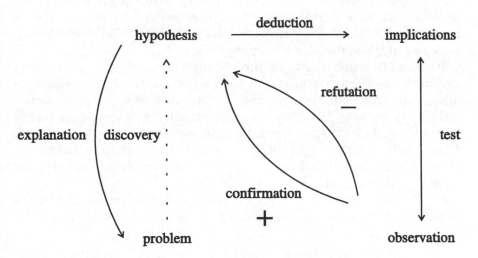

FIG. 21. The hypothetico-deductive model of science

Thus, in normal cases there will be a great number of different rival theories, which nevertheless are empirically equivalent. This formulation seems to imply, as Quine (1960) has claimed, that theory-choice in science is *underdetermined by data*.[15] To close the gap between empirical evidence and theories, Quine argues that theory-choice has to appeal to the criterion of simplicity. Many sociologists of science take advantage of this thesis and suggest that the choice of theories has to be based on or even appeal to extra-scientific social factors (cf. Ch. 9).

There are many objections to this simple empiricist picture of theory-choice. Let us say that two theories T and T′ are *empirically equivalent* if and only if EC(T)=EC(T′). This guarantees, assuming a neutral observational language $L_0$ for T and T′, that theories T and T′ have the same *deductive* connections to empirical statements. As Laudan (1990*a*) argues, this does not imply that they are equally well confirmed by the evidence e in $L_0$. This is correct, for the reason that confirmation depends essentially on the *probabilistic* relations between theory and evidence. This is seen in a striking way in the case of statistical hypotheses: they usually do not deductively entail any empirical statements, but give them conditional probabilities (e.g. a normal distribution of errors of measurement for a given unknown quantity). Nevertheless, there are cognitive—even empirical—criteria for making rational choices between such 'empirically equivalent' hypotheses, if they give different probabilities to different potential observations.

In the same way, the testability of a theory postulating theoretical entities requires that the truth of this theory should make a difference, at least with some probability, to some observable phenomena. Testing theories may thus be 'hypothetico-inductive' rather than hypothetico-deductive (cf. Niiniluoto and Tuomela 1973).

It should be emphasized that the scientists need not believe or accept one of the available hypotheses in each situation. Among the options of a cognitive problem there is always the *suspension of judgement*—technically speaking, this amounts to the acceptance of the disjunction of all rival hypotheses as the strongest conclusion warranted by the evidence (Levi 1967). In other words, if the evidence is not strong enough, the scientists may suspend judgement and look for more evidence, instead of adopting extra-scientific criteria of acceptance.

Conflicting theories, if interpreted realistically, cannot be true at the same time. But fortunately we do not have to consider at the same time

---

[15] For discussions on the underdetermination thesis, see Newton-Smith (1981), Laudan (1990*a*; 1996).

all logically possible theories; our choice is limited to the relevant ones which are able to solve the initial problem of explanation. For some problems it is difficult to find even one satisfactory theory. Moreover, there may be situations where all the relevant rival theories that are not yet excluded by the problem situation and empirical evidence are truthlike. In this case, the underdetermination argument would fail to block the tentative inference from data to a truthlike theory (cf. Niiniluoto 1989; MacIntosh 1994). But it is not clear that this would be always the case: for example, Cushing (1994) considers the possibility that the standard Copenhagen interpretation of quantum mechanics and Bohm's non-local hidden variable theory of quantum mechanics, which have entirely different ontologies, are empirically equivalent.

Perhaps the strongest counter-argument is the following: the underdetermination argument presupposes that there is a clear, context-independent distinction between empirical and non-empirical. This is questioned by the thesis of the theory-ladenness of observations. What counts as observational evidence depends on the available instruments and on the accepted theoretical background assumptions. There is no unique and fixed 'upper limit' of the observable (cf. Newton-Smith 1981; Churchland and Hooker 1985; Laudan 1990a).

Indeed, if we do not endorse naive empiricism, then we have to acknowledge that rival hypotheses in science are usually evaluated relative to some background assumptions which may include tentatively accepted theories. Thus, even when T1 and T2 are empirically equivalent as such, their relations to the empirical evidence may be different in the light of the background assumptions.

The important insight that theory-choice takes place in a context of background assumptions was expressed by the concepts of paradigm and disciplinary matrix (Kuhn), research programme (Lakatos), and research tradition (Laudan). The grounds for choosing between theories may include, besides empirical evidence, background theories, regularity assumptions, conceptual frameworks, exemplars from earlier research, and axiological principles.

The underdetermination argument can of course be repeated on the level of research programmes. This is what Kuhn did in his claim that the choice between paradigms is not dictated by 'logic and experiment', but involves persuasive argumentation, conversions, and gestalt switches.[16]

---

[16] For discussion on Kuhn's account of revolutionary theory-change, see Dilworth (1981). Kuhn (1993) denies that a group of scientists could experience a gestalt switch. Cf. Thagard (1992).

Lakatos's interesting suggestion was that it is possible rationally to appraise research programmes by their *rate of progress* (cf. Laudan 1977). Such programmes are like vehicles of transportation that carry the scientists forward in their competition for new results. Even though there is always the possibility that a programme is only temporarily running out of steam, and will be recovered by new improvements, most scientists are opportunists who jump to the most rapidly advancing research programme. In the light of this metaphor, it is important that the concept of scientific progress can be understood in methodological terms appropriate to scientific realism (see Section 6.6).

We are now back in the axiological question of Section 6.2: what are the aims or desiderata of scientific enquiry? Kuhn's (1977) own favourite list includes accuracy, consistency, scope, simplicity, and fruitfulness. Even though truth is not included here, it might be the case that such desiderata in fact have interconnections with each other, and there may be hidden links with truth after all (cf. Section 6.4). For example, accuracy and scope seem to be indicators of the two main ingredients of the concept of truthlikeness: truth and content. A good strategy for methodology would be to study methodological rules which conditionally assume these desiderata as the aims of science. Here the optimization model of theory-choice, illustrated in Sections 6.1 and 6.4 with the concepts of truth, information, and systematic power, turns out to be a very flexible conceptual tool.

For example, it can be shown that the realist effort in truth-seeking is compatible with the idea that, in the context of applied research (cf. Niiniluoto 1993), the choice between hypotheses may be influenced by practical, extra-scientific interests. In other words, the decision-theoretical framework is able to conceptualize situations where both epistemic and practical utilities are involved and interact. This can happen in cases where some predictive model is intended to constitute the basis of some action or policy. A good example is given by Helen Longino (1989). Linear and quadratic models have been proposed for measuring the health risks of radiation. The loss (negative utility) of a mistaken model could be equated with its distance from truth, if the problem is purely theoretical and belongs to basic research. However, if the safety standards are adopted by implementing the model in practice for the public and the workers in nuclear facilities, then it is safer to overestimate the health risks than to underestimate them. Hence, the practical interest of protecting people from radiation justifies a loss function that gives higher penalties for too low risk estimates. This kind of case is especially interesting, since the same loss function can reflect the 'pure' cognitive value (i.e. distance from the truth) and weight it with a pragmatic human interest.

The Quinean conclusion that simplicity *has* to be used as a criterion of theory-choice is not adequate, since it gives a simplified picture of scientific enquiry. But, of course, there are methodological situations where simplicity *may* play an important role. The classical question, ever since the days of Ptolemy (cf. Section 5.4), has been the relation of simplicity and truth.

Hans Reichenbach (1938) made a distinction between *descriptive* and *inductive simplicity* (cf. Niiniluoto 1994*e*). The former concerns choice between theories which are 'logically equivalent, i.e. correspond in all observable facts' (p. 374), the latter theories 'which are equivalent in respect to all observed facts, but which are not equivalent in respect to predictions' (p. 376). According to Reichenbach, preference for descriptive simplicity is a matter of convenience, while inductive simplicity indicates higher probability and truth.

Reichenbach's concept of equivalence is ambiguous. It may mean logical equivalence (including intertranslatable theories like matrix and wave formulations of quantum mechanics) and empirical equivalence (in the sense defined above). This gives us two formulations of the Principle of Descriptive Simplicity:

> Of two logically equivalent theories, prefer the one which (DS$_1$) is descriptively simpler.

> Of two empirically equivalent theories, prefer the one which is descriptively simpler. (DS$_2$)

As logical equivalence entails empirical equivalence, DS$_2$ entails DS$_1$, but not vice versa.

The first of these principles, DS$_1$, is relatively uncontroversial as a practical rule. If two theories are known to be equivalent, there cannot be any purely cognitive differences between them: they make the same claims about reality, they have the same truth value, they are equally accurate relative to observations, and equally worthy of rational belief or acceptance as true. However, greater simplicity may amount to an enormous advantage in *cognitive fruitfulness* and *practical economy*: a simple formulation of a theory is often easy to work with, to employ in the quest of further knowledge, or to apply for practical purposes (e.g. in calculation of predictions, teaching of students, programming of computers, etc.). Hence, principle DS$_1$ is a good rule for choosing among the equivalent formulations of our theory that one which is most convenient for our current purposes.

On the other hand, the stronger principle DS$_2$ is problematic, since two empirically equivalent theories may have non-equivalent theoretical parts.

If we accept theoretical realism, which allows that theoretical terms are interpreted and theoretical statements have a truth value, then two empirically equivalent theories may have different truth values. Thus, $DS_2$ expresses the idea that theoretical truth is irrelevant—or at least less important than simplicity. This view is a traditional element of empiricist instrumentalism.

For example, Heinrich Hertz required in *Die Principien der Mechanik* (1894) that a physical theory should be admissible (i.e. logically consistent), correct (i.e. agree with all phenomena), and appropriate (i.e. distinct and simple). (See Hertz 1956.) To explain these notions, let us form an equivalence class of consistent theories which are empirically equivalent to each other (e.g. all theories that have the same empirical consequences as Maxwell's equations). Then a member of this class is distinct, if it makes explicit the 'essential relations' of its objects; it is simple, if it does not contain any 'superfluous or empty relations'. This amounts to a clear formulation of $DS_2$. According to Mach, Hertz's criterion of appropriateness 'coincides' with his criterion of the economy of thought (Mach 1960: 318).

The step from $DS_1$ to $DS_2$ could be justified by the Thesis of Translatability, advocated by Logical Positivism. This 'dogma of empiricism' (Quine 1953) claims that all terms and statements in science can be reduced to the observational language by means of explicit definitions (cf. Section 5.1). Therefore, it would imply that equivalence and empirical equivalence coincide. But I do not see that Reichenbach could accept such a defence of $DS_2$, given his early rejection of Carnap's phenomenalism. In any case, it should not be accepted by scientific realists. Hence, the only legitimate applications of descriptive simplicity concern cases covered by $DS_1$, where the compared theories are fully equivalent, not merely empirically equivalent.

The idea of inductive simplicity also has many different interpretations. First, it may concern what Reichenbach called the context of discovery, or what others have called the pursuit of a theory: a simple hypothesis is chosen as the object of further enquiry, testing, and elaboration. The principle

> Of theories equivalent relative to the observed facts, pursue     $(IS_1)$
> the one which is the simplest

can be defended in terms of *economy*, projection 'along the lines of least resistance', effective search strategy, quick testability, and 'rapid strategy of progress' (Rescher 1990). Indeed, Rescher extends this 'simpler-models-first-heuristics' for the whole context of scientific enquiry.

A simple theory, he says, 'lightens the burden of cognitive effort'. If a simple solution accommodates the data at hand, 'there is ... no good reason for turning elsewhere'. We 'opt for simplicity' not because it is 'truth-indicative', but because it is 'teleologically cost-effective for the most effective realization of the goals of inquiry' (ibid. 3–5).

The economic defence of simplicity may be justifiable in terms of the decision-making strategy that Herbert Simon has called *satisficing*. (Giere (1988) has argued that scientists in fact are satisficers, rather than optimizers.) Given some criteria, fix a minimum level that a satisfactory or 'good enough' solution has to reach. Then—instead of trying to find the optimal solution among all possible solutions—you should accept the first minimally satisfactory solution that you hit upon. In the context of science, this means that we cannot and need not always try to generate and consider all possible hypotheses, but rather we accept for pursuit the first satisfactory hypothesis we are able to find. This is usually the simplest solution to our problem. It seems to me that satisficing can be viewed as a special case of optimization, where waste of time and money is included as a loss in the decision problem (Niiniluoto 1994*e*).

If the preference for simplicity is applied in the cases where a theory is accepted for practical purposes, e.g. for prediction or action, the following special case is obtained:

> Of theories equivalent relative to the observed facts, accept        (IS$_2$)
> for practical purposes the one that is the simplest.

But this is clearly problematic, as Shrader-Frechette (1990) has illustrated with examples of applied science in public policy. Preference for ontological simplicity, she points out, may lead to 'dangerous consequences'. Thus, a rule such as IS$_2$ is unsatisfactory, since it does not take into account the losses and risks of alternative choices (as the Bayesian decision theory does), and it does not allow for the possibility of withholding the decision and searching for better solutions or more data.

On the other hand, simplicity as *manageability* or *applicability* has a role in applied science. If a theory is defined by equations which cannot be solved for the relevant case, it is a normal practice to introduce some 'simplifications' or 'approximations' in the theory—even when we know that this will lead us away from truth (cf. Section 5.3). If we have to choose between a calculated prediction or no prediction at all, simplicity may be favoured even at the expense of accuracy and truth (Niiniluoto 1984: 262).

Reichenbach's own interpretation of inductive simplicity—unlike the economic formulations IS$_1$ and IS$_2$—applies to the context of cognitive justification:

Of theories equivalent relative to the observed facts, accept      (IS$_3$)
the simplest one as the best candidate for truth.

In Reichenbach's view, the simplest theory is the most probable candidate
for truth, and it will also 'furnish the best predictions'.

Assuming that the simplicity S(h) of a hypothesis h, or its complexity
K(h), can be measured, it could be included as an *additional* factor in the
formula of expected utility U(h/e) of h given evidence e (cf. Levi 1967). It
might be used also as a *secondary* factor which distinguishes hypotheses
with the same expected utility U(h/e). But in these cases it is not clear that
the chosen hypothesis would generally be the 'best candidate for truth'.
However, appeal to simplicity as an additional factor in theory-choice may
be justified in basic science at least in those cases where the form of a quantitative law can be derived from already accepted theories: in such cases
the improved accuracy of a complex function does not 'pay', if the law
cannot be incorporated within the established theoretical framework.

Eino Kaila defined in 1935 the *relative simplicity* of a theory h as the
ratio between the multitude of empirical data derivable from e and the
number of logically independent basis assumptions of h (see Kaila 1939;
1979). Thus, the relative simplicity RS(h, e) of h given e is defined by

$$RS(h, e) = syst(h, e)/K(h). \tag{19}$$

This measure, Kaila observed, is proportional to the 'explanatory power' of
a theory. (He operated with a deductive or non-probabilistic notion of systematic power.) And *if* it could be exactly defined and measured, relative
simplicity RS(h, e) would also define the 'inductive probability' of h on e.

An interesting feature of Kaila's concept of relative simplicity is that its
application as a decision rule immediately justifies Reichenbach's Principle of Descriptive Simplicity, i.e. DS$_1$ and DS$_2$. If theories h and h' are
equivalent or empirically equivalent, then (at least in Kaila's sense)
syst(h, e)=syst(h', e), and formula (19) recommends us to prefer h to h' if
and only if K(h)<K(h') or S(h)>S(h').

Kaila's definition is essentially equivalent to the concept of *explanatory
unification* of Friedman (1974) and Kitcher (1989), and *explanatory coherence* of Thagard (1992). These notions elaborate the idea that a good
theory should contain powerful but simple explanatory schemata. If logical
strength were the only desideratum, it would be easy to satisfy by making
the theory more and more complex—and eventually a logical contradiction would entail every statement; therefore it seems natural to opt for
strong but still simple theories.

Kaila's proposal is also related to Laudan's (1977) definition of scientific
progress in terms of the difference between the empirical problem-solving
capacity of a theory (cf. syst(h, e)) minus the 'conceptual problems' of h (a

variant of K(h)). Where Kaila uses the ratio of two factors, Laudan employs their difference, but I do not see that this makes an important distinction between their approaches. (For a similar case, see (10) and (11).)

The concept of relative simplicity has further an interesting connection to measures of beauty in 'algorithmic aesthetics'. Stiny and Gips (1978) propose that the aesthetic value of a text x (sequence, figure, picture, composition, etc.) is defined by $L(x)/K(x)$, where $L(x)$ is the length of x and $K(x)$ is the Kolmogorov complexity of x. This is directly analogous to (19). However, this is not a good definition of beauty, since the aesthetic value should start to decrease if the regularity of x (or $1/K(x)$) becomes too large.

On the other hand, Kaila does not have arguments to show that relative simplicity $RS(h, e)$ would behave exactly like probability. It is nevertheless plausible to assume that posterior probability $P(h/e)$, or increase of probability $P(h/e)-P(h)$, is proportional to $syst(h, e)$: a hypothesis is confirmed by the empirical data it explains (cf. (10)). If a connection of this kind is established, relative simplicity has a similar intuitive motivation to Elliot Sober's (1975) account, where theory-choice is determined by two 'irreducibly distinct goals', namely support and simplicity.[17]

The most common attempt to justify something like $IS_3$ is through prior probabilities. It is tempting to assume—as Jeffreys and Wrinch first suggested in 1921—that greater simplicity is associated with higher prior probability:

Among rival theories, h is simpler than h′ iff $P(h)>P(h')$.[18]          (SP)

This assumption with Bayes's Theorem guarantees that, in the context of hypothetico-deductive theorizing, greater simplicity entails larger posterior probability:

Assuming (SP), $h \vdash e$, and $h' \vdash e$, it holds that $P(h/e)>P(h'/e)$          (20)
iff h is simpler than h′.

This is one possible formulation of Reichenbach's thesis of Inductive Simplicity.

In spite of Popperian contrary suggestions that simplicity should always be associated with prior *im*probability, it seems that assumption (SP) might hold in some special cases. But as a general principle it expresses the old dictum: *simplex sigillum veri*. This is a highly dubious metaphysical doctrine:

---

[17] Sober does not measure support by posterior probability and simplicity by content, however. In my view, Sober's definition is not an explicate of simplicity, but rather of the degree of completeness of an answer to a question. For more recent work, see Forster and Sober (1994) and Sober (1990).

[18] See Hesse (1974), Quine (1966).

why on earth should nature be simple? Why should there be any a priori reasons to regard simpler theories as more probable than their rivals?[19]

The problem of inductive simplicity appears in a new light if we replace the strong HD-condition h⊢e with $0<P(e/h)<1$. When our theories make evidence e only probable to some degree, results like (20) are not valid any more. Instead of the questionable (SP), we may then study whether a posteriori preference for simple theories could be a consequence of likelihoods $P(e/h)$. In other words, simple theories need not be assumed to be probable a priori, since they turn out to be probable a posteriori. This expectation turns out to be true in Hintikka's system of inductive logic: when evidence e is large enough, the simplest or most parsimonious constituent compatible with e will also be the most probable given e (cf. Niiniluoto 1994e).

The most important case of inductive simplicity has been the problem of *curve fitting*. Suppose we are interested in the lawful connection between two quantities x and y. Our hypotheses are thus of the form $y=f(x)$, where f is a function. Let our evidence $E=\{\langle x_i, y_i \rangle \mid i=1, \ldots, n\}$ consist of a finite set of pairs of measurements of the values of x and y. Then the problem of curve fitting is often presented in the following form:

> Given the points E, find the simplest curve that passes     (CF)
> through them.

This rule, Reichenbach (1938) claims, is 'not to be regarded as a matter of convenience', but it 'depends on our inductive assumption: we believe that the simplest curve gives the best predictions'.

Most philosophers agree that the simplicity of a curve depends on the order of its equation: a linear function $y=ax+b$ has degree 2, since it is determined by two points, a quadratic function $y=ax^2+bx+c$ has degree 3, etc. Some of them explain their preference for simple curves by prior probability (Jeffreys), some by falsifiability (Popper) or testability (Friedman). Kaila pointed out that a simple curve of degree m through the points of E has large relative simplicity, measured in this case by n/m (cf. (19)). For a fixed number n of observations, we prefer a hypothesis with a small degree m. The same argument has recently been reinvented by Gillies (1989) in his Principle of Explanatory Surplus (measured by the difference n−m, instead of Kaila's ratio n/m).

However, the problem (CF) appears in a new light if we take seriously the fact that numerical measurements always contain observational errors. A curve going through all the observed points, even if they were

---

[19] Einstein's conception of simplicity was motivated by the idea that the world is a beautiful, harmonious mathematical construction. This view has captivated mathematical realists from Plato to Galileo and modern physicists. See Hesse (1974).

rounded by mean values, would *overfit* the data (Forster and Sober 1994). Therefore, the typical method in regression analysis is first to fix a desired level of simplicity, and then among these simple hypotheses to seek the one which is closest to the observed data. Thus, CF is replaced by

> Among hypotheses of a fixed level of simplicity, choose the    (CF')
> one which has the minimum distance from the evidence E.

For example, let E be as above and let FL be the class of linear functions of the form $f(x)=ax+b$. Then the distance between E and a hypothesis f can defined by the Square Difference:

$$D(f, E)=\sum_{i=1}^{n} (y_i-f(x_i))^2.$$

Then CF' recommends the use of Least Square Difference (LSD):

> Among linear functions in LF, choose the one f which    (21)
> minimizes the difference D(f, E).

The function f that satisfies (21) is the *least false* member of the class LF.[20] This idea takes us from the domain of 'inductive' simplicity to the theory of truthlikeness.

Using Akaike's Theorem, Forster and Sober (1994) have further shown that there are rational criteria for the choice of the class of functions in the curve-fitting problem CF'.

All these considerations show that there are methodological contexts where simplicity may play a significant role. They can be motivated by reasonable realist principles, without invoking metaphysical justifications or instrumentalist interpretations.


## 6.4 From empirical success to truthlikeness

A scientific realist typically insists that the cognitive aim of scientific enquiry should contain some 'veric' epistemic utility (cf. Sintonen 1984)—such as truth or truthlikeness. As we saw in Section 6.2, Laudan (1984a), on the other hand, has argued that truth (of theories) should be excluded, since it is a 'utopian' aim for science: we do not have any method of knowing that this goal has been reached or even approached to any extent. Instead, problem-solving ability serves for Laudan as an acceptable and accessible goal

---

[20] The log-likelihood measure used by Forster and Sober (1994) is equivalent to this LSD distance. Another distance function, the maximum of the differences $|y_i-f(x_i)|$, i=1, ..., n, is used by W. Patryas. Cf. Niiniluoto (1986b; 1987a).

which can be effectively recognized or calculated—independently of such problematic notions as truth.

Let us agree for a while, at least for the purposes of the argument, with Laudan that truth or closeness to the truth is not directly included in the epistemic goal of enquiry. It may still be the case that empirical success in the sense accepted by Laudan (and by all empiricists and instrumentalists who demand that theories should save the phenomena) serves as an *indicator of the truth or truthlikeness* of a theory. (In the same way we saw in Section 6.3 that sometimes simplicity and truth may go together.)

The simplest of such arguments is well known. Let g be a theory with a non-zero prior probability $P(g)>0$. Assume that g has actual empirical success, i.e. there is a true non-tautological empirical statement e derivable from g. Hence, $P(e/g)=1$ and $P(e)<1$. Then, by Bayes's Theorem (4.4),

$$P(g/e)=P(g)P(e/g)/P(e)=P(g)/P(e)>P(g). \tag{22}$$

This means that *actual empirical success increases the probability* of the truth of a theory. In other words, problem-solving effectiveness with respect to observed facts serves as a fallible indicator of the truth of a theory. Moreover, this increase of probability is higher the more surprising or novel the predicted statement e is (i.e. the smaller $P(e)$ is).

A similar but less general argument can be formulated with estimated verisimilitude ver. If e′ is a novel prediction derivable from theory g, not included in the old evidence e, then in many typical cases we have $ver(g/e\&e')>ver(g/e)$. For example, if the problem $B=\{h_1, h_2\}$ includes two alternative hypotheses, where $h_2=\sim h_1$, and if $h_1$ but not $h_2$ entails e′, then $ver(h_1/e\&e')>ver(h_1/e)$.

Another way of arguing for the same conclusion is the following. Assume that we choose information content as a truth-independent epistemic utility: $u(g,t)=u(g,f)=cont(g)$. Then, by (8), the expected utility is also

$$U(g/e)=P(g/e)cont(g)+P(\sim g/e)cont(g)=cont(g). \tag{23}$$

This leads to unsatisfactory results: (23) is maximized by choosing h to be a contradiction. Further, (23) would imply that more logical strength means always increasing cognitive success:

$$\text{If } g \vdash g', \text{ then } U(g/e)>U(g'/e). \tag{24}$$

For example, Newton's theory becomes better if we add to it the claim that the moon is made of cheese![21] The same problem arises if we replace cont with a measure for systematic power or problem-solving effectiveness,

---

[21] This is a problem also with some theories of truthlikeness, the 'naive definition' of Miller and Kuipers. See Niiniluoto (1987a; 1998a).

such as (6): if u(g, t)=u(g, f)=syst(g, e), then U(g/e)=syst(g, e), and the undesirable consequence (24) follows again. This appears to be fatal to Laudan's (1977) analysis of scientific progress, since it is not clear that the additional penalty for conceptual problems could save his measure from the trouble with (24).

In the light of this analysis, the real problem with Laudan's account is not his measure as such, but rather the idea that problem-solving effectiveness could be treated as a truth-independent criterion of success. What we should do with a measure like syst(g, e) is to treat it as a *truth-dependent* epistemic utility. This has been done already by Pietarinen (1970): if theory g is true, then by accepting it we gain all of its systematic power; but if g is false, by accepting g we lose the systematic power of the true alternative theory ~g. Thus, u(g, t)=syst(g, e) and u(g, f) =–syst(~g, e). This implies, by (6), that

$$U(g/e)=P(g/e)syst(g, e)–P(\sim g/e)syst(\sim g, e)=P(g/e)–P(g/\sim e) \quad (25)$$
$$=[P(g/e)–P(g)] / P(\sim e).$$

Maximizing this value of U(g/e) is equivalent to choosing that g which is best confirmed by evidence e (cf. (10)). Again we see that high expected systematic power serves as an indicator for the truth of a theory.

This vindication of the HD method at the same time gives partial justification to *abduction*, construed as *inference to the best explanation* (IBE).[22] In Peirce's original formulation, a theory g is found to explain a surprising fact e, and this gives a reason to think that theory g is true. In the weakest form, the conclusion only says that g is testworthy or a candidate for further testing. In a slightly stronger form, IBE is a way of finding indirect confirmation for a hypothesis. In the strongest form, the best explanation has high information content and high posterior probability, and by (10) it is the best confirmed and thus most acceptable theory. But a careful formulation would be needed if IBE is understood as an acceptance rule, since it is well known that high probability alone cannot be a sufficient condition of acceptance (cf. Levi 1967).

There is one way of avoiding these arguments: to claim that the prior probability P(g) of a genuine universal theory g must be zero. This assumption—shared by Carnap and Popper—is a very strong and highly questionable metaphysical supposition, since it gives the prior probability one (relative to empty evidence) to the factual claim that there are no true universal laws about the world (Niiniluoto and Tuomela 1973). In other

---

[22] Abduction is often understood to provide a logic of discovery, but Peirce himself considered its validity in terms of truth-frequencies. IBE, or abduction as a method of justification, is discussed by Laudan (1984a), Niiniluoto (1984), Thagard (1988), van Fraassen (1989), Lipton (1991; 1993), Psillos (1994a; 1996).

words, the confirming power of empirical success is blocked only by adopting dogmatically a scepticist position towards the possibility that a theory
even *might* be true.

Van Fraassen (1989) has also argued against IBE in defending his
constructive empiricism (cf. Section 5.1). As IBE is always restricted to a
set of historically given or formulated hypotheses, it may lead to 'the best
of a bad lot'. How could we know that the true hypothesis is among those
so far proposed? And as this set is in any case very large, its 'random
member' must be quite improbable. It has been pointed out that this criticism, if valid, would create serious troubles for van Fraassen's own 'constructive empiricism', since the assessment of the empirical adequacy of
rival theories also involves an inductive step from finite evidence (Psillos
1996). In the Bayesian framework these worries have a straightforward
answer: we always consider cognitive problems as sets B of mutually exclusive and jointly exhaustive hypotheses (cf. Section 3.5), where one of them
may be the 'catch-all hypothesis' (cf. Papineau 1996*a*: 10). In the simplest
case, this set contains only two elements, a hypothesis h and its negation
~h. So trivially one and only one element of this set B is true (see also
Lipton 1993).

Of course it may happen that no element of B is clearly superior to
others, but then suspension of judgement is the most rational conclusion.
To improve the situation, new evidence is needed, or alternatively the
problem set B has to be expanded by the introduction of new concepts
(cf. Niiniluoto 1987*a*). The extended cognitive problem then contains new
rival explanations which may be evaluated by IBE.

In some special cases, we may indeed have good reasons to think that
an interesting theoretical hypothesis has probability zero, since it is too
sharp (e.g. a point hypothesis about a real-valued parameter). However, if
hypothesis h has a $\varepsilon$-neighbourhood $U_\varepsilon(h)$ with a non-zero probability, and
the disjunction of the elements in $U_\varepsilon(h)$ entails evidence e, then an argument similar to (22) shows that $PAT_{1-\varepsilon}(h/e) > PAT_{1-\varepsilon}(h)$, i.e. e increases the
probable approximate truth of h.

It might also be the case that the cognitive problem B is based upon a
counterfactual idealizing assumption b, so that all the elements of B are
known to be false. Then no rational rule recommends us to accept the best
element of B as true. Instead, our target h\* is the 'least false' element of B,
i.e. the complete answer that would be true if b were true. Even if an idealized law or theory is not true, a scientific realist can nevertheless assert that
it may be highly truthlike (cf. Section 5.4). However, in that case, we cannot
expect a hypothesis in B to entail exactly any true empirical statement. But
still we may judge that $h_i$ seems to be more truthlike than $h_j$ if the empiri-

cal predictions of $h_i$ are closer to the observed evidence e than those of $h_j$, where the distance between two empirical statements is definable by some statistical measure of fit (e.g. $\chi^2$, LSD) (Niiniluoto 1986c).

So even in those cases where a hypothesis fails to have a finite probability, our measures allow us to make at least comparative appraisals of cognitive success in the realist sense.

The opponents of realism may still remain u1.impressed by our results, since they may suspect that their truth depends on some peculiar or artificial features of our measures. But this is unfair, since the general results (22) and (25) are valid for any probability measure P.

Van Fraassen (1989) argues further that the attempt to give an extra bonus to a hypothesis on the basis of its explanatory power would lead to an incoherent probability function (for criticism, see Kvanvig 1994). But this is not the correct Bayesian way of giving credit for explanatory success. For cases where the theory entails the evidence such 'plausibility' considerations (simplicity, systematic power, coherence with accepted background theories) are usually built into the prior probability $P(g)$ of g. But, if g docs not entail e, it may also happen that the explanatory success of g relative to e manifests itself in the rise of the posterior probability $P(g/e)$. Similar accounts of 'inductive simplicity' were mentioned in Section 6.3.

Measures like P, ver, and PAT indicate that there is an *upward path* from empirical success to the truthlikeness or approximate truth of a theory. It is clear that this path is *fallible*: there is no way of conclusively *proving* the truth or verisimilitude of scientific theories, and it would be unfair to require a scientific realist to accomplish or even attempt such a task.

Laudan's 1981 article 'The Confutation of Convergent Realism' (see Laudan 1984a) presented an important challenge to this realist thesis. With reference to Boyd (1973) and Putnam (1975), Laudan assumes that scientific realists should accept the following two principles:

If a theory is approximately true, it is empirically        (L1)
successful.

If a theory is empirically successful, then it is probably        (L2)
approximately true.

L1 says that there is a 'downward path' from approximate truth (alternatively: truthlikeness) to empirical success, while L2 expresses the converse 'upward path'. Laudan then points out that there are a plethora of theories in the history of science which were by our lights non-referring (e.g. ether, phlogiston, and caloric theories), but nevertheless enjoyed considerable empirical success. Assuming that non-referring theories cannot be approximately true, i.e.

> If a theory is approximately true, its central terms are          (L3)
> referring,

such theories are counter-examples to L2. Moreover, if a theory can be empirically successful without being approximately true, then the underlying idea of L1, namely that approximate truth is a good or even the best explanation of empirical success, becomes doubtful (cf. Section 6.5).

McAllister (1993) has recently suggested that phlogiston theory was not empirically successful, nor approximately true, which would block Laudan's attack on L2. However, his argument relies on a narrow notion of success as the proportion of true empirical consequences derivable from a theory. Certainly a theory can be highly successful if all of its (most informative) predictions are false but approximately correct.

It has been more usual to defend realism by rejecting the link L3: non-referring theories (e.g. ideal gas theory) can be approximately true (Hardin and Rosenberg 1982; Niiniluoto 1985c). Psillos (1994b) has recently shown in detail how the caloric theory of heat (supported by Lavoisier, Laplace, and Black) had a large amount of empirically confirmed content (e.g. laws of experimental calorimetry, law of adiabatic change, Carnot's theorems) which was preserved in the later theories of Clausius and Joule. Psillos suggests that this successful part of the theory was approximately true, but also independent of the referential failure of the caloric hypothesis (namely heat as a material substance consisting of fine particles). Thus, L1 and L2 seem to be saved by rejecting L3.

There is a gap in Psillos's argument: he moves from discussion of confirmation (indicators of truth) to a claim about approximate truth. But even if this gap can be filled by our concepts of AT and PAT, there still remains the problem that his claim concerns only those non-theoretical statements of the caloric theory which do not contain the theoretical term 'caloric'.

More generally, Kitcher (1993) points out that in the examples mentioned by Laudan the theoretical postulates were not really needed for the derivation of the successful empirical content of the theory. This observation shows clearly that L2 is a misleading simplification, and should be replaced by something like

> If a theory is empirically succesful, and its theoretical          (L2′)
> postulates are indispensable to the derivation of the
> empirical consequences, then the theory is probably
> approximately true (or probably truthlike).

Similarly, as we shall see in the next section, L1 is too simplified to hold generally.

A historical case giving plausibility to this thesis L2′ is Newton's theory of gravitation: its ability to unite Kepler's and Galileo's laws from different empirical domains and to provide a framework for the concretization of empirical regularities and rules of action (see the example of ballistics discussed in Section 5.3) gives support to its probable truthlikeness (cf. Niiniluoto 1994$d$). Another example could be the ideal gas theory: its concretization by van der Waals's law supports the thesis that this theory, when interpreted as referring to real gas, is approximately true. But it is even more interesting to illustrate the force of L2′ by phlogiston theory, since this allows us to employ the discussion of charitable theoretical reference in Section 5.2.

It can be argued that phlogiston theory had some empirical success which was derived from its theoretical postulates (see Niiniluoto 1984; 1985$c$). This theory made an improvement on earlier accounts of combustion by realizing that fire is not a substance (or element) but a process. By postulating the existence of a theoretical entity or kind F, it explained that some pieces of stuffs $A_i$ (i=1, . . . , n) burn (B) under certain conditions (C), and some other stuffs $D_j$ (j=1, . . . , m) do not burn in these conditions:

$$\forall i \forall x(A_i x \rightarrow Fx) \tag{T}$$
$$\& \forall j \forall x(D_j x \rightarrow \sim Fx)$$
$$\& \forall x(Cx \rightarrow (Fx \equiv Bx)).$$

T entails then

$$\forall i \forall x(A_i x \ \& \ Cx \rightarrow Bx) \tag{$\alpha$}$$
$$\forall j \forall x(D_j x \ \& \ Cx \rightarrow \sim Bx). \tag{$\beta$}$$

This derivation uses essentially the theoretical term F, but on the other hand it is independent of the interpretation of F. This means that the empirical statements ($\alpha$) and ($\beta$) are derivable from the Ramsey sentence $T^R$ of T (cf. Section 5.1).

But the next step of the phlogiston theory was radically false: it claimed that F indicates a material stuff that leaves a body in burning and calcination; the later oxygen theory of Lavoisier asserted that F refers to the ability of a body to absorb a gas, oxygen, which is united to a body under the process of burning. On this level the phlogiston theory turns out to have a low degree of truthlikeness as a whole—in spite of the relative success of its part T.

The principles DR3 and DR4 with a threshold requirement (cf. Section 5.2) allow us to define a charitable concept of reference which after all satisfies L3: if theory T gives a sufficiently truthlike description of some real entity, T does refer to it. However, this does not lead us back to

Laudan's confutation of realism, since the relevant examples now support the modified principle L2′: the empirical success of the predictions ($\alpha$) and ($\beta$) of the phlogiston theory supported the theoretical assumptions T; by our lights, this theory refers to oxygen (or to the ability to absorb oxygen) by DR3 and DR4. The phlogiston theory as a whole is not truthlike, and fails to be referring even by the charitable DR3 and DR4.

Another aspect of L2′ is illustrated by Ptolemy's astronomical theory.[23] As it was a remarkably successful theory, and it essentially used a system of epicycles to save the astronomical phenomena, L2′ suggests that the postulation of such epicycles was probably a truthlike hypothesis. Two comments are in order here. First, one might argue that epicycles as such were not really indispensable for the account of the data, but they became necessary only after Ptolemy's false assumption that the earth is the immovable centre of the system. Secondly, as long as no better theory had been proposed, it was indeed rational to regard Ptolemy's well-developed theory as the most truthlike of the existing astronomical theories—in particular, better than the isolated heliocentric hypothesis of Aristarcus (cf. Wachbroit 1986; Niiniluoto 1987b). Thirdly, it is important to emphasize once more that any rule like L2′ is fallible and may admit counter-examples—in the same way as a rule of induction may rationally assign a high epistemic probability to a generalization on the basis of repeated observational successes, but the generalization after all turns out to be false.

## 6.5  Explaining the success of science

Further reasons for preferring realism to instrumentalism and anti-realism become evident when we ask for an *explanation* of the success of science.[24]

It cannot be denied that science has been extremely successful on two practical levels. First, the method of science provides a rational way of resolving cognitive disputes about the nature of our universe. The relative success of science over other ways of forming belief systems (such as myths, religions, pseudo-sciences, etc.) can be explained by such epistemic virtues or ideals of science as its self-corrective methods of research, causal interaction with research objects, critical attitude, and public argumentation (Sections 1.2 and 4.4). This relative and historically progressive

---

[23] I am grateful to Professor Antonio Dieguez Lucena for raising this question.

[24] For discussion on this issue, see Smart (1963), Putnam (1978), van Fraassen (1980), Laudan (1984b), Boyd (1984; 1990), Tuomela (1985), Niiniluoto (1990a; 1990b), Brown (1994).

epistemic success of science over its rivals is either denied or left unexplained by those sceptics and relativists who fail to find *any* distinguishing features in the procedural rationality of science. It is over-explained by those dogmatists who falsely claim that science possesses an *infallible* method for finding certified truths. Our theories about science should leave room for both consensus and dissensus within the scientific community (cf. Laudan 1996).

Secondly, science has been practically successful also in the empirical and pragmatic senses: its theories have entailed successful predictions and have served as effective tools of human action. Theories postulating theoretical entities have yielded surprising novel predictions even in fields they were not designed to cover. Reliable predictions and rules about means and ends have enabled human beings to enhance their interaction with nature and to pursue their practical goals efficiently. Occasional losses and failures do not change this overall picture. This *empirical and pragmatic success* of science is a fact about which both instrumentalists and realists agree. But they will typically disagree on the best way of explaining this fact.

John Bernal (1969) wanted to use the practical success of science to explain its epistemic success: the 'continually renewed interconnection with industry' explains the 'progressive growth of science' (p. 1237). Even though laboratory practice is an important element in the critical testing of theories in natural science, Bernal's thesis is clearly exaggerated. There are progressive areas of science which, at least for a long time, develop independently of industrial applications. Therefore, the connection to industry generally fails to explain the existence of theoretical revisions and revolutions which arise within a scientific tradition.

A scientific realist turns the table around and wishes to explain the empirical and pragmatic success of science by its cognitive success. 'Realism is the only philosophy that does not make the success of science a miracle', as Putnam (1975) once put it. But here we have to be careful about the explanandum and the explanans, if we wish to reach 'the ultimate argument for scientific realism' (Musgrave 1988).

The explanation of success cannot concern all scientific theories at the same time—the realist is not committed to the claim that all scientific theories are true and empirically successful in the same way (cf. Kyburg 1983). Rather, the explanation concerns a typical theory T (say, Newton's mechanics): the explanandum is that T has been, and continues to be, successful in making both expected and surprising (novel) empirical predictions. If T were strictly true, the truth of all of its deductive consequences would immediately follow. But theoretical predictions are often at best approximately correct. Then the explanans cannot be the truth of T:

for example, Newton's highly successful theory is not true. Instead, the explanans should be taken to be the truthlikeness or approximate truth of T.

Levin (1984) suggests that 'the explanation of the success of a theory lies within the theory itself'. Indeed, the minimalist can avoid truth-talk by replacing

T is empirically successful, because T is true                              (26)

with

T is empirically successful, because T.                                     (27)

These principles are not in any way trivial. The success of the genetic theory is a consequence of the fact that genes exist. For some theories, (27) amounts to a probabilistic explanation (e.g. quantum mechanics gives a probabilistic explanation of the observable results of the two-slit experiment). Moreover, (27) fails for theories which accidentally work well (within some limited range of applications) without being true. For example, the success of a pseudo-scientific medical theory may require a psychological explanation.

Levin's elimination strategy does not work for

T is empirically successful, because T is truthlike.                         (28)

The success of Newton's theory in engineering applications results from its approximate truth (cf. Laymon 1982; Niiniluoto 1994d).

Rescher (1988) argues that the success of a theory is typically explained by another theory. For example, Einstein's theory explains why Newton's mechanics is successful under some conditions (for small velocities) and unsuccessful under other conditions. This is indeed a correct observation (cf. Section 5.3), but it is in no way in conflict with the schema (28): the truthlikeness of T means that there is a true theory T' which is close to T.

How does the 'downward path' from the truthlikeness of a theory to its empirical success work? As we know from classical logic, a true statement logically entails only true consequences. Hence, if a theory is true, all of its empirical predictions (if there are any) are true as well. The same principle holds for approximate truth, if we consider consequences derivable from one premiss on the same level of generality:[25]

---

[25] This additional condition is needed if generalizations and singular statements are compared to different targets (the true constituent vs. the true state description) (see Niiniluoto 1987a). Another warning about (29) is that it holds only when the conjunction of the premisses is approximately true. As Weston (1992) points out (see also Miller 1994), degrees of approximate truth are not generally preserved in *modus ponens*: let h be false

If theory T is approximately true, its deductive consequences are also approximately true.        (29)

(Cf. Fig. 11 in Ch. 3.) For truthlikeness, a similar condition does not hold, since deductive consequences of a truthlike theory may have low information content (i.e. high $\Delta_{sum}$-value). But the mixed principle (18) holds (again for the same level of generality): if a theory is truthlike, the degree of approximate truth of its deductive predictions has to be relatively high.

The situation is more complicated when theory T is a generalization and its predictions are singular. One difficulty is that there are quantitative laws, studied in non-linear systems theory and chaos theory, which are *unstable* in the sense that small differences in the antecedent conditions lead to great differences in the calculated predictions (see Ford 1983; Earman 1986). The errors of antecedent conditions are multiplied if T is a rapidly growing function (see Niiniluoto 1987a: 396). Hence, if the dynamic theory T is strictly true (but unstable) and the antecedent condition e is approximately true (but false), the deductive consequences of T&e may be very far from the truth.

On the other hand, for theories satisfying continuity or stability conditions, the approximate truth of the theory and the initial condition puts restrictions on the approximate truth of its consequences. No general results of the following form can be proved: if T is more truthlike than T′, all predictions from T are closer to the truth than those from T′.[26] But more precise results can be obtained in special cases, when the type of statements and the distance function $\Delta$ are fixed. For example, if $y=f_1(x)$ and $y=f_2(x)$ are two curves such that $f_1$ is uniformly closer to the true curve $f_*$ than $f_2$ in an interval I, then for *all* $a \in$ I the singular prediction $f_1(a)$ is closer to the truth $f_*(a)$ than prediction $f_2(a)$. But if $f_1$ is closer to the truth than $f_2$ by the Minkowskian metric $\Delta^p$ for small p (see (29) in Ch. 3), then the predictions from $f_1$ are closer to the truth than those from $f_2$ *on average*.

but approximately true, and let g be any statement, then h→g is true and therefore also approximately true; hence, g follows by *modus ponens* from two approximately true premisses, but there is no guarantee that it is approximately true. However, this is not a counterexample to (29), since here the conjunction of the premisses, namely h&(h→g), is equivalent to h&g, and this need not be approximately true.

[26] Kuipers (1992) gives detailed proofs of theorems of this sort. However, his comparative concept of truth approximation presupposes that one theory is uniformly better than another, and this guarantees a similar uniform relation between their empirical consequences. Kuipers also proposes methodological rules which are related to the 'upward path': theory T may be preferred to another theory T′ if T is more successful than T′ relative to the evidence so far. However, it is problematic that new evidence can never reverse this judgement (see Zwart 1998): for example, if new evidence falsifies T, theories T and T′ will be incomparable for Kuipers. My corresponding assessments are revisable: when ver(T/e)>ver(T′/e), it may still be the case that ver(T/e&e′)<ver(T′/e&e′).

The Tchebyscheff or supremum metric (i.e. $\Delta^p$ with p=∞) guarantees that the *maximum* predictive error from $f_1$ is smaller than that from $f_2$ (see Niiniluoto 1987*a*) (see Fig. 22).

Recent work on the concepts of truthlikeness and approximate truth can thus show in which precise sense, and to what extent, the assumption that a theory is 'close to truth' helps to explain the practical success of its observational predictions.

Boyd (1990) suggests further that realism should be able to explain 'the reliability of scientific methods'. Successful prediction is only a special case of such a task. In Section 6.2, we have seen that the general form of methodological rules in science is given by technical norms: if your goal is A, and you believe you are in situation B, then you ought to do X. Such rules may concern, for instance, observations by instruments, experimental design, statistical tests of hypotheses, concept and theory formation, and rules for theory revision. In the same way that truthlike theories may help to derive successful norms of this type in applied research (see Section 5.3), truthlike knowledge about the world (situation B) and about the causal regularities between action X and desired result

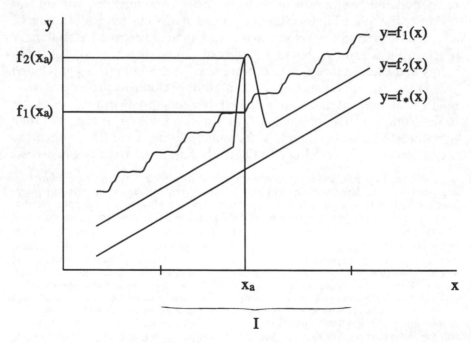

FIG. 22. Distances between curves

A in situation B helps to establish methodological norms and explain their reliability.

The 'ultimate' argument for scientific realism consists now of the claim that truthlikeness and approximate truth give *satisfactory* and *best* explanations of the success of science. This gives support, by inference to the best explanation, for thesis (R5) of Section 1.3. This argument is abductive, hence non-demonstrative, but gains strength from the fact that realism is not only the best, but also the *only* satisfactory explanation of the success of science.

This conclusion of scientific realism has been challenged by two different counter-arguments of philosophers with instrumentalist leanings. The first is the *pragmatist* strategy of denying that the concept of truth could be defined independently of practical success: the classical idea of truth as correspondence with reality should be replaced by the view that 'true' and 'useful' have the same meaning, i.e. truth is defined in terms of pragmatic success (see Section 4.6). This strategy leads, however, to the undesirable consequence that the pragmatist has *no* explanation for the practical success of science any more: the explanatory schemata

> Science is pragmatically successful, since its theories are sufficiently truthlike (30)

> Theory $T_1$ is pragmatically more successful than theory $T_2$, since $T_1$ is more truthlike than $T_2$ (31)

are transformed into trivial tautologies:

> Science is pragmatically successful, since its theories are pragmatically successful (32)

> Theory $T_1$ is pragmatically more successful than theory $T_2$, since $T_1$ is pragmatically more successful than $T_2$. (33)

This refutes Fine's (1986*a*) 'Metatheorem 1', alleging that an anti-realist has an equally good explanation for the success of science as a realist.[27]

The second strategy has been supported by methodological anti-realists like Bas van Fraassen (1980) and Larry Laudan (1984*b*), who retain the

---

[27] See Niiniluoto (1990*a*). In praising Fine, Davidson (1990) fails to note this problem. Similarly, Sober (1990), who claims that the realist's miracle argument is a weak abductive argument, fails to observe that the alternative empiricist argument 'a theory T is predictively successful, since T is empirically adequate' only gives a trivial self-explanation. (To avoid the triviality, the explanandum might be construed as the success of theory T in a particular type of application i and the explanans as the empirical adequacy of T relative to a class I of applications. Then the success of T in i is explained by the fact that i belongs to the class of the successful applications I of T. But this is almost trivial again, when compared to the realist's explanation of why T is successful in the whole class I of its applications.)

classical concept of truth even for theories, but find it altogether irrelevant in the analysis of scientific progress. They suggest that science *is* practically successful (in making true observational predictions, or in solving empirical problems), but this is not a fact in need of any explanation. Van Fraassen points out that it is no wonder our theories 'work', since we *choose* those theories which 'survive' in the 'fierce competition'. Laudan remarks that the problem-solving capacity of our theories, or their reliability in predicting nature and intervening in the natural order, needs no explanation in terms of their truth or truthlikeness, since we use testing procedures and strategies of experimental design which select more reliable theories than other techniques.

I find these excuses insufficient. Consider an analogy: why are our cars faster than cars fifty years ago? It is not sufficient to say that we buy faster cars now than earlier (cf. van Fraassen), or that we produce in our factories faster cars than earlier (cf. Laudan). Our explanatory question demands an account of the relatively permanent ability of a car to perform successfully in terms of its speed. We need to identify some property (such as the structure of its engine) which relates the behaviour of this artefact to its functioning in its natural environment.

Similarly, an explanation of the ability of a scientific theory to yield successful predictions, not only in cases it was originally designed or selected to handle but in novel and surprising types of cases as well, has to refer to some permanent property of the theory, which describes its relation to the world. Truthlikeness is the best—even the only—property I know that could serve this function. Hence, relative success in the pursuit of epistemic values is the best explanation for the practical success of science.

## 6.6  Rationality and progress in science

The concepts of 'rationality' and 'progress' are sometimes used as synonyms. However, it is appropriate to divorce these notions.

By using the terms of Section 6.2, we may say that *rationality* is a methodological concept. It concerns the way in which scientists in fact pursue their goals. Therefore, it is also historically relative: in assessing the rationality of the choices made by past scientists, we have to study the aims, standards, methods, alternative theories, and available evidence accepted within the scientific community, or within the relevant research programme, at that time (cf. Doppelt 1983; Laudan 1987*a*).

On the other hand, *cognitive progress* is a goal-relative concept which should be distinguished from neutral descriptive terms (change, development) and from methodological terms (rationality). Cognitive progress is an axiological concept: the step from A to B is progressive if B is an improvement on A, i.e. B is better than A relative to the ends or values of scientific enquiry (cf. Niiniluoto 1980; 1985c; 1995).

Progress, as a result-oriented or achievement word, should also be distinguished from process-oriented terms like quality or skill (i.e. competence in the performance of some task; how well something is done). There is no necessary connection between quality and progress, even though the high quality of research is a good probabilistic indicator of progress (cf. Niiniluoto 1987b).

As we noted in Section 6.4, scientists normally work within research programmes. In the Lakatosian picture, science is a competition of rival programmes, where the winners are decided by their rate of progress. However, the competition would not make much sense if each programme had complete freedom to define its own goals and standards of progress. This kind of value-relativity is one interpretation of Kuhn's incommensurability thesis (cf. Laudan 1984b), but Kuhn himself argued that there are desiderata of theory-choice common to all science (consistency, accuracy, scope, simplicity, and fruitfulness) (see Kuhn 1977: ch. 13). We have also claimed in Section 6.2 that axiological principles (linked with the notion of progress) are constitutive of science.

Hence, as Laudan (1987a) says, progress in science should be evaluated by 'our lights' or by 'our standards'. But here the agreement among present-day philosophers ends: they support different values of science—and, hence, different 'theories of scientific progress' (cf. Niiniluoto 1984). In the earlier sections, I have already observed the fundamental difference between the realist philosophers whose axiology includes truth (or some related 'veric' epistemic utility, such as truthlikeness) and those who deny the relevance of truth as a value in science.

Laudan (1977) formulated an *arationality assumption* which claims that 'the sociology of knowledge may step in to explain beliefs if and only if those beliefs cannot be explained in terms of their rational merits'. But, as Laudan (1984a) himself has convincingly shown, principles of rationality have changed in the course of the history of science. So *whose* theory of rationality should be used in the applications of the arationality principle?

Laudan's initial idea was to apply the best theory of rationality that *we* have. But, as Laudan acknowledged later, it is more natural to explain a person's belief by referring to his or her *own* conception of rationality:

a was in a situation s                                                     (34)
a thought that it is rational to believe in p in situation s
Hence, a believed in p.

This is a special case of a more general model of rational explanation (cf. Hempel 1965).

To apply this idea to science, let SC be the scientific community, $V_0$ the accepted standards of rationality or 'scientific values' in SC, and $e_0$ the available evidence for SC at time $t_0$. Further, let $U_V(T, e)$ be the *epistemic value* of theory T on evidence e relative to standards $V$.[28] Then a *rational explanation* of the preferences of SC at $t_0$ would look like the following:

SC preferred T over T' at $t_0$ because $U_{V_0}(T, e_0) > U_{V_0}(T', e_0)$.     (35)

It may happen that *our* current standards of rationality V would yield a different evaluation:

$U_V(T, e_0) < U_V(T', e_0)$.

Therefore, (35) allows what Doppelt (1983) has called 'moderate relativism of rationality'.

Schema (35) explains scientific preferences in terms of their 'rational merits'. Laudan's (1984a) reticulational model suggests that the acceptance of values V in SC could be explained by the theories and methods adopted in SC (cf. Section 6.2). But it seems to me that—in addition to this possibility—the choice of values may be justified in many other ways as well. Among them we may have reliance on metaphysical, epistemological, aesthetic, ethical, and social principles. A sociologist of knowledge may at least in some cases give a good explanation why values $V_0$ were accepted in a community at a given time (e.g. why Catholic astronomers tended to support instrumentalism) or why only evidence $e_0$ was available at $t_0$ (e.g. religious or ethical limitations on experimenting with human bodies). For reasons that will become clear in Section 9.1, I call this the Weak Programme of the sociology of science (see Niiniluoto 1991a).

The schema (35) could be applied also in those cases where a scientist's choices are determined by non-scientific values—such as personal profit, power, and glory. In that case, $U(T, e)$ would not be a measure of the epistemic value of T, but rather some other subjective or social utility. Even in these cases a preference may be instrumentally rational relative to the goals. But it is another question whether such action is compatible with the constitutive norms of science (cf. Section 8.4).

In spite of the moderate relativism of rationality, the concept of *cognitive progress* in science should be defined in a non-relative way by referring to *our* standards. What these standards are is the central issue

---

[28]  Cf., for example, formulas (7)–(10), (20), and (22).

debated within the philosophy of science (Niiniluoto 1984; 1985$c$; 1995).[29] For the empiricists, progress means more certified or well-confirmed observational statements; on the level of theories, this means more empirical success (cf. Section 6.1). The instrumentalists combine this with the ideas of simplicity, theoretical systematization of observations, and problem-solving ability of theories. For the scientific realists, progress means cognitively more successful, truthlike, and explanatory theories.[30]

It is important to stress here that a scientific realist need not claim that all actual steps of theory-change in science have been and will be progressive (cf. Niiniluoto 1984; 1987$a$). A realist wishes to give a truth-related criterion for making meaningful statements about progress, and this is quite compatible with the possibility that some steps in the development of science have been regressive. But a critical fallibilist differs from the sceptics in claiming that on the whole the methods of science have been able to promote progress in science (see thesis (R5) of Section 1.2 again).

My specific proposal here as a critical scientific realist is to use the concept of truthlikeness Tr to define an absolute concept of progress— and estimated verisimilitude ver to define an evidence-relative notion of estimated or evidential progress (Niiniluoto 1979; 1980).[31] Thus,

> The step from theory T to theory T' is *progressive* iff    (36)
> Tr(T, h\*)<Tr(T', h\*).

[29] Besides cognitive progress in the content of scientific knowledge, there are also other types of progress in science: pragmatic progress (i.e. more successful predictions and rules of action), institutional progress (i.e. the improvement of the working conditions of scientists and their social status), and progress in methods (i.e. improvement of scientific methods) (see Boyd 1984). Kitcher (1993) gives an interesting list of some dimensions of progress. The relations of scientific progress and social progress are discussed in Ch. 10.

[30] In Niiniluoto (1984), I distinguished realism about scientific theories and realist theories of scientific progress. Problem-solving approaches usually deny both of them (see Kuhn 1962; Laudan 1977; Rorty 1998), but I have suggested that the problem-solving capacity of a theory could also be measured realistically in terms of truthlikeness (see Section 5.1). It is conceivable that a theoretical realist would reject the idea that science is approaching closer to truth (cf. Worrall 1982; Watkins 1984). On the other hand, Duhem (1954) added to his instrumentalism a peculiar doctrine of approach to a 'natural classification', so that in a sense he advocated a realist view of progress.

[31] Kitcher's (1993) account of progressive changes of successive 'consensus practices' also appeals to the notion of verisimilitude, but he illustrates this notion only in two simple cases: generalizations (using the number of exceptions as the criterion) and singular quantitative statements (pp. 120–3). Kitcher is optimistic that his multidimensional notion of scientific practices helps to 'bypass' the 'artificial problems that have been at the focus of much logically ingenious work on verisimilitude'. I do not believe this is warranted. Even though closeness to truth is only one dimension of progress (or, for me, two combined dimensions), if it is taken seriously at all, there is no excuse for avoiding the hard work in this area. Aronson, Harré, and Way (1994) defend a realist theory of progress by their own explication of verisimilitude in terms of type-hierarchies.

The step from theory T to theory T' *seems progressive* on evidence e iff ver(T/e)<ver(T'/e).                    (37)

Progress in the sense (36) is relative to the target h* and the cognitive interests built into the definition of the min-sum-measure of truthlikeness. Thus, (36) presupposes that T and T' are regarded as rival answers to the same cognitive problem. It is possible that comparability is achieved by first translating T and T' to a common extended framework (cf. Section 5.2).

Estimated progress (37) instead involves epistemic considerations through the evidence e and the probability measure P used to define the function ver. I have earlier called it 'apparent' progress, in contrast to 'real' progress defined by (36), but this may be misleading, since it seems to imply subjectivity in a negative sense. The point is of course that we do not have direct access to truthlikeness relations involving Tr, but in general they have to be estimated by the available evidence, and such epistemic assessments of progress are fallible—just as all human knowledge claims are.

In brief, (36) states that we have made progress in approaching a target, i.e. in solving a cognitive problem, even if we do not know it. (37) states that we have evidential reason to think that progress has been made. In the spirit of the fallibilist definition of knowledge (see (2) in Ch. 4), these two notions could be united into a combined notion of cognitive progress, where both real and estimated progress takes place (cf. Cohen 1980; Barnes 1991; but see Miller 1994).

Simple special cases of (36) and (37) include the following. Unlike the models of expansion, revision, and contraction in the study of belief change (Gärdenfors 1988; Levi 1991), these results essentially involve the notions of truth and truthlikeness.

(*a*) *Learning from experience.* On the most rudimentary level, scientific progress does not yet involve theory-change, but takes place on the empirical level—by new observations, experiments, and phenomena.[32] My definitions cover cases of this sort as well. Suppose that we learn the truth of a non-tautological empirical statement e. Then our cognitive problem can be represented by $\{e, \sim e\}$, and the target h* is e. Our earlier 'theory' T is $e \lor \sim e$ (i.e. ignorance), and the new 'theory' T' is e. Then trivially (36) holds, since $Tr(e \lor \sim e, e) = 1 - \gamma' < Tr(e, e) = 1$, and (37) holds, since $ver(e \lor \sim e, e) = 1 - \gamma' < ver(e/e) = 1$.

(*b*) *Accumulation of truths.* Let $g \in D(B)$ be a partial non-complete true answer to problem B. Let $g' \in D(B)$ be another true answer, which is non-tautological, different from g, and not logically entailed by g. Then the step from g to g&g' is progressive. This follows from principle (35) in

---

[32] This aspect of scientific progress has been discussed by Kaiser (1993).

Chapter 3 that among true statements truthlikeness increases with logical strength. If g and g' are known with certainty on evidence e, i.e. a strong concept of knowledge with a certainty condition is assumed, so that $P(g/e)=1$ and $P(g'/e)=1$, then we have also $ver(g/e)<ver(g\&g'/e)$, i.e. the step from g to g&g' seems progressive on evidence e.

(c) *Gain in true information.* Let $g_0 \in D(B)$ be a tautology and $g \in D(B)$ a non-tautological truth which is not certain on evidence e. Then $P(g_0/e)$ $=1>P(g/e)$, but $Tr(g_0, h^*)<Tr(g, h^*)$. This illustrates the difference between the concepts of progress as increasing truthlikeness and progress as increasing certainty.

(d) *Closeness to the truth.* Let $g_0 \in D(B)$ be tautological, and let $h_i \in B$ be false. Hence, $P(g_0/e)=1>P(h_i/e)$. Here $Tr(g_0, h^*)=1-\gamma'$ is smaller than $Tr(h_i, h^*)$ if $\Delta_{*i}$ is small. Thus, the step from ignorance to a falsity which is sufficiently close to the truth counts as real progress. Here it is also possible that this conclusion is legitimized by estimated verisimilitude as well: we may have $ver(g_0/e)=1-\gamma'<ver(h_i/e)$.

(e) *Truth content.* By the truth content principle (37) of Chapter 3, a logical weakening of a false theory g improves truthlikeness if the weakening is made by adding the strongest truth $h^*$, i.e. the step from g to $g \vee h^*$ is progressive. If $h^*$ is sufficiently probable, this step is also estimated to be progressive.

(f) *Replacement.* Let $h_i$ be a false complete answer, and let $h_j$ be another complete answer which is closer to the truth than $h_i$. Then the replacement of $h_i$ by $h_j$ is progressive.

(g) *Conceptual enrichment.* Suppose that g is the complete true answer to the cognitive problem B with target $h^*$, i.e. $g=h^*$. Then g cannot be any further improved with respect to its truthlikeness relative to B. But if the language L for B is enriched by new concepts (not explicitly definable in terms of L), then a new extended problem B' in the enriched language L' is obtained, where $D(B) \subseteq D(B')$. Progress towards the new target $h'^*$, which is logically stronger than $h^*$, now becomes possible.

General results of this kind can be applied in two ways (cf. Niiniluoto 1985a). In retrospective applications, T and T' are theories that have actually been proposed and supported in the history of science (e.g. Newton's mechanics and Einstein's special relativity theory, Priestley's phlogiston theory, and Lavoisier's theory of oxygen). Then definition (36) shows that, as Popper (1972) argued against Kuhn (1962), it *makes sense* to speak about historical progress in science as approaching the truth.[33] But definition (37) also allows us to make *fallible appraisals* of such theory

---

[33] Popper took Kuhn's (1962) criticism perhaps too lightly in his rebuttal of the 'Myth of the Framework' (see Lakatos and Musgrave 1970), since we have seen that the explication of the concept of truthlikeness is relative to a cognitive problem involving a conceptual frame-

sequences relative to our current knowledge e (where e may include the best theories that we now possess). For example, the step from impetus theory to Galileo's mechanics can be evaluated relative to our current theories. Here truthlikeness is a tool of historical reconstruction.[34]

On the other hand, in prospective applications, e is our present knowledge situation, T and T' are alternative theories that we contemplate as rival solutions to a cognitive problem. In this case, verisimilitude—understood as the epistemic utility to be maximized in science—is a tool in epistemology.

While definitions (36) and (37) concern cases of theory-change, we may also define a concept of cognitive improvement which concerns the status of a theory when evidence is increased:

> New evidence e' (added to old evidence e) *cognitively*        (38)
> *improves* theory T if and only if ver(T/e)<ver(T/e&e').

(See Hilpinen 1980.) Here we see again the difference between real and estimated progress. It may happen that e' confirms and cognitively improves a false theory T in the sense of (38), so that P(T/e)<P(T/e&e') and ver(T/e)<ver(T/e&e'), but nevertheless replacing our present theory with the false T would not be really progressive in terms of Tr.

An interesting variant of (38) covers the *correction of presuppositions*. Suppose that the cognitive problem B is defined relative to a presupposition b, but later work indicates that b is false.[35] Then we may revise B into a new cognitive problem B' with another, more realistic presupposition b'. Then some bad answers in D(B) may turn out to be good in D(B').

---

work. Still in his last papers, where he insists that science produces 'knowledge of nature', Kuhn repeats that he denies 'all meaning to claims that successive scientific beliefs become more and more probable or better and better approximations to the truth' (Kuhn 1993: 330). As a consequence of incommensurability, he argues, Aristotelian propositions about force and motion cannot be expressed even in an enriched Newtonian vocabulary. I agree that, if this is the case, we should not try to make wholesale comparisons between Aristotle's and Newton's physics, but rather look for partial translations between them (cf. Section 5.2) and compare their consequences for specific applications. Kuhn himself admits that Aristotle made statements, e.g. about the movements of a projectile after it leaves the mover's hand, which 'we can make in a Newtonian vocabulary and can then criticize' (ibid. 340). Analysis of scientific change in terms of increasing truthlikeness should focus on examples of such paths of local and piecemeal progress.

[34]  As historical case studies of truthlikeness, Hettema and Kuipers (1995) discuss theories of atoms (Rutherford, Bohr, Sommerfeld), and Kieseppä (1996) Galileo's mechanics.

[35]  For example, b might state that the atomic weight of an element is a unique natural number, while b' corrects this assumption by introducing the concept of isotype. For presuppositions of questions, see Kleiner (1993).

# 7

# Internal Realism

Hilary Putnam, famed for his vigorous defence of scientific realism, dramatically announced in 1976 his conversion to 'internal realism', which he contrasted with 'metaphysical realism'. Putnam's new position, which has stimulated an extraordinarily lively discussion, belongs to the tradition of Kantianism in its denial that the world has a 'ready-made' structure, and to pragmatism in its linkage between truth and the epistemic concepts of verification and acceptance (Putnam 1981). It also has interesting relations to Nelson Goodman's ideas about 'worldmaking', and to Thomas Kuhn's claims about theory-relative 'worlds'.

Putnam's restless search has already led him to 'repent' much of what he said in relation to the 'unhappy label' of internal realism (see Putnam 1994). Still, for the project of critical scientific realism, I think it is useful and instructive to consider these issues in detail.

I shall argue in this chapter that a reasonable realist should accept neither metaphysical nor internal realism in Putnam's sense. Semantical realism is compatible with ontological pluralism: the non-epistemic correspondence theory of truth can be combined with the idea that objects can be individuated and identified in alternative ways through different conceptual systems.

## 7.1 Ways of worldmaking

Traditional religions taught that in the beginning of time the world was created by God. According to some myths, like Plato's *Timaeus*, it was not the highest of the gods, but only his assistant, a demiurge, who was ordered to do the hard work of making the world. Philosophers like Spinoza, whose God exists in nature, not as a supernatural deity, still made a distinction between *natura naturans* (creative nature) and *natura naturata* (created nature), human beings belonging to the side of the creatures. In Hegel's idealism, nature is nothing but the alienated form of objective spirit.

Philosophical naturalism, which accepts the thesis of ontological realism (cf. Ch. 2), regards material nature (or Popper's World 1) as the original lawlike reality. It has existed eternally, or come to its present phase of development in a momentary event (like the Big Bang of modern cosmology), but has not been created by any supernatural force or agent.[1] Plants, animals, and human beings have been 'created' or 'emerged' from this nature by biological and cultural evolution.

Both of these doctrines, divine creationism and evolutionary naturalism, fail to pay sufficient attention to human activity: the human agents are not only passive products and spectators of the reality outside them, but also industrious participants in the processes within the world.

Marxism and pragmatism are two philosophical schools that have given emphasis to human material praxis: man is a tool-making animal who is in causal interaction with his environment through hands, instruments, and sense organs.[2] This conscious and planned interaction brings about intended and unintended effects in nature—in this sense human beings transform or 're-create' the world. This interaction is also the critical element in the development of human cognition, since it makes possible the transmission of information about reality to the human mind (Section 4.4). In science, more or less passive observation is supplemented by the experimental method, where the enquirer actively manipulates nature and thereby poses questions for nature to answer.[3]

With Hegelian influence, praxis philosophy has often been in dire straits over idealism. Western Marxism, especially the Frankfurt school and the so-called practical materialists, took inspiration from Marx's youthful writings and Georg Lukács's equation of alienation and reification, and ended up with the thesis that nature in itself, independent of human interaction, is an empty category.[4] Pragmatism, especially James's pluralist 'radical empiricism' and Schiller's 'humanism', took the world—or worlds in plural—to be a malleable product of individual human actions.[5]

An ontological realist insists that World 1 is ontologically (but not causally) mind-independent: even if we can interact with it and transform it through our actions, we are not the creators of nature. A reasonable non-reductionist realist also admits that there is the special ontological

---

[1] Modern cosmologists argue that time began with the Big Bang, so that it is not meaningful to ask what happened before it.

[2] Benjamin Franklin's definition of man as a 'tool-making animal' was quoted by Karl Marx in *Capital*. For praxis philosophy, see Bernstein (1971).

[3] For the experimental method, see Hacking (1983). The metaphor of putting questions to nature was used earlier by Bacon and Kant. For the applications of 'erotetic logic' to the philosophy of science, see Hintikka (1988b) and Kleiner (1993).

[4] See Marx (1975), Lukács (1971), Markovic (1968), and Schmidt (1971). Cf. Chalmers (1976).

[5] Pihlström (1996) gives a survey of the problem of ontology within classical and neo-pragmatism.

domain of material artefacts and human-made abstractions, i.e. the Popperian World 3. As it is a product of human activity, we may say, if we will, that 'we' have 'created' it. But even this way of speaking may be too voluntaristic, since the existence of culture and society in some form is always a precondition of human activity: the function of our individual and social actions is to reproduce, transform, modify, and extend this reality (Bhaskar 1979).

Ontological subjective idealism takes the idea of human activity too seriously and too literally: the human mind becomes the creator of the whole world. Kant criticized 'the mystical and visionary idealism' of Bishop Berkeley (Kant 1950: 41). His 'transcendental idealism' instead started an important project of studying how our mental structures and acts influence the contents of our beliefs and cognition, i.e. 'the sensuous representation of things'. But to interpret this epistemological function as a process where a special 'world' of phenomena or things-for-us is 'constituted' (as Kant himself did in the standard interpretation) is misleading (cf. Section 4.3): *epistemic* terms like 'perception', 'belief system', 'knowledge', 'representation', and 'world picture' should not be replaced by *ontological* terms like 'world', 'nature', and 'reality'. The human construction of *knowledge* should not be confused with the construction of the *reality*.

This distinction can be illustrated by the concept of *Umwelt*, suggested by the German biologist Jakob von Uexüll. All non-living material things and living animals exist as parts of the same physical environment. But each species has also its specific environment: those aspects of objective nature it is attentive to through its senses and interested in by virtue of its basic needs. The natural human *Umwelt* does not contain all the sounds, smells, and tastes that are central (i.e. accessible and vitally important) to ants, bats, and dogs (cf. Nagel 1986). In this sense, *Umwelt* is a species-relative part of objective nature.

However, for von Uexüll, this concept had also a subjective element. As soon as we proceed to discuss the contents of perceptions, beliefs, knowledge, expectations, etc. of some cognitive agent X, we are giving an epistemic account of the-world-as-conceived-by-X or the-nature-as-it-appears-to-X (cf. Drummond 1990). In traditional scholastic terms, this *world-for-X* has 'intentional inexistence' in the mind or consciousness of X. As a part of the Popperian World 2, facts about the propositional attitudes of X are partly a reflection of objective nature, but also partly a 'creation' of X, since its features depend on the way X perceives the sensory stimulus and how X's brain produces an image of the world. In this respect, human beings have an inborn tendency to see their *Umwelt* as consisting of rigid objects, bodies, or things. The world-for-X is not only how the reality is seen-as by X, but also how it is believed to be by X. In this sense, the 'world' of our ancestors 'contained' fairies, brownies, angels, and evil spirits, which have disappeared from our enlightened and secularized 'world'.

After the 'linguistic turn', many traditional philosophical doctrines about mind-dependence were reformulated in terms of language-dependence. Subjective idealism gave way to *linguistic* or *conceptual idealism* which denies the existence of reality ontologically independent of linguistic or conceptual frameworks. In this view, the world is 'a text' or 'a textual construction'. If interpreted literally (which certainly is not the only possible interpretation here), linguistic idealism is advocated by radical versions of Saussurean semiology, poststructuralism, postmodernism, and deconstructionism. 'There is nothing outside of texts', is the famous slogan of Jacques Derrida.[6]

The tendency towards linguistic idealism arises from the conviction that the world is responsive to our linguistic ways of describing it. Peter Strawson (1950) formulated this view by arguing that 'facts are what statements (when true) state; they are not what statements are about'.[7] Thomas Kuhn (1962) is famous for the claim that in some sense the world changes with theories: after a paradigm shift the scientists 'live in different worlds' (pp. 111, 193). Putnam's (1981) internal realism claims that objects are relative to theories or constituted by linguistic frameworks.

Similar claims are often made in connection with perception. Many empiricists have claimed that we do not see external objects but only 'sense data'. N. R. Hanson (1958) argued that when Ptolemian and Copernican astronomers look at a sunset they 'see different things'. However, it is quite compatible with direct perceptual realism that all seeing is seeing as, and all perceptions are laden with concepts and theories (Section 4.5). The relevant formula is 'A sees b as c' or 'A sees b as an F', where 'c' and 'F' occur within the scope of the epistemic seeing operator, but b occurs outside it (cf. Hintikka 1975; Niiniluoto 1982). Excluding cases of hallucination, b refers to an element of the external world (i.e. World 1). The perceptual awareness (that this is c, or that this is an F) is a mental state of the perceiver, and thus belongs to World 2. Seeing b as an F does not presuppose that A correctly identifies b or any of its properties, or that he even knows that he is looking at b. But the fact that these conditions hold

---

[6]  For discussion, see Rorty (1982) and Norris (1996). According to Dillon (1995), Derrida denies mind-independent reality. But Derrida's polemics against the 'transcendental signified' might involve only the rejection of Platonic concepts or meanings.

[7]  Strawson's view is discussed and criticized by Searle (1995).

sufficiently often in normal circumstances makes perception a reliable source of information about the mind-independent world.

According to Rescher's formulation of conceptual idealism, what is mind-dependent is 'not reality itself (whatever that might be), but reality-as-we-picture-it' (Rescher 1982). This thesis as such may seem trivially true (the world-for-X depends on X), but nevertheless it is a highly interesting task to study *how* our mind constitutes the world-for-us. Edmund Husserl's phenomenology, Rudolf Carnap's phenomenalistic *Aufbau* (1967), and Ernst Cassirer's (1965) neo-Kantian account of the structuring of the perceptual world can be understood as different answers to this how-question. In his later work, Husserl emphasized the intersubjective and cultural nature of our common *Lebenswelt* or 'life-world' (Husserl 1970); this way of speaking is continued in the phrase 'the social construction of reality' (Berger and Luckmann 1971). Martin Heidegger's notion of the world also belongs to this Kantian and phenomenological tradition: the human *Dasein* is always a 'being-in-the-world', and the world is always already projected and reflected through human concepts and practices.[8]

Thus, for many philosophers the terms 'world' and 'reality' refer to something that belongs to Worlds 2 and 3.[9] Some of them, at least occasionally for some purposes, put the objective world 'in brackets'. As long as they and we know what they are talking about, there is no harm in this way of speaking from a realist's viewpoint. The realist will be alerted only when the existence of a mind-independent world is denied, when the figments of our imagination or superstition are claimed to be 'real', or when support is sought for scepticist or instrumentalist conclusions.

A deliberate blurring of the distinction emphasized above takes place in Nelson Goodman's neo-pragmatist monograph *Ways of Worldmaking* (1978).[10] With his characteristic style and subtlety, Goodman describes how 'multiple actual worlds' (not possible worlds as alternatives to the actual one) are 'made' by such operations as composition and decomposition, weighting, ordering, deletion and supplementation, and deformation. It is clear that these operations of worldmaking include material activities (e.g.

[8] Heidegger's conception of truth as *aletheia*, as the direct openness or uncovering of the world, can be interpreted as a form of anti-representationalism. The same view is developed in his theory of art (see Kusch 1989). For discussions of Heidegger's problematic relations to realism and naturalism, see Dreyfus and Hall (1992).

[9] When Ludwig Fleck (1979) talks about the 'genesis' and 'development' of scientific 'facts', he is really speaking about the socially accepted beliefs of the scientists. When Shapin (1994) writes about the 'social history of truth', he makes it explicit that here his concept of 'truth' does not go beyond accepted beliefs.

[10] For discussions of Goodman, see Scheffler (1980), Siegel (1987), Putnam (1990), Devitt (1991), Harris (1992), and McCormick (1996).

painting tables) besides conceptual and epistemic activities. The 'worlds' may contain material artefacts produced by artists, things represented by works of art and scientific theories, perceptions organized by our concepts and interests, beliefs about items and kinds, etc.

Certainly the human world is full of extraordinarily fascinating artefacts, concepts, beliefs, and theories. All of them are handled—some even created—in various ways by human activities. But why speak of 'worlds' in this connection? Goodman sometimes talks of 'world-versions' instead of 'worlds'. This is reasonable, but it makes his theses less exciting or less radical than they first appear: the actual human-made World 3 surely contains multiple irreconcilable constructions by means of 'the symbol systems of the sciences, philosophy, the arts, perception, and everyday discourse'. And the claim that we can have 'no world without words or other symbols' (ibid. 6) is almost a triviality, if it speaks about world-versions.

There is thus an interpretation of Goodman which makes sense to a realist: he is speaking about World 2 and World 3, and need not take any standpoint toward World 1. Even the question whether all versions are 'of one and the same neutral and underlying world' (ibid. 20), and whether they in some sense 'conflict' with each other (ibid., p. x), does not make much sense in this context. But, as a pluralist and relativist, Goodman is not satisfied with this alternative. He wants to replace the objective notion of truth with the relative concept of 'rightness'. Further, he insists that there is no world 'in itself'. When Scheffler (1980) pressed Goodman to clarify whether stars are of our making, the answer was an emphatic yes: 'We have to make what we find, be it Great Dipper, Sirius, food, fuel, or stereo system' (Goodman 1984: 36). (See also McCormick 1996.)

The critics of Goodman have wondered whether his 'irrealism' is coherent at all, and whether it should be understood literally or metaphorically. Goodman himself has insisted that he should be understood literally (see Goodman 1984: 42). Thus, he clearly wishes to make the radical claim that the project of worldmaking goes all the way from artefacts to what the realist takes to be objective, non-relative physical reality. So is he simply confusing Worlds 1 and 3?

To answer this question, we have to ask whether it is possible to defend the view that the whole of reality, even the physical world, is in some sense made by us—without collapsing to idealism. Perhaps the most interesting attempt in this direction comes from Putnam's internal realism: 'the mind and the world jointly make the mind and the world.'[11] This view is

---

[11] A surprisingly similar statement can be found in the forgotten pragmatist F. C. S. Schiller: 'And I can see no reason why the view that reality exhibits a rigid nature unaffected by our treatment should be deemed theoretically more justifiable than its converse, that it

discussed in the next two sections. I think it fails in its aim, but still a rational reconstruction can be given to some of its intended elements.

## 7.2 Putnam on internal realism

Putnam announced his rejection of metaphysical realism in his presidential address to the American Philosophical Association in 1976 (see Putnam 1978). He emphasized then that, according to internal realism, realism should be understood as an empirical theory which explains the success of science (cf. Section 6.5). But this aspect of his view has gradually faded away at the same time as the influence of Dummett's anti-realism and classical pragmatism has strengthened.

Perhaps Putnam's clearest formulation of the metaphysical–internal distinction is given in *Reason, Truth and History* (1981: 49). The 'externalist perspective' (or 'God's Eye point of view') of *metaphysical realism* (MR) includes three theses:

> The world consists of some fixed totality of mind-       (MR1)
> independent objects.
>
> There is exactly one true and complete description of 'the       (MR2)
> way the world is'.
>
> Truth involves some sort of correspondence relation
> between words and external things or sets of things.       (MR3)

On the other hand, *internal realism* (IR) accepts the denials of MR1, MR2, and MR3:

> What objects does the world consist of? is a question that       (IR1)
> it only makes sense to ask within a theory or description.
>
> There is more than one 'true' description of the world.       (IR2)
>
> Truth is some sort of idealized rational acceptability.       (IR3)

There is a literal sense in which IR1 is trivially true. If we ask how many tables there are in this room, anyone accepts that the answer depends on our definition of 'table'. Similarly, if we formulate the question in IR1, the answer depends on the definition of 'object' (Hilpinen 1996). Do we count

is utterly plastic to our every demand—a travesty of Pragmatism which has attained much popularity with its critics. The actual situation is of course a case of interaction, a process of cognition in which the "subject" and the "object" determine each other, and both "we" and "reality" are involved, and we might add, *evolved*' (see Schiller 1912: 11). See also Putnam (1978; 1983b; 1987; 1990; 1994). Pihlström's (1996) dissertation is a careful and well-informed analysis of the possibility of 'pragmatic realism' in the Putnamian spirit.

tables, legs (and other parts) of tables, molecules, and protons among objects? Putnam's (1987) own favourite example compares the Carnapian world (with three individuals) and the Polish logicians' worlds (with the seven mereological sums formed from three individuals). These two descriptions are easily seen to be intertranslatable (cf. Quine 1969). So this example simply makes a point about our variable ways of using the concept of 'object'—but not more. It does not yet succeed in saying anything about the ontological plurality of the world.

As both MR and IR are intended to be versions of realism, the most natural reading of them excludes subjective idealism and thus presupposes the existence of a mind-independent world (cf. principle OR in Ch. 2). MR1 says that this world has a 'fixed' o. unique structure. It thus combines ontological realism and ontological monism. IR1 instead attempts to formulate the view of *ontological pluralism*: the world is mind-independent, but it has several structures relative to acceptable 'descriptions' or 'theories'.

In 'Why there isn't a ready-made world' (Putnam 1983*b*), Putnam reformulated IR1 precisely to this form:

> The world is not ready-made; its structure is relative to     (IR1′)
> conceptual frameworks.

This thesis is non-trivial. It denies that the world has any built-in structure, and claims the structure of the world is created through conceptual activities, variously called 'conceptualization', 'reification', 'articulation', 'organization', or 'structuring'. In other words, the world is carved or sliced into pieces (objects, properties, essences, facts, causal relations, etc.) only relative to descriptions, theories, or conceptual schemes.[12] In Raimo Tuomela's (1985) Sellarsian terms, IR1′ denies the ontological Myth of the Given.

While MR2 assumes that the whole truth about everything is uniquely determined, IR2 asserts the plurality of truths.

According to Putnam (1978), the existence of a fixed correspondence between words and mind-independent things would imply that

> Truth is a radically non-epistemic notion.                    (MR3′)

Instead, IR3 claims that an epistemically 'ideal' theory could not be false.[13] Truth is equated with acceptability or verifiability under ideal conditions.

---

[12] Putnam later criticized this cookie cutter metaphor, since it seems to involve the idea of a world without any properties. Cf. below, however. Some of Putnam's (1983*b*) remarks suggest that he is only opposing essentialism.

[13] Putnam's model-theoretic argument attempted to prove that the ideal theory cannot be false. One of the problems of this argument is the assumption that the world is simply a collection of individuals on which one can impose any structure. For criticism, see Niiniluoto (1987*a*: 142–3).

This appeal to ideal conditions, rather than to verification here and now, is an important weapon in Putnam's (1981) criticism of cultural relativism.

Putnam clearly thought that the MR-theses and the IR-theses go together in natural 'packages'. It is of course possible to find, with some variations, more or less articulated formulations of MR. Classical examples include many traditional metaphysical systems, Russell's logical atomism, and Wittgenstein's *Tractatus* (before its closing aphorisms), where the world, as the totality of facts, is pictured by the language. An 'absolute' conception of reality is defended by Williams (1985) and a 'view from nowhere' by Nagel (1986). Different formulations of IR are given by Putnam (1981), Rescher (1982), and Tuomela (1985).

However, it seems equally clear to me that theses MR1, MR2, and MR3 (and thereby their negations IR1, IR2, and IR3) are logically independent of each other. Therefore, they allow us to define, besides the 'pure' doctrines MR and IR, six other 'mixed' positions.[14]

One of these mixed views combines ontological realism with an epistemic theory of truth. For example, the version of 'internal realism' defended by Brian Ellis (1988) accepts an epistemic notion of truth (IR3), and the existence of various 'epistemic perspectives' (IR2), but at least starts from the assumption that the world has a categorial ontological structure (MR1).

Before studying some of these mixed views, let us note that Putnam's dichotomy allows a realist to advocate either the correspondence theory of truth (MR3) or the pragmatist theory of epistemic truth (IR3). It may be debated whether the redundancy theory (or disquotational theory) is sufficient for someone who wishes to be called a 'realist'; Putnam (1990) himself, in advocating a substantial notion of truth, disagrees on this issue with Horwich (1990) (and so do I, see Section 3.4; cf. also Putnam 1994). But at least the nominalist Hartry Field (1982), who takes space-time points as the ultimate individuals, suggests that a metaphysical realist could combine MR1 with the redundancy theory.

Kuhn (1991) in turn combines something like the internalist theses IR1 and IR2 with the redundancy theory. When Kuhn states that a conceptual scheme is not a 'set of beliefs'—and that sharing such a scheme involves a common structure, not its embodiment in the head of an individual— I think he can be interpreted as denying that truth is an epistemic concept in the sense of IR3. Still, Kuhn rejects the correspondence theory. This

---

[14] I have defended one of these mixed positions in Niiniluoto (1980; 1984; 1987a; 1996a). See also Field (1982), Aune (1986; 1987), Wolterstorff (1987), Brown (1988), Boyd (1989), Newton-Smith (1989), Devitt (1991), and Searle (1995). Cf. the discussion in Pihlström (1996).

means that Kuhn's position cannot be classified as MR or IR (see below, however).

Field (1982) has argued that MR1 does not imply MR2, which 'should not be taken as a component of any sane version of realism'. Putnam's reply appeals to the following point: if by MR1 the world consists of a fixed set I of individuals and a set P of their properties and relations (and nothing else), then there is an ideal language L which speaks of I and P. Such a language L need not be denumerable. But the set $Tr_L$ of true sentences of L, which is well defined by MR3, is then the set of all truths, as MR2 requires. Another way of formulating this argument is to say that, by MR1, the world is (or can be represented by) a set-theoretical structure W=(I, P). If L is a language which gives a complete description of W, then $Tr_L$ is the theory of W (in the model-theoretical sense), i.e. Th(W)={h in L|W⊨h}.

This debate seems to conflate different senses of 'exist' and 'language'. Field is right that *we* need not actually have a unique complete language L, even if MR1 holds. If the structure W=(I, P) is infinitely complex (e.g. I contains all past, present, and future individuals, P contains predicates and n-place relations for all finite n, higher-level relations between lower-level relations), then L would be an infinitary language which need not be finitely definable at all. Further, the set of truths $Tr_L$ in L may fail to be finitely or even recursively axiomatizable. Moreover, the world W of the metaphysical realist might include, besides individuals and relations, laws and potencies as well. Infinitary languages describing such a complex world may 'exist' as set-theoretical entities, but the situation is different, if language is supposed to be something that a human brain or mind is able to process. To say with Putnam's argument that such an ideal language 'exists' is indeed a very strong idealization. It would be more plausible to say that the infinitely complex world is inexhaustible in the sense that each *human* language L covers only a fragment of it (cf. Niiniluoto 1980; 1984: ch. 5).[15]

We have formulated in Section 2.4 a special form of metaphysical realism, which takes tropes or property-instances to be the ultimate elements of reality. This tropic realism does not imply a unique language for describing the world. Putnam's argument for deriving MR2 from MR1 does not hold

---

[15] Grim (1991) has recently argued, by using diagonalization methods of set theory, that $Tr_L$ for a given language L does not constitute a *set*. This is not quite conclusive, since the argument appeals to set-theoretical or metalinguistic truths about $Tr_L$ which need not be included in L. Moreover, there are versions of set theory which admit a universal set (i.e. the set of all sets), and they could include $Tr_L$ as a set. But at least Grim's claim adds a further obstacle to the derivation of MR2 from MR1.

here: the predicates of the ideal language do not refer to tropes, but rather to properties that are human-made classes of similar tropes, and therefore the language can always be chosen in alternative ways.

MR2 is indeed a very strong principle, since it may be taken to entail MR1: if there is a unique truth about everything, this description should also contain some privileged way of speaking about 'objects', so that it will also tell in a unique way which objects there are in the world.

But who then would be willing to accept the strong thesis MR2? Somewhat surprisingly, one answer appears to be Wilfrid Sellars (1968), whose scientific realism starts from a criticism of the Myth of the Given (i.e. rejection of MR1 in favour of IR1') and concludes with the equation of truth as assertability relative to the ideal 'Peirceish' conceptual system.

This observation indicates that MR2 should be divided into two different theses. The first says that we already possess, a priori as it were, an ideal language for describing reality:

> There is an a priori privileged language for describing the      (MR2')
> world.

This claim is denied by Tuomela's (1985) rejection of the 'linguistic Myth of the Given'. But another version of MR2 says that such a language will be found a posteriori when science approaches its 'Peirceish' limit:

> There is an a posteriori privileged ideal language for      (MR2")
> describing the world.

In Sellarsian realism, with its *scientia mensura* principle, the scientific community reaches in the asymptotic limit the ultimate 'God's Eye perspective', and truth is defined as assertability relative to this perspective. This means that Sellars combines the theses IR1', MR2", and IR3.[16]

More generally, the combination of MR2 and IR3 is typical to most versions of epistemic, pragmatist, or coherence theories of truth: a sentence is true if and only if it follows from, or coheres with, the set of all true beliefs (cf. Section 4.6). These theories presuppose the existence of an ideal belief state which contains all truths about the world. If MR2 fails, then these epistemic theories of truth collapse.

Putnam (1990) has clarified his earlier discussion of truth as ideal acceptability (IR3) by emphasizing that the ideal state does not simultaneously concern any truth whatsoever—there is no single state of justification that would entail all truths. This is important for Putnam, for otherwise IR3 would conflict with his IR2. Putnam also says that the ideal

---

[16] For Sellars, see Rosenberg (1980), Pitt (1981), and Tuomela (1985).

knowledge situation is an idealization like frictionless planes, but it can be approximated in actual situations.

Peter Unger (1975) has claimed that our understanding of truth assumes that a sentence is true if and only if it expresses the whole truth about everything or else is a part of the whole truth. As the concept of the whole truth about the world is inconsistent (i.e. Unger rejects MR2), Unger concludes that truth is impossible.

Unger's argument fails, however, to shake such theories of truth as do not rely on the fiction of the whole truth about everything. Such accounts are given by non-epistemic notions of truth, in particular by the correspondence theory, which defines truth as a relation between a statement and the world, not between a statement and the set of true beliefs.[17]

We have seen in Section 3.4 that Tarski's definition does not presuppose MR2, since it makes truth relative to a language L. The same holds of the concept of truthlikeness (Section 3.5). If the theses MRI' or MR2" were correct, we could of course uniquely define the degrees of truthlikeness relative to the ideal conceptual framework, but this is not an assumption that is needed for the notion of verisimilitude (cf. Niiniluoto 1980; 1987a). The choice of the relevant language is one of the contextual factors which determines the cognitive problem and its target. Conceptual frameworks are selected on the basis of our cognitive and practical purposes, and they can always be improved and made descriptively more complete. Realism with truthlikeness can survive without the assumption MR2" which might be said to express the Myth of the Taken.

As we saw in Section 4.6, Putnam (1994) has recently acknowledged, against Dummett, the possibility of recognition-transcendent truths, so that he must give up IR3 in its original form. Putnam is not favouring the correspondence theory, either, but rather moving to the 'Wittgensteinian' view that there is no definition of truth in the strict sense (Putnam 1995: 11; see also Davidson 1996).

Putnam (1994) has also expressed doubts about the whole distinction between metaphysical and internal realism. IR was construed above as consisting of the negations of the MR-theses, relative to the assumption OR of ontological realism. The claim was that IR is true and MR false. This presupposes that both of them (and OR) are meaningful statements.[18] But if

---

[17] Kusch (1991b) has presented Unger's thesis as an argument against critical scientific realism. It is a two-edged sword, however, since Unger also claims that beliefs and emotions do not exist—and thereby would destroy most programmes within philosophy and sociology of science (cf. Ch. 9).

[18] Popper's demarcation criterion is not symmetric with respect to negation: universal generalizations are falsifiable, but their negations (existential statements) are not. Current forms of verificationism are usually symmetric, since they speak about coming to know the truth value of a proposition. On this criterion, MR is meaningful if and only if IR is.

one accepts a modern version of the verificationist theory of meaning, one might rather assert that the problem with MR is not its *falsity* but its *incoherence*: it is a picture which 'fails to make sense'. But then likewise IR, as the negation of MR relative to OR, is meaningless (cf. Putnam 1987; 1990).

This line of thought is illustrated by the fact that the formulations of MR and IR refer to 'the world'. When IR1′ states that 'the world is not ready-made', the famous cookie cutter metaphor is implied: the world is like a cake which we can cut into pieces in different ways by our concepts. This means that objects and properties do not exist objectively, but only relative to human-made conceptual systems. However, the result is a difficult meta-physical position, since the world 'out there' before our conceptual activities appears to be without objects, properties, or any structure at all—indeed, a kind of 'noumenal jam' (cf. Tuomela 1985). As a pure abstraction, without any features or determinations, it seems to be the same as Hegel's *nothingness* or a neo-Kantian *Grenzbegriff*. In Rorty's (1982) words, it is a 'world well lost'. If the mind-independent existence of this world is denied, the position collapses to subjective or linguistic idealism. If we attempt to claim that the world contains mind-independent individuals (cf. Tuomela 1985), the position reduces to a nominalistic version of metaphysical realism. Thus, it may seem that the best way out of this impasse is to announce that the talk about this world is meaningless, i.e. to be a strong rather than weak anti-realist about the world (cf. Section 2.2). In particular, one should give up the sharp line between properties 'discovered' in the world and properties 'projected' onto the world (Putnam 1987), so that likewise the distinction between Worlds 1, 2, and 3 is without ground.

Difficulties with the concept of the world can be seen also in the problem of finding a satisfactory interpretation of Kuhn's later work. Kuhn (1990) has remarked that Putnam's internal realism has 'significant parallels' to his own view. Recent discussion of Kuhn has suggested two alternatives for understanding the nature of the world. Hoyningen-Huene (1993) interprets Kuhn as accepting a Kantian distinction between the stable world-in-itself and variable phenomenal worlds. In contrast to Kant, there is a plurality of phenomenal worlds, introduced by the 'taxonomies' created by new 'lexicons'. But, in harmony with Kant, there is perceptual and referential access only to the phenomenal worlds, so that paradigm changes in science induce changes on the level of world-for-us. If this 'Darwinian Kantianism' (or 'Whorfian Neo-Kantianism', as Irzik and Grünberg (1998) call it) is the correct interpretation of Kuhn, he fails—like Kant and later Kantians—to make sense of the world-in-itself.

Ian Hacking (1993) suggests that Kuhn is a nominalist: THE WORLD consists of individuals, and lexical categories introduce classes of individuals. When language changes, the world of individuals remains stable, but the world of kinds of individuals changes. This alternative leads us back to the strange picture of the world consisting of individuals which are not yet of any kind. It also fails to explain why we apply a concept to some individuals and not to others (cf. Section 2.4).

Putnam's (1981) own formulation of internal realism has been called 'transcendental nominalism' (Hacking 1983), since it takes objects to be human-made constructions by means of conceptual frameworks. Such objects are accessible to us, as they are of our own making. But, as we have seen, this view is also laden with the traditional difficulties of the Kantian position.

In spite of these difficulties, I think that the real world can be regained. In the next section, I defend the claim that there is a reasonable version of realism which is neither 'metaphysical' nor 'internal' in Putnam's sense. It avoids the problematic thesis MR2 by combining the correspondence theory of truth (MR3) with the pluralist principle IR2 and with a refined version of IR1 which accepts a minimal ontological realism but does not imply 'conceptual idealism'.

## 7.3 World-versions and identified objects

In her criticism of Putnam's internal realism and Goodman's irrealism, Susan Haack (1996a) points out that these views are shifting up and back between a momentous tautology ('you can't describe the world without describing it') and a seductive contradiction ('incompatible descriptions of the world can both be true').

Indeed, it is a trivial tautology that our descriptions of the world are always relative to languages. This does not imply that the reality itself is relative to language. In the following, I try to express this common-sense argument in a more detailed and illuminating way.

A scientific realist accepts the minimal ontological assumption that there is an actual world (Popperian World 1) independent of human minds, concepts, beliefs, and interests. Let us call it THE WORLD. If you wish, this assumption may be called 'metaphysical'. But it can be defended by transcendental and a posteriori arguments (Section 2.5). All the evidence of common sense and science assures us that THE WORLD does exist now and existed long before the emergence of humankind on earth. Human beings are evolutionary products of THE WORLD, and they have learned to interact with this reality and to transform it according to their needs. They have also invented languages for communication and representation, and are able to describe THE WORLD in various conceptual frameworks (Section 3.1).

Should we refrain from saying anything about THE WORLD, apart from its existence? If we try to describe THE WORLD at all, it is not the pre-categorized independent reality any more (cf. Pihlström 1996). The answer to this horror of metaphysics is, in my view, simply that THE WORLD does not change in any way when we give descriptions of it. (At most some new physical entities, like tokens of sounds and letters, are added as documents of these descriptions.) This is the crux of its mind-independence. In the same way, when I describe (or test hypotheses about) how the planets revolve around the sun, or how the atomic nucleus is constituted by elementary particles and forces between them, the solar system and the atom do not change. When we baptize a newly born baby, the child obtains a new cultural property (the proper name by which she will be known in the community), but as a physical object she does not change (or, in other words, a mere Cambridge change occurs; cf. Section 2.5). More generally, when we 'structure' THE WORLD by our concepts, it is not THE WORLD that changes, but rather our *world view*. For these reasons, I do not think it is at all incoherent to speak about the mind-independent WORLD. And we can even have fallible rational beliefs about the features of this WORLD through science.

Against Kant (and later linguistic idealists), we have good scientific reasons to believe that THE WORLD has a physical spatio-temporal structure and obeys natural causal laws (cf. Section 2.4). Thus, the mind-independent WORLD is a *lawlike flux of causal processes*. Pihlström (1996: 134) suggests that this thesis implies at least a moderate version of MR1. Whether this is the case depends on the intended meaning of MR1. My formulation does not speak about mind-independent individuals, and it is not quite clear whether 'object' in MR1 is meant to cover such entities as processes and laws. Brown (1994) gives a metaphysical realist treatment of laws as the elements of reality, but I do not take real dispositions and potencies to be Platonic entities, nor claim that the composition of the world is exhausted by its laws.

For a realist who rejects anti-realism about the past there must also be a legitimate sense of saying that electrons, planets, stones, trees, and dinosaurs existed before human beings invented languages or conceptual schemes. The suspicion that this is philosophically problematic arises easily from the following fallacy: the equivalence

$$x \text{ exists at } t \text{ iff the sentence '}x \text{ exists' is true at } t \qquad (1)$$

implies that the left side is false at those moments of time $t$ when a concept or a sentence referring to $x$ does not yet exist. But the correct form of (1) is x exists at t iff the sentence 'x exists at t' is true.                    (2)

The metalinguistic sentence on the right side is temporally indefinite, and if it is true now it is true at any time. Even if the sentence 'Dinosaurs exist' was not yet invented at $t_0$=100 million BC, it is nevertheless counterfactually true that 'Dinosaurs exist' would have been a true sentence at $t_0$, if someone had formulated it at $t_0$.[19] In any case, as it is true now that 'Dinosaurs existed at $t_0$', by (2) dinosaurs existed at 100 million BC—at a time when no human beings and languages existed.

Internal realism, in the form which claims that objects are relative to conceptual schemes, runs into troubles with this issue. Certainly no one wants to assert that we now *causally* produce entities existing in the past. A charitable interpretation suggests that objects are human constructions only in a 'metaphorical' sense (Wolterstorff 1987), but then it remains a mystery what Putnam would literally mean. Sometimes it is assured that an internal realist can accept all the same counterfactuals about the past as the metaphysical realists, or that the statement 'Dinosaurs existed at $t_0$' is true in the 'world-version' legitimized by science. But the realist's claim is not only that the statement about dinosaurs belongs to our current scientific theory, but that it is a claim about dinosaurs in the past. If this claim is true, how could the existence of past objects be in some 'conceptual' sense dependent on our present activities?

It is essential to this realist view that THE WORLD has contained and contains 'full' or 'thick' *objects with all of their mind-independent features*, not only ghostly bare particulars of the nominalists. Dinosaurs did have such properties and parts as weight, length, colour, bones, skin, legs, and eyes.

There are many alternative ontological theories about the nature of such objects as constituents of THE WORLD. As we saw, there is a danger that a strong version of MR1 (e.g. a theory of transcendent or immanent universals) would lead to the unacceptable MR2. In this respect, a theory of tropes (or perhaps a combined substance and trope theory, as mentioned in Section 2.4) seems more attractive.

As events can be taken to be tropes as well, tropic realism fits the idea of world flux. If tropes, or spatio-temporally located property-instances, are understood as the ultimate 'elements' of reality, this amounts to a form of metaphysical realism in the sense of MR1. But, on the other hand, tropic realism allows that physical objects (as mereological sums of tropes) and properties (as classes of similar tropes) can be formed in different ways. Thus, various kinds of 'ontologies' (in the normal sense of the world) can

---

[19] This problem worries Crispin Wright (1993).

be built up from tropes. Further, physical objects have characters that are distinctly mind-independent, but it is not assumed that some of these traits are their 'essential' properties. In this sense, tropic realism is compatible with ontological pluralism. What is more, no privileged language is assumed, i.e. MR2' and MR2" are denied.

But can we also make sense of the thesis IR1'? A natural answer to this question is obtained if we distinguish existence and identification from each other.[20] It is clear that dinosaurs were *identified* as dinosaurs, i.e. as a special kind of physical object or organism, only through a human language. To individuate something as a particular, it has to be distinguished from other things; to identify a particular as a dinosaur, at least some of its characters or properties have to be described. These identifications involve human activities (thinking, perceiving, using language, etc.), as Rescher (1982) convincingly argues. Rescher further asserts that to be *identifiable* is mind-involving as well, since the realm of possibility is mind-dependent, but this is less convincing. If an object x has *some* mind-involving relative properties (e.g. x can be identified, seen, thought, etc., by human beings), x itself may nevertheless exist in a mind-independent way. The possibility of the identification of a physical thing, like a dinosaur or a chair, is indeed based on its mind-independent features (location in space and time, causal continuity, qualities).[21]

We may thus make a distinction between *UFOs* ('unidentified flying objects') and *IFOs* ('identified flying objects'). THE WORLD contains UFOs, which are not our constructions, or produced by us in any causal sense. But these UFOs are not 'self-identifying objects' in the bad metaphysical sense feared by Putnam: they are potentially identifiable by us, as extended elements or 'chunks' of the world flux, by means of continuity, similarity, and mind-independent qualities. IFOs, on the other hand, are in a sense human-made constructions, objects under a description, and hence exist only relative to conceptual schemes. Dinosaurs existed as UFOs at 100 million BC, but the related IFOs exist only after the invention of the concept 'dinosaur'.

One might question whether there is any reason to speak about the existence of IFOs at all. Perhaps we should acknowledge only ordinary objects, UFOs, in our ontology? (Cf. Musgrave 1989.) However, as IFOs are

[20] I defended this view first in my paper for the 1992 congress on realism in Beijing (see Niiniluoto 1996a). The present account is somewhat different. The same position is argued forcefully in Wolterstorff (1987). See also the 'modest realism' in Brown (1988).

[21] Hintikka and Hintikka (1989) argue that objects are typically individuated by means of criteria appealing to spatio-temporal continuity. (For another, perspectival, method of individuation, see Hintikka 1975.) Objects are identified as certain kinds by means of their physical properties.

public human constructions, in our framework they can be counted as World 3 entities.

Again it may seem that we are compelled to accept metaphysical realism in the sense of MR1. But the distinction between UFOs and IFOs leaves open the concept of an *object*. Dinosaurs may be 'objects', but so may dinosaur heads and nails, mereological sums of animal heads, clouds of dust, and molecules. The question about the number of objects in this room, or in the whole world, certainly depends on how we wish to define an 'object'. Nature itself does not define it, and the 'totality' of all objects is not 'fixed'.[22] MR1 in its literal sense is not implied. Moreover, our freedom to choose conceptual frameworks suggests also that IR1′ holds in the sense that there are many alternative structures in the world.

Hence, even if we reject conceptual idealism ('all objects are IFOs'), our realism is compatible with a version of IR1: THE WORLD does not contain self-identifying individuals, but can be categorized into objects in several alternative, overlapping ways relative to conceptual schemes. For example, depending on the choice of a suitable conceptual framework, THE WORLD can be 'sliced' or 'structured' to a system of momentary events, mass points, physical systems, etc.

The distinction between UFOs and IFOs may seem to resemble Kant's *Dinge an sich* and *Dinge für uns*, in the two-world account (cf. Section 4.4), but there is a crucial difference in interpretation. A UFO is not an unknowable noumenon: it is not inaccessible but rather inexhaustible, something that can be described and identified in an unlimited number of ways. An IFO is not a phenomenal veil which hides a UFO from us, and it is not the content of our knowledge about the reality. Rather, it is a part of THE WORLD as described relative to a conceptual framework, and, after we have introduced the relevant language, it is up to the reality to 'decide' what kinds of IFOs there are.

Here it is natural to use the cookie cutter metaphor, after all: a UFO is a mereological part of THE WORLD, and an IFO is the UFO as a conceptually created 'slice'. A cake can be sliced into pieces in a potentially infinite number of ways, and the resulting slices are human constructions made out of the parts of the cake. It is important to see that a UFO corresponding to an IFO is not defined negatively, as a propertyless bare particular, i.e. as nothing, but rather it is a complex entity, and the IFO as it were gives a partial description of it (i.e. of those of its properties expressible in the

[22] See Hilpinen (1996). We have already noted above in Section 7.2 that Putnam's (1987) much discussed example of a world with three physical objects (for Carnap) and seven objects, their mereological sums (for Polish logicians), fails to establish anything about the metaphysical status of objects.

L is *true in THE WORLD* if it is true in $W_L$. In other words, for any L, truth about world-version $W_L$ is truth about THE WORLD as well.

In this way we have combined semantical realism (MR3) with a pluralistic view of language (IR2) and ontology (IR1'): our conception of truth is clearly a version of the correspondence theory, but it is not metaphysically suspect in the sense feared by the internal realists.

Putnam (1994) has recently stated that he repents some of his statements about internal realism. Against (some trends in) James and Goodman, he now asserts that the world is not a product of our minds, but it is 'as it is independently of the interests of the describers'. He also argues that we are not starmakers: objects should not be said to be relative to language. I think this is a significant change in Putnam's thinking. His conclusions agree with our position developed in this section. But we have also tried to show in which way it makes sense to speak about objects (IFOs) and facts ($W_L$s) that are relative to conceptual frameworks. This gives a possibility of interpreting Goodman and Kuhn without giving any support to their relativism. But this is not our only notion of object or fact. Our mixed position between metaphysical and internal realism attempts to make sense even of distinctions (external vs. internal, independence vs. dependence of minds and schemes) that Putnam still regards as unintelligible 'metaphysical phantasies'.

chosen language L). In this sense, the existence and the properties of IFOs depend on the reality, and knowledge about IFOs gives us truthlike information about the UFOs.

The distinction between UFOs and IFOs generates a corresponding distinction between THE WORLD and linguistically relative *world-versions*. Every interpreted language or conceptual system L whose terms have a meaning through social conventions (Section 3.1) 'picks out' or determines a structure $W_L$, consisting of objects, properties, and relations, and exhibiting THE WORLD as it appears relative to the expressive power of L. The elements of the domain of $W_L$ are thus IFOs identified relative to L. For example, if language L contains the predicates 'human being', 'man', 'woman', and 'parent', the structure $W_L$ consists of human beings classified by their sex and by their family relations. If the terms 'man' and 'woman' are defined in some different way, another language L' and another structure $W_{L'}$ are obtained.[23]

Such structures $W_L$ are *fragments* or 'versions' of THE WORLD.[24] This view can be regarded as a formulation of the internalist principle IR1', since it allows reality to be structured in many ways. It also denies the sort of metaphysical realism MR2'' which assumes the existence of an ideal 'Peirceish' language L such that THE WORLD=$W_L$ (see Niiniluoto 1980; 1987a).

It is important to emphasize that the concept of $W_L$ is not epistemic: if a community shares the lexicon (to use Kuhn's phrase) or language L, $W_L$ is not what they *believe* about the world, or what they can warrantedly assert about the world, but rather *the way the world is* relative to L (to use Goodman's phrase). In other words, if a member of this community has false beliefs (expressible in L), then his 'life-world' differs from $W_L$.

---

[23] This is an important theme in contemporary debates on sex and gender. The male–female distinction may be based, for instance, on sexual organs, chromosomes, or behavioural patterns. Each such definition creates its own structure $W_L$. In this sense, it is correct to say that nature itself does not dictate how male and female should be defined, so that the choice is a cultural affair. On the other hand, when a definition is specified, it is an objective matter of fact which individuals belong to males and which to females (or, perhaps, outside these classes).

[24] If our theory T in language L contains idealizational assumptions (e.g. assumes the existence of frictionless planes), then structure $W_L$ plays the role of the 'real system' and the interpretation of T the role of 'models' in Fig. 20 of Ch. 5. If L contains idealized concepts that only make sense relative to idealizational assumptions I, so that I is taken to be the set of the meaning postulates of L, an alternative way of understanding $W_L$ would be the following: $W_L$ is what the real system would be if I were true (cf. Section 3.5 for cognitive problems relative to false presuppositions). Then the statement that $W_L$ is a 'fragment' of THE WORLD needs a qualification: $W_L$ is 'close' to the real system, and the distance or likeness depends on the strength of the counterfactual assumptions I. In this case, truth about $W_L$ is at best truthlike about THE WORLD.

This account of course allows that persons sharing the same language L can have different beliefs or 'life-worlds' about the structure $W_L$.

The world-versions thus give us a natural interpretation of Goodman's thesis that there is no unique way the world is, but rather the number of these ways equals the number of essentially different linguistic frameworks. However, this account does not lead to relativism, since all structures $W_L$ are fragments of the same WORLD—and therefore *cannot be incompatible* with each other.

It can also be suggested that the world-versions $W_L$ could be explications of Kuhn's notion of a 'world with a taxonomy'. In this case he is not a relativistic Kantian (Hoyningen-Huene) or a nominalist (Hacking), but a critical realist. This interpretation would also make his view compatible with the correspondence theory of truth.[25]

I have earlier suggested that THE WORLD consists of 'potential facts' which become 'actual' in the structures $W_L$ when we impose some concepts upon mind-independent reality (Niiniluoto 1987a: 177). This way of talking is perhaps not very attractive. The point is to illustrate the idea that, as soon as we choose a language L, it is THE WORLD itself which chooses the structure $W_L$. It may be more natural to say that THE WORLD contains *unidentified facts*, while $W_L$ contains *identified facts*. This corresponds to Searle's (1995) view—against Strawson (1950)—that a fact is just anything in virtue of which some statement is true in the correspondence sense (without denying, with Searle, that facts are also complex objects with an internal composition).

It might be objected that my suggestion leads back to unacceptable metaphysics. Martin Kusch (1991b) has argued that my WORLD is something like Schopenhauer's *das Ding an sich*, a blind will: how can THE WORLD, which does not have any inherent or unique categorial structure, 'choose' the structure $W_L$?

The metaphorical talk about 'choices' can be understood here as easily as in decision theory and game-theoretical semantics (cf. Hintikka 1996): in the game of exploring reality, the choice of the language L is my first move, and it is followed by 'Nature's choice' of the structure $W_L$. The game continues with my attempt to study the secrets of $W_L$. And all true information about $W_L$, namely about a fragment of THE WORLD, also tells us something about THE WORLD.

One of Putnam's motivations for his internal realism was the assumption

---

[25]  In his last papers, Kuhn (1993) says that puzzle-solving produces knowledge of nature, but still the objective of research cannot be characterized as 'match with external reality' (pp. 330, 338). To repeat my point, Kuhn fails to see here that truth about $W_L$ is also truth about THE WORLD.

---

that we have no way of referring to mind-independent objects. As a solution in the Kantian spirit, he suggested that reference becomes possible if the objects are of our own making through conceptual frameworks. It is of course correct that reference is always established by a linguistic description—and, as Putnam (1981) points out, this holds even of causal theories of reference, since causal relations are also described in language. In this sense, it might seem that we can refer only intralinguistically to IFOs. But, following Peirce, we may distinguish the immediate and the dynamic object of a referring expression: the former is the object-as-it-is-described by the referring expression, the latter the object as such independent of descriptions (see Section 3.1). In the theories of reference formulated in Section 5.2, it is real objects as UFOs that satisfy the relevant descriptions.[26] Hence, by referring in language L to IFOs relative to L we also refer to the corresponding UFOs. This account makes no assumption about a unique and 'magical' relation of reference, or about Platonic correspondences (cf. Putnam 1983b: p. xiii), since language–world relations as results of interpretations are human constructions (see Section 3.1).

A similar conclusion applies to the concept of truth. Truth is relative to interpreted languages, but again there is no unique way of fixing such interpretations. As each $W_L$ is a structure for language L, we can directly apply Tarski's model-theoretical definition of truth for sentences of L (cf. Section 3.4). For each L, we can define the class of truths in L:

$$Tr_L = Th(W_L).$$

This agrees with IR2, and does not imply the problematic MR2, since the union of all classes $Tr_L$ over 'all possible languages' L (whatever that might mean) is not well defined.

Putnam's main objection to the correspondence theory of truth is that we do not have any concept-free access to reality.[27] If THE WORLD were simply a noumenal jam, it would not make much sense to say that some statement is true about it, since there would be nothing to be represented, or nothing that would make the statement true. However, our account shows that the Tarskian semantic definition relates sentences (of some language L) to world-versions relative to L. But, as $W_L$ is uniquely determined by L and THE WORLD, this approach also allows us to define an objective notion of truth about mind-independent reality: a sentence h in

---

[26]  Such satisfaction may be only approximate or truthlike. Cf. n. 24.
[27]  Cf. Putnam (1981; 1983b), Tuomela (1985; 1990), and Wolterstorff (1987). Määttänen (1991) developes and defends the idea that we can be in a preconceptual contact with reality through our actions. This is an important aspect of the 'sub-symbolic' connectionist models of human mind.

# 8

# Relativism

The relations of relativism and realism are problematic, since both doctrines exist in several variations, and some philosophers would deny both doctrines (Section 8.1). In this chapter, I defend a moderate 'constructivist' form of moral relativism against moral realism (Section 8.2), and similarly consider the prospects of moderate cognitive relativism (Section 8.3). I conclude that a slide from relativism about justification to stronger forms of relativism about truth and reality is unwarranted, and should be rejected by a reasonable realist. The implications for debates on the feminist philosophy of science are also discussed (Section 8.4).

## 8.1  Varieties of relativism

Relativism is in fact a bundle of different doctrines. Their interrelations depend on philosophical background assumptions. Some forms of relativism may be right, some wrong.[1]

The two main types of relativism are (in a broad sense) *cognitive* and *moral*. Here is a classified list of some 'cognitive' categories which might be taken to be 'relative' in some respect:

*ontological*
- objects
- facts
- world
- reality

*semantical*
- truth
- reference
- meaning

---

[1] For good discussions of relativism, see Meiland and Krausz (1982), Hollis and Lukes (1982), Bernstein (1983), Margolis (1986; 1991), Haack (1987), Siegel (1987), Laudan (1990*b*; 1996), and Norris (1996). See also Niiniluoto (1991*a*; 1991*c*).

*epistemological*
- perception
- belief
- justification
- knowledge

*methodological*
- inference
- rationality
- progress.

A corresponding list of 'moral' categories may include at least

- customs
- values
- ethics
- law
- politics
- religion.

On the other hand, there is a great variety of factors which some category might be taken to be *relative to*:

- persons
- groups
- cultures
- environments
- languages
- conceptual frameworks
- theories
- paradigms
- points of view
- forms of life
- gender
- social class
- social practices
- social interests
- values.

Relativity to individual persons has been called 'subjectivism' and 'protagoreanism' (Margolis 1986); this is the usual interpretation of the *homo mensura* doctrine of Protagoras: 'man is the measure of all things' (Schiller 1912). Relativity to cultures is 'cultural relativism'; relativity to languages or conceptual/theoretical frameworks is usually called 'conceptual relativism', 'framework relativism' (Elkana 1978), or 'incommensurabilism'; relativity to viewpoints is 'perspectivism'; relativity to gender is 'gender relativism'; and relativity to social factors is 'class relativism' or 'social relativism'.

If a relativist thesis claims that 'x is relative to y', we have proposed twenty choices for x and fifteen for y. Without any attempt at being complete in our classification, we have thus found already 20×15=300 types of relativism. Many of them are familiar: reality and truth are relative to persons (Schiller's 'humanism'), truth is relative to historically conditional points of view (Nietzsche's 'perspectivism'), objects and facts are relative to languages (Putnam's 'internal realism'), perceptions are relative to theories ('theory-ladenness of observations'), meanings are relative to conceptual frameworks ('meaning variance'), beliefs are relative to gender (feminist standpoint theories), ethics is relative to social class (Marxism), values and rationality are relative to cultures, etc.

Depending on philosophical assumptions, there are also systematic interconnections between different relativist theses. For example, if a point of view is defined by a class position or by the possession of a conceptual system, perspectivism becomes identical with class relativism or framework relativism, respectively. If it is assumed that women have a language characteristically different from the male language (cf. Spender 1982; Harding and Hintikka 1983), then linguistic relativism entails gender relativism.

It is also clear that some variants of relativism exclude each other. For example, Protagoreanism, which claims that each individual person has his or her subjective beliefs or values, is incompatible with class and gender relativisms.

We may also distinguish *local* and *global* forms of relativism. The former restricts its claim to a specific category X, while the latter generalizes this claim to all categories. For example, global subjectivism asserts that everything is relative to individual persons, but local subjectivism may be restricted, e.g. to morality only.

## 8.2 *Moral relativism*

Let us start our discussion in the domain of morality, where I think a plausible defence of a modest form of relativism can be given (Niiniluoto 1991c; 1992c). This provides a useful contrast to cases where I am inclined to reject relativism. It also allows us to sharpen our notion of relativism.

Human beings have supported, at different times and places, various customs, moral codes, legal orders, political systems, and religious doctrines. Such a diversity and variation is a basic *fact* about human culture and social life. In particular, it was the fact of the *relativity of morality* that enlightened the pioneers of social anthropology, such as Edward Westermarck, who started to study 'the origin and development of moral ideas' (see Stroup 1982).

The relativity or diversity of morality is thus a fact that is open to empirical investigation—from both historical and contemporary perspectives. It is also the task of science to give an *explanation* of this fact. Such explanations usually have the form of statistical arguments, which link the moral views M supported by a person, group, or culture A with some conditions C about the needs, interests, character, family background, education, or social position of A (see Brandt 1959: chs. 5–6). The diversity of moral ideas is thus explained by variations of biological, psychological, or social factors.[2]

If relativity is a fact which can be socially explained, are we thereby committed to *moral relativism*?[3] It is important to understand why the answer to this question is no.

Despite the relativity of moral views, a *moral realist* may still claim that moral values exist in some objective (human-independent) sense. According to Brink (1989: 7), moral realism is the view that 'there are moral facts and true moral claims whose existence and nature is independent of our beliefs about what is right and wrong'. A Platonist version of realism locates values in the transcendent realm of ideas. For G. E. Moore (1929), goodness is a real but non-natural property of human acts or persons. 'Naturalist' realists in ethics reduce morality to some natural properties definable in descriptive (physical or mental) vocabulary (see Boyd 1988; Brink 1989). It would follow from such versions of realism that absolute moral judgements of the form

$a$ is good                                                                                        (1)
$a$ is right
$a$ is holy

have truth values (when $a$ is some object, act, or state of affairs) (cf. Sayre-McCord 1988). Thus, if two systems of moral views contradict each other, both of them cannot be correct.

Moral realism (especially its metaphysical and religious versions) is often combined with epistemic absolutism, which claims that one of the

---

[2] This determination need not imply social determinism: a tendency of condition C to bring about views M leaves room for personal judgements, arguments, and decisons. In spite of powerful mechanisms of education, enculturation, and indoctrination, a socially embodied tradition is not always reproduced and accepted, but sometimes given up individually and collectively.

[3] For discussion of moral relativism, see Brandt (1959), Mackie (1977), Harman (1977), Williams (1985), and Sayre-McCord (1988).

moral systems can be known to be true, and the others are known to be mistaken. But, to account for the fact of ethical diversity, a moral realist may also be a fallibilist about moral knowledge (cf. Boyd 1988), who thinks that the choice of the right moral ideas always remains uncertain and thus some of us may be mistaken in these matters (cf. Mackie 1977: 36).

A particularly interesting form of absolutism accepts that all moral views are socially determined, but claims that one of the perspectives is the right one. The strategy of some Marxist philosophers to overcome ethical relativity was to urge that the morality of the 'most progressive class' (i.e. the working class) is the right one, since it is in the direction of the presumed objective laws of history (see Redlow *et al.* 1971). This view may be regarded as a secular version of the religious doctrine that an act is good if it works in the direction of God's will.

The relativity of morality is thus compatible with absolutist and fallibilist versions of moral realism. Hence, if one wishes to defend relativism, it is not sufficient to appeal to the fact of moral diversity within human cultures. Relativism is not a factual claim about the historical evolution and diffusion of moral views, but a philosophical thesis about their truth and justification.

More generally, as a philosophical doctrine, the relativist thesis that 'X is relative to Y' claims that Y is the necessary or ultimate *medium* for the existence of X (for example, there cannot be visual perceptions without a viewpoint or location of the perceiver), or Y is the best, only, or ultimate *standard* or *measure* for X (for example, political systems as human constructions have to be assessed and decided by persons or cultures).

In Haack's (1996*a*) terms, what I call mere relativity (X varies depending on Y) is 'shallow relativism', and proper philosophical relativism (X makes sense only relative to Y) is 'deep relativism'.

In attacking moral realism, relativists have to dissociate their position also from the stronger rebuttals of moral absolutism. Such traditional attacks include moral *nihilism*, which denies the existence of moral values in any sense, and moral *scepticism*, which denies all knowledge about moral values. J. L. Mackie's (1977) 'error theory' admits that moral statements are cognitively meaningful, but they are all false. Semantical anti-realism in ethics denies that moral judgements have truth values.[4] Nihilism,

---

[4] For example, emotivism (A. J. Ayer) analyses moral judgements as exclamations expressing emotions, and prescriptivism (C. L. Stevenson, R. M. Hare) as commands. Sayre-McCord (1988) classifies these views as examples of moral instrumentalism, in analogy with instrumentalism concerning scientific theories. A related sophisticated approach is Blackburn's (1993) 'quasi-realism' which attempts to justify some aspects of realist talk about morality on anti-realist premisses.

scepticism, and anti-realism are negative doctrines. Relativism in the deep sense is, instead, a positive thesis which accepts that moral views may be true or justified in some *relativized* sense.[5]

But how could the thesis of relativism be formulated? Let us approach this problem by starting from the philosophical problems concerning moral realism.

Some versions of moral realism rely on questionable metaphysical assumptions (such as Platonic ideas, God's will, or the telos of history) which are untestable by any factual information or lack explanatory power relative to any known aspect of the world. Even though such assumptions have been part of many traditional philosophical world views, from the viewpoint of scientific realism there does not seem to be any ground for accepting or supporting them (cf. Section 1.2). Similarly, non-natural moral properties are 'queer', if they are assumed to belong to the fabric of the world (Mackie 1977). The independent existence of moral values is unnecessary for the explanation of moral observations and beliefs: if I see an act of violence and judge it to be morally wrong, the appeal to 'real' moral facts does not add anything to the explanation of my views (Harman 1977; but see Sayre-McCord 1988).

Further, the attempts to reduce values to physical or mental facts commit what G. E. Moore (1929) called *the naturalist fallacy*: for example, if 'good' is defined as that which satisfies human desires, we can open the question of whether the satisfaction of such desires is always morally good or not. I think this kind of objection can be raised also against Richard Boyd's (1988) attempt to extend scientific realism to the domain of moral realism: according to his version of naturalism, goodness is a physical property, but it does not have an 'analytic' or reductive definition at all. However, Boyd gives a characterization of moral goodness in terms of a 'cluster' of 'human goods' which 'satisfy important human needs' (such as the need for love and friendship), together with psychological and social mechanisms (such as political democracy) which contribute to their 'homeostatic' unity. Knowledge of this property is to be obtained by observation and by attempts to reach a 'reflective equilibrium'. I fail to see why such a complex cluster of various types of elements should characterize a physical property, and how this approach hopes to evade Moore's open question strategy.

Putting these anti-metaphysical and anti-reductionist points together, moral realism is wrong, since there simply seems to be no independently

---

[5] See Meiland and Krausz (1982: 2), Margolis (1991).

existing 'moral reality' to which moral judgements could be in the relation of correspondence. Hence, there are no objective grounds for thinking that absolute moral judgements of the form (1) have truth values.[6]

Moral realism fails to appreciate the fact that *morality is human-made*—a historically depeloping social construction. According to what may aptly be called *moral constructivism*, moral values as social artefacts belong to Popper's World 3.[7] Besides rejecting naturalist attempts to reduce morality to the physical World 1, this view also excludes the claim of moral *subjectivism* which takes morality to be simply a matter of personal attitude or feeling, hence an element of World 2. The constructivist view of morality as a social fact helps us to understand why a moral system has binding or coercive force (in Durkheim's sense) within the community where it has been constituted and accepted.

If moral facts are part of the 'fabric' of World 3, it is possible to make true or false statements about morality relative to some socially constructed system of moral ideas (e.g. an ethical theory or the moral code of a human community). Instead of absolute statements (1), we have *relativized* statements of the form

In system S, a is good                                    (2)
In system S, a is right
In system S, a is holy,

where S is identified by its content or by its acceptance in some community. For example,

In Christian ethics, respect for your parents is good.    (3)
In the moral code accepted in Finland, stealing is wrong.
In the Islamic religion, Mecca is a holy city.

Statements of the form (3) have truth values as assertions about World 3, and can be results of descriptive and interpretative social and cultural sciences.[8]

---

[6] The situation is similar in religion, I believe. Gods do not exist, but were created by men as idealized pictures of themselves. Therefore—excluding descriptive statements about the history, psychology, and sociology of religion—genuinely religious judgements about gods and their attributes are not true. (According to Carnap's analysis, some of them are false, some lack truth values; see Ayer 1959.)

[7] See Niiniluoto (1984: ch. 9; 1985*b*). Cf. Harman (1977). For social facts as results of agreement, see Gilbert (1989) and Searle (1995).

[8] In the philosophy of law, statements of the type (2) are usually called norm propositions (von Wright 1963*a*). For the applicability of the correspondence theory of truth to norm propositions in legal dogmatics, see Niiniluoto (1981; 1985*b*). For the opposing view,

The relativization of value statements (2) agrees with our earlier remarks on the fact of moral relativity. There are, and have been, moral views such that

> In system $S_1$, a is good                                    (4)
> In system $S_2$, a is bad.

Another way of expressing this relativity is to use predicates of *relative goodness*:

> a is good-for-x                                               (5)
> a is right-for-x,

where x is a member of a community supporting the moral system S.[9] For example,

> Respect for parents is good-for-Christians                    (6)
> Stealing is morally-forbidden-for-the-Finns

are just other ways of formulating the claims (3). Even 'universally' accepted principles about human rights (if there are any) have the form (3), since they are relative to the moral system accepted by humanity at a given time.

Note that we have maintained an important *fact–value dichotomy* as the difference between ordinary factual statements and value statements of the form (1). We have also opposed attempts to collapse this distinction by reducing values to 'natural' elements of World 1 or World 2. But at the same time we have been able to go beyond this dichotomy by claiming that relativized value statements of the form (4) may express facts about World 3. Again, such facts about World 3 do not express absolute principles of morality, since there is always the prospect of changing or transforming the social reality in World 3.

Relativism as a philosophical thesis has to add something to the fact of relativity. I shall call *modest relativism* the claim that relativization is an

and defence of the consensus theory in this connection, see Aarnio (1987). Another example of statements of type (2) is judgements of scientific quality, relative to some standards (see Niiniluoto 1987d). Bohlin (1998) suggests that my analysis of quality agrees with social constructivism in science studies; this is natural, since I favour a constructivist view of values, even though I am opposed to social constructivism concerning facts about nature (cf. Ch. 9).

[9] Statements of the form (5) can also be understood as true or false assertions about instrumental values: a is good-for-x if a satisfies the needs of x or a is an effective means for the purpose x (e.g. Milk is good-for-babies, Tractors are good-for-farming). (See von Wright 1963b.) Some 'naturalized' theories attempt to reduce all value statements to facts about instrumental values, but thereby they accept nihilism about intrinsic values. For instrumental rationality, see Rescher (1988).

essential or uneliminable aspect of moral judgements: (4) and (5), as state-ments with a truth value, cannot be reformulated without reference to system S or auditory x.

It is important to emphasize that modest relativism does not entail *radical moral relativism* which claims that all moral systems are equally good or equally well justified. This is a highly questionable doctrine for several reasons. Attempts at formulating it usually stumble over the problem of incoherence: theses like 'it is a basic human right that every-one may decide his or her own morality' or 'as rights are always relative to a society it is wrong for people in one society to interfere with the values of another society' are internally inconsistent, since they support relativist theses with absolutist premises (cf. Williams 1982: 171).

Unlike radical relativism, modest relativism is compatible with the idea of *moral progress* and moral *regress*. This was argued in detail by Wester-marck's *Ethical Relativity* (1932). He started from the plausible hypothesis that morality has developed from retributive emotions, i.e. from impartial feelings of approval and disapproval. As most theories of emotions today emphasize, emotions are not pure qualitative feelings but also contain in some way or another a cognitive component.[10] The adequacy of emotions can then be assessed at least partly by considering the correctness of their cognitive aspect. For example, xenophobia (as a kind of fear) is usually based on irrational beliefs about the threat of strangers. In particular, as Westermarck tried to argue in his merciless criticism of what he con-sidered as old-fashioned and inhuman aspects of the ethical doctrines of Christianity, ethical views can be evaluated on this basis—without accepting a realist view of morality.

Moral systems can also be evaluated and compared in terms of higher-order principles (such as consistency, universalizability, agreement with moral intuition, harmony with other valuations) which are explicated in philosophical ethics.[11] Factual knowledge is also relevant to the assessment of values, since we can have significant historical evidence concerning the consequences of the adoption of value systems (e.g. the present ecological crisis leads us to criticize the ideology that takes nature to be just a resource for human exploitation). Personal and collective experiences, improvement

---

[10] Some theories assume that emotions contain judgements without assent, while some cognitive theories go so far as to identify emotions with certain types of beliefs or assertions (e.g. I fear a dog iff I believe that the dog threatens me). A representative collection of essays on this theme is A. O. Rorty (1980).

[11] See Brandt (1959), Häyry (1992), Niiniluoto (1992c). Rorty defends the idea of moral progress without Moral Truth by appealing to a kind of universalizability principle: moral progress means 'an increase in our ability to see more and more differences among people as irrelevant' (1998: 11).

of human knowledge, critical conversation of humanity, and systematic ethical theories have taught us to give better and better articulations of the conditions of good human life. These lessons are codified in such agreements as the Declaration of Human Rights by the United Nations. But, in my view, the twentieth century—with its wars, concentration camps, and the recent wave of nihilist egoism—has also exhibited morally regressive trends.

The idea that moral knowledge can be improved by the critical discussion of the free citizens of democratic nations has led to the suggestion that moral *objectivism* could be defended without presupposing moral realism in the ontological sense. Thus, Jürgen Habermas (1983) defines the truth (or rightness) of normative statements as the ideal consensus reached in discourse free from domination and undemocratic asymmetries. Hilary Putnam (1990; 1995) criticizes moral relativism by arguing that the basic insights of American pragmatism, namely the consensus theory of truth and fallibilism, apply equally well to science and ethics.[12]

It seems to me, however, that this line of argument again leads only to relativized moral judgements, conditional on some more basic value assumptions. In particular, the discourse ethics of Habermas presupposes the principles of equality and democracy—and thus it at best gives relative statements of the form (2), where the system S is defined to be the basic moral beliefs of the ideal democratic community.

Against the consensus theory of moral truth, it is also possible to raise Quine's (1960) famous queries about Peirce: why should we think that moral beliefs converge to some ideal limit, and why should such a limit be unique? A consensus theory of factual truth fails for similar reasons (cf. Section 4.6).

It thus seems clear that the appeal to long-run moral objectivity does not overcome modest relativism—even though it may help in refuting radical relativism. The fundamental reason for this conclusion is the failure of moral realism: as morality is a social construction, progressively constituted by the consensus of human communities, there is no independent or 'external' criterion for saying that the consensus reached actually in a finite time or ideally in the limit is the 'true' or 'right' one.

## 8.3  Cognitive relativism

What lessons for cognitive relativism can be derived from our discussion of moral relativism?

---

[12]  This way of collapsing the fact–value dichotomy is an attempt to extend the epistemic definition of truth from factual to value or normative statements. Cf. Section 4.6.

The first thing to observe is that cognitive relativism (in Haack's 'deep' sense) cannot be established merely by appealing to well-known facts about the *relativity* of human perceptions, beliefs, and standards of rationality. For example, individual and cultural variety of beliefs is a constant feature of our history: members of different communities have held conflicting belief systems, such that

According to belief system $B_1$, it is the case that p                    (7)
According to belief system $B_2$, it is the case that ~p.

But this at best only amounts to the existence of agents $x_1$ and $x_2$ such that

$x_1$ believes that p                                                       (8)
$x_2$ believes that ~p.

Such doxastic diversity does not imply any radical form of relativism, which would claim that all belief systems are equally good.[13]

The second point is that even the *explanation* of doxastic diversity fails to establish relativism. As we shall see in more detail in Chapter 9, the so-called 'strong' and 'empirical' programmes of 'the sociology of knowledge' (or, more properly, the sociology of belief) have attempted to show by case studies that the beliefs of scientists can be explained in terms of social factors. But an argument that social conditions C tend to produce beliefs B leaves open the decisive questions whether the beliefs B were justified and true.

Thirdly, cognitive disagreement is by no means unusual within science, either: the history of science shows that even the most warranted beliefs have varied at different places and times. This can be rationally explained by the fact that different scientific communities—besides the possibility that they have had access to different observational evidence and explanatory theories—have adopted different methodological practices and epistemological standards. Thus not only beliefs (cf. (7)), but also *assertions* (i.e. what are taken to be *justified* beliefs) are relative:

According to standards of justification $J_1$, it is assertable     (9)
    that p
According to standards of justification $J_2$, it is assertable
    that ~p.

The history of science is full of examples of this kind (cf. Donovan, Laudan, and Laudan 1988). For example, the hypothetico-deductive method warrants the tentative acceptance of explanatory theories postulating

---

[13] See Feyerabend (1987: 76). Cf. Haack (1987).

theoretical entities (see Laudan 1981*b*), while such inferences are not legitimized by the more restricted empirical and inductive methods. Another
example is provided by the standard Neyman–Pearson methods of statistical testing: a null hypothesis may be rejected if the significance level is
chosen as .01, but it may be acceptable on the level .05.

Examples of this type may be also established by the programme of
*social epistemology* (Fuller 1988) which analyses the sensitivity of knowledge production to the social structures within the scientific community
and society at large. Such studies may give results of type (9), where the
standards J are socially embedded and explained.

Again, these examples do not imply radical cognitive relativism. Such
a position is defended by Barnes and Bloor (1982), whose 'equivalence
postulate' states that 'all beliefs are on a par with one another with respect
to the causes of their credibility' (p. 23), so that 'for the relativist there is
no sense attached to the idea that some standards or beliefs are really
rational as distinct from merely locally accepted as such' (p. 27) (see also
Feyerabend 1987). Barnes and Bloor see their opponents as 'granting
certain forms of knowledge a privileged status' (p. 22). But absolutism (one
privileged set of standards) and radical relativism (all standards are
equally good) is a false dichotomy: moderate relativism allows that there
are different standards but some of them are epistemically better than
others.

Indeed, the standards of justification J in (9) are intended to be epistemological and methodological (cf. Ch. 6), and it is possible rationally
and critically to evaluate such standards within the philosophy of science.
For example, inductive, abductive, and hypothetico-deductive methods
have been studied in detail in the theory of scientific inference. Peirce
suggested that such modes of inference are assessed in terms of their
'truth-frequencies'. This is illustrated by the Neyman–Pearson tests:
the significance level indicates the probability that the null hypothesis is
rejected when it is true.[14]

Helen Longino (1990; 1996), defending 'contextual empiricism' in her
comments on feminist research, considers a large class of cognitive values
in science (such as accuracy, consistency, and simplicity), but concludes that
typical 'non-cognitive' values (like novelty and ontological heterogeneity)
may serve cognitive purposes well. Of values like applicability to current
human needs and diffusion of power she says that they are 'more relevant
to decisions about what theories or theoretical frameworks to work on

---

[14] In the Peircean spirit, Goldman (1986) suggests how scientific standards can be
appraised by their ability to produce true results. See also Laudan's (1984*a*) reticulational
model for the mutual evaluation of theories, methods, and values in science. Cf. Section 6.2.

than to decisions about plausibility' (Longino 1996: 48). This analysis is compatible with the thesis that there are values or standards of justification which are constitutive of science, and among these standards truth-related values are primary, but otherwise they are not governed by a uniquely fixed system of weights of importance (see Section 6.2).

There is a strong form of social externalism which starts from the idea that theory-choice in science is always 'underdetermined' by evidence or 'rational' factors, and concludes that the remaining gap has to be filled by social factors (cf. Section 6.3). In its extreme form, represented by Collins (1981), the influence of nature in the formation of scientific knowledge is taken to be 'small or non-existent'. But this position, when understood literally, should not be called 'relativism' any more, since it denies the very idea of cognitive justification—and therefore collapses into some kind of cognitive scepticism or anarchism (see, however, Section 9.1).

Fourthly, as Plato already observed, global forms of cognitive relativism face the serious problem of *incoherence* (see Siegel 1987). Suppose a Y-relativist makes the claim

All beliefs are relative to Y. (R)

Then is R itself an absolute or relative claim? In the former case, global relativism is given up as self-refuting. In the latter case, the relativist might consistently urge that R is indeed Y-relative as well (cf. Kusch 1991a). But then relativism is 'self-vitiating' in the sense that its views cannot be communicated to anyone else but its own believers (cf. Preston 1992).

Fifthly, attempts to formulate cognitive relativism by means of the concept of *relative truth* do not look promising.[15] The claim

p is true-for-x (10)

should mean something more than

x believes that p, (11)

for otherwise we come back to the 'innocent' relativity of beliefs (8). More-over, the analysis of (10) is as such question-begging, if it relies on the concept of absolute truth.

[15] For relative truth, see Swoyer (1982). Statements with indexical expressions seem to provide a special case where the relative truth predicate makes sense ('I am a Finnish male' is true-for-Ilkka-Niiniluoto and false-for-Barbara-Streisand), but in the logician's sense they correspond to open formulas (which lack truth values) rather than genuine sentences. As statements like 'Ilkka Niiniluoto is a Finn' are objective non-relative truths, this case does not give any support to relativism concerning truth. In particular, this means that truth is not relative to such properties of the knowing subject A as A's sex, gender, race, nationality, age, religion, and social class.

Similar problems arise with perspectivism, which makes truth relative to viewpoints (cf. Hautamäki 1986). The relativization of statements of the form

It is the case that p from viewpoint v                                     (12)

can be avoided by the reformulation

The world is such that it appears-p-from-the-viewpoint-v                   (13)

(cf. Niiniluoto 1991a). For example, the perspectival relativity of visual perceptions is based on underlying non-relative invariances in the world, and such laws help to explain, for instance, why a coin with a certain physical shape looks round from one viewpoint and flat from another.

Joseph Margolis (1991) has promised 'the truth about relativism'. He admits that strong forms of cognitive relativism with relativized truth values are self-defeating, but argues for a 'robust' relativism with many 'truth-like values' instead of bivalence. He grounds this view in an ontological picture of the world as a flux without permanent invariances, but does not otherwise develop it in technical details.

The concept of truthlikeness seems to provide a tool that is missing in Margolis's project. If knowledge is defined by the fallibilist criterion (2) of Ch. 4, which requires only that the known proposition is truthlike (or approximately true), and we allow that two rational persons may have different evidential reasons (clause (c')), then the pair of statements

$x_1$ knows that p                                                          (14)
$x_2$ knows that q

may be consistent even when p and q are incompatible with other. But if knowledge is understood in the sense of the classical definition (1) of Ch. 4, which satisfies the success condition that known propositions are true, then p and q in (14) cannot be incompatible with each other. The fallibilist account of knowledge thus allows some cognitive variation and flexibility which is excluded by the classical definition of knowledge.

In the case of morality, we defended a modest form of relativism in the preceding section: value statements are incomplete unless they contain a reference to a system of moral ideas. We have seen that a similar *modest cognitive relativism* applies to *assertions*: a claim that a belief is justified is always relative to some standards of justification (cf. (9)). Moreover, we have no good grounds for urging that we already possess some ultimate ideal or perfect system of standards. This relativity also concerns our estimates of epistemic probability and verisimilitude (Section 4.5). But we have already argued that this does not lead to radical cognitive relativism, since scientific methods and methodologies can be evaluated by their epistemological soundness and by the success of the research programmes based upon them—and thereby the standards of scientific justification have in fact improved with the progress of science (cf. Boyd 1984).

Modest relativism about assertions does not imply a corresponding relativism about *truth* and *reality*. Putnam's (1981) neo-pragmatist strategy in arguing against cultural relativism first appeals to the idea of 'ideal' conditions of justification and then links truth to 'ideal acceptability'. This approach, if successful, would avoid the relativity of assertions of type (9). (For criticism, see Moser 1990.) But, in my view, its weakness lies in the fictional presupposition that such ideal conditions of justification could ever be fully specified (cf. Section 4.6). Therefore, I think there is reason to favour a version of scientific realism which distinguishes relative epistemological and methodological terms (such as justification, estimated verisimilitude, and rationality) from non-relative ontological and semantical concepts (like reality and truth).

A scientific realist accepts the ontological thesis that nature is prior to and independent of our thinking or consciousness (Ch. 2). On this basis, it is possible to formulate the correspondence theory of truth, where truth is a relation between a statement and reality—and this relation holds independently of human beliefs, desires, and interests (see Section 3.4). This means that claims of the form (7) can be *de-relativized* (unlike claims of type (2)):

It is the case that p,                                                        (15)

or simply

p,                                                                            (16)

is a statement which has a truth value independently of any relativization to belief systems. Similarly, the statement (16) has its truth value independently of whether we can justify it or not. The key idea is the following: in constructing languages or conceptual frameworks, we create tools for putting questions to nature. But it is up to nature to 'decide' how it answers our questions (cf. Section 7.3). In other words, given a language L, the structure of the world $W_L$ relative to L is independent of our beliefs and interests, and the truth value of a statement p in L depends on its relation to $W_L$.

On the other hand, we have seen that the concepts of truthlikeness (Section 3.5) and scientific progress (Section 6.6) are pragmatically relative to cognitive interests and to conceptual frameworks which serve to define the targets of the relevant cognitive problems. This kind of relativity is not a threat to scientific realism, but rather a dynamic aspect of the development of science (cf. Niiniluoto 1991*a*).

The conclusions of scientific realism have been challenged by the 'social constructivists' who claim that reality itself is a social construction. Sometimes this relativistic thesis is just given by a slide from knowledge to truth and reality (see Knorr-Cetina 1983: 12), but it has been also argued that theoretical entities are created in the course of enquiry through the negotiation and consensus of laboratory communities (Latour and Woolgar 1979). As we have seen above, social constructivism is a plausible account for the creation of moral facts in World 3. But when applied to theoretical entities in science (e.g. electrons, quarks, hormones), such constructivism would lead at least to modest local relativism about truth and reality, since it treats natural scientific objects as World 3 entities—and thereby reduces (at least partly) World 1 to World 3. I argue against this view in Section 9.3.

Another trend in science studies is to assume anti-realism about nature and realism about society (see Fuller 1989: 3). This move might save the constructivist from some infinite regress arguments, since otherwise the basis of a social construction should be socially constructed etc. (Niiniluoto 1991*a*). But I find it extremely implausible to think that our beliefs about nature would somehow be more robust or real than nature itself—to me this sounds like an echo of Hegelian objective idealism.

To summarize, I have argued here that the diversity of human beliefs is a fact which has plausible historical explanations. I have also suggested that—in analogy with modest moral relativism—modest cognitive realism is defensible for assertions, i.e. claims about justified beliefs. Such relativity is reflected also in our estimates of verisimilitude and scientific progress. But this form of relativism does not imply radical cognitive relativism, and it cannot be extended to the concepts of truth and reality. For strong forms of cognitive relativism, it is not even clear that anyone has given a coherent formulation (cf. Harris 1992).

So it seems that relativism fails precisely at those points where it conflicts with scientific realism. In brief, from a realist's viewpoint, relativism is either innocent or incoherent.

## 8.4  *Feminist philosophy of science*

*Feminist epistemology* has become an important part of the programme of feminist science and philosophy.[16] It is evident that relativism is bound to

---

[16] In this section, which is based on Niiniluoto (1996*b*), I am indebted to advice and comments by Sara Heinämaa and Ritva Ruotsalainen.

be an important theoretical problem for feminist epistemology, since the whole project involves at least a lure of *gender relativism*: being a woman is supposed to make a relevant difference in the theory of knowledge. For us, it is instructive to consider this type of relativism which concentrates on the special nature and situation of the knowing subject.

If gender relativism is formulated as a radical thesis about truth (cf. Section 8.3), it seems to make pointless the emancipatory enterprise of feminism as a political movement: the talk about male *bias* does not make sense any more on this view, since that would presuppose some objective standard of truth and falsity. If the results of 'androcentric' science are true-for-males, then does it help very much to claim that they are false-by-the-feminine-standards? If the feminists presented their own claims (e.g. about the social position of women as oppressed) only as true-from-the-female-viewpoint, not as assertions which correspond to reality, who would take them seriously?

The first advocates of women's liberation argued that the exclusion of women from academic posts was unwarranted and unjust, since women are in general *equally good* for teaching and research positions as men. There is nothing that prevents women, when they have the right kind of education, from using the methods of science as well as men. Indeed, whatever differences there may be between the two sexes, they are irrelevant for the evaluation of a person's academic potential. This anti-relativist view was associated with the moderate programme of Women's Studies as a new academic discipline which adds new problems and topics to the curriculum and research agenda of the earlier 'androcentric' science.

This view was further supported by the argument that the dominant male philosophers, often unintentionally, have tended to associate characteristics considered masculine (such as rationality and objectivity in a special sense) to their allegedly universal picture of 'man', 'human being', and 'reason' (Lloyd 1984), and thereby justified the exclusion of the more emotional and subjective women. But when these stereotypical *gender differences* were emphasized, it was a short step to the 'gynocentric' conclusion that after all they are crucially important. Thus, it was claimed that the current methods of science are 'sexist', and should be criticized in all fields (cf. Bowles and Klein 1983). This radical view suggests a second potential task for feminist epistemology: it should try to show that there is a special kind of *woman's knowledge*, obtained by typically feminine methods or means.

Feminist epistemology, following this line, took the task of proving that there is a feminine language, mind, and thinking different from the masculine. Anthropologists suggested that this is a mentality difference, due to the traditional roles of men and women in social occupations and domestic life. Nancy Chodorow, in her psychoanalytic object–relations theory, argued that male and female personalities are constructed in different ways, because sons and daughters have different relations to their mother. This explains, Chodorow asserted, why men are attached to the subject–object distinction and to the urge to dominate and control external reality. Carolyn Merchant (1983) and Evelyn Fox Keller (1985) pointed out that precisely these features are typical of the experimental method of modern natural science, as formulated by Francis Bacon in the early seventeenth century.

Merchant's historical analysis is very interesting and important, since modern science indeed gave up the ancient idea of Nature as a maternal or female organism. But, for the same reason, I think she takes too literally the crude sexual metaphors that Bacon used in his description of the experimental method. Baron Verulam was a man of his time, and in advertising his method of learning he chose his rhetoric for his male audience (especially James I, a notorious witch-hunter and male chauvinist by our standards). Men later used more refined and elegant ways of talking about their passionate 'love of truth' or their wish to 'uncover' the 'veiled' and 'hidden secrets' of nature. Instead of domination, this relation is often one of admiration and worship. Even Bacon knew that 'nature to be commanded must be obeyed' (see Bacon 1960).

It may be a historical fact that the methods of science have been influenced by models taken from sexual relations, witch trials, interrogation of witnesses in court (see Kant 1930: p. xxvii), and the virtues of seventeenth-century British gentlemen (Shapin 1994). But it would be an instance of a genetic fallacy to try to evaluate the goodness of these methods by their historical origins.

Nevertheless, it is fascinating to play with the idea that the appeal of scientific methods could have a link to the patterns of human sexuality and gender. If the manipulation and cross-examination of nature in experiments is seen as masculine, then similarly the hermeneutic method of *Verstehen* or emphatic understanding has been regarded as typically feminine. This method employs emotions, instead of excluding them, and aims at the unity of subject and object.[17] It has also been suggested that,

---

[17] See the description of Barbara McClintock's important biological work in Tuana (1996): McClintock wanted to know 'intimately' every plant in the field, to 'listen' to them carefully, and to 'find a great pleasure' in studying them. I think this is comparable to the accounts of male scientists of their 'love of truth'. As Tuana observes, this is very different from 'the accounts of detached, disinterested observers' (p. 24). I agree that scientists (both male and female) should be passionate searchers for truth. The mistaken ideal of detached researchers is based on the rationalist view of emotions as disturbances—this view fails to see the importance of emotions as motives of scientific work. On the other hand, I still hold that emotions are not criteria of acceptance in the context of justification.

instead of propositional knowledge, female knowledge is typically intuitive and tacit.

The suggestion that there are *masculine and feminine scientific methods* is in fact one of the possible forms of gender relativism in science. Thereby this kind of feminist programme has also become a target of the criticism that the feminine research methods relying on 'feminist consciousness' (cf., for example, Stanley and Wise 1983) are too 'soft' and 'personal' to be scientific. It is no wonder that many feminists have wished to reconsider or denounce such views. In her introduction to the influential book *Feminism and Methodology* (1987), Sandra Harding argues 'against the idea of a distinctive feminist method of research' (p. 1).

Harding's *feminist standpoint theory* accepts fallibilism, but asserts that 'women's experiences, informed by feminist theory, provide a potential grounding for more complete and less distorted knowledge claims than do men's' (Harding 1987: 184). 'Women's and men's characteristic social experiences provide different but not equal grounds for reliable knowledge claims', she adds, so that 'we all—men as well as women—should prefer women's experiences to men's' (ibid. 10).

Harding says that 'standpoint theorists are not defending any form of relativism', since women's and men's experiences are not claimed to be equal grounds for knowledge claims (ibid. 186). This means that in her vocabulary relativism is always assumed to have what I call the radical form (see also Harding 1993: 61).[18] In my terms, however, Harding's basic position here is moderate gender relativism, since she insists on the difference between two types of experiences, but also expresses her preference ordering of them. At the same time, Harding's bold thesis that women's experiences should be preferred by both men and women makes her a sort of objectivist, since it asserts the existence of a privileged framework for doing science. To paraphrase Protagoras, as far as there is scientific knowledge about society and nature, woman is the measure of all things.[19]

Harding is not urging that women are more intelligent than men, or equipped with superior mental powers. Rather her argument is based on the *social position* of women as 'oppressed' and 'marginalized': in fighting against their oppressors the women achieve 'a truer (or less false) image of social reality'.

As women's position in society is not a historical constant, Harding's position is not objectivist in Bernstein's (1983) sense, which requires the

[18] Radical relativism in feminist epistemology has been supported by Spender (1982).
[19] However, Harding admits that 'men sympathetic to feminism' might do some useful 'phallic critique' (Harding 1987: 11).

existence of a 'permanent, ahistorical matrix or framework' for doing science. But this seems to mean also that women would lose their epistemic advantage if the feminists took power in society.

Nancy Hartsock (1983) derives the feminist standpoint view directly as a transformation of the *Marxist* view that the proletariat in capitalist society is in an epistemically privileged position in relation to the bourgeoisie. Similarly, Marxist ethics combined moral class relativism with an objectivist twist: the morality of the 'most progressive class' is the right one, since it is in the direction of the presumed objective laws of history (cf. Section 8.2).

The Marxists had a grand narrative to support the privileged historical position of the working class. Similar stories about the feminine class are hardly more plausible. This is not the only problem in the relation of Marxism and feminism.

A radical version of Western Marxism argued that the 'logic of capital' deforms or distorts all human thinking, and therefore there is a difference between 'bourgeois physics' and 'socialist physics' (cf. discussions in Sandkühler 1975). Another version asserted that the economic value forms are constitutive of the forms of thinking in natural and social science. This emphasis on social factors is reminiscent of the Soviet doctrine in Stalin's era: that social practice may change the laws of genetics was a background of the Lysenko case (cf. Roll-Hansen 1989). But here the academic Marxist school was even more orthodox than the official Marxist-Leninists in the Soviet Union: Stalin himself wrote in 1950 an article to support the view that the laws of logic and grammar are, like the laws of geometry, independent of social and economic structures.

Pierre Duhem's polemics against 'German science' and the accusations of Einstein's 'Jewish physics' in the Third Reich are notorious examples of the ways in which science has been relativized to nationalist and racist purposes. To many of us they sound outdated, something that should be eliminated from science.[20] Is the standpoint thesis of the superiority of

---

[20] Giere (1996) points out that current post-positivist theories of sciences do not exclude the possibility of 'gender bias' in the overall processes of scientific enquiry. Such a bias may enter, e.g. through the choice of subjective prior probabilities. He concludes that 'as disquieting as it may seem to many, we shall have to learn to live with the empirical possibility of "Jewish science"' (p. 12). I find this formulation problematic. Sane philosophies of science should exclude 'Jewish science' in the sense that the credibility of scientific claims should not be defended by criteria or arguments which appeal to the race, religion, or gender of the scientist. If there is 'gender bias' in science in this sense, feminist philosophy should fight against it. On the other hand, it is quite legitimate that various cultural interests influence the choice of problems that are studied by scientific methods.

'feminist research' to bad 'androcentric science' any better than the idea of 'socialist physics'?

Why should we think that the marginalized people at the bottom of social hierarchies are epistemologically superior? Harding's answer seems to be based on the assumption that social science studies 'problems' of some individuals or groups: 'a problem is always a problem *for* someone or other' (Harding 1987: 6). Therefore, these different social groups have an important role in the context of discovery, i.e. in the generation of questions that are asked in science. Further, when hypotheses about the life of these groups are investigated, it is certainly important to test them against the experience of the members of these groups (cf. Giere's (1996) useful classification of research problems).

Arguments along these lines are sufficient to show that some research problems may be generated by *problems for women* (e.g. the social status of feminist mothers), and that *hypotheses about women* (e.g. how women experience motherhood) should be tested by studying women's experiences. This is what was originally on the agenda of moderate Women's Studies. But they do not yet show why women are the best research experts in the study of women's problems.

Harding's thesis that all science should preferably be based on *women's experiences* remains unwarranted. All marginalized people are not women, and not all members of the 'oppressor group' are male. And all research problems are not generated from people's everyday experiences.[21]

Another argument suggests that men fail to recognize social problems, since they still rule and largely create the societal structures. But, again, certainly there are also marginalized men. Moreover, this argument in fact turns upside down the traditional conception of maker's knowledge (see Hintikka 1974): the more men participate in the making of society, the more (not less) knowledge they should have about it.

Harding (1993) has recently clarified her position by saying that 'marginalized lives provide the scientific problems and the research agendas—not the solutions—for standpoint theories'. But, if this is her view, then it is difficult to see what remains of her original thesis that women's experiences should always be preferred as 'grounds of knowledge claims'. If we really wish to 'maximize objectivity' in social research, it no doubt is desirable to have persons with different social backgrounds among the community of investigators (i.e. the membership in the scientific community should be open to all who have the will and talent for higher academic education). This diversity may enhance the critical discussion

---

[21] For the generation of research problems from earlier theories and paradigms, see Rescher (1984) and Kleiner (1993).

and questioning within the scientific community. It may even be bene-
ficial to have members with 'antiauthoritarian' and 'emancipatory' values
(cf. Harding 1986: 27). But, by this principle, a community which includes
*both men and women* is better than any genderwise homogeneous group.
And if 'strong' or self-reflective objectivity is not achieved because social
values held by the whole scientific community will not be identified or
detected (Harding 1993: 57), then the research community of Women's
Studies should include non-feminists, too.

Maybe the only way to support the claim that a purely feminine community of investigators is preferable to one with mixed genders would be
a transformation of the Marxist doctrine that the 'logic of capital' distorts
human thinking. Thus, Du Bois (1983) believes that the force of patriarchy
deforms all thinking: 'We are observer and observed, subject and object,
knower and known. When we take away the lenses of androcentrism and
patriarchy, what we have left is our own eyes, ourselves, and each other.'
In other words, when male domination is eliminated, the way is reopened
to a Cartesian transparent subject and foundationalist naive empiricism.
This kind of return to feminine objectivism is rejected by Harding.

Harding's (1993) aim is to show that it is possible to have genuine knowledge that is 'fully socially situated'. This makes her position resemble what
the Marxist epistemologists used to call the *double determination view* of
scientific knowledge. The knowledge claims are results partly of the interactions of the scientists with an independently existing reality, partly of the
social situation of the scientists in their culture and community. This view
is compatible with critical scientific realism: the truth or truthlikeness of
a scientific claim depends on its correspondence with reality, but the discovery and justification of such a claim may be intertwined with features
of the social situation. While the *norm* of objectivity precludes personal or
social wishes and interests being explicitly presented as reasons for accepting or rejecting hypotheses ('I find this theory acceptable, since its truth
would give me an advantage . . .'), real-life scientists as fallible and limited
human beings may in fact be influenced in this task by their non-scientific
values. However, critical self-reflection and openness to objections by
other scientists help to make science, as Peirce put it, a self-corrective
enterprise (cf. also Popper 1963).

Feminist *postmodernism* (see Nicholson 1990) has challenged the standpoint theory by arguing that it is a 'universalizing mistake' to speak in the
name of an abstract 'woman'. White middle-class heterosexual women of
North America and Western Europe cannot have the voice of black, Asian,
Native American, or lesbian women. When Harding (1986; 1993) admits that
these divisions lead to 'different feminisms' that 'inform each other', gender

relativism is lost and transformed to Protagorean subjectivism: there will then be literally as many feminisms as feminists, since eventually smaller and smaller class divisions end with singletons of one member only.

Postmodernism deconstructs gender relativism also in the sense that it questions all universal generalizations about the nature of women. Feminist postmodernists see themselves as continuing an anti-essentialist project with plural and complexly constructed conceptions of social identity.

To complete the deconstruction of feminist epistemology (in the traditional sense), the postmodernists argue that epistemology, as a project of finding ultimate and firm grounds for knowledge claims, is tied to the historical development of the ideology of modern Western culture. In this view, standpoint theories belong to the past. What remains is the successor project of epistemology, the endless discourse or conversation on women and femininity—in particular, by questioning the masculine–feminine and sex–gender distinctions.

We may also add that of course an important part of feminist writing will belong to philosophy and the critique of ideology, which has taken its model from emancipatory social science. Conceptual and normative questions are here based upon philosophical reflections and arguments.

Social *constructivism* has been recommended for feminist philosophy by Elizabeth Potter (1993) (see Ch. 9 n. 7). But the relativist idea that men and women 'construct' their own 'realities' has also been effectively criticized by Grimshaw (1986).

It seems to me that the common mistake of postmodernism and social constructivism is their belief that anti-foundationalism about science entails anti-realism. A similar conclusion is made by the so-called feminist empiricists. Fallibilist realism provides an alternative that they all ignore.

Harding defines *feminist empiricism* as the view that 'sexism and androcentrism (in science) are social biases correctable by stricter adherence to the existing methodological norms of scientific inquiry' (Harding 1986: 24). This is perhaps not the best formulation, since the leading feminist empiricists, like Longino (1990) and Nelson (1990), hardly think that we already possess a ready and finished pattern of methodological norms. Reasonable empiricists will agree with Richard Boyd (1984) that the progress of science takes place both in its content and in its methods and methodology.[22]

---

[22] While a feminist empiricist thinks that the self-corrective methods of research are the best means of eliminating whatever 'sexist bias' there may be in the *content* of scientific knowledge, there is another kind of meta-level social bias in the *attitudes and institutions*, and its correction can take place by ethical norms and measures of science policy (rather than by methodological norms). This distinction is emphasized in Harris (1992).

When Lynn Hankinson Nelson (1990) bases her feminist empiricism on Quine's philosophy (see also Nelson and Nelson 1996), she associates her view with empiricism in the sense opposed to theoretical realism. Quine's account of language, truth, and the web of belief has a strong leaning towards theoretical relativism (see e.g. the criticism in Harris 1992).

Realism and relativism are of course not the only relevant alternatives in the philosophy of science—for example, Laudan (1990*b*) is both an anti-realist and an anti-relativist. But it seems fair to say that there is surprisingly little discussion of realism within feminist philosophy. Linda Alcoff (1987) has rightly emphasized the importance of this question to the feminist movement. But when she contrasts the correspondence theory of truth with the 'constructive' notion of truth (which she associates with the 'Continental' philosophers Foucault and Gadamer), I do not understand why the former is claimed to make truth 'abstract' and 'universal': Tarskian truth can be applied to singular and temporal statements; and not only languages, but their interpretations and thus the correspondences between languages and the world as well, have to be created by human activities (cf. Ch. 3).

The term *feminist realism* is used in a recent collection of articles (Nelson and Nelson 1996) by Ron Giere and Ilkka Niiniluoto. In my view, critical fallibilist scientific realism would give the best epistemological background for feminist research within Women's Studies, understood as an empirical interdisciplinary attempt to find new descriptive knowledge about nature, mind, culture, and society. It would preserve all the advantages that feminist empiricism has over standpoint theories and postmodernism. It would help us to understand how new research on issues important to feminism may complement and correct the earlier biased views. It insists that truth is not relative to persons or gender, but accepts that different communities have used varying methods of justifying knowledge claims—and that these methods can still be improved. It can combine the ideas that scientific enquiry is always socially situated and cognitively progressive, without falling into the traps of radical relativism.

Finally, I wish to show that the realist view of science is not incompatible with a positive programme of feminist politics. Feminist enquiry (besides the philosophical and descriptive lines mentioned above) could take its model from *applied social sciences* like social policy studies or peace research. A typical 'design science' studies conditional recommendations or *technical norms* of the form

> If you want G, and believe you are in situation B, then you      (TN)
> ought to do Z.

(see Section 6.1). Such statements can in principle be supported in a *value-neutral* way by showing that doing Z in situation B is most likely to bring about the goal G. Thus, TN is a statement that has a truth value in the realist sense, and so it can be a result of scientific enquiry. On the other hand, TN is *conceptually value-laden* in the sense that it contains a description of a goal G. In applied social science, G may range from the maintenance of the status quo to radical and even utopian aims. G could also be a goal which expresses the interests and political purposes of a particular social group, like women or some marginalized minority (e.g. black feminists, lesbians). In this case, TN represents *research for* that group. When descriptive social studies show that the actual situation is of type B, then the normative conclusion 'You ought to do Z!' is *true for* the members of this group (Niiniluoto 1985*b*). Examples of such technical norms might be the following: 'If you wish to improve the academic position of women scholars, and you live in the present situation in Finland, you ought to do Z' and 'If a black mother wishes to improve her condition of life in the United States, she should do W.'

This is, I think, an attractive model of genuinely *feminist* research, since all the values and political goals of this movement can be packed into the goal G. The traditional principle of value-neutrality is nevertheless respected, as long as commitment to G does not influence the assessment of the causal connections between the means Z and the end G in situation B. The type of action needed to achieve the desired goal is highly context-dependent via the situation B. In this way, empirical research may be combined with feminist politics.

# 9

# Social Constructivism

Epistemology has traditionally concentrated on the knowledge of individual agents. The terms 'rational' and 'social' are often taken to be opposite to each other. However, Charles Peirce has already argued that the true subject of knowledge is the indefinitely large scientific community (see Section 4.4). Among philosophers, Ludwig Wittgenstein deserves credit for his arguments about the social character of language. Following Popper and Kuhn, philosophers of science have slowly started to understand that the adequate understanding of the production of scientific knowledge requires consideration of practices of enquiry and argumentation rooted within the community of scientists.

The scientific community has been studied by the sociology of science since the 1930s, with Robert Merton as a leading figure. This work has increased our knowledge about science in two important ways. First, it has studied empirically the internal structure of the scientific community—institutions, research groups, publications, goals, values, norms, reward systems, assessment of quality, controversies, etc., that operate in the actual work of the scientists.[1] Secondly, it has investigated the scientist's role in society at large and the functions of science in relation to other social institutions and activities.[2]

New trends became fashionable in the sociology of science in the 1970s. With influences from Kuhn and the new philosophy of science, they criticized Merton's picture of the ethos of science.[3] Other inspiration came from Karl Mannheim's 'sociology of knowledge' (i.e. the attempt to show how human beliefs vary in different cultures), and from the phenomenological thesis that reality is 'socially constructed' (cf. Section 7.1). Philosophers and sociologists working in Edinburgh were also influenced by the later Wittgensteinian relativism (which links language to 'forms of life') and the 'externalist' studies of the history of science (which link the development of scientific knowledge to the society where the scientists are

---

[1] A classical exposition of these themes is Merton (1973).
[2] See Ben-David (1971), Ziman (1994).
[3] See Merton (1973), Mulkay (1977; 1979). Merton's ethos, which is at least compatible with scientific realism, will be discussed in Section 10.3.

working). On this basis, new programmes took on the task of giving social explanations of the beliefs of the scientists.[4]

Even though some advocates of these approaches have tried to disguise themselves as 'neutral' observers who go to scientific laboratories like good anthropologists without any prejudice about their object of study, they in fact make very strong philosophical assumptions and conclusions. This is, I think, an adequate reason for treating them as fellow philosophers and assessing their claims as part of the dispute between realism and anti-realism (Niiniluoto 1991a).

I shall argue that, in spite of its misleading appearance, the 'Strong Programme' of the Edinburgh school is not really a serious threat to scientific realism (Section 9.1), but rather a form of empiricist naturalism based upon a radically nominalist (in my view, mistaken) Wittgensteinian 'finitism' about language (Section 9.2). In considering Harry Collins's relativist programme and Bruno Latour's social constructivism, it is likewise interesting to ask whether they resist charitable interpretations which would reconcile them with realism (Section 9.3).

## 9.1 The Edinburgh programme: strong or wrong?

The Edinburgh school (David Bloor, Barry Barnes, Steven Shapin) has been the most influential of the sociological approaches to scientific knowledge. The theoretical principles of the 'Strong Programme' were formulated in Bloor's *Knowledge and Social Imagery* (1976). An early statement was given in Bloor (1973) which attempts to extend Mannheim's sociology of knowledge to the field of mathematics— and refuses to limit the sociology of mathematics to the 'sociology of error', i.e. to cases where the standards of mathematical reasoning have been violated. Generalizing from this case, Bloor wants to show that science in all of its areas and aspects can be subjected to scientific sociological enquiry.

Bloor's approach has been extensively criticized, among others, by Martin Hollis, Steven Lukes, Larry Laudan, and J. R. Brown, who claim that his principles are either empty, trivially true, or wrong.[5]

---

[4] See Berger and Luckmann (1971), Wilson (1970), Bloor (1976), and Shapin (1994). For current work in the social studies of science and technology (STS), see Jasanoff *et al.* (1995).

[5] See Laudan (1977), Hollis and Lukes (1982), Brown (1984; 1989), Sayers (1987), Haack (1996b). See also McMullin (1988; 1992). In his preface to the 2nd edn., Bloor (1991) asserts with remarkable self-confidence that 'attacks by critics have not convinced me of the need to give ground on any matter of substance'. In my reading, this statement is possible only due to ambiguities in the interpretation of the Symmetry principle.

The *Strong Programme* aims to give a scientific explanation of 'the very content and nature of knowledge' (Bloor 1976: 1). Here knowledge means, instead of 'true belief', whatever the scientists collectively 'take to be knowledge' (ibid. 2). The principle of *Causality* says that the explanation of scientific beliefs should use the 'same causal idiom' as any other science (ibid. 3). *Impartiality* requires that both true and false, or both rational and irrational, beliefs should be causally explained, and *Symmetry* demands that both kinds of beliefs should be explained by the same types of factor (ibid. 4–5). Finally, *Reflexivity* indicates that the programme should apply to itself.

It is clear that the Strong Programme is consciously based upon heavy philosophical assumptions. Bloor's book is indeed advertised on the back cover as 'a forceful combination of materialism, relativism and scientism'. He gives no concessions to the idea that there might be methodological differences between the natural and social sciences: 'the search for laws and theories in the sociology of science is absolutely identical in its procedure with that of any other science' (ibid. 17). (This view is usually called methodological monism.) Moreover, 'in the main science is causal, theoretical, value-neutral, often reductionist, to an extent empiricist, and ultimately materialistic like common sense' (ibid. 141).

Another statement of the programme was given in a joint article of Barnes and Bloor (1982), who call their view 'a relativist theory of knowledge'. Instead of claiming that all collectively accepted systems of belief are equally true or equally false, they formulate an 'equivalence postulate' to the effect that for all beliefs 'the fact of their credibility is to be seen as equally problematic', i.e. both true and false (rational and irrational) beliefs have to be explained in the same way by searching for their local causes of credibility (pp. 23–5). This is a combination of the earlier principles of Impartiality and Symmetry.

In spite of Bloor's methodological monism and his principle of Reflexivity, it has seemed to many of his critics that there is a dramatic difference in his descriptions of science on two levels (see e.g. Niiniluoto 1991*a*). As the *method* of the sociologist of science, science for Bloor satisfies very strict—and some of us would say old-fashioned-positivist, empiricist, inductivist, and causalist principles. But as the *object* of sociological study, science (including physics and mathematics) for Bloor is 'a social phenomenon' whose methods, results, and objectivity are relative to social interests and causally influenced by social factors. It seems as if Bloor is assuming the objectivity of science in order to prove that science is not objective.

The feeling that there is something perplexing here arises from the fact that the Edinburgh school is usually seen as a successor—or even the prime successor—of the *externalist* approach to the history of science. Among Soviet Marxists, Boris Hessen's 1931 study of the 'social and economic roots' of Newton's *Principia* is a classic in this tradition: it sees Newton's mechanics as a response to the economic needs of seventeenth-century British society. Another famous case study is Paul Forman's 1971 thesis that the German scientists in the Weimar Republic 'sacrificed physics' to 'the *Zeitgeist*': their readiness to accept indeterminism and to find a failure of causality in atomic processes was primarily due to hostile social-intellectual pressures from the mystical and anti-rational public.[6] The *internalists*, instead, argue that such theoretical changes are typically due to intra-scientific reasons, such as the cognitive problem situation, available evidence, and rational arguments in favour of the competing theories. It is clear that analytic philosophers of science have traditionally favoured the internalist view. Kuhn's (1962) compromise suggests that internalism is valid within the periods of normal science, but extra-scientific influences can become decisive during periods of crisis and scientific revolution.

The Edinburgh school has produced a remarkable series of case studies of its own. For example, Shapin has argued that the disputes about phrenology in nineteenth-century Scotland were correlated with social class position. The supporters of phrenology came from the middle class with the interest of finding practical knowledge in the purpose of egalitarian social reforms, while its opponents came from the academic circles in the upper class. The structure of such an externalist *interest explanation* is then

> The members of the community C belong to social class S.  (1)
> The members of S have the social interest I.
> The members of C believed that theory T would promote interest I.
> Therefore, the members of C believed in theory T.

Sometimes it is suggested that the third premiss in (1) is superfluous: Bloor (1991) claims that social interests 'don't have to work by our reflecting on

---

[6] Another type of externalism does not think that the social conditions *cause* beliefs, but rather they serve to *constitute* the research domain of natural science. Pietilä (1981) refers in this connection to Alfred Sohn-Rethel's Marxist theory of value forms. Cf. the discussion on 'bourgeois' and 'socialist' physics, and 'androcentric' and 'feminist' science, in Section 8.4. Kusch (1991a), in the spirit of Michel Foucault, argues that the relation between knowledge and social power is internal rather than external.

them', but sometimes 'they just *cause* us to think and act in certain ways' (p. 173).

Some philosophers urge that explanation by motives cannot be causal.[7] Bloor suggests that the basis for objections to interest explanations is the 'fear of causal categories', but I do not think that such 'desire to celebrate freedom' is the only reason for reluctance about explanatory arguments of the form (1).

Indeed, most of Bloor's opponents would accept the idea that scientific beliefs—or perhaps rather theoretical preferences and choices in science—can be explained. This is allowed even by Laudan's (1977) 'arationality principle' (cf. Section 6.6). Rational explanation of the form (34) in Section 6.6 can likewise be construed as causal. Further, the explanation of a belief may refer to its *reasons*, i.e. to other beliefs from which it has been derived by rational *inference*:

> Scientific community C believes that p, because C has          (2)
> received the information that q and C thinks that q entails
> or supports p.

This scheme allows cases where p is deducible from the accepted evidence q, but also situations where q inductively confirms p or p is the best explanation of q. As a special case of (2), where q is identical with p, C's belief that p is explained by the fact that C has received the information that p from a *source* C accepts (e.g. observation or experiment):

> Scientific community C believes that p, because its members          (3)
> have repeatedly perceived that p in a systematic observation
> or experiment.

At least the fashionable causal theories of knowledge are ready to construe the connective 'because' in (2) and (3) as expressing a causal relation (Pappas and Swain 1978; Goldman 1986). As perception is fallible, though often reliable, it can cause false beliefs among the scientists. Moreover, false sentences can be correctly deduced from false premises, or induced from true premises. Hence, models (2) and (3) can impartially be applied both to true and false beliefs. Other types of causal explanations of beliefs might be invoked in everyday life (e.g. a hallucination due to the use of drugs), but their role in science is accidental. Radical *internalists* might then claim that *all* scientific beliefs are causally explainable by

---

[7] This is the position of 'analytical hermeneutics' which has been influenced by the later Wittgenstein. As we shall see in the next section, Bloor is also an admirer of Wittgenstein, but his interpretation favours naturalism and methodological monism. The causalist view of the explanation of action is defended by Tuomela (1977) and Davidson (1980).

their reasons, so that their meta-methodological position would satisfy all of Bloor's four principles of Causality, Impartiality, Symmetry, and Reflexivity.

This argument shows that the original target of Bloor's criticism was not clearly defined. Bloor's attack was directed against the idea that social processes distort knowledge, so that sociological explanations are needed only for scientific beliefs that fail to be true or rational. But the idea that truth would 'explain itself' is odd in the context of empirical science, since beliefs about the world have to be obtained by some processes of investigation and reasoning. The principle of Impartiality may have some bite against such aprioristic views about mathematics which claim our mathematical knowledge to be based on direct intuition ('I believe that two plus two is four, because two plus two is four') (cf. Bloor 1973), but even a Platonist may allow that knowledge about arithmetic requires some psychological processes like calculation, inference, and proof.

The peculiar formulation of the principle of Impartiality is less serious than the ambiguities with the principle of Symmetry. The argument above shows that *social externalism*—the demand that the sociology of science explains beliefs *always* by *social* factors—does not follow from the four basic principles of the Strong Programme, but rather is an addition to its artillery. Moreover, it seems that Bloor is committed to such social externalism: even though he argued already in Bloor (1973) against I. C. Jarvie's 'misconception' that personal and class interests are the only basis of explanation in the sociology of knowledge, he only suggested adding to them other 'features of social life'. Hence, it may seem fair to agree with Laudan (1982; 1996) that the Symmetry requirement is an instance of questionable 'premature dogmatizing'.

But what about the many illuminating case studies? Certainly such works are worthwhile and may increase our understanding of science in its social context. But it should also be clear that the social externalist thesis cannot be *proved* by case studies. Inferences about causal connections are uncertain in most special cases.[8] For example, why should the

---

[8] An example from feminist debates illustrates this problem. Elizabeth Potter (1993) has tried to illustrate the gender-relative nature of 'social negotiations' in natural science by a case study of Boyle's Law of Gases. The knowledge that the air has spring and weight, she argues, was 'influenced by class and gender considerations'. Robert Boyle, a Puritan and an opponent to attempts to liberate women from the domestic sphere, supported the mechanistic natural philosophy. He defeated the organicist or hylozooist view, which was associated with Hermes, Paracelsus, and Campanella, and advocated by the radical men and women of the 'mob'. Potter concludes that Boyle's work had 'direct implications for women of that period'. It should not surprise anyone that scientific knowledge may be highly *non-neutral* in society, since it often corrects popular everyday conceptions and prevailing

upper-class position of Scottish philosophers have any causal role in their argumentation against the doctrine of phrenology? At best the case studies show that social factors *sometimes* play *some* role in explaining the success of some idea in a cultural or social climate. Much more evidence would be needed for the inductive generalization that social factors always determine scientific beliefs.

Moreover, the inductive generalization will be refuted by single cases where rational non-social factors seem to be sufficient to explain the choices within the scientific community. Without denying the importance of the relevant social context, the successes of Harvey, Galileo, Kepler, Newton, Lavoisier, Einstein, Heisenberg, and Crick could give such examples. There are also cases where scientific evidence and argumentation have been able to achieve a victory over strong social or religious opposition (e.g. Darwin's theory of evolution).

Bloor has given a response to the counter-argument that scientific beliefs could be internally and rationally explained by schema (2): even explanatory reasons are 'social' (see Brown 1989). This defensive move has the danger that the whole Symmetry principle is watered down: if *everything* is social, the thesis is empty.

Bloor's real argument is more interesting, however. He suggests that 'epistemic factors' are really 'social factors', since 'the link between premise and conclusion is socially constituted'. Here Bloor is not denying the possibility of internalist explanations of the form (2), but insists that we need social and historical factors to explain why community C took reason q to support p or applied q in a particular way; this is clearly a complement to the argument (2). This might be called the *Weak Programme* of the sociology of knowledge, since it suggests that a sociologist may step in to explain the premises of scientific beliefs *after* a philosopher has first given a rational explanation of them (cf. Section 6.6).[9]

I think this Weak Programme may legitimately be applied to partially explain the reasoning and the weighting of evidence by scientists in many

doctrines. If there were women in Britain who were devoted to what turned out to be a mistaken theory, Boyle's rejection of that theory and the step toward a more truthlike account of gases certainly had 'direct implications' for these women. What Potter fails to show, I think, is that gender considerations played any causal role in Boyle's evaluation of the experimental evidence available at his time.

[9] I have used this term in Niiniluoto (1991a). Sometimes this term has been used simply to refer to Merton's sociology of science. D. Chubin and S. Restivo (in Knorr-Cetina and Mulkay 1983) speak about 'the Weak Programme' which does not use the hard method of science in the social study of science. Bloor (1991) equates 'the Weak Programme' with the 'distortion paradigm', but I do not assume that the social influences need to have a distorting effect.

special cases. The acceptance of scientific evidence and the link between scientific evidence and conclusions depend on the standards of scientific inference and method adopted in the relevant scientific community (cf. Longino 1990)—and such standards have varied in the history of science. But, as Papineau (1988) points out, this partial influence of social factors does not imply that scientific practice is not generally reliable (in Goldman's sense) for generating true or truthlike theories.

Furthermore, the suggestion that the warranting link between a reason q and a belief p *always* needs a *social* explanation (in terms of extra-scientific, political, religious, etc. factors) would not be plausible (cf. Haack 1996*b*). An interesting case can be made for the thesis that social factors may influence the assessment of philosophical arguments (Kusch 1995). But the compelling nature of deductive and mathematical reasoning needs no special social explanation (apart from the rather trivial condition that the scientist must have learned elementary logic and mathematics), as such inferences are *per definitionem* necessarily truth-preserving.[10]

Any comprehensive framework for science studies should acknowledge that the opinions of the scientific communities may depend on a variety of different types of factor—among them 'internal' reasons, arguments, prejudices, mistakes, persuasive communication, and 'external' social influences. The fact that the subjects of scientific knowledge are always socially situated does not preclude their interaction with the objects of knowledge. This is the basic principle of the 'double determination view' of scientific knowledge (cf. Section 8.4). Case studies should show what factors were indeed active and what their interplay really was. Instead of sweeping generalizations (like the Symmetry thesis), the task for a theory of science would be to provide a plausible model which shows *where* and *how* external factors may play a role in scientific practice.

Bloor's (1991) reply to his critics suggests that the message of the Edinburgh school has been widely misunderstood. It should not be confused with the extreme relativism of Collins (see below). According to Bloor, the

---

[10] The development of mathematics has an interesting social history. In particular, the standards of mathematical concept formation and proofs have progressed through debates. Our present state of mathematics is 'contingent', since it could be different. There are conflicting schools in the foundations of mathematics (such as Platonism, constructivism, intuitionism) and even alternative 'deviant' systems of logic. Bloor (1976) uses these points in his attack on the 'necessity' of mathematical truth. I agree with Bloor's anti-Platonism, but I think the Popperian conception of World 3 is enough to save realism in mathematics (cf. Section 2.2 and Niiniluoto 1992*b*). We have also argued in Section 3.2 for a notion of analytic truth which is relative to a language (with meaning postulates). Logical entailment is necessarily truth-preserving relative to the stipulation of the meaning of the logical connectives. These stipulations can be made in alternative ways, but as long as these definitions are accepted, logical truth is not open to negotiation.

claim that 'knowledge depended exclusively on social variables' would be 'absurd':

The strong programme says that the social component is always present and always constitutive of knowledge. It does not say that it is the *only* component, or that it is the component that must necessarily be located as the trigger of any and every change: it can be a background condition. Apparent exceptions to covariance and causality may be merely the result of the operation of other natural causes apart from social ones. (Ibid. 166)

In particular, Bloor accepts natural causal stories about sensory experience (cf. (3)) and causal explanations with a 'naturalistic construal of reason' (cf. (2)) (ibid. 177). Cognitive science and the sociology of knowledge are 'really on the same side', since they are both naturalistic (ibid. 170).

Bloor's main point appears now to be *naturalism* rather than sociologism. The Symmetry thesis does not require that all explanations should refer to social interests, but it legitimizes all arguments appealing to natural causes. Thus, even though 'sensory causes' as explanations of beliefs were mentioned in a footnote to Bloor (1973), I think the original formulation of the Strong Programme was highly misleading. Explanation 'by the same type of factors' is now so extremely wide a notion that it excludes only non-natural causes involving Platonist or idealist ontologies. In this respect, it is compatible with most versions of scientific realism.

In a recent book, Barnes, Bloor, and Henry (1996) do their best to convince their readers that they are indeed good empiricists. They emphasize that all scientists use 'realist strategies' (p. 12). In a very clear way, they also dissociate their position from the 'idealist' sociological approach to scientific knowledge which 'denies the existence of an external world and gives no role to experience in the generation of knowledge and belief' (pp. 76, 202).

What Bloor calls the 'idealist' account of science is advocated in the *Empirical Programme of Relativism* of Harry Collins. This approach, which has also led to a number of interesting historical case studies, explicitly adopts a relativistic position where 'the natural world has a small or non-existent role in the construction of scientific knowledge' (Collins 1981). He emphasizes the unlimited 'interpretative flexibility' of empirical data, and illustrates the social mechanisms by which scientific controversies over such interpretations are settled. Collins (1985) has also argued that the validity of induction in science has only a conventional character.[11] But if this is the case, why should we have any reason to believe that the 'empir-

---

[11] Collins argues that the notion of repetition of the 'same' experiment involves arbitrary social decisions. For criticism, see Hesse (1988).

ical' results of the sociologists of science, or inductions from their results, have any content which is a contribution of the social world of science that they study?

Anti-realism about nature is sometimes adopted as a *methodological*, rather than ontological, principle: in studying scientific beliefs, you should bracket nature and its possible influence, and concentrate on the social determinants of belief. If this is Collins's view, he is not an 'idealist' in the ontological sense. Ingemar Bohlin (1998) motivates this rule with the desire to avoid 'whig history': it would not be impartial to use our current theories in the evaluation of historical case studies, so that it is better methodologically to pretend that we have no knowledge about nature.

In my view, this principle would deprive us of the most important idea of current causal theories of knowledge: the justification of a belief crucially depends on our causal interaction with the object of the belief. This is also an essential feature of knowledge-seeking in science (see Section 4.4). For example, in evaluating the controversy between Galileo and the astronomers of the Church, it is of the utmost importance to know whether Galileo's telescope allowed him to be in causal interaction with Jupiter's moons. A methodology which brackets this question can only lead to a badly misleading historiography of science.[12]

More generally, I think that the attempt to make the historian and sociologist of science into a Baconian empiricist who has purified his mind from all 'idols' or prejudices (see Bacon 1960) is based upon the wrong ideal. Observations in science are theory-laden, and similarly historiography of science is laden with philosophical background assumptions (Agassi 1963). When historical episodes are evaluated relative to our current theories (see Section 6.6 for such an application of the ver-measure), the realist is not giving a question-begging attempt to *prove* that science makes progress, as Bohlin suspects. Retrospective assessments of the historical development of science are as fallible as our current theories.

In a recent book, written by Collins jointly with Trevor Pinch, the emphasis is on the uncertainty of scientific conclusions—a view which is well in harmony with fallibilist critical realism. The authors seem to be committed to a form of theoretical realism when they assert that the correct outcome in the dispute over gravity waves depends in part upon 'whether there are, or are not, gravity waves' (Collins and Pinch 1993: 138).

---

[12] Feyerabend was aware of this issue: his *Against Method* (1975) attempts to argue that Galileo's telescope was so bad that there was no point in the Church astronomers using it. See also Kitcher (1993: 168).

## 9.2 Finitism

To understand more deeply the position of the Edinburgh school, one should still consider its way of combining empiricism, materialism, and sociology. Bloor and Barnes have recognized the need to give independent philosophical support for their approach. In *Knowledge and Social Imagery* (1976), Bloor argues that the necessity characteristic of logical and mathematical thought is due to socially relative practices and 'negotiations'. Deriving inspiration from Wittgenstein's remarks on the foundations of mathematics, Kuhn (1962), and Hesse (1974; 1980), Bloor and Barnes have both suggested that social factors influence science primarily through the 'conventional character' of language and conceptual classifications (cf. Barnes 1981). In *Wittgenstein: A Social Theory of Knowledge* (1983), Bloor further argues that our thinking or mental states are socially constructed.

This strategy of argumentation as such does not lead to any conclusions which violate reasonable realist views. Human languages do have an important 'conventional' element: they are 'social constructions', the meanings of words are based upon conventions accepted and sustained in the linguistic community, and the choice of conceptual frameworks reflects human interests or social purposes (cf. Section 3.1). This is a fairly standard view of language among philosophers—from Peirce to Wittgenstein, Carnap, and Popper. It can be accepted as a part of scientific realism, instead of the physicalist view of languages (cf. Section 3.4), and without embracing Dummettian anti-realism (cf. Section 4.6) or Putnamian internal realism (cf. Ch. 7). It can be combined with the realist view about truth as correspondence. Many philosophers of mind would also accept that all humans are social beings who in their practices are always conditioned by the culture that they also transform. The human self indeed is a social and cultural construction, i.e. a World 3 entity (cf. Section 5.4). It does not follow that truth *about* languages (or about other social constructions in Popper's World 3), or truth expressible *in* these languages, is somehow relative to social interests (see e.g. Olivé 1987). And it does not follow that particular *beliefs* formulated in scientific languages have to be explained by social factors.

Given that I largely agree with Bloor about the social character of language, where is the possible difference in our views? The clue can be found in Bloor's (1974) early paper, where he rejects Popper's World 3 as a non-naturalistic or 'mystified' form of Platonism. In my view, the doctrine of World 3 instead shows how to be an anti-psychologist in logic and mathematics without being a Platonist, or how to be a constructivist and realist in mathematics at the same time (Niiniluoto 1992*b*). This contrast leads to a crucial difference: Bloor (1991) is convinced that concept application follows the principles of *finitism*, which is a narrow nominalist, conventionalist, and constructivist view.

Bloor discusses separately the applications of finitism to meaning and beliefs. All fallibilists will acknowledge that the application of concepts involves epistemic uncertainty: in claiming that the table in front of me is red, my perception may be mistaken; in claiming that it is two metres long, my measurement may be only approximate. For some important terms in everyday and scientific language, my use of them may be wrong, since I am ignorant of their proper criteria; but fortunately, according to the Division of Linguistic Labour (Putnam 1975), the community will usually include experts who are able to make the relevant distinctions.

For our purposes, it is more interesting to consider Bloor's finitism in relation to semantics. Here the starting point is Wittgenstein's definition of meaning as use, which involves the idea that language is a social institution, i.e. an activity based upon rules rather than mere behavioural regularities. (In the same way, it is not just a regular custom that cars drive on the left side in Great Britain and on the right side in Finland, but this behaviour is governed by socially accepted traffic regulations.) The doctrine of finitism then asks to what extent rules in fact are able to determine the applications of concepts.

According to Bloor's (1991) finitism, 'meaning is constructed as we go along': the future applications of a concept are not 'fully determined by what has gone before'. As they can always be contested and negotiated, the meanings have the 'character of social institutions' (ibid. 164, 167). This view is based on the model of ostensive learning (to which all definitions ultimately have to appeal): basic classificatory terms are introduced by pointing out exemplars or paradigm cases, and the further applications are made on the basis of similarity or resemblance (Kuhn 1962; Barnes, Bloor, and Henry 1996). This account does not identify the meaning as an 'algorithm fully formed in the present, capable of fixing the future correct use of the term, of distinguishing in advance all the things to which it will eventually be correctly applicable' (ibid. 55). Hence, meanings are never fully determined, and their future applications are always to some extent open—and thus liable to social negotiations.

Let us distinguish four different cases concerning the extent in which future applications of a concept are determined by rules:

All future cases are determined.                                        (F1)

Some future cases are determined, some undetermined.        (F2)

The future cases are only partially determined.                    (F3)

All future cases are undetermined.                                 (F4)

The alternative F1 suggests a fairly innocent interpretation of the thesis that we never know how our kind terms 'are going to be used' (ibid. 55). When the meaning of a concept has been institutionally agreed (by a dubbing ceremony, social convention, or definition), it may be *changed* later. This could be the case even when the meaning has been completely determined, so that F1 holds. The pressure for change may come from cognitive or social reasons, when the earlier use of the terms turns out to be inadequate (cf. Papineau 1996*b*: 19). It is no doubt true that there may be very strong political or ideological passions involved with the definition or refining of concepts—the distinction between 'male' and 'female' is a good example. Such conceptual change is certainly an important aspect of science (cf. Thagard 1992), as illustrated by the history of the concept of 'mass' in physics (see Kuhn 1990). Another example is the change in 1960 from the earlier ostensive definition of 'metre' (the platinium-iridium bar in Paris serving as the standard of length) to a new theoretical definition (the length equal to 1650763.73 wavelengths *in vacuo* of the radiation corresponding to the transition between the levels $2p_{10}$ and $5d_5$ of the isotype 86 of Krypton). This definition cannot even be understood without knowledge of modern physics, but it fixes the length of one metre in terms of a lawlike physical fact—and F1 seems to hold as long as the laws of nature do not change.

The finitist may object that the standard conceptions of meaning are too idealized or unrealistic if they assume that the extension of a term is fixed in all possible worlds (Montague) or (in a more Wittgensteinian mode) its use is fixed in all alternative situations. Here I agree that many of our terms in natural and scientific languages are vague in the sense that *all* of their future and potential applications are not predetermined by rules or specifications, i.e. F1 is too strong. However, it would be an instance of the All-or-Nothing Fallacy to conclude that the use of such terms is *never* determined: F4 is not the negation of F1, as F2 is also an alternative to F1. Condition F2 characterizes cases of *vagueness*: here indeterminacy concerns only problematic borderline cases, so that a term may still have antecedently specifiable clear positive and negative applications. We have no difficulties in applying the predicate 'red' to ripe strawberries, but the borderlines to oranges and grapes may be unsharp. Hence, from the fact that all future cases are not determined, it does not follow that an arbitrary 'next case' is undetermined.

Another alternative to F1 is F3 which allows that the next cases are in some way *partially* determined by rules. This case is treated in fuzzy logic:

the extension of a predicate is a 'fuzzy set', so that each object has some degree of membership (between 0 and 1) in this set.

It would be very problematic for a finitist to make the claim F4 in a strong form: if the future applications were always fully undetermined by rules, all concepts would be semantically completely indeterminate. If this were the case, human communication (if possible at all) would have to be explained by merely behavioural regularities in our use of language, which conflicts with the institutional viewpoint where we started.

In his latest book, Bloor (1997) gives a systematic defence of the view of rules and meanings as *social institutions*. Roughly speaking, an institution **I** exists for a group G if and only if the members of G mutually believe (accept) that **I** exists.[13] Again I agree with this social approach to rules, but not with Bloor's radical nominalism.[14] In rejecting 'meaning determinism', Bloor gives up the idea that rules exist 'in advance of our following them' (ibid. 21). Instead, 'we create meaning as we move from case to case' (ibid. 19). This seems to claim that we do not have any capacity to construe rules which have implications in advance for the next case; hence, even F3 is not a viable position, and the strong condition F4 seems to be implied.

The key to the doctrine of finitism comes from the Wittgensteinian idea of *rules*. Wittgenstein's famous account of rule-following in his remarks on the foundations of mathematics, and in his private language argument, has inspired anti-realistic interpretations of mathematics (Michael Dummett, Crispin Wright). Saul Kripke (1982) formulated a scepticist problem of rules: when a finite sequence of numbers is given, we may be unable to tell which rule has been followed in its construction, or perhaps there is even no fact about such a rule to be known.

A clear formulation of the problem of rule-following is given by Philip Pettit (1992). A rule should satisfy the 'objective condition' that it is applicable to an indefinite number and variety of situations, and the 'subjective condition' that it should be identifiable and effective in a finite mind. A rule-in-extension, as an infinite class of pairs, does not satisfy the subjective condition. A rule as an abstract function would be a Platonic entity which also fails to satisfy the subjective condition. If a rule is, instead, specified by giving a finite number of earlier instances, the objective

---

[13] For an analysis of social institutions as conventions in David Lewis's sense, see Searle (1995).

[14] Bloor's nominalism is clear when he claims that predicates do not have extensions: 'particular things, or individual objects, exist in advance, but not classes of things' (Bloor 1997: 24). Here I agree with Bloor that classes are human constructions, but not with his finitist assumption that the only way of constructing classes is by adding one member after another.

condition is not satisfied, since the earlier cases can be extrapolated in an infinite number of ways.

Bloor's (1973) early discussion of mathematics is based on such Wittgensteinian problems, and in his finitism they are extended to concepts and beliefs as social institutions. For example, the finite sequence <3, 6, 9, 12> does not uniquely determine its next member, and it is up to us to decide whether it is 15 or something else. I think we should acknowledge this as a fact. There is nothing in mathematics, whether Platonist or not, which presupposes that such sequences have a unique or predetermined continuation (*pace* Bloor 1973). The problem of extending such a finite sequence is not a *mathematical* problem, and does not tell us anything interesting about the viability of the sociology of mathematics. In some contexts, the sequence may exemplify an underlying rule (for example, you try to guess what rule I had in mind). Sequences of this sort are often used in intelligence tests, but there the idea is to pick out the simplest rule that they instantiate, and similar behaviour can be taught even to computers. However, if the sequence consists of the digits in the decimal expansion of $\pi=3.1415926\ldots$, then the problem belongs to mathematics—and there are well-known algorithms for continuing the sequence, and no reference to social 'negotiations' is needed.

The last point about mathematics may be generalized: *infinite mathematical sequences can be defined by a finite specification.* This solves Pettit's puzzle at least in mathematics. For example, an infinite sequence can be defined by $<3n|n\in N>$, i.e. the members of this sequence are $a_n=3n$ for $n=1, 2, 3, \ldots$ More precisely, this sequence is defined recursively by the conditions

$$a_0=3 \tag{4}$$
$$a_{n+1}=a_n+3.$$

Similarly, when the number zero 0 and the successor operation $S(x)=x+1$ are given in arithmetic,[15] the sum of two natural numbers is defined recursively:

$$x+0=x \tag{5}$$
$$x+S(y)=S(x+y)$$

---

[15] The problem of extending finite sequences already presupposes that the concept of natural number is known and understood. In Peano arithmetic, zero 0 and successor function S are the two undefined primitive concepts, and anything that satisfies Peano's axioms may be taken to be 0 and S. Simple explicit constructions of these notions can be given in set theory.

for all x and y in N. Definition (5) specifies a rule that can be applied to an infinite number of special cases. It can be identified by a finite description in World 1, and by a finite mind in World 2, but it defines the sum function as a public entity in World 3.

Against general forms of rule scepticism, this analysis shows that in mathematics it is possible to have rules which define sequences with the property F1. For the possibility of rules in language, it is remarkable that our mastery and understanding of the syntax and semantics of natural languages is also largely based on recursive principles (as shown by Chomsky's work on generative grammars and Tarski's definition of truth). In human languages, there are also methods of explication (cf. Carnap 1962) which aim at making vague and fuzzy concepts more precise.

More generally, against radical nominalism about rules, I think it is important to emphasize that social customs and norms as World 3 entities are in a sense more than their *actual* instances in human behaviour. Here the doctrine of World 3 differs from finitism.[16] Thus, if linguistic meaning is identified with 'use' following Wittgenstein's suggestion, it should not be understood only as the sum of actual uses so far, but at least some future and potential uses should be included as well.

I conclude that Bloor's attack on 'meaning determinism' does not show the incoherence of the idea of rule-governed linguistic meaning (in the sense F1). It is still feasible to maintain the realist principle defended in Chapter 7: we choose the language L, and the world decides which sentences of L are true. There are also semantic methods that the realist can employ in treating the cases F2 and F3: statements with vague and fuzzy concepts may be assigned degrees of truthlikeness (see Niiniluoto 1987a). The meanings that are created by linguistic communities may be incomplete, but they can be refined and changed. There are cases where debates about meaning are influenced by 'social' factors, but this is a natural consequence of the fact that language is a social institution.

Radical social relativism about truth and scientific beliefs would need stronger premisses than the conventional character of human languages

---

[16] If the world is deterministic, the laws of nature (construed in a non-Humean or non-nominalistic way) fix sequences of events in the strong sense F1. If the world is indeterministic, and governed by probabilistic laws, the alternative F3 holds. On the other hand, F4 would correspond to an atomistic or lawless world. Bloor (1997) gives a very interesting illustration of finitism: the price of a commodity in a market economy is not determined by the past, but is fixed at each instance of time by a complex process of social pressures and negotiations. My guess is that this situation should be described by F3 rather than by F4.

and the social nature of human minds. We shall now turn to the programme
of 'constructivism' that has attempted to establish such premisses.[17]


## 9.3 Life in laboratory

Among the sociologists of science, the *constructivist* programme appears
to be currently the most popular approach. Its classical works are Bruno
Latour's and Steve Woolgar's *Laboratory Life: The Social Construction
of Scientific Facts* (1979) and Karin Knorr-Cetina's *The Manufacture of
Knowledge* (1981).[18]

The constructivists are interested in the actual production of scientific
knowledge within research groups working in laboratories. As their
method they typically use participant observation by an 'outsider' in the
laboratory witnessing the strange behaviour of the 'tribe' of scientists. This
'ethnographic study of scientific work' (Knorr-Cetina 1983) thus attempts
to approach science in the same way as an anthropologist investigates
foreign cultures.

In a well-known passage, Pierre Duhem described the experience of a
layman in a physical laboratory:

Go into this laboratory; draw near this table crowded with so much apparatus: an
electric battery, copper wire wrapped in silk, vessels filled with mercury, coils, a
small iron bar carrying a mirror. An observer plunges the metallic stem of a rod,
mounted with rubber, into small holes; the iron oscillates and, by means of the
mirror tied to it, sends a beam of light over to a celluloid ruler, and the observer

---

[17] Among the social approaches to science, one should mention *social epistemology*. This
is the title of Steve Fuller's (1988) book and of a new journal he has founded. The scope of
social epistemology includes studies of collective cognitive rationality and consensus formation (e.g. Habermas, Lehrer, Goldman), and as such does not question the possibility of
realism. Kusch (1991*a*), appealing to the underdetermination thesis and Foucault's notion
of power, defends social relativism about science by the counterfactual: we would not have
scientific knowledge if there were no networks of social power within the scientific community and within the relations between science and society. I agree that science would not
exist without social practices and norms concerning research organization, funding, science
policy, universities, research institutes and laboratories, libraries and journals, a reward
system, authority, methodology, and ethics. (See also Longino 1990; Kitcher 1993.) It is also
plausible that in some cases social valuations and interests (personal vanity, lust for
resources and power, politics, and religion) have influenced the contents of the beliefs of
scientists (not only the choice of the problems that they study or programmes that they
pursue). These points about the fallibility of the scientists do not imply radical forms of relativism about scientific knowledge, truth, and reality.

[18] See also Knorr-Cetina and Mulkay (1983), Latour (1987; 1992), Woolgar (1988), Knorr-
Cetina (1995). For comments, see Tibbets (1986), Brown (1989), Hacking (1988), Niiniluoto
(1991*a*), McMullin (1992), Nickles (1992), and Haack (1996*a*).

follows the movement of the light beam on it. There, no doubt, you have an experiment; by means of the vibration of this spot of light, this physicist minutely observes the oscillations of the piece of iron. Ask him now what he is doing. Is he going to answer: 'I am studying the oscillations of the piece of iron carrying this mirror'? No, he will tell you that he is measuring the electrical resistance of a coil. If you are astonished and ask him what meaning these words have, and what relation they have to the phenomena he has perceived and which you have at the same time perceived, he will reply that your questions would require some very long explanations, and he will recommend that you take a course in electricity. (Duhem 1954: 145)

A similar situation was repeated some decades later, in 1975, when Duhem's young compatriot Bruno Latour—without training in chemistry, biology, and social studies of science—entered R. Guillemin's biochemical laboratory at La Jolla, California. *Laboratory Life* (1979) is an exciting and lively description of Latour's adventures in the wonderland of Guillemin's laboratory. It has inspired a whole generation of young sociologists who now go to laboratories with the same fervour as the first anthropologist travelled a hundred years earlier to do field work among wild and exotic cultures.

The 'anthropological' study of the everyday laboratory practices of science may give very interesting new perspectives on the construction of scientific *beliefs* or *knowledge* in the scientific community. Hacking (1988) appreciates what Latour's studies tell us about the use of the experimental method as a scientific group work. But the constructivists wish to interpret this process more radically as a construction of scientific *facts*, theoretical *entities*, and even *reality*. They further think that this interpretation 'makes unnecessary the use of ad hoc epistemological explanations' (Latour and Woolgar 1986: 166). In his 1986 postscript, Latour notes that some philosophers of science have recently shown sympathy towards the sociology of knowledge, so that 'perhaps it is not any more productive to reject all attempts to philosophize about science'. But still Latour proposes 'a ten-year moratorium on cognitive explanations of science' (ibid. 280).

However, it is again clear that the constructivist programme is committed to very strong philosophical assumptions. In criticizing the prejudices of philosophers Latour reveals his own preconceptions. Already the decision to employ observation by an outsider who has freed his mind from all prejudices about science is laden with the rhetoric of naive Baconian inductivism, positivism, and behaviourism.

Latour and Woolgar admit that their 'observer' is not in a more privileged position than 'research informants', but they believe in the methodological value of the 'outsider' approach (ibid. 278). Latour thus starts from an 'agnostic position': 'There are, as far as we know, no a priori reasons for supposing that scientists' practice is any more rational than that of outsiders' (ibid. 30). It is an interesting idea to study scientific activities by suspending judgement about the rationality of science. But as the story goes on, Latour urges that the *falsity* of this supposition follows from his anti-epistemological starting point:

The notion that there is something special about science, something peculiar or mysterious which materialist and constructivist explanations can never grasp, . . . will remain as long as the idea lingers that there is some peculiar thinking process in the scientist's mind. (Ibid. 168)

This idea, which would save the *ad hoc* epistemological concepts of which 'we have tried to rid ourselves', is 'inconsistent with our argument so far'. Thus, Latour's story involves a fallacious slide from

I don't assume that science is rational

first to

I assume that science is not rational

and finally to

I prove that science is not rational.

Woolgar (1988: 12) repeats the conclusion that 'there is no essential difference between science and other forms of knowledge production'.

This conclusion has been transformed from a methodological principle to the superdogma of the constructivist school (see also Russell 1983). In her recent survey of the empirical study of 'the creation of knowledge at the workbench and in notebooks, in scientific shop talk, in the writing of scientific papers', Knorr-Cetina (1995) asserts that 'one immediate result of all laboratory studies was that nothing epistemologically significant was happening in these instances' (p. 151). How could such a momentous conclusion be an 'immediate result'? By what criteria of 'epistemologically significant'? And if this 'result' were correct—e.g. there were only sociological differences between modern medical laboratories, Zande magic, and Renaissance astrology—would not that undermine the credibility of the empirical studies of science as well?

As an illustration of possible epistemological interpretations of laboratory work we may refer to Latour's (1983) interesting observation about the 'Pasteurization' of France. His point is that Pasteur did not study 'nature' in his laboratory, but only phenomena in artificial conditions. To make his work successful in practice outside laboratory, Pasteur had to extend these artificial conditions to cover the whole of society.

From the realist's viewpoint, this is illuminating but not surprising. Galileo had to test his law of free fall in special circumstances, because his law contained idealizations. Manipulation of nature in controlled experimentation is needed especially for the reason that scientific theories typically are *idealizational*, and state what would happen in counterfactual situations (see Section 5.3). More generally, the constructivist sociologists of science agree with instrumentalism in taking the laboratory phenomena as the *objects* of investigation in the natural sciences—instead of treating them as *evidence* for theoretical claims about the world outside the laboratory, as realism does (see Section 5.1). Laboratory work is not random collection of empirical data, as the naive inductivists assume (cf. Hempel 1965), but is designed to test theoretical hypotheses and thereby to contribute to solving cognitive problems. It is this feature that makes it epistemologically interesting.

The most central idea of the constructivist programme is expressed by the claim that scientific reality is an artefact, created by selective, contextual, and socially situated scientific laboratory practices and negotiations.

The constructivist interpretation is opposed to the conception of scientific investigation as descriptive, a conception which locates the problem of facticity in the relation between the products of science and an external nature. (Knorr-Cetina 1983: 118–19)

As 'scientific objects are produced in the laboratory',

it is the thrust of the constructivist conception to conceive of scientific reality as progressively emerging out of indeterminacy and (self-referential) constructive operations, without assuming it to match any pre-existing order of the real. (Ibid. 135)

According to Woolgar (1988: 65–7) scientific objects like pulsars do not exist prior to their discovery, but they are 'constituted' by 'representational practices' and 'the social network'.

In the Latour–Woolgar story, Guillemin's laboratory used 200 tons of pig brains to synthesize one milligram of Thyrotropin Releasing Factor (TRH)—a substance in the hypothalamus that releases a hormone, thyrotropin, from the pituitary. For this work, Guillemin received (with Schally) the Nobel Prize in 1977.

Latour interprets TRH as an artificial laboratory construction, and the fact that TRH is Pyro-Glu-His-Pro-NH$_2$ as a social construction. Scientific facts are created by a consensus, or by the acceptance of a statement, which is preceded by experiments, measurements, inscriptions, debates, and negotiations.

We do not wish to say that facts do not exist nor that there is no such thing as reality. In this simple sense our position is not relativist. Our point is that 'out-there-ness' is the *consequence* of scientific work rather than its cause. (Latour and Woolgar 1986: 180)

It is clear that this statement leads to a form of anti-realism: theories cannot be compared to a pre-existing external reality. As reality in this view is a consequence of scientific work, it cannot exert any causal influence on the process of constructing scientific knowledge.[19]

We have seen that the causal impact of reality on beliefs is an important element of Peirce's conception of scientific method (Section 4.4), causal theories of knowledge, and even Bloor's naturalism. It is not quite easy to locate the constructivists precisely in a coordinate system of contemporary philosophy of science. Knorr-Cetina has noted the resemblance of her view to Merleau-Ponty's phenomenology and Goodman's world-making. Woolgar's example of pulsars reminds us of the Goodmanian project of starmaking (see Section 7.1). Similarities to other classical (John Dewey) and contemporary pragmatists, as well as Gaston Bachelard (see Castelão-Lawless 1995) and practical materialists (Lukács 1971), are also evident. For example, referring to Latour, Rorty (1998: 8) wishes to get rid of the notion that quarks and human rights differ in 'ontological status'. But there are also important differences. Where the anti-relativist consensus theorists (like Putnam and Habermas) follow Peirce in speaking about epistemically ideal research and discourse communities, the sociological constructivists talk about finite and sharply localized communities (such as Guillemin's laboratory).

Moreover, the subtitle of Latour and Woolgar's book is clearly taken from Berger and Luckmann's phenomenological *The Social Construction of Reality* (1971). However, while Berger and Luckmann are clearly speaking about the constitution of social reality (or World 3), Latour is making a statement about theoretical entities in natural science. For this reason, I think it is interesting to compare Latour's account of TRH to rival philosophical views about the status of theoretical terms (Niiniluoto 1991*a*).

---

[19] Trevor Pinch and Wiebe Bijker suggested in 1984 the application of constructivist ideas in the study of technology: successful and unsuccessful machines should be studied symmetrically (cf. Bloor), and machines work because they have been accepted by relevant social groups, and not vice versa (cf. Latour) (see Bijker and Law 1992; Bijker 1995). As such the idea that machines are socially constructed fits much better with technological artefacts (in World 3) than with theoretical entities in physics and biology. But again the order of explanation becomes problematic. In one sense, it is of course correct that technological tools (like cars) work as they do by virtue of the activities of the engineers. But in another sense, material artefacts have objective physical properties, and these properties explain their capacity to work well (cf. Section 5.5).

Scientific realists typically think that theories attempt to match pre-existing entities in reality (cf. Ch. 5). A weaker version of theoretical realism, the so-called entity realism, agrees that theoretical entities do exist, in spite of the lack of truth of theoretical laws. Instrumentalism brackets the existence of theoretical entities, or regards them at best as useful fictions.

A position between instrumentalism and realism is represented by those philosophers who think that theoretical entities are 'constructions'. For example, phenomenalists (like the young Carnap) claimed that theoretical terms can be explicitly defined by means of observational ones, so that theoretical entities are (to use Russell's phrase) *logical constructions* out of sense data. A mentalist interpretation of this stance, favoured by some 'constructivist' philosophers of mathematics, regards theoretical entities as *mental constructs* in the human mind. Finally, theoretical entities may be viewed as results of *material constructions*, i.e. as experimentally produced artefacts. Examples of these artefacts include radioactive substances and synthetic materials produced in physical and chemical laboratories.

Latour's account of TRH is not identical with any of the above views. He treats TRH as an artificial construction of Guillemin's laboratory team, but the process he describes is not an instance of a logical, mental, or material construction. Perhaps definitions and theories, but not hormones, may be 'logically constructed' from the researchers' measurements, statements, and inscriptions. TRH can hardly be a 'mental construction' in the researcher's brain, either, since its production needs masses of pig brains.

Also the alternative of 'material construction' is excluded.[20] For example, the team at La Jolla did not simply bring about the substance TRH—in the same causal sense as, for example, neutrinos can be 'created' in an accelerator by bombing heavy nucleii with α-particles and by letting the free neutrons decay into protons, positrons, and neutrinos. Such a causal creation takes place, even if we know nothing about neutrinos. Instead, Latour urges that facts about TRH were consequences of the eventually reached *consensus* in the laboratory community:

[20] Referring to Andrew Pickering's work on the 'construction' of weak neutral currents and quarks, Nickles (1992) suggests that Latour and Woolgar, too, presuppose material and interpretative practices for the construction of reality. This does not change the peculiar role of paperwork, discourse, dropping modalities, and consensus in Latour's account. Nickles further points out that in material laboratory constructions we can make sense of a phenomenon existing potentially and 'waiting to be discovered'. Similarly, Brown (1989) argues that the material construction of new physical phenomena in laboratory is not a social construction, since the potential for their existence 'has always been there'. For example, it is not up to us to invent the nature and properties of transuranic elements, even though they are produced for the first time in laboratories.

experiments
measurements
inscriptions  → consensus  → fact
negotiations

An important part of this process involves changes in the 'modalities' of statements which eventually lead to a 'closure' of the negotiation. Latour's social construction, mediated by a consensus, is thus epistemic or doxastic in a peculiar sense.

There are indeed cultural entities and institutions (such as language, legal order, state), and cultural non-physical properties of material artefacts (such as their function, meaning, monetary value), which presuppose the existence of a social consensus in the relevant community (see e.g. Searle 1995). These entities and properties belong to World 3. From the realist's viewpoint, to understand theoretical entities in natural science in the same way would be a confusion between Worlds 1 and 3.

The realist can further argue that the order from consensus to theoretical entities is mistaken. Take first an example from the common-sense framework: we are able to agree, by our perceptual and linguistic abilities, that the thing in front of us is a table. The existence of this table cannot be explained by this consensus, but rather our ability to reach a *consensus can be explained by the permanent existence of the table* (cf. Section 2.5). A critical realist extends this account of everyday objects (as ontologically prior to our perceptions and opinions about them) to scientific objects. The available fossil evidence warrants an abductive reasoning to the existence of dinosaurs more than 300 million years ago, and the previous existence of these animals (a long time before a concept identifying them was invented) and the traces they have left for posterity explain our present consensus. Similarly, the agreement of Guillemin's team did not create TRH, but rather the previous existence of a substance controlling metabolism and maturation in animal and human bodies, together with the use of scientific methods of experimentation, explains the fact that the 'negotiations' did reach an agreement that TRH exists and is Pyro-Glu-His-Pro-NH$_2$.

Only this order of explanation makes sense of the further fact that other laboratories have also been able to *discover* the *same* substance with the same structure as Guillemin. And if it were literally true to claim that scientists construct theoretical entities, then they would be also *causally and morally responsible* for them. But this would lead to absurdities: certainly the workers of R. Gallo's laboratory, which first identified the HI-virus, cannot be blamed for the later and earlier infections that this virus (i.e. other tokens of this virus-type) has caused and will cause. (Again we see that anti-realism runs into trouble with the reality of the past.)

It is not only the case that the critical realist can present a more plausible story about theoretical discoveries in science than a social constructivist. The same facts—our ability to construct and manipulate theoretical entities—that Latour uses for defending his special brand of anti-realism have been employed by Hacking (1983; 1988) as 'an experimental argument' for entity realism. Essentially the same idea—derived from the Plato–Vico idea that Maker's Knowledge has a higher epistemic status than Spectator's Knowledge—was a key element of Friedrich Engels's 1886 criticism of Kantian agnosticism:

In addition there is yet a set of different philosophers—those who question the possibility of any cognition, or at least of an exhaustive cognition, of the world. To them, among the more modern ones, belong Hume and Kant . . . The most telling refutation of this as of all other philosophical crotchets is practice, namely, experiment and industry. If we are able to prove the correctness of our conception of a natural process by making it ourselves, bringing it into being out of its conditions and making it serve our own purposes into the bargain, then there is an end to the Kantian ungraspable 'thing-in-itself'. The chemical substances produced in the bodies of plants and animals remained just such 'things-in-themselves' until organic chemistry began to produce them one after another, whereupon the 'thing-in-itself' became a thing for us, as, for instance, alizarin, the colouring matter of the madder, which we no longer trouble to grow in the madder roots in the field, but produce much more cheaply and simply from coal tar. (Engels 1946: 24.)

Here Engels makes a stronger claim than the entity realist Hacking: our ability to produce chemical substances (similar to TRH) serves as a proof of our knowledge about their existence *and* properties.

Perhaps a critical reader may suspect that my reading of Latour's strange position is unfair. To do justice to him, I mention three possible charitable interpretations of social constructivism. Encouragement for such discussion comes from Latour's (1992: 292) (remembering his moratorium[21]) surprisingly generous remark: 'The idea that science studies may ignore philosophy altogether, . . . or not build up its own metaphysics and ontology is foreign to me.'

---

[21] Tibbets (1986) argues with fervour for the thesis that the advocates of the empiricist relativist and constructivist programmes 'simply refuse to play according to the rules and guidelines established by traditional philosophy': when terms like 'truth', 'reality', 'facts', and 'knowledge' appear, they are 'reconstructed in sociological terms'. Tibbets fails to show why these programmes nevertheless wish to conduct empirical case studies and inductions from them in the style of traditional methodology and philosophy.

First, Brown (1989: 83) points out that Latour's argument ignores the difference between a *fact* and what is *believed to be a fact*.[22] For a fallibilist, all theoretical statements (e.g. about TRH) and beliefs about reality are always conjectural. If the talk about 'constructing facts' really means only the creation of conjectural theories about the world, Latour would be a good Popperian who has used misleading terms to express his view.

Secondly, the incommensurability view, inspired by Kuhn's and Feyerabend's holistic theory of meaning, can be seen to imply the doctrine that each theory defines those 'theoretical constructs' it speaks about. For example, each theory of electrons speaks about its own 'electrons' which satisfy its axioms. But when theories change, the postulated ontologies are also radically ruptured. To speak of electrons independently of any theory does not make any sense on this view, which also represents a relativist position about theoretical entities. In this sense, the creation of a theory about TRH at the same time creates TRH as a 'theoretical construct'. We have argued in Section 5.2 that this view is based on a wrong theory of meaning and reference. A theoretical realist interprets rival theories as speaking of the *same unknown entities*, identified indirectly through their causal role and influences, so that successive theories may give conjectural but increasingly accurate descriptions of the nature of these things.

Thirdly, in order to refer by a word to physical objects (such as 'table', 'horse', 'electron') a consensus about the meaning of these words is presupposed. Latour's story could be understood as a description of how Guillemin's team 'constructed' the *definition* or *criteria* for TRH (see Brown 1989: 84). Internal realists think that the existence of all objects is relative to such linguistic definitions. This nominalist doctrine involves a kind of magical theory of the creation of objects by naming or defining (cf. Section 7.3). To claim that the reality of physical objects depends on a preceding consensus about their definition or agreement on their existence also runs against the reasons for distinguishing World 1 and World 3. But if by TRH one means the *identified object* under a linguistic description, then the dependence on the theoretical description can be understood. An interpretation in this direction has recently been suggested by Knorr-Cetina (1995: 161) as a response to Giere's (1988) criticism: the constructivist account 'does not preclude the possibility

[22] Latour's way of speaking about 'facts' resembles Ludwig Fleck's pioneering work in 1935 (see Fleck 1979, with Kuhn's preface). Fleck analyses the way in which empirical scientific facts 'originate' through the work of 'thought collectives'. Both thinking and facts are 'changeable' for him.

that some physical correlate of this entity existed, unidentified, tangled up with other materials, before scientists turned attention to this object', and thus provided for 'the encounterability' of this object 'within forms of life'.

My initial literal interpretation makes Latour an original thinker who runs into absurd consequences. The three charitable interpretations make him an ordinary Popperian, Kuhnian, or Putnamian who has not formulated his view in a clear way. Anyone who is not satisfied with these alternatives should construct a new proposal for us to negotiate.

These alternative interpretations are not directly very topical for Latour any more. In his recent work, he makes a fluent attempt to go beyond modernism and postmodernism (see Latour 1993): the modern way of thinking with the dichotomies society/nature or taken/found is unable to deal with 'hybrids' or 'quasi-objects' like holes in the ozone layer or mad cow disease. In conclusion, he recommends 'one more turn after the social turn' (Latour 1992). But his new position takes from the earlier one some ingredients that I consider fallacious.

With Michael Callon (cf. Jasanoff *et al.* 1995), Latour advocates a principle of Generalized Symmetry which tries to overcome the Kantian dichotomy of subject/object or society/nature. In his view, Bloor and Collins are 'asymmetric' in requiring that society explain nature. Using the actor-network model (cf. Latour 1987), with human and non-human 'actants', one should treat nature and society symmetrically: they are both 'results of the practice of science- and technology-making'. 'The activity of nature/society making becomes the *source* from which societies and natures originate' (Latour 1992: 282). At the same time, the distinction between natural objects and artefacts is blurred. This ontological view, where action precedes nature and society, seems to be a form of practical materialism (cf. Section 7.1).

I do not find this ontology very promising.[23] One of its problems is the threat of an infinite regress: from which source do the activities of science and technology originate? Further, in processes and actions it is already possible and easy to distinguish material, mental, and social aspects. There are processes with non-human actants, without mental and social aspects,

[23] The ontological problems with 'hybrids' are genuine and worth studying—and again illustrate the power of the World 3 terminology. Whether holes are existing 'entities' is an old puzzle for ontological theories. But holes in the ozone layer, produced unintentionally by human activities, clearly belong to World 1: recall that nature is not claimed to be causally independent of human activities (see Section 2.3). A material artefact has a World 1 kernel, shaped by a human designer, but it becomes a World 3 entity when the kernel is joined with its cultural properties (see Section 2.4).

e.g. a fusion reaction in the sun, and they need no co-authoring from 'technoscience' in order to become nature. The Lysenko case (see Roll-Hansen 1989) reminds us that facts about nature proved to be resistant against practical manipulation, i.e. the growth and heredity of plants could not be changed by any actions of the believers of the 'practice criterion'. Nature did not result from science- and technology-making.

# 10

# Realism, Science, and Society

Scientific realism and its alternatives are philosophical positions which can be defended and criticized from the perspectives of ontology, semantics, epistemology, axiology, and methodology. In the earlier chapters, we have gone through various kinds of rational arguments for and against realism.

In Section 9.2, I suggested a Weak Programme of the sociology of science which should study the motivations and reasons why certain views about science have been socially attractive or accepted in different communities and different times.[1] It is clear that the problem of realism itself provides a highly interesting case study for such an approach. Realism has gained support because such a defence of scientific knowledge has been expected to be socially, economically, and morally desirable. Similarly, realism has been opposed by thinkers who, for one reason or another, wish to undermine the epistemic authority of science. In Section 10.1, historical illustrations of such views are given—from the ancient philosophical schools to the present day Science Wars.

In Section 10.2, I consider more systematically the question concerning the cultural value of science. It is argued that one can overcome the usual contrast between two views, one defending science as an instrumental value and the other as an intrinsic value. At the same time, excessive forms of 'scientism' can be avoided.

Finally, in Section 10.3, attention is given to critics who wish to emphasize the values of freedom (Paul Feyerabend) and solidarity (Richard Rorty) over and above the ideals of scientific method and objectivity. Against these contrasts, I argue that the existence and advance of science in the critical realist's sense can promote good human life in a democratic society. But this is possible only on the important condition for

---

[1] See Niiniluoto (1991a). Kusch (1995), who calls his programme the Sociology of Philosophical Knowledge (SPK), has recently studied the sociology of philosophical arguments in connection with the debates on psychologism at the turn of the century. He accepts Bloor's principle of Impartiality (cf. Section 8.1) in the sense that no standpoint is adopted concerning the truth or falsity of the considered philosophical views. Barnes and Bloor (1982: 47) ask the sociological question of what 'might account for the remarkable intensity of the Faith in Reason', and answer that 'relativism is disliked because so many academics see it as a dampener on their moralizing'.

science policy that science as a social institution is able to maintain its truth-centred methodological and ethical norms.

### 10.1 Social reasons for realism and anti-realism

Most schools of Greek philosophy were devoted to the search of wisdom (Greek *sophia*) in a sense which combines epistemological and ethical questions in an intimate way. A proper type of knowledge was assumed to be conducive, or even necessary, to a happy life (Greek *eudaimonia*).

For Socrates and Plato, this connection is expressed by the slogan 'virtue is knowledge': philosophical wisdom, enlightened by the idea of goodness, gives access to the true and the good.

For Aristotle, knowledge-seeking is a natural disposition of all men. Knowledge can be organized into systematic bodies of theoretical sciences (concerned with truth about the world) and practical sciences (concerned with human action). Ethics and politics as practical sciences help the human intellect to know the ends of good life and thereby to make the right choices in deliberation.

For the Epicureans, materialist philosophy gives the foundation for a peaceful life, where, as Lucretius states in his poem, men are oblivious to the fear of death and gods. Similarly, *ataraxia* or unperturbed mind is guaranteed for the Stoics by the true principles of philosophy. All these views share the assumption that *knowledge of infallible truths is a necessary condition of human individual happiness.* To be an owner of truths is thereby a moral virtue for a person.

In the medieval synthesis of Greek philosophy and Christian theology also, the mental possession and contemplation of truths was regarded as the highest state of man; error and ignorance were sins. Such truths included, besides the doctrines of religion, also the achievements of the Aristotelian sciences—interpreted in the realist way as truths about reality (see Section 5.4). The great scholastic teachers of the Catholic Church thus combined realist views of religion and science in their world view.

A radically different view of eudaimonism was offered by the relativist and sceptical schools of antiquity. According to Protagoras, 'man is the measure of all things': systems of belief, ethics, religion, and state are all human-made, and there are no universally valid truths in these areas. Therefore, Protagoras suggested, we can make our life comfortable by adopting those beliefs that happen to prevail in our own community.

Similar practical wisdom was taught by the sceptical tradition, from Pyrrho of Elis (fourth century BC) to the Academic sceptics (Archesilaus,

Carneades) and Sextus Empiricus (second century AD). (See Burnyeat 1983.) These philosophers sought good life from *epoche*, suspension of judgement. They had many important theoretical arguments against the possibility of knowledge—senses may deceive us, reasoning may be flawed, alternative views can be supported by equally strong arguments—but they also thought that *epoche* saves the wise man from dogmatism and fanaticism, and thereby gives him peaceful tranquillity. In other words, suspension of judgement, *denial of knowledge is a necessary condition of a happy life*.

The withholding of assent in theoretical matters leaves room for practical action which follows 'probability' or 'verisimilitude' (Carneades, Cicero). At least according to Burnyeat's interpretation, this term referred to appearances of things in contrast to realities beyond the appearances.[2] Such a life with appearances follows 'the guidance of nature, the compulsion of the feelings, the tradition of laws and customs, and the instruction of arts' (Sextus Empiricus 1985). In P. P. Hallie's words, a Pyrrhonian sceptic lives peacefully 'according to the institutions of one's own country and the dictates of one's own feelings, experience, and common sense'.[3]

Ancient sceptics are thus epistemological anti-realists in the sense that they deny knowledge of reality behind the appearances. Augustine objected to this position in his *Contra Academicos*: a man who does not attain truth cannot be happy. Every man 'earnestly desires' the truth, and if he cannot find it, he should 'get a grip on himself and refuse to desire truth so that, since he cannot possess it, he may thus avoid being of necessity unhappy'.[4] The fact that man can live happily is, therefore, a proof of his ability to find the truth.

Another kind of criticism of human knowledge (especially *scientia* as the sort of wisdom offered by science) was based upon mystical and religious views which wished to warn man of hubris, namely of the temptation to penetrate into the area of forbidden secrets. Many ancient and medieval myths and tales (the tree of knowledge in Genesis, Prometheus, Icarus, Faust) suggested that human efforts toward new inventions were somehow dangerous or connected to evil forces (von Wright 1993). This kind of anti-realism was founded on moral, rather than epistemological, arguments: there are ethical limitations to the legitimate area of human knowledge.

---

[2] For other interpretations, which make Carneades and Cicero forerunners of critical realism, see Niiniluoto (1999*b*).
[3] See the foreword to Sextus Empiricus (1985).
[4] See Augustine (1950: 46). This argument is well known as 'sour grapes'. A modern version has been put forward by Laudan: as truth is a utopian goal, it is not rational to pursue it (cf. Section 6.2).

When Pyrrhonian scepticism was revived in the sixteenth century, its arguments were first directed against the Protestant religion and against science (in both the Aristotelian and emerging modern forms). This attack was combined with fideism, i.e. the thesis that the sufficient foundation of religion is faith without any rational supporting reasons. Michel de Montaigne and most other 'nouveaux Pyrrhoniens' thus employed the devastating 'war machine' of scepticism to support a fideist conception of Catholicism (see Popkin 1979). It was only later, most notably with David Hume in the eighteenth century, that the sceptical position was equally directed against science and religion.

The desire to *leave room for faith* has been a forceful motive for anti-realism about science. When the new Copernican system seemed to shake the pillars of the doctrines of the Church, an instrumentalist interpretation of astronomical theories was proposed as a remedy. Cardinal Bellarmine told Galileo in 1619 that the teaching and application of the heliocentric system was allowed, if it was presented hypothetically, merely as a tool for saving the phenomena, not as a truth about the universe, since such a 'dangerous attitude' would 'arouse all Scholastic philosophers and theologians' and 'injure our holy faith by contradicting the Scriptures' (cf. Section 5.4).

The instrumentalist view thus served here as a conservative reaction to defend religious doctrines from the advances of science. This is clear also from Pierre Duhem's case; he described his instrumentalist position (namely the inability of natural science to give real explanations) as the 'physics of a believer' (Duhem 1954). The same tendency is visible in those thinkers who often adopting narrow empiricism and theoretical anti-realism about science, hail the alleged cognitive limitations of indeterminist quantum physics as a starting point for religious speculations.[5]

The main founders of modern science were realists about scientific theories, but their grounds were at least partly metaphysical: Galileo's Platonism, Kepler's deification of the sun, Newton's theological cosmology (cf. Burtt 1954). The champions of scientific revolution also insisted that the new physics and astronomy could be conclusively proved. However, it was well known already at the time that successful predictions cannot strictly speaking prove a hypothetical theory: as Clavius correctly pointed out, such an inference would involve the fallacy of affirming the consequent (Blake, Ducasse, and Madden 1960). For this reason it is conceivable that Galileo—perhaps intentionally—exaggerated the certainty of his demonstrations, since he had to fight with the Church, a powerful adversary.

[5] For example, Laurikainen (1985; 1987), who appeals to Wolfgang Pauli on this issue, finds in quantum mechanics a proof of the possibility that God, as a Spirit with free will, may interfere with the rational order of nature. Cf. Section 5.4.

Francis Bacon also claimed certainty on the basis of his inductive experimental method (see Bacon 1960). His programme for the advancement of learning re-established the link between truth and happiness with a threefold optimism: the right methods will rapidly bring about new scientific results; this knowledge enhances man's power over nature; and this increased power helps to subdue miseries and foster human happiness. Knowledge in the realist sense, as certified truth about the 'forms' of 'nature', is thus desirable, since it is *useful for the purposes of developing technological know-how*. This idea has continued to be a characteristic assumption of the modern age, of the scientific-technological revolution, of the rise of new forms and institutions of applied research, and of the philosophical schools of Marxism and pragmatism (cf. Section 10.2).

Bacon argued for the legitimacy of science also in terms of religion: humanity lost its original mastery of nature in the fall of Adam, but science is designed gradually to restore this power through useful inventions. When this work is finished, the Millennium will commence.[6]

The modern era is characterized by the ideals of individualism, freedom of thought, democracy, equality, and progress. It is often said that in this period science conquered the place that religion occupied in the premodern age. But in fact academic institutions have largely been willing to live in peaceful coexistence with the Church—science and religion have run into conflict only occasionally (e.g. Darwinism, creationism). The universities and the Church (especially in Protestant countries) have often joined forces in a combat against superstition, magic, and occultism in their old and New Age forms.

Relief from superstition was the great theme of the Enlightenment. It led to the revival of the Greek ideal of *paideia*, i.e. universal education for the whole of mankind. The new public system of schools was founded on the conviction that *it is better to know than to be ignorant*. All human beings are born with the desire to *learn*, and it is their basic human *right* to have the opportunity to have access to the best and most up-to-date knowledge. Science is an indispensable tool for producing such knowledge. As Kant expressed it, having the courage to use one's own reason prepares a person for adulthood (see Siegel 1988). Critical thinking thus helps an educated and enlightened citizen of a democratic society to build a *scientific world view* (see Section 1.2).

The conviction that science is the most reliable source of knowledge led to a powerful combination of epistemological optimism and scepticism:

---

[6] See Bacon's writings in Farrington (1964). See p. 132 for Bacon's reference to Daniel 12: 4.

accept the results of science, but reject religion and metaphysics as unknowable and meaningless. Different forms of this view can be found among realists, positivists, empiricists, Kantians, pragmatists, and Marxists. It is also popular within contemporary movements of secular critical thinking who call themselves 'free thinkers', 'humanists', and 'sceptics'.[7]

This *pro-science* attitude still allows for realist and anti-realist interpretations of scientific theories. The former sees theories as bold, fallible, verisimilar accounts of reality beyond the observables; the latter takes science to be only an economical systematization of observable phenomena and regularities with predictive and manipulative power.

The desire *to strengthen the epistemic authority of science vis-à-vis* superstition and religion has sometimes encouraged interpretations of science that exaggerate the certainty of its conclusions and thus are in conflict with critical realism. Dogmatic realists have assumed that science employs infallible mechanical methods which yield incorrigible, certain, and practically applicable knowledge. This quest for certainty has also been a motive for eliminating the more or less hypothetical theoretical parts of science. Comte's positivism restricted scientific knowledge to the observational level where certainty is supposed to be guaranteed, and gave strong emphasis to the useful applications of science (see Comte 1970). The desire to support the scientific world view was also the background of Mach's positivism (see Mach 1960).[8] The verificationism of the logical positivists and the new forms of semantical anti-realism attempt to defend science by showing that scepticism is meaningless.[9] Such programmes emphasizing the scientific world view are sometimes seen as providing a useful image for promoting the status of science and scientists in society.[10]

But, as we have seen in earlier chapters, the dogmatic quest for certainty can be criticized on logical, epistemological, and methodological grounds: according to critical scientific realism, science is a fallible but progressive attempt to approach closer to the truth about reality. Therefore, it is also important to ask why such fallible science should still be individually and socially desirable.

---

[7] The *Skeptical Inquirer* is a leading journal in this field.

[8] The contrast to Duhem shows that instrumentalism may be supported by almost opposite social reasons.

[9] These forms of empiricism are anti-realist with respect to theories, but they differ from the sceptical form of anti-realism which claims that we live only in a world of 'appearances'. An empiricist like van Fraassen (1980) demands that the observational consequences of scientific theories should be true.

[10] For the development of the profession of scientist, mainly as late as the 19th century, see Ben-David (1971). Tuomela (1985), who favours critical Sellarsian realism, suggests that scientific realism is 'the scientists' own philosophy'.

An important way of answering this question was given already by the Academic sceptics. In Augustine's dialogues, Licentius asserts that 'the end of a man is to seek the truth perfectly' (Augustine 1950: 45). The self-image of a scientist is thus not one who *possesses* knowledge, or has some privileged access to truth, but more humbly one who *seeks* the truth. This idea was built into the nineteenth-century educational programme of universities which, in Wilhelm von Humboldt's famous words, aimed at *Bildung durch Wissenschaft*, edification by means of research. Modern fallibilists, like Peirce and Popper, then modified the ancient assumptions by suggesting that, at least for the scientists, persistent *truth-seeking* is a precondition of personal happiness. At the same time, critical realism maintains the thesis that the scientific method, in spite of its fallibility, is nevertheless the best way of seeking the truth. Moreover, the anti-dogmatic *critical attitude* that is characteristic to this conception of scientific enquiry is seen to be a key element of democratic education and good social life in an 'open society'.[11]

Attempts to overcome the debate between realism and anti-realism have led to positions which are seriously concerned with the social status of science. A sophisticated example is Richard Rorty's (1989; 1991) version of pragmatism with its anti-representational view of language. Rorty's philosophical arguments appeal mainly to Sellars, Quine, and Davidson (cf. Section 3.1), but his most central thesis, with reference to Dewey, is ethical or social: anti-representationalism has a crucial link to the *tolerance and solidarity of Western liberal democracy* (see also Section 10.3). Rorty can thus be seen as a true heir to Pyrrhonian scepticism: his recipe for good human life includes the suspension of judgement between the metaphysical positions of realism and anti-realism, the adoption of the advantages of science as a depository of Baconian rules of action, and conformity to the contingent ethical standards of his own local culture.

Appealing to Dewey, Rorty (1998: 7) argues that the replacement of 'objectivity' in the realist sense with 'intersubjective agreement' would 'put an end to attempts to set up a pecking order among cultural activities' (e.g. hard science vs. soft science, science vs. the arts). This is hardly convincing: a realist may appreciate other areas of culture and life even more highly than science (cf. Section 10.2), and an anti-realist might find his own criteria for setting up pecking orders.

Putnam's (1990) internal realism (cf. Ch. 7) is also partly based on the conviction that his account of science and ethics gives 'realism with a

---

[11] This is the social message of Popper's 'critical rationalism'. Siegel (1988) discusses philosophical issues about rationality, education, and critical thinking.

human face'. The combination of the view that the world is not ready-made with an anti-relativistic epistemic account of truth is for Putnam an ethically commendable hypothesis, something that can be justified relative to human praxis (cf. Pihlström 1996).

If nature were our construction, perhaps we would also take a morally responsible attitude towards it. This might be presented as an ethical justification of social constructivism (cf. Ch. 9). But constructivist views may also lead to voluntarist illusions that it is always easy to change and improve the state of nature, or alternatively to indifference towards nature as a social construction rather than as containing hard facts. The realist instead gives emphasis to the factuality (Peircean 'secondness') of the world, i.e. its ability to resist our will. As the world is not of our making, we should have a theory of reference and truth which establishes a semantical link between language and the world. In this spirit, Bhaskar (1990) argues that the Rortyan anti-representational view, which denies realist correspondence truth about ecological facts, leads to indifference about ecological problems and thereby strengthens tendencies towards ecocatastrophe. Hans Radder (1996) raises the question of whether normative policy recommendations are at all legitimate in present STS studies, e.g. whether there is anything in the social constructivist account of the global warming issue in climate science that urges us to be more precautionary in practice.[12]

Finally, it is important to note that *anti-science* attitudes also exist in realist and anti-realist versions. The former look upon science as a producer of natural and social evils, which are worse the more its rules of action are based upon reality; such criticism often fears the alleged 'positivistic' and 'mechanistic' nature of natural science. Indeed, the 'hard' image of science as certified knowledge with industrial applications has also made science a target for the 'romantic' critics (from Rousseau and Herder in the eighteenth century to many contemporary postmodernists and communitarians) who fear that science ignores, or even destroys, that which is historically unique, particular, authentic, and morally significant in human life. The critics point out that Hard and Big Science has led to the atom bomb, the risks of nuclear power, exploitation of natural resources, consumer society, pollution of nature, and the ecological crisis. These facts have led many philosophers who still have faith in human reason in science to question the legitimacy of the modern scientific-technological form of life and the myth of progress (see von Wright 1993).

---

[12] A similar argument has been put forward in connection with feminism (cf. Section 8.4): if there are no objective standards of knowledge, then Women's Studies is not in a position to correct 'male bias' in science. Realism is therefore desirable, if the women's political movement wishes to have success in its effort to improve science.

The socially undesirable effects of science and technology have also lent support to the 'rage against reason'[13] within contemporary philosophy—from Nietzsche's perspectivism, Heidegger's *Gelassenheit*, Adorno's and Horkheimer's 'Dialectics of Enlightenment' and 'Critique of Instrumental Reason', to Foucault's 'power produces knowledge', Derrida's deconstruction of the Western 'metaphysics of presence', and French and American postmodernism. Paul Feyerabend's 'epistemological anarchism' belongs to this list as well (see Section 10.3). These anti-realist views are usually indifferent or hostile to natural science, wish *to undermine the epistemic authority of science in society*, and work to replace it with other human practices.

Some of the most influential scholars in the social studies of science, who seem to be disappointed about the social and political functions of science and technology in the modern world, have joined the critics in defending anti-realist interpretations of the epistemic credentials of science.

But the scientific empire strikes back. A new 'anti-antiscience' movement, consisting of scientists concerned about the rise of postmodernism and social constructivism, has joined in a counter-attack on the critics of science. What is known as *Science Wars* was started in the 1990s with the so-called Sokal Affair, aiming at making postmodern literary jargon ridiculous (cf. Sokal and Bricmont 1998). Paul Gross and Norman Levitt's (1994) book attacks the 'higher superstition' of 'the academic left'.

Science Wars is a new stage in an ancient battle over the social status of science. It is possible to look at it from a sociological perspective and ask what the interests of the armed forces are. Elisabeth Lloyd (1996), herself a distinguished mainstream analytic philosopher of science, has presented a sharp analysis of the debate. According to Lloyd, the main issue is a conflict regarding 'the control and dissemination of information concerning scientific activities'. Those who have risen to defend science against anti-science wish to maintain the image of science as a trustworthy authority in order to ensure social and economic order and in order to defend the professional interests of the natural scientists. They fail to see that the 'demystification' of science in science studies is not a hostile attempt to discredit science—and, behaving like 'military intelligence', they make themselves guilty of using the strategies of discreditation and exclusion against their 'enemies'.[14]

On the other hand, Alan Sokal himself has made it clear that his defence of the realist view of science is partly based on his left-wing political ideals.

[13] This term is used by Richard Bernstein in McMullin (1988). Cf. Norris (1996).
[14] For example, Lloyd has no difficulty in showing that Gross and Levitt have a biased and prejudiced view about the feminist contributions to science (1996: 239, 257).

Thus, while the warriors of anti-antiscience may have their own black-and-white pictures, misidentified targets, and overemphasis on the objectivity of scientific knowledge, they seem to have genuine worries about threatened social values: Enlightenment rationality, the functioning of democracy, and the funding of scientific research (see Segerstråle 1996).

There is one point where, in my view, Lloyd goes too far in her interpretation. She says that many reactions against the 'relativism' and 'irrationality' of science studies arise from a mistaken 'exclusivity doctrine' which claims that social and internal explanations of science are exclusive and competing rather than complementary. As a matter of fact, I think this exclusivity doctrine is mistaken, as shown by my defence of the Weak Programme (Section 9.2) and the double determination view of scientific knowledge (Section 8.4). But certainly the spread of the doctrine has been fuelled by the well-known statements *against* rational standards of belief by Barnes and Bloor, against explanations in terms of TRASP (true, rational, successful, progressive) by Collins, and against epistemological explanations of science by Latour. Strategies of exclusion and discredit have worked in both directions.

Finally, in closing this section, it is good to remember that when a realist or anti-realist defends his or her position in terms of its utility or social desirability, this is not an argument for the truth of the position—unless a simple equation of being true and useful is assumed. In spite of the old Marxist definition of ideology as 'false consciousness', to show that a certain image of science fulfils an ideological function in society is not a proof of its falsity (cf. Niiniluoto 1984: 229): true beliefs, too, can serve the interests of some social group. Indeed, how could it be otherwise? The survey in this section seems to show that all possible views about the relations between scientific knowledge and social values have found their supporters in history: one and the same view about science has been linked to very different social interests, and the same moral or political attitudes have led to very different positions about science.

## 10.2  Science as cultural value

To study more systematically the cultural value of science, it is useful to start from L. J. Cohen's (1997) question of whether there is a professional moral duty for scientists to be realists. According to Cohen, this conclusion can be defended by the following argument: (i) if knowledge is an end in itself, and (ii) if realism is part of the best methodology in pursuing knowledge, then (iii) a scientist has an ethical obligation to be a realist.

I agree that this is a valid inference as a form of practical syllogism which connects ends with the best means of pursuing them. We have also seen reasons to support premiss (ii) in Chapter 6, in the strong form which takes the empirical success of science to indicate the truth-likeness of its best theories. (In this sense, some methodological anti-realists may in fact be realist without knowing it.) For a critical realist, (ii) does not claim that all (or even most) of the results of scientific enquiry are true. It does not deny the possibility that a true idea could some-times occur to us by 'revelation' or by some other non-scientific means, but this would be an accident only without any warrant to its conclu-sion. Moreover, (ii) does not imply that science will answer all important questions about reality—there is no a priori guarantee of the complete success of science in this sense. Instead, the point of (ii) is that the method of science is designed so that it helps us to correct our errors and to bring us closer to the truth, and in this respect it is more reliable than its rivals.

In order to assess premiss (i), it is instructive to consider first an alternative view. J. D. Bernal, the well-known British historian of science, was a convinced and eloquent supporter of the optimistic Enlightenment tradition. Science is a cultural value, he argued with Bacon and Marx, since it serves as an efficient and indispensable tool of social progress (see Bernal 1939; 1969).

In his *Science in History* (1969), Bernal distinguished five different senses of science: (1) institution, (2) method, (3) cumulative tradition of knowledge, (4) a major factor in the maintenance and development of production, (5) one of the most powerful influences moulding beliefs and attitudes to the universe and man (p. 31). The 'progressive growth of science comes from its continually renewed interconnection with industry' (p. 1237): science solves problems that have primarily emerged from practical issues of 'economic necessity' (p. 39), and it brings about 'recipes' describing 'how to do things' (p. 40) and rational means for the conscious planning of social production and order. 'Science implies socialism', as Bernal wished to put his thesis (p. 11).

Especially in his work in the late 1960s, Bernal was painfully aware of the possibility that science, if not free and socially responsible, can also be 'distorted for mean and destructive ends' (p. 1309). The danger, as he saw it, arises from 'idealistic' theories of science (p. 497).

The ideal of pure science—the pursuit of Truth for its own sake—is the conscious statement of a social attitude which has done much to hinder the development of science and has helped to put it into obscurantist and reactionary hands. (p. 41)

But if able to avoid taking refuge in a 'cosmic pessimism' (p. 661), natural and social sciences together will remove both known and yet unrecognized 'evils', cure diseases, 'maintain life and happiness for all', discover 'new good things' and 'new and effective bases of organization for social action' (p. 1310), and transform society to 'one free from exploitation' (p. 1309).[15]

Bernal's Baconian optimism and Marxist rhetoric are not very fashionable today. We simply know too much of the evils, oppression, and regress that have been brought about in the name of science and technology. But still we may admire the courage of Bernal's personal visions and hopes.

We may also agree that science—in spite of its many present-day destructive associations—at least *has been* and still *may be* a 'cultural value'. However, there is reason to challenge Bernal's characterization of *how* and *why* science is a valuable form of activity in our culture, and to disagree with Bernal about the role of epistemic values (such as truth) in the mission of science.

Cultural values may be expressed as an axiological system which states what kind of things or aims are regarded as possessing intrinsic and derived value (cf. Rescher 1969). In general, an *axiological system* $A = \langle V, B, I \rangle$ consists of three elements:

First, V is a hierarchical ordering of *intrinsic values* which are regarded as valuable in themselves, without relation to other aims. Intrinsic values may be, for example,

- hedonistic: happiness
- vitalistic: life, health
- economic: money, wealth
- political: power, liberty, equality, justice, peace
- social: love, friendship
- epistemic: knowledge, truth
- aesthetic: beauty
- religious: holiness, sanctity.

The dominant type of intrinsic value is a central characteristic of an axiological system—and expresses the 'ethos' of a culture where such a system is widely supported. Secondly, B is a system of *beliefs* which state

---

[15] Bernal obviously had in mind the atomic bomb and other military applications of science. This artefact was a result of applied research and development (i.e. science-based engineering). The Manhattan Project did not pursue 'truth for its own sake'. That characterization may rather apply to such pioneers in physics as Ernest Rutherford. Perhaps Bernal's thesis is only that the supporters of the ideal of pure science are often naive and do not realize the evil purposes for which their work will eventually be used.

how (or by what means) the intrinsic values in V may be pursued. Thirdly, I is a set of *instrumental values* which serve, according to beliefs B, as effective tools or intermediate steps for reaching or promoting intrinsic values V.

In what sense then could science be regarded as a cultural value? Bernal's position seems to be clear: his intrinsic values are primarily political and social (good social life, justice, liberty, freedom from exploitation) with hedonistic and vitalistic elements (happiness, health). Economic goals are for him instrumental values, since they help us to achieve good life free of misery. And science as a pursuit of knowledge is also an instrumental value in the service of industry and social organization. Bernal's conception of science is thus *instrumentally oriented* in the sense that he regards epistemic values as means to ends that belong to the sphere of the social applications of scientific knowledge—and explicitly denies the idea that truth could be valued for its own sake.

The instrumental orientation view of science may exist in many variants, since it may be combined with many different axiological systems. Science may be taken to be a tool for technological and economic progress (as many pragmatists think; cf. Rescher 1977; 1978), for rational social life (as many Marxists thought), or for *Bildung* as the education of rationally thinking human individuals (as the Enlightenment philosophers and many of their Romantic successors urged).

An alternative to such instrumental orientation is to include *epistemic values* (such as truth and information) among the *intrinsic* values of our axiology (cf. Section 6.2); this is premiss (i) of Cohen's argument. This conception of science may be called *cognitivism*, since it takes the essence of science to be the rational pursuit of knowledge, i.e. justified true information about reality, by systematic methods of enquiry (cf. Levi 1967).

Cognitivism may again exist in many variants. Bernal's criticism of the ideal of 'intrinsic and pure knowledge' is directed at a special version of cognitivism which regards Truth (with a capital 'T') as the *only* basic value, and therefore remains indifferent or even hostile to the attempts to apply scientific knowledge to the needs of mankind in a socially responsible way. However, cognitivists may quite well accept, besides truth, other intrinsic values (such as beauty, health, justice, freedom, etc.) in their axiology. Thereby they may also accept that the best results of scientific enquiry, besides their intrinsic epistemic value, also possess instrumental value relative to the goals of good life.

In this sense, cognitivism need not accept *scientism*, understood as an axiological view which gives intrinsic value only to science. Indeed, against scientism in this sense, a critical scientific realist may appreciate as 'ends in themselves' also other domains of human life and culture (such as family, art, etc.).[16] (Cf. Section 10.1.)

Concerning Bernal in particular, the rhetorical opposition between instrumental orientation and cognitivism becomes thus largely unnecessary, if we realize that an axiological system may attribute to the same goal (such as truth) *both intrinsic value and instrumental value* (relative to the other intrinsic values in the system) *at the same time* (Niiniluoto 1990b).

The contrast between cognitivism and instrumental orientation does not become irrelevant or empty through this observation, however. It still has important consequences concerning scientific method and science policy. First, in assessing the validity of a truth claim in science, a scientist may appeal only to its epistemic value or to evidential indicators of such values, but not to its extra-scientific instrumental value. Predictive and pragmatic success may on some conditions be a fallible criterion of truth (cf. Section 6.1), but this is not a licence for wishful thinking or repression. For example, it is not an argument in favour of (or against) a scientific hypothesis that its truth would be nice and useful (or awkward and harmful) relative to our practical interests.[17]

Secondly, while a cognitivist regards it as valuable and rational to pursue 'pure' basic science, or curiosity-oriented fundamental research, even if the obtained knowledge perhaps never leads to any useful 'practical' applications, an instrumentalist has to justify the rationality of *all* scientific activity as some form of 'strategic' or 'applied' research.[18] This is one of the reasons why I prefer a *socially responsible form of cognitivism* to the kind of instrumentalism represented by Bernal.

A further reason for preferring cognitivism is based on the observation that *the empirical and pragmatic success of science can be explained by its cognitive success*—not the other way round, as Bernal suggests (see Section 6.5). Even if you value the practical applications of science more highly than advances on the cognitive level, the most effective way of pursuing them is

[16] The artistic creation of beauty may be an end in itself, which coexists in an axiological system as an intrinsic value along with the scientific pursuit of truth. I think it can be argued that art may also serve important epistemic functions as well. The construction of new systems of representation and viewpoints may be useful for the imagination needed in scientific concept and theory formation. Moreover, a work of art (e.g. a fictional historical or psychological novel) may also give truthlike information about reality (cf. Niiniluoto 1986d). However, an artist usually does not even attempt to justify his work as a truth claim. If he did this successfully, he would turn into a scientist. (This is a modification of the story of the caterpillar turning into a butterfly, told by Kemeny (1959) to illustrate the relation between philosophy and science.)

[17] Recall, however, Longino's example about the combination of truth-oriented and practical criteria in the same loss function (Section 6.3).

[18] Cf. Niiniluoto (1984: ch. 10; 1993), Irvine and Martin (1984). For the nature of applied science, see also Section 8.4.

via powerful theories. 'Theory is the most practical thing conceivable', as Ludwig Boltzmann put this (Bolzmann 1974: 35). Hence, instead of being a dangerous and reactionary ideology, as Bernal urged, the pursuit of epistemic values is an indispensable and explanatory element in guaranteeing that science is able to serve as a source of cultural value in society.

## 10.3 Science in a free society

The questioning and self-criticism of human reason is an important task of philosophy, but it should not be based upon black-and-white horror-stories or glimmering pictures of science. In this concluding section, I shall argue that such a reflective project serves to highlight the crucial need to secure the normative structure of scientific activities.

In a series of remarkable books, *Against Method* (1975), *Science in a Free Society* (1978), and *Farewell to Reason* (1987), Paul Feyerabend launched an attack on received views about science. Building upon his work on incommensurability and radical meaning variance (cf. Section 5.2), which was partly based upon his early endorsement of eliminativist scientific realism, Feyerabend argued against the idea of Scientific Method: there are no universal or context-independent methodological rules which the scientist should not sometimes break in the name of progress. As there is no fixed method, science is not associated with any special kind of Reason and Knowledge. This means that science does not have any special epistemic authority, either, and in a free society it should be treated as equal to other doxastic traditions.

Feyerabend was a prolific author, who sometimes liked to wear his dadaist cap (and wanted to shock orthodox thinkers and to tease Popper in particular), but sometimes preferred to formulate his position with more precision and caution (cf. e.g. Feyerabend 1978; Munévar 1991). His criticisms of overly narrow and rigid conceptions of science and infallible reason are often penetrating and joyful, but his theoretical arguments for his *epistemological anarchism* are not very convincing. He argues from the non-existence of absolute methods, which would be valid in all circumstances, to the famous principle 'anything goes', but—even as a reductio of excessive rationalism—this seems to be again an example of the All-or-Nothing Fallacy.[19]

---

[19] 'Anything goes' is not Feyerabend's own methodological recommendation, but his caricature of the rationalist's predicament (see Feyerabend 1978: 188; cf. Lloyd 1997). But a reasonable scientific realist may take methodological rules to be context-dependent in the strong sense that they are designed to work in our universe (see Boyd 1990; cf. the treatment of situation-relative technological norms in Section 6.2). Feyerabend (1984b), in raising

After having given up the notions of justification and falsification, he sees human knowledge as 'an ever increasing ocean of mutually incompatible (and perhaps even incommensurable)' theories, myths, and fairy tales, where nothing is ever settled and 'no view can ever be omitted' (Feyerabend 1975: 30). If this kind of proliferation really were the correct description of enquiry (or its goal), then the rule 'anything goes' would be almost trivially correct! But, paradoxically, this defence of 'permanent revolutions' in science has driven Feyerabend to an extremely cumulativist account of science where no view is ever omitted (see Niiniluoto 1984: 161).

In his later work, Feyerabend (1984a) compared science to art, and was led to an anti-realist position that Preston (1997) characterizes as voluntaristic constructivism: nature as described by our scientists is 'a work of art that is constantly being enlarged and rebuilt by them', and in response to other kinds of cultural activities the universe 'really' contains gods and other non-scientific entities.

Feyerabend's most enduring and significant philosophical influence came from John Stuart Mill's classic *On Liberty* (1859) (see below). I think it is appropriate to view Feyerabend as a Pyrrhonian sceptic in epistemology and an absolutist in morality who puts *liberty* (as negative freedom, or freedom from constraints) as the highest intrinsic value on the top of his axiological system. From the perspective of his values, he finds methodological norms, external facts, and objective truth to be undesirable restrictions, tyrants which should be deposed.[20]

What was a moral project or crusade for Feyerabend is—somewhat surprisingly—a fact for many contemporary sociologists of science. Where the philosophical anarchist is annoyed by what he perceives as the overly strong or dominant status of scientific research and education in our society, the relativist and constructivist sociologists of science declare that scientific research has no epistemic advantage over other belief systems (see Ch. 9; cf. Russell 1983). I still remember my first astonishment at finding this agreement between Feyerabend and 'philosophically neutral' sociologists (see Mulkay 1977; Niiniluoto 1991a).

Feyerabend's plea for liberty gives us reason to ask whether freedom could be an *alternative* to truth. Many philosophers would object that

---

the positivist physicist Ernst Mach to a hero of scientific thinking, somewhat surprisingly seems to propose empirical testability as a sound and generally valid methodological principle in science (cf. Niiniluoto 1986a). He claims that Mach's rejection of atomic theories was 'reasonable', since he followed a principle accepted 'by most scientists and by almost all modern philosophers of science', namely that 'pure constructions of thought' have 'no place in science' since 'statements about them are untestable in principle'.

[20] Here Feyerabend agrees with the views of Michel Foucault.

freedom and truth cannot be distinguished in this way. Perhaps the strongest formulation is given by Habermas (1983): according to his consensus theory, truth is defined as the ultimate result of discourse in a community without domination. Every member of the community should be in a symmetrical position and free to present his or her questions and arguments. By this dialogical criterion, *freedom is conceptually a necessary condition of truth*.

In my view, however, it is too strong to make freedom a necessary or a sufficient condition of truth. A dominated member of an asymmetric community may with good luck discover something that is true (cf. Harding 1986). And a group of free and democratic minds in symmetric discourse is not likely to reach truth about any factual matter at all if its members do not have access to the external world through interaction.

On the other hand, it is plausible to think that *freedom* is a necessary condition or *constitutive of justification*. Good reasons cannot be given for or against a scientific claim if all possible critical questions about it are not allowed. Hence, freedom is necessary to knowledge (but through its link to the requirement of justification rather than that to truth). A classical formulation of this general principle of *freedom in thinking* was given by Mill (1859).

Mill gave three different reasons for freedom of opinion. First, we cannot be sure that the view we are opposing is false. Secondly, even when our opinion is correct, it is important that the opposing view may be presented as a challenge and also criticized for its weakness. Thirdly, two conflicting views may both contain some elements of truth (cf. the notion of partial truth). Here we see that Mill is not claiming that freedom is necessary or sufficient to truth, but he is speaking about the public presentation and acceptance of opinions.

Mill's first reason is clearly related to Popper's fallibilism. The second reason is an important stricture against dogmatism inside the scientific community, and thereby motivates Feyerabend's principle of *proliferation*: for the progress of science it is important to multiply existing alternatives to the current theories. It also shows that it is socially desirable to be *tolerant* with respect to belief systems which are alternatives to scientific knowledge. Thus, the principle of freedom of religion permits every citizen freely to endorse his or her beliefs in spite of their possible irrationality.

It has been suggested by Lloyd (1997) that Feyerabend's whole project should be understood in the light of his commitment to Mill's principles. Feyerabend once remarked that astrology bores him 'to tears', but still it 'deserves a defence'. According to this interpretation, Feyerabend is not really endorsing the wild ideas of witchcraft, faith healing, and Chinese medicine, but rather is engaged in the noble defence of minority opinions.[21]

Feyerabend's relativism differs from Mill, however, at least in the sense that he does not believe in the progress of science toward the truth. What is more, from the Millian tolerance toward different opinions it does not follow that there is no such thing as epistemic authority within science (cf. Kitcher 1993), or that science does not have any difference from, or epistemic advantage against, pseudo-science.

Feyerabend defended, in the name of 'freedom', among other things, the Catholic Church, creationism, astrology, and voodoo against the 'tyranny' of science. I think he should have been more alerted by the fact that religions and pseudo-sciences are typically *dogmatic* belief systems. The ideal of science, instead, is to rely on critical self-corrective methods which accept no incorrigible internal dogmas, permanent authorities or holy scriptures, and no external violations of its autonomy. In this respect, science attempts to be the only knowledge-seeking institution where collective self-deception in the long run is impossible.

Mill's conditions for good science have been abolished in totalitarian societies. The autonomy of science can flourish only in a society which is willing to support *self*-corrective scientific institutions (cf. Rescher 1978) and is wise enough to let the scientific community resolve cognitive problems by means of the critical method.

There is thus a link between science and the values of liberal, democratic, Western society, as Richard Rorty (1989) argues, following John Dewey. However, I think it is problematic to connect these values to an anti-representational doctrine of language and science. If my account of the success of science and its explanation is correct (cf. Section 6.5), you cannot simply exploit science and science-based technologies with Baconian virtues without at the same time 'buying' their realist explanation.

It is also wrong to draw, as it were, a dichotomy between 'objectivity' and 'solidarity'—after all, Rorty is famous for abolishing rather than creating dichotomies! The right answer to Rorty's question 'solidarity or objectivity?' is 'yes, both!' We should have solidarity with the values of

---

[21]  Note, however, that what is a minority opinion is a relative matter. In post-war central Europe, where Feyerabend was educated by the last member of the Vienna Circle, Viktor Frank, analytic philosophy and scientific realism were (and in most places still are) minority positions. At least judging by the enormous flow of pseudo-scientific information in contemporary media, one may claim that the scientific world view has been reduced to a minority position today in Western countries. And Mill's principle of proliferation would also justify something that Feyerabend disapproved of: the importation of Western science and religion as new alternatives to the cultures in the east and south.

our community and the whole of humanity, but we can achieve this by pursuing objective truth in science.

Rorty (1991) thinks that the emphasis on objectivity is a disguised form of the idea of a scientist as a kind of priest of a non-religious culture who mediates between us and something non-human: what God was for the pre-modern culture, nature is for the moderns, and both of them will be rejected in the new postmodern (non-religious and non-scientific) culture. A quite different interpretation is possible, however. At least the Christian religion is extremely human-centred: man is the image of God, and he has the right to rule and subdue other creations of God. The pragmatism of Rorty (like that of James, Dewey, and Putnam) continues this human-centred perspective of the world: contempt of objectivity can be claimed to be a remnant of the comfortable position where we did not have to relate ourselves to anything (like World 1) that is by its nature non-human.

But what, more precisely, is the connection between science and democratic values? Feyerabend has given an answer in his principle of 'democratic relativism' which says that 'citizens, and not special groups have the last word in deciding what is true or false, useful or useless in society' (Feyerabend 1987: 59). This principle contains two subtheses; in my view, the first of them is incorrect, the latter correct.

First, who decides what is true and false? Let us illustrate this with an actual example. Today some historians claim that the persecution of Jews and concentration camps never existed. The parliament of Germany has passed a law which makes the public dissemination of this opinion criminal. This is a way in which society defends itself against neo-fascist movements. But it does not mean that the citizens decide what is *true*. The idea that historical 'truth' is political might arise from the use of 'truth' as meaning 'accepted belief' or from an anti-realist view about the past. Scientific realists avoid such absurdities by insisting that the truth about the holocaust is determined by the fact that Auschwitz really existed.

The truth is not decided by the citizens, but not by the scientists, either. (And not by police, as pointed out by Russell 1940.) As I just said, truth about history is determined by historical facts which are independent of us. What is open to us is to improve our knowledge of history and reinterpret its meaning for ourselves.

More generally, the link between science and Western values does not mean that the *method* of science is itself 'democratic'. As Popper has emphasized, critical and public discussion among scientists is an important element of the research process. But no simple principle of 'cognitive egalitarianism' applies inside or outside the scientific community. Science is a system of *expert knowledge*. When we need knowledge—for cognitive, educational, or practical purposes—about elementary particles, we consult nuclear physicists; when about the Third Reich, we consult professional historians. When editors of journals decide about the acceptability of submitted papers, they consult referees who are the best among their peers in the particular issue discussed in the article. The opinions of such experts are fallible, but they are the best we can get, if they are based upon free enquiry, careful consideration of the evidence, and critical discussion among colleagues. These opinions have epistemic authority within science and society at large—but not because the scientists are better, more intelligent, or more virtuous than other citizens, and because we have to trust such gentlemen (Shapin 1994), but because they use public, critical methods of investigation, and the reliability of their claims can be evaluated.

When experts disagree, matters are not settled by a vote, but the strongest argument should win. Suspension of judgement is also a possible rational standpoint in some matters. Science does not have ready answers to all cognitive problems. It is even possible that some cognitive problems will remain forever unsolved by science (cf. Section 10.2).

So the 'democratization of science' cannot mean that the distinction between expert and lay knowledge disappears.[22] Instead, it should mean the democratization of the *membership in the scientific community*: in a free society, a career in science should be in principle and in practice open to all who have enough talent, motivation, and energy to go through the professional education. Possibilities and conditions of this membership should not depend on nationality, sex, race, and wealth (cf. Section 8.4).

It should also mean democratization in *the public distribution of knowledge*, which thereby also redistributes power within society (see Fuller 1993). Up-to-date results of scientific knowledge should be accessible to every interested citizen through systems of education and channels of public communication.

Further, it should mean the democratization of *science and technology policy*.[23] Here we come to the correct part of Feyerabend's 'democratic relativism': the citizens will ultimately decide what is 'useful or useless in society'. Here the issue is not what is true and false, but what areas of research and development are financed by public funds, to what purposes scientific knowledge is applied, what are the ethical limits of genetic technology and animal experimentation, how technological projects are

---

[22] For a challenging discussion of this issue, see Fuller (1993). Fuller's 'democratic presumption' says that 'science can be scrutinized and evaluated by appropriately informed lay public', but this is ambiguous between several interpretations.

[23] I have discussed issues of science and technology policy in Niiniluoto (1997c).

assessed in social and moral terms, and what kinds of risk are socially acceptable. Good examples of such democratic methods include 'consumer panels' and 'consensus conferences' where lay members of society assess the consequences of alternative technologies on what they regard as good life.

Expert knowledge about factual matters plays a partial role in the analysis of such questions, but ultimately the policy issues involve decisions about *values* that are not derivable from the results of empirical science. The moderate moral relativism defended in Chapter 8 is thus a natural ally of democracy, since it excludes the possibility that scientists and philosophers could function as 'dictators' in society by deciding the choices of intrinsic values by the methods of science. To be sure, factual knowledge about nature, history, and society is in many ways relevant to the rational consideration and change of values: 'decisionism', which regards values as arbitrary, purely subjective choices, is not plausible (Habermas 1971). In questions concerning the aims and decisions of individuals, groups, and societies, scientists can give reliable information about the present situation and the probable consequences of alternative courses of action or alternative technological projects. But there remains the possibility of disagreement about acceptable social goals among rational citizens— and this is not settled by science, but by democratic procedures of decision-making.

But on what conditions is science able to fulfil all these important functions in a democratic society? I said above that trust in science depends on the fact that the community of its practitioners is employing the critical method of scientific enquiry. It is clear that the validity of this condition, in turn, depends on the normative structure of science.

Scientific activities are governed by at least four types of social norms, most of them unwritten. First, there is *etiquette*, i.e. rules for decent or appropriate behaviour in academic events, like conferences and doctoral disputations. Secondly, the *ethics* of science concerns morally acceptable and unacceptable scientific practices—such as honesty in collecting and reporting data, fairness with respect to colleagues, avoidance of unnecessary harm to the objects of enquiry, and responsibility for the use of the results.[24] Thirdly, *methodology* expresses the adequate ways of seeking knowledge (cf. Section 6.2). Fourthly, there is *legislation* concerning society in general and scientific institutions in particular.

A classical account of the normative structure of science was given in Robert Merton's formulation of *the ethos of science* (see Merton 1973).

---

[24] For the ethics of science, see Tranøy (1988). The Committee on the Conduct of Science appointed by the National Academy of Sciences in the USA has published a useful guidebook *On Being a Scientist* (Washington, 1989).

His principles state that science is a collective group activity of seeking new knowledge, where the scientists do not pursue their own personal advantage (Disinterestedness), publish their results for the whole community (Communism), and evaluate knowledge claims by pre-established impersonal criteria (Universalism) and by critical scrutiny in terms of empirical and logical criteria (Organized scepticism). Reference to race, nationality, religion, class, and personal qualities is excluded in scientific argumentation—and so is appeal to personal profit in the assessment of knowledge claims. These norms are fairly close to the received view about science within the analytic tradition. John Ziman (1994) argues that they have served the progress and productivity of science by encouraging personal creativity and openness to public debate.

Some of the norms (such as the fair play principle in attributing credit for scientific discoveries and ruling out plagiarism) have the function of keeping up the motivation of the scientists in the pursuit of novel results. But it is very important to realize that many norms in science, in both ethics (e.g. rules against fabrication of data and fraud) and methodology (e.g. rules for testing statistical hypotheses), are *truth-centred*: they are designed to guarantee the reliability and self-corrective nature of scientific enquiry. In other words, these social norms are epistemologically, not only sociologically, highly relevant and interesting.

The existence of methodological and moral norms for the conduct of scientists shows that the Feyerabendian dream about unlimited freedom cannot be realized in science. And it should not be, either, since such norms (or many of them) are *constitutive* of the enterprise that we call science (cf. Section 6.2). Anarchism as the hope of absolute negative freedom is thus doomed to failure.

The anarchists fail to realize that the 'restricting' rules (methods, moral maxims) guarantee *positive freedom* to science, i.e. they *enable* the researchers to pursue the goals of enquiry. The existence of objective facts and truths, and methods aiming at them, independently of the scientist's personal wishes or group interests, is what makes intersubjective agreement possible in science. And such objectivity also means that truth is above human authority: instead of being a 'tyrant', truth guarantees that we are *free*, since no social pressure on *us* has the power of changing the truth. In a slightly different sense, knowledge helps us to protect ourselves against manipulation (see Siegel 1988).

Important sociological studies have indicated many ways in which the Mertonian principles are violated by the actual behaviour of scientists: examples include cases of domination, self-interest, fraud, and secrecy (see Mulkay 1979). Such violations do not yet show that the Mertonian norms are not *valid* any more: the invalidity of a norm means that it may be violated without a sanction. This is not the case with scientific misbehaviour, as the increased interest in ethical codes and committees in academic science indicates.

If truth-centred norms are constitutive of science, as I have claimed, they cannot be overthrown as an old-fashioned 'ideology'—in the same way as, for instance, the old ideology of amateurs competing in the Olympic Games has been transformed into the new ideology of sport as a profession. Therefore, one should be deeply concerned and worried about the future of science in Western societies. Research and development (R&D) is largely tied up with military and commercial purposes in a way which does not satisfy the Mertonian demands of publicity and critical conversation. Even academic research in the universities is dominated by national science policies which aim at short-term economic benefits and industrial applications. Big science with laboratories is becoming increasingly expensive. Demands of accountability and the mechanical use of science indicators encourage biased behaviour with respect to the ethical norms. John Ziman (1994), in surveying the present conditions of research, asserts that the Mertonian normative framework CUDOS (Communalism, Universalism, Disinterestedness, Originality, Scepticism) is now replaced by PLACE (Proprietary, Local, Authoritarian, Commissional, Expert work). All these developments may endanger the epistemological abilities and credentials of scientific enquiry—and harm scientific progress.

Cynical observers claim that science in the traditional sense is already corrupted, spoiled, and lost. However, realism is a philosophy which encourages us to fight for science, for its methods and ethics. If anything, this is a good social reason for keeping up the high spirit of critical realism about science.

# References

AARNIO, A. (1987). *The Rational as Reasonable*. Dordrecht: D. Reidel.

ABRAHAM, W. J. (1985). *An Introduction to the Philosophy of Religion*. Englewood Cliffs, NJ: Prentice-Hall.

ACKERMAN, R. (1961). 'Inductive Simplicity', *Philosophy of Science*, 28: 152–60.

AGASSI, J. (1963). *Towards a Historiography of Science*. The Hague: Mouton.

AJDUKIEWICZ, K. (1978). *The Scientific World-Perspective and Other Essays*. Dordrecht: D. Reidel.

ALCOFF, L. (1987). 'Justifying Feminist Social Science', *Hypatia*, 2/3: 85–103.

—— and POTTER, E. (eds.) (1993). *Feminist Epistemologies*. London: Routledge.

ALLISON, H. E. (1983). *Kant's Transcendental Idealism: An Interpretation and Defense*. New Haven: Yale University Press.

ALMEDER, R. (1983). 'Scientific Progress and Peircean Utopian Realism', *Erkenntnis*, 20: 253–80.

ANKERSMIT, F. (1989). 'The Use of Language in the Writing of History', in H. Coleman (ed.), *Working with Language*. Berlin: Mouton de Gruyter, 57–81.

ARMSTRONG, D. M. (1978). *Universals and Scientific Realism*, vols. i–ii. Cambridge: Cambridge University Press.

—— (1989). *Universals: An Opinionated Introduction*. Boulder, Colo.: Westview Press.

ARONSON, J. L., HARRÉ, R., and WAY, E. C. (1994). *Realism Rescued: How Scientific Progress is Possible*. London: Duckworth.

AUGUSTINE (1950). *Against the Academics*. Westminster: Newman Press.

AUNE, B. (1986). *Metaphysics: The Elements*. Oxford: Blackwell.

—— (1987). 'Conceptual Relativism', in Tomberlin 1987: 269–88.

AYER, A. J. (ed.) (1959). *Logical Positivism*. New York: Free Press.

BACON, F. (1960). *The New Organon*. Indianapolis: Bobbs-Merrill.

BACON, J. (1995). *Universals and Property Instances: The Alphabet of Being*. Oxford: Blackwell.

BALZER, W., MOULINES, C. U., and SNEED, J. D. (1987). *An Architectonic for Science: The Structuralist Program*. Dordrecht: D. Reidel.

—— PEARCE, D., and SCHMIDT, H.-J. (eds.) (1984). *Reduction in Science: Structure, Examples, Philosophical Problems*. Dordrecht: D. Reidel.

BARNES, B. (1981). 'On the Conventional Character of Knowledge and Cognition', *Philosophy of the Social Sciences*, 11: 303–33.

—— and BLOOR, D. (1982). 'Relativism, Rationalism and the Sociology of Knowledge', in Hollis and Lukes 1982: 21–47.

—— —— and HENRY, J. (1996). *Scientific Knowledge: A Sociological Analysis*. London: Athlone.

BARNES, E. (1991). 'Beyond Verisimilitude: A Linguistically Invariant Basis for Scientific Progress', *Synthese*, 88: 309–39.

——(1995). 'Truthlikeness, Translation, and Approximate Causal Explanation', *Philosophy of Science*, 62: 215–26.

BARWISE, J., and ETCHEMENDY, J. (1987). *The Liar*. Oxford: Oxford University Press.

BAUDRILLARD, J. (1984). 'The Precession of Simulacra', in B. Wallis (ed.), *Art after Modernism: Rethinking Representation*. New York: New Museum of Contemporary Art, 253–81.

BECKERMANN, A., FLOHR, H., and KIM, J. (eds.) (1992). *Emergence or Reduction: Essays on the Prospects of Nonreductive Materialism*. New York: Walter de Gruyter.

BELL, J., and SLOMSON, A. (1969). *Models and Ultraproducts*. Amsterdam: North-Holland.

BEN-DAVID, J. (1971). *The Scientist's Role in Society: A Comparative Study* (2nd edn. 1984). Chicago: University of Chicago Press.

BENNETT, J. (1988). *Events and their Names*. Oxford: Oxford University Press.

BERGER, P., and LUCKMANN, T. (1971). *The Social Construction of Reality*. Harmondsworth: Penguin Books.

BERGMAN, G. (1967). *Realism: A Critique of Brentano and Meinong*. Madison: University of Wisconsin Press.

BERNAL, J. D. (1939). *The Social Function of Science*. London: Routledge.

——(1969). *Science in History*. Harmondsworth: Penguin.

BERNSTEIN, R. (1971). *Praxis and Action: Contemporary Philosophies of Human Activity*. Philadelphia: University of Pennsylvania Press.

——(1983). *Beyond Objectivism and Relativism*. Oxford: Blackwell.

BHASKAR, R. (1975). *A Realist Theory of Science*. Leeds: Leeds Books.

——(1979). *The Possibility of Naturalism: A Philosophical Critique of Contemporary Human Sciences*. Brighton: Harvester Press.

——(1989). *Reclaiming Reality*. London: Verso.

——(1990). 'Rorty, Realism and the Idea of Freedom', in Malachowski 1990: 198–232.

BIGELOW, J. (1994). 'Sceptical Realism: A Realistic Defense of Dummett', *Monist*, 77: 3–26.

BIJKER, W. E. (1995). 'Sociohistorical Technology Studies', in Jasanoff *et al.* 1995: 229–56.

——and LAW, J. (eds.) (1992). *Shaping Technology/Building Society: Studies in Sociotechnical Change*. Cambridge, Mass.: MIT Press.

BLACKBURN, S. (1993). *Essays in Quasi-realism*. Oxford: Oxford University Press.

BLAKE, R. M., DUCASSE, C. J., and MADDEN, E. H. (1960). *Theories of Scientific Method: The Renaissance through the Nineteenth Century*. Seattle: University of Washington Press.

BLOOR, D. (1973). 'Wittgenstein and Mannheim on the Sociology of Mathematics', *Studies in History and Philosophy of Science*, 4: 173–91.

——(1974). 'Popper's Mystification of Objective Knowledge', *Science Studies*, 4: 65–76.

——(1976). *Knowledge and Social Imagery*. London: Routledge & Kegan Paul.

BLOOR, D. (1983). *Wittgenstein: A Social Theory of Knowledge*. Houndmills: Macmillan Educations.

——(1991). *Knowledge and Social Imagery* (2nd edn. with afterword). Chicago: University of Chicago Press.

——(1997). *Wittgenstein, Rules and Institutions*. London: Routledge.

BOHLIN, I. (1998). *Sken och Verklighet: Kvalitetet inom Universitetsvärlden i Relativistisk Belysning*. Stockholm: BVN.

BOHM, D. (1980). *Wholeness and the Implicate Order*. London: Kegan & Paul.

BOLTZMANN, L. (1974). *Theoretical Physics and Philosophical Problems*. Dordrecht: D. Reidel.

BONILLA, J. P. Z. (1992). 'Truthlikeness without Truth: A Methodological Approach', *Synthese*, 93: 343–72.

BOWLES, G., and KLEIN, R. D. (1983). *Theories of Women's Studies*. London: Routledge & Kegan Paul.

BOYD, R. (1973). 'Realism, Underdetermination and a Causal Theory of Evidence', *Noûs*, 8: 1–12.

——(1979). 'Metaphor and Theory-Change', in A. Ortony (ed.), *Metaphor and Thought*. Cambridge: Cambridge University Press, 356–408.

——(1984). 'The Current Status of Scientific Realism', in Leplin 1984: 41–82.

——(1988). 'How to Be a Moral Realist', in Sayre-McCord 1988: 181–228.

——(1989). 'What Realism Implies and What it Does Not', *Dialectica*, 43: 5–29.

——(1990). 'Realism, Approximate Truth, and Philosophical Method', in Savage 1990: 355–91.

——(1992). 'Constructivism, Realism, and Philosophical Method', in J. Earman (ed.), *Inference, Explanation, and Other Frustrations*. Berkeley and Los Angeles: University of California Press, 131–98.

BRANDOM, R. (1994). *Making it Explicit*. Cambridge, Mass.: Harvard University Press.

BRANDT, R. B. (1959). *Ethical Theory*. Englewood Cliffs, NJ: Prentice-Hall.

BRINK, D. O. (1989). *Moral Realism and the Foundations of Ethics*. Cambridge: Cambridge University Press.

BROAD, C. D. (1925). *The Mind and its Place in Nature*. London: Routledge & Kegan Paul.

BROPHY, J., and PAOLUCCI, H. (eds.) (1962). *The Achievement of Galileo*. New Haven: College and University Press.

BROWN, C. (1988). 'Internal Realism: Transcendental Idealism?', in *Midwest Studies in Philosophy*, xii: *Realism and Antirealism*. Minneapolis: University of Minnesota Press, 145–55.

BROWN, H. I. (1977). *Perception, Theory, and Commitment: The New Philosophy of Science*. Chicago: University of Chicago Press.

BROWN, J. R. (ed.) (1984). *Scientific Rationality: The Sociological Turn*. Dordrecht: D. Reidel.

——(1989). *The Rational and the Social*. London: Routledge.

——(1994). *Smoke and Mirrors: How Science Reflects Reality*. London: Routledge.

BRZEZINSKI, J., CONIGLIONE, F., KUIPERS, T., and NOWAK, L. (eds.) (1990). *Idealization*, i: *General Problems*. Amsterdam: Rodopi.

BUNGE, M. (1961). 'The Weight of Simplicity in the Construction and Assaying of Scientific Theories', *Philosophy of Science*, 28: 120–49.

——(1973). *Philosophy of Physics*. Dordrecht: D. Reidel.

——(1977–9). *Treatise on Basic Philosophy*, vols. iii–iv. Dordrecht: D. Reidel.

——(1981). *Scientific Materialism*. Dordrecht: D. Reidel.

BURGE, T. (1986). 'Individualism and Psychology', *Philosophical Review*, 45: 3–45.

BURNYEAT, M. (ed.) (1983). *The Sceptical Tradition*. Berkeley and Los Angeles: University of California Press.

BURTT, E. A. (1954). *The Metaphysical Foundations of Modern Science*. New York: Doubleday.

CAMPBELL, K. (1990). *Abstract Particulars*. Oxford: Blackwell.

CARNAP, R. (1936–7). 'Testability and Meaning', *Philosophy of Science*, 3: 419–71; 4: 1–40.

——(1942). *Introduction to Semantics*. Cambridge, Mass.: Harvard University Press.

——(1949). 'Truth and Confirmation', in Feigl and Sellars 1949: 119–27.

——(1962). *The Logical Foundations of Probability* (2nd edn.). Chicago: University of Chicago Press.

——(1963). 'Intellectual Autobiography', in Schilpp 1963: 1–84.

——(1966). *Philosophical Foundations of Physics*. New York: Basic Books.

——(1967). *The Logical Structure of the World and Pseudoproblems in Philosophy*. Berkeley and Los Angeles: University of California Press.

CARTWRIGHT, N. (1983). *How the Laws of Physics Lie*. Oxford: Oxford University Press.

——(1991). 'Can Wholism Reconcile the Inaccuracy of Theory with the Accuracy of Prediction?', *Synthese*, 89: 3–13.

——(1994). 'Fundamentalism vs. the Patchwork of Laws', *Proceedings of the Aristotelian Society*, 93: 279–82.

CASSIRER, E. (1944). *An Essay on Man*. New York: Doubleday.

——(1965). *The Philosophy of Symbolic Forms*, vols. i–iii. New Haven: Yale University Press.

CASTELÃO-LAWLESS, T. (1995). 'Phenomenotechnique in Historical Perspective: Its Origins and Implications for Philosophy of Science', *Philosophy of Science*, 62: 44–59.

CHALMERS, A. (1976). *What Is This Thing Called Science?* Milton Keynes: Open University Press.

CHISHOLM, R. (1970). 'Events and Propositions', *Noûs*, 4: 15–24.

CHOTKOWSKI LA FOLLETTE, M. (ed.) (1982). *Quality in Science*. Cambridge, Mass.: MIT Press.

CHURCHLAND, P. M. (1979). *Scientific Realism and the Plasticity of Mind*. Cambridge: Cambridge University Press.

——(1988). *Matter and Consciousness* (rev. edn.). Cambridge, Mass.: Bradford Books, MIT Press.

CHURCHLAND, P. M. (1989). *A Neurocomputational Perspective: The Nature of Mind and the Structure of Science*. Cambridge, Mass.: MIT Press.

——and HOOKER, C. A. (eds.) (1985). *Images of Science*. Chicago: University of Chicago Press.

CHURCHLAND, P. S. (1986). *Neurophilosophy: Toward a Unified Understanding of the Mind/Brain*. Cambridge, Mass.: MIT Press.

COHEN, L. J. (1980). 'What has Science to do with Truth?', *Synthese*, 45: 489–510.

——(1989). *An Introduction to the Philosophy of Induction and Probability*. Oxford: Oxford University Press.

——(1997). 'Are There Ethical Reasons for Being, or not Being, a Scientific Realist', in Dalla Chiara *et al.* 1997: 145–53.

COHEN, R. S., HILPINEN, R., and RENZONG, Q. (eds.) (1996). *Realism and Anti-realism in the Philosophy of Science: Beijing International Conference*. Dordrecht: Kluwer.

——and LAUDAN, L. (eds.) (1983). *Physics, Philosophy and Psychoanalysis*. Dordrecht: D. Reidel.

COLLINS, H. M. (1981). 'Stages in the Empirical Programme of Relativism', *Social Studies of Science*, 11: 3–10.

——(1985). *Changing Order*. London: Sage.

——and PINCH, T. (1993). *The Golem: What Everyone Should Know about Science*. Cambridge: Cambridge University Press.

COMTE, A. (1970). *Introduction to Positive Philosophy*. Indianapolis: Bobbs-Merrill.

COX, D. (1997). 'The Trouble with Truth-Makers', *Pacific Philosophical Quarterly*, 78: 45–62.

CRANE, T. (1992). 'Mental Causation and Mental Reality', *Proceedings of the Aristotelian Society*, 92: 185–202.

CUMMISKEY, D. (1992). 'Reference Failure and Scientific Realism: A Response to the Meta-induction', *British Journal for the Philosophy of Science*, 43: 21–40.

CUSHING, J. T. (1994). *Quantum Mechanics: Historical Contingency and the Copenhagen Hegemony*. Chicago: University of Chicago Press.

——DELANEY, C. F., and GUTTING, G. M. (eds.) (1984). *Science and Reality*. Notre Dame, Ill.: University of Notre Dame Press.

DALLA CHIARA, M. L., DOETS, K., MUNDICI, D., and VAN BENTHEM, J. (eds.) (1997). *Structures and Norms in Science*. Dordrecht: Kluwer.

DANCY, J., and SOSA, E. (eds.) (1992). *A Companion to Epistemology*. Oxford: Blackwell.

DAVIDSON, D. (1980). *Essays on Actions and Events*. Oxford: Oxford University Press.

——(1984). *Inquiries into Truth and Interpretation*. Oxford: Oxford University Press.

——(1990). 'The Structure and Content of Truth', *Journal of Philosophy*, 87: 279–328.

——(1996). 'The Folly of Trying to Define Truth', *Journal of Philosophy*, 93: 263–78.

DENNETT, D. (1978). *Brainstorms: Philosophical Essays on Mind and Psychology*. Montgomery: Bradford.

DESCARTES, R. (1968). *Discourse on Method and the Meditations*. Harmondsworth: Penguin Books.

DEVITT, M. (1991). *Realism and Truth* (2nd edn.). Oxford: Blackwell.

——and STERELNY, K. (1987). *Language and Reality*. Oxford: Blackwell.

DEWEY, J. (1938). *Logic: The Theory of Inquiry*. New York: Holt.

——(1941). 'Propositions, Warranted Assertibility, and Truth', *Journal of Philosophy*, 38: 169–86.

DILLON, M. (1995). *Semiological Reductionism: A Critique of the Deconstructionist Movement in Postmodern Thought*. Albany, NY: State University of New York Press.

DILWORTH, C. (1981). *Scientific Progress: A Study Concerning the Nature of the Relation between Successive Scientific Theories*. Dordrecht: D. Reidel.

DONOVAN, A., LAUDAN, L., and LAUDAN, R. (eds.) (1988). *Scrutinizing Science: Empirical Studies of Scientific Change*. Dordrecht: Kluwer.

DOPPELT, G. (1983). 'Relativism and Recent Pragmatic Conceptions of Scientific Rationality', in N. Rescher (ed.), *Scientific Explanation and Understanding*. Lanham, Md.: University Press of America, 107–42.

DREYFUS, H. L., and HALL, H. (eds.) (1992). *Heidegger: A Critical Reader*. Oxford: Blackwell.

DRUMMOND, J. J. (1990). *Husserlian Intentionality and Non-foundational Realism: Noema and Object*. Dordrecht: Kluwer.

DU BOIS, B. (1983). 'Passionate Scholarship: Notes on Values, Knowing and Method in Feminist Social Science', in Bowles and Klein 1983: 105–16.

DUHEM, P. (1954). *The Aim and Structure of Physical Theory*. Princeton: Princeton University Press.

——(1969). *To Save the Phenomena: An Essay on the Idea of Physical Theory from Plato to Galileo*. Chicago: University of Chicago Press.

DUMMETT, M. (1978). *Truth and Other Enigmas*. London: Duckworth.

——(1982). 'Realism', *Synthese*, 52: 55–112.

DURBIN, P. (ed.) (1980). *A Guide to the Culture of Science, Technology, and Medicine*. New York: Free Press.

EARMAN, J. (1986). *A Primer on Determinism*. Dordrecht: D. Reidel.

——(1992). *Bayes or Bust? A Critical Examination of Bayesian Confirmation Theory*. Cambridge, Mass.: A Bradford Book, MIT Press.

ECO, U. (1986). *Semiotics and the Philosophy of Language*. Bloomington, Ind.: Indiana University Press.

ELKANA, Y. (1978). 'Two-Tier-Thinking: Philosophical Realism and Historical Relativism', *Social Studies of Science*, 8: 309–26.

——et al. (eds.) (1978). *Toward a Metric of Science: The Advent of Science Indicators*. New York: Wiley & Sons.

ELLIS, B. (1988). 'Internal Realism', *Synthese*, 76: 409–34.

ENGELS, F. (1946). *Ludwig Feuerbach and the End of Classical German Philosophy*. Moscow: Progress.

ESPAGNAT, B. d' (1983). *In Search of Reality*. New York: Springer-Verlag.

ETCHEMENDY, J. (1988). 'Tarski on Truth and Logical Consequence', *Journal of Symbolic Logic*, 53: 51–79.

FARRINGTON, B. (1964). *The Philosophy of Francis Bacon*. Chicago: University of Chicago Press.

FAYE, J., and FOLSE, H. (eds.) (1994). *Niels Bohr and Contemporary Philosophy*. Dordrecht: Kluwer.

FEIGL, H. (1950). 'Existential Hypotheses: Realist versus Phenomenalistic Interpretations', *Philosophy of Science*, 17: 35–62.

——and SELLARS, W. (eds.) (1949). *Readings in Philosophical Analysis*. New York: Appleton-Century-Crofts.

FESTA, R. (1993). *Optimum Inductive Methods*. Dordrecht: Kluwer.

FETZER, J. (1981). *Scientific Knowledge: Causation, Explanation, and Corroboration*. Dordrecht: D. Reidel.

——(1991). *Philosophy and Cognitive Science*. New York: Paragon House.

FEYERABEND, P. (1962a). 'Explanation, Reduction, and Empiricism', in H. Feigl and G. Maxwell (eds.), *Minnesota Studies in the Philosophy of Science*, vol. ii. Minneapolis: University of Minnesota Press, 28–97.

——(1962b). 'Problems of Microphysics', in R. G. Colodny (ed.), *Frontiers of Science and Philosophy*. Pittsburgh: University of Pittsburgh Press, 189–283.

——(1975). *Against Method*. London: New Left Books.

——(1978). *Science in a Free Society*. London: Verso.

——(1984a). *Wissenschaft als Kunst*. Frankfurt am Main: Suhrkamp.

——(1984b). 'Mach's Theory of Research and its Relation to Einstein', *Studies in History and Philosophy of Science*, 15: 1–22.

——(1987). *Farewell to Reason*. London: Verso.

FIELD, H. (1972). 'Tarski's Theory of Truth', *Journal of Philosophy*, 69: 347–75.

——(1973). 'Theory Change and the Indeterminacy of Reference', *Journal of Philosophy*, 70: 462–81.

——(1980). *Science without Numbers*. Princeton: Princeton University Press.

——(1982). 'Realism and Relativism', *Journal of Philosophy*, 79: 553–67.

FINE, A. (1979). 'How to Count Frequencies: A Primer for Quantum Realists', *Synthese*, 42: 145–54.

——(1984). 'The Natural Ontological Attitude', in Leplin 1984: 83–107.

——(1986a). 'Unnatural Attitudes: Realist and Instrumentalist Attachments to Science', *Mind*, 95: 149–79.

——(1986b). *The Shaky Game: Einstein, Realism, and the Quantum Theory*. Chicago: University of Chicago Press.

FINE, K. (1975). 'Vagueness, Truth, and Logic', *Synthese*, 30: 265–300.

FLECK, L. (1979). *Genesis and Development of a Scientific Fact*. Chicago: University of Chicago Press.

FODOR, J. (1987). *Psychosemantics: The Problem of Meaning in the Philosophy of Mind*. Cambridge, Mass.: MIT Press.

FOLSE, H. (1985). *The Philosophy of Niels Bohr: The Framework of Complementarity*. Amsterdam: North-Holland.

——(1987). 'Niels Bohr's Concept of Reality', in Lahti and Mittelstaedt 1987: 161–79.

FORD, J. (1983). 'How Random is a Coin Toss?', *Physics Today*, 40–7.

FORSTER, M., and SOBER, E. (1994), 'How to Tell When Simpler, More Unified, or Less *ad hoc* Theories Will Provide More Accurate Predictions', *British Journal for the Philosophy of Science*, 45: 1–36.

FOSTER, M. H., and MARTIN, M. L. (eds.) (1966). *Probability, Confirmation, and Simplicity*. New York: Odyssey Press.

FREGE, G. (1950). *The Foundations of Arithmetics*. Oxford: Blackwell.

FREUD, S. (1973). *Introductory Lectures on Psychoanalysis*. Harmondsworth: Penguin Books.

FREUDENTHAL, G. (1984). 'The Role of Shared Knowledge in Science: The Failure of the Constructivist Programme in the Sociology of Science', *Social Studies of Science*, 14: 285–95.

FRIEDMAN, K. (1972). 'Empirical Simplicity as Testability', *British Journal for the Philosophy of Science*, 23: 25–33.

FRIEDMAN, M. (1974). 'Explanation and Scientific Understanding', *Journal of Philosophy*, 71: 1–19.

FULLER, S. (1988). *Social Epistemology*. Bloomington, Ind.: Indiana University Press.

——(1989). *Philosophy of Science and its Discontents*. Boulder, Colo.: Westview Press.

——(1993). *Philosophy, Rhetoric, and the End of Knowledge: The Coming of Science and Technology Studies*. Madison: University of Wisconsin Press.

GÄHDE, U. (1997). 'Anomalies and the Revision of Theory-Elements: Notes on the Advance of Mercury's Perihelion', in Dalla Chiara *et al.* 1997: 89–104.

GÄRDENFORS, P. (1988). *Knowledge in Flux: Modeling the Dynamics of Epistemic States*. Cambridge, Mass.: MIT Press.

——(1990). 'Frameworks for Properties: Possible Worlds vs. Conceptual Spaces', in L. Haaparanta, M. Kusch, and I. Niiniluoto (eds.), *Language, Knowledge, and Intentionality*. Acta Philosophica Fennica 49. Helsinki: The Philosophical Society of Finland, 383–407.

GAVROGLU, K., GOUDAROULIS, Y., and NICOLACOPOULOS, P. (eds.) (1989). *Imre Lakatos and Theories of Scientific Change*. Dordrecht: Kluwer Academic Publishers.

GIEDYMIN, J. (1971). 'The Paradox of Meaning Variance', *British Journal for the Philosophy of Science*, 22: 30–40.

GIERE, R. (1988). *Explaining Science: A Cognitive Approach*. Chicago: University of Chicago Press.

——(1989). 'Scientific Rationality as Instrumental Rationality', *Studies in History and Philosophy of Science*, 20: 377–84.

——(1996). 'The Feminism Question in the Philosophy of Science', in Nelson and Nelson 1996: 3–15.

GILBERT, M. (1989). *On Social Facts*. London: Routledge.

GILLIES, D. (1989). 'Non-Bayesian Confirmation Theory and the Principle of Explanatory Surplus', in A. Fine and J. Leplin (eds.), *PSA 1988*, vol. ii. East Lansing, Mich.: Philosophy of Science Association, 373–80.

GOLDMAN, A. (1967). 'A Causal Theory of Knowing', *Journal of Philosophy*, 64: 357–72.

——(1986). *Epistemology and Cognition*. Cambridge, Mass.: Harvard University Press.

GOODMAN, N. (1951). *The Structure of Appearance* (3rd edn. 1977). Cambridge, Mass.: Harvard University Press.

——(1972). *Problems and Projects*. Indianapolis: Bobbs-Merrill.

——(1978). *Ways of Worldmaking*. Hassocks: Harvester Press.

——(1984). *Of Mind and Other Matters*. Cambridge, Mass.: Harvard University Press.

GRIM, P. (ed.) (1982). *Philosophy of Science and the Occult*. Albany, NY: State University of New York Press.

——(1991). *The Incomplete Universe: Totality, Knowledge and Truth*. Cambridge, Mass.: MIT Press.

GRIMSHAW, J. (1986). *Feminist Philosophers: Women's Perspectives on Philosophical Traditions*. Brighton: Wheatsheaf Books.

GROSS, P., and LEVITT, N. (1994). *Higher Superstition: The Academic Left and its Quarrels with Science*. Baltimore: Johns Hopkins.

————and LEWIS, M. (eds.) (1996). *The Flight from Science to Reason*. New York: New York Academy of Sciences.

GRÜNBAUM, A. (1973). *Philosophical Problems of Space and Time* (2nd edn.). Dordrecht: D. Reidel.

GURWITSCH, A. (1967). 'Galilean Physics in the Light of Husserl's Phenomenology', in McMullin 1967: 388–401.

HAACK, S. (1978). *Philosophy of Logics*. Cambridge: Cambridge University Press.

——(1987). ' "Realism" ', *Synthese*, 73: 275–99.

——(1993). *Evidence and Inquiry: Towards Reconstruction in Epistemology*. Oxford: Blackwell.

——(1996a). 'Reflections on Relativism: From Momentous Tautology to Seductive Contradiction', in J. Tomberlin (ed.), *Philosophical Perspectives*, x: *Metaphysics*. Oxford: Blackwell, 297–315.

——(1996b). 'Towards a Sober Sociology of Science', in Gross, Levitt, and Lewis 1996: 259–65.

HAAPARANTA, L., and HEINÄMAA, S. (eds.) (1995). *Mind and Cognition: Philosophical Perspectives on Cognitive Science and Artificial Intelligence*, Acta Philosophica Fennica 58. Helsinki: Philosophical Society of Finland.

HABERMAS, J. (1971). *Toward a Rational Society*. London: Heinemann.

——(1983). *Moralbewusstsein und kommunikatives Handeln*. Frankfurt am Main: Suhrkamp.

HACKING, I. (1983). *Representing and Intervening*. Cambridge: Cambridge University Press.

——(1988). 'The Participant Irrealist at Large in the Laboratory', *British Journal for the Philosophy of Science*, 39: 277–94.

——(1993). 'Working in a New World: The Taxonomic Solution', in Horwich 1993: 275–310.

HAMMINGA, B., and DE MARCHI, N. (eds.) (1994). *Idealization in Economics*. Amsterdam: Rodopi.

HANSON, N. R. (1958). *Patterns of Discovery*. Cambridge: Cambridge University Press.

HANSSON, B. (1988). 'Risk Aversion as a Problem of Conjoint Measurement', in P. Gärdenfors and N.-E. Sahlin (eds.), *Decision, Probability and Utility*. Cambridge: Cambridge University Press, 136–58.

HARDIN, C., and ROSENBERG, A. (1982). 'In Defence of Convergent Realism', *Philosophy of Science*, 49: 604–15.

HARDING, S. (1986). *The Science Question in Feminism*. Ithaca, NY: Cornell University Press.

——(ed.) (1987). *Feminism and Methodology*. Bloomington, Ind.: Indiana University Press.

——(1993). 'Rethinking Standpoint Epistemology: What is "Strong Objectivity"?', in Alcoff and Potter 1993: 49–83.

——and HINTIKKA, M. B. (eds.) (1983). *Feminist Perspectives on Epistemology, Metaphysics, Methodology and Philosophy of Science*. Dordrecht: D. Reidel.

HARMAN, G. (1977). *The Nature of Morality*. New York: Oxford University Press.

HARRÉ, R. (1986). *The Varieties of Realism*. Oxford: Blackwell.

——and MADDEN, E. H. (1975). *Causal Powers*. Oxford: Blackwell.

HARRIS, J. F. (1992). *Against Relativism: A Philosophical Defense of Method*. La Salle, Ill.: Open Court.

HARTSOCK, N. (1983). 'The Feminist Standpoint: Developing the Ground for a Specifically Feminist Historical Materialism', in Harding and Hintikka 1983: 283–310. (Reprinted in Harding 1987: 157–80.)

HAUGELAND, J. (ed.) (1981). *Mind Design*. Cambridge, Mass.: MIT Press.

HAUTAMÄKI, A. (1986). *Points of View and their Logical Analysis*, Acta Philosophica Fennica 41. Helsinki: The Philosophical Society of Finland.

HÄYRY, M. (1992). 'Moral Relativism and the Philosophical Criticism of Other Cultures', *Science Studies*, 5/1: 53–6.

HEALEY, R. (1981). 'Comments on Kochen's Specification of Measurement Interactions', in *PSA 1978*, vol. ii. East Lansing, Mich.: Philosophy of Science Association, 277–94.

——(1989). *The Philosophy of Quantum Mechanics: An Interactive Interpretation*. Cambridge: Cambridge University Press.

HEISENBERG, W. (1962). *Physics and Philosophy*. New York: Harper Torchbooks.

HEMPEL, C. G. (1935). 'On the Logical Positivist Theory of Truth', *Analysis*, 11: 49–59.

——(1952). *Fundamentals of Concept Formation in Empirical Science*. Chicago: University of Chicago Press.

——(1958). 'The Theoretician's Dilemma: A Study in the Logic of Theory Construction', in H. Feigl, M. Seriven, and G. Maxwell (eds.), *Minnesota*

*Studies in the Philosophy of Science*, vol. ii. Minneapolis: University of Minnesota Press, 37–98.

——(1965). *Aspects of Scientific Explanation*. New York: Free Press.

——(1983). 'Valuation and Objectivity in Science', in Cohen and Laudan 1983: 73–100.

HENKIN, L., *et al.* (eds.) (1974). *Proceedings of the Tarski Symposium*. Providence, RI: American Mathematical Society.

HERTZ, H. (1956). *The Principles of Mechanics*. New York: Dover.

HESSE, M. (1974). *The Structure of Scientific Inference*. London: Macmillan.

——(1980). 'The Strong Thesis of Sociology of Science', in *Revolutions and Reconstructions in the Philosophy of Science*. Brighton: Harvester Press, 29–60.

——(1988). 'Socializing Epistemology', in McMullin 1988: 97–122.

HETTEMA, H., and KUIPERS, T. (1995). 'Sommerfeld's *Atombau*: A Case Study in Potential Truth Approximation', in T. Kuipers and A. N. Mackor (eds.), *Cognitive Patterns in Science and Common Sense*. Amsterdam: Rodopi, 273–97.

HILPINEN, R. (1980). 'Scientific Rationality and the Ethics of Belief', in R. Hilpinen (ed.), *Rationality in Science*. Dordrecht: D. Reidel, 13–28.

——(1996). 'On Some Formulations of Realism, or How Many Objects Are There in the World?', in Cohen, Hilpinen, and Renzong 1996: 1–11.

HINTIKKA, J. (1968). 'The Varieties of Information and Scientific Explanation', in B. van Rootselar and J. E. Staal (eds.), *Logic, Methodology and Philosophy of Science*, vol. iii. Amsterdam: North-Holland, 151–71.

——(1974). *Knowledge and the Known*. Dordrecht: D. Reidel.

——(1975). *The Intentions of Intentionality*. Dordrecht: D. Reidel.

——(1984). 'Das Paradox transzendentalen Erkenntnis', in E. Schaper and W. Vossenkuhl (eds.), *Bedingungen der Möglichkeit*. Stuttgart: Klett-Cotta Verlag, 123–49.

——(1988*a*). 'On the Development of the Model-Theoretic Viewpoint in Logical Theory', *Synthese*, 77: 1–36.

——(1988*b*). 'What is the Logic of Experimental Inquiry?', *Synthese*, 74: 173–90.

——(1996). *The Principles of Mathematics Revisited*. Cambridge: Cambridge University Press.

——(1997). *Lingua Universalis vs. Calculus Ratiocinator: An Ultimate Presupposition of the Twentieth Century Philosophy*. Dordrecht: Kluwer.

——and HINTIKKA, M. B. (1989). 'Toward a General Theory of Individuation and Identification', in *The Logic of Epistemology and the Epistemology of Logic*. Dordrecht: Kluwer, 73–95.

——and SUPPES, P. (eds.) (1970). *Information and Inference*. Dordrecht: Reidel.

HODGES, W. (1986). 'Truth in a Structure', *Proceedings of the Aristotelian Society*, 86: 135–52.

HOLLIS, M., and LUKES, S. (eds.) (1982). *Rationality and Relativism*. Oxford: Blackwell.

HOOKER, C. A. (1972). 'The Nature of Quantum Mechanical Reality: Einstein Versus Bohr', in R. G. Colodny (ed.), *Paradigms and Paradoxes: The*

*Philosophical Challenge of the Quantum Domain*. Pittsburgh: University of Pittsburgh Press, 67–302.

——(1987). *A Realist Theory of Science*. Albany, NY: State University of New York Press.

HORWICH, P. (1990). *Truth*. Oxford: Blackwell.

——(ed.) (1993). *World Changes: Thomas Kuhn and the Nature of Science*. Cambridge, Mass.: MIT Press.

HOWSON, C. (ed.) (1976). *Method and Appraisal in the Physical Sciences: The Critical Background to Modern Science, 1800–1905*. Cambridge: Cambridge University Press.

——and URBACH, P. (1989). *Scientific Reasoning: The Bayesian Approach*. La Salle, Ill.: Open Court.

HOYNINGEN-HUENE, P. (1993). *Reconstructing Scientific Revolutions: Thomas S. Kuhn's Philosophy of Science*. Chicago: University of Chicago Press.

HUSSERL, E. (1970). *The Crisis of European Sciences and Transcendental Phenomenology*. Evanston, Ill.: Northwestern University Press.

IRVINE, J., and MARTIN, B. (1984). *Foresight in Science: Picking the Winners*. London: Frances Pinter.

IRZIK, G., and GRÜNBERG, T. (1998). 'Whorfian Variations on Kantian Themes: Kuhn's Linguistic Turn', *Studies in History and Philosophy of Science*, 29: 207–21.

JAMES, W. (1907). *Pragmatism: A New Name for Some Old Ways of Thinking*. New York: Longmans, Green & Co.

JAMMER, M. (1974). *The Philosophy of Quantum Mechanics*. New York: John Wiley & Sons.

JARDINE, N. (1979). 'The Forging of Modern Realism: Clavius and Kepler against the Sceptics', *Studies in History and Philosophy of Science*, 10: 141–73.

——(1986). *The Fortunes of Inquiry*. Oxford: Oxford University Press.

JASANOFF, S., MARKLE, G. E., PETERSEN, J. C., and PINCH, T. (eds.) (1995). *Handbook of Science and Technology Studies*. London: Sage Publications.

JENNINGS, R. C. (1987). 'Tarski: A Dilemma', *Inquiry*, 30: 155–72.

JOHNSON, L. E. (1992). *Focusing on Truth*. London: Routledge.

KAILA, E. (1926). *Die Prinzipien der Wahrscheinlichkeitslogik*, Annales Universitatis Fennicae Aboensis, series B, IV, no. 1. Turku: University of Turku.

——(1939). *Inhimillinen tieto*. Helsinki: Otava.

——(1979). *Reality and Experience*. Dordrecht: D. Reidel.

KAISER, M. (1991). 'Progress and Rationality: Laudan's Attempt to Divorce a Happy Couple', *Inquiry*, 34: 433–55.

——(1993). *Aspekte des wissenschaftlichen Fortschritts*. Frankfurt: Peter Lang.

KAMPPINEN, M., and REVONSUO, A. (eds.) (1994). *Consciousness in Philosophy and Cognitive Neuroscience*. Hillsdale, NJ: Lawrence Erlbaum Associates.

KANT, I. (1930). *The Critique of Pure Reason*, trans. J. M. D. Meiklejohn. London: Bell & Sons.

——(1950). *Prolegomena to any Future Metaphysics*. Indianapolis: Bobbs-Merrill.

KELLER, E. F. (1985). *Reflections on Gender and Science*. New Haven: Yale University Press.

KEMENY, J. (1959). *A Philosopher Looks at Science*. New York: Van Nostrand.

KIESEPPÄ, I. (1996). *Truthlikeness for Multidimensional, Quantitative Cognitive Problems*. Dordrecht: Kluwer.

KIM, J. (1973). 'Causation, Nomic Subsumption, and the Concept of Event', *Journal of Philosophy*, 70: 217–36.

KIRKHAM, R. L. (1992). *Theories of Truth: A Critical Introduction*. Cambridge, Mass.: MIT Press.

KITCHER, P. (1989). 'Explanatory Unification and the Causal Structure of the World', in Kitcher and Salmon 1989: 410–505.

——(1993). *The Advancement of Science: Science without Legend, Objectivity without Illusions*. Oxford: Oxford University Press.

——and SALMON, W. (eds.) (1989). *Scientific Explanation*. Minneapolis: University of Minnesota Press.

KLEINER, S. A. (1993). *The Logic of Discovery: A Theory of the Rationality of Scientific Research*. Dordrecht: Kluwer.

KNORR-CETINA, K. (1981). *The Manufacture of Knowledge: An Essay on the Constructivist and Contextual Nature of Science*. Oxford: Pergamon Press.

——(1983). 'The Ethnographic Study of Scientific Work: Towards a Constructivist Interpretation of Science', in Knorr-Cetina and Mulkay 1983: 115–40.

——(1995). 'Laboratory Studies: The Cultural Approach to the Study of Science', in Jasanoff *et al.* 1995: 140–66.

——and MULKAY, M. (eds.) (1983). *Science Observed: Perspectives on the Social Study of Science*. London: Sage Publications.

KOCHEN, S. (1985). 'A New Interpretation of Quantum Mechanics', in Lahti and Mittelstaedt 1985: 151–69.

KORDIG, C. R. (1971). *The Justification of Scientific Change*. Dordrecht: D. Reidel.

KORNBLITH, H. (ed.) (1985). *Naturalizing Epistemology*. Cambridge, Mass.: Bradford Books, MIT Press.

KRAJEWSKI, W. (1977). *Correspondence Principle and the Growth of Knowledge*. Dordrecht: D. Reidel.

KRANTZ, D., LUCE, R. D., SUPPES, P., and TVERSKY, A. (1971). *Foundations of Measurement*. New York: Academic Press.

KRAUSZ, M. (ed.) (1989). *Relativism: Interpretation and Confrontation*. Notre Dame, Ind.: University of Notre Dame Press.

KRIPKE, S. (1980). *Naming and Necessity*. Oxford: Blackwell.

——(1982). *Wittgenstein on Rules and Private Language*. Oxford: Blackwell.

KROON, F. (1988). 'Realism and Descriptivism', in Nola 1988: 141–67.

KUHN, T. S. (1962). *The Structure of Scientific Revolutions* (2nd enlarged edn. 1970). Chicago: University of Chicago Press.

——(1977). *The Essential Tension*. Chicago: University of Chicago Press.

——(1983). 'Rationality and Theory Choice', *Journal of Philosophy*, 80: 563–70.

——(1990). 'Dubbing and Redubbing: The Vulnerability of Rigid Designation', in Savage 1990: 298–318.

——(1991). 'The Road since Structure', in A. Fine *et al.* (eds.), *PSA 1990*, vol. ii. East Lansing, Mich.: Philosophy of Science Association, 3–13.

——(1993). 'Afterwords', in Horwich 1993: 311–41.

KUIPERS, T. (ed.) (1987). *What-Is-Closer-to-the-Truth?*, Poznań Studies in the Philosophy of Science. Amsterdam: Rodopi.

——(1992). 'Truth Approximation by Concretization', in J. Brzezinski and L. Nowak (eds.), *Idealization*, iii: *Approximation and Truth*. Amsterdam: Rodopi, 159–79.

KUOKKANEN, M. (1990). 'Does Pearce's Challenge Refute Stegmüller's Thesis? A Discussion Note', *Science Studies*, 3/2: 75–81.

——(ed.) (1994). *Idealization*, vii: *Structuralism, Idealization and Approximation*. Amsterdam: Rodopi.

KUSCH, M. (1989). *Language as Calculus vs. Language as Universal Medium: A Study in Husserl, Heidegger and Gadamer*. Dordrecht: Kluwer.

——(1991*a*). *Foucault's Strata and Fields*. Dordrecht: Kluwer.

——(1991*b*). 'Koko totuus totuudesta', *Tiede ja edistys*, 16/4: 284–97.

——(1995). *Psychologism: A Case Study in the Sociology of Philosophical Knowledge*. London: Routledge.

KVANVIG, J. L. (1994). 'A Critique of van Fraassen's Voluntaristic Epistemology', *Synthese*, 98: 325–48.

KYBURG, H. E., JR. (1983). 'The Scope of Science', in N. Rescher (ed.), *Limits of Lawfulness*. Lanham, Md.: University Press of America, 53–60.

LAHTI, P., and MITTELSTAEDT, P. (1985). *Symposium on the Foundations of Modern Physics*. Singapore: World Scientific.

————(1987). *Symposium on the Foundations of Modern Physics 1987*. Singapore: World Scientific.

LAKATOS, I. (1976). 'History of Science and its Rational Reconstructions', in Howson 1976: 1–39.

——and MUSGRAVE, A. (eds.) (1970). *Criticism and the Growth of Knowledge*. Cambridge: Cambridge University Press.

LANGER, S. K. (1953). *Feeling and Form*. London: Routledge & Kegan Paul.

LATOUR, B. (1983). 'Give Me a Laboratory and I Will Raise the World', in Knorr-Cetina and Mulkay 1983: 141–70.

——(1987). *Science in Action*. Milton Keynes: Open University Press.

——(1992). 'One More Turn after the Social Turn . . .', in McMullin 1992: 272–94.

——(1993). *We Have Never Been Modern*. Cambridge, Mass.: Harvard University Press.

——and WOOLGAR, S. (1979). *Laboratory Life: The Social Construction of Scientific Facts*. London: Sage Publications.

————(1986). *Laboratory Life: The Construction of Scientific Facts*. Princeton: Princeton University Press.

LAUDAN, L. (1973). 'The Trivialization of the Self-Corrective Thesis', in R. Giere and R. Westfall (eds.), *Foundations of Scientific Method: The Nineteenth Century*. Bloomington, Ind.: Indiana University Press, 275–306.

——(1977). *Progress and its Problems: Toward a Theory of Scientific Growth*. London: Routledge & Kegan Paul.

LAUDAN, L. (1981*a*). 'The Confutation of Convergent Realism', *Philosophy of Science*, 48: 19–49.

——(1981*b*). *Science and Hypothesis*. Dordrecht: D. Reidel.

——(1982). 'More on Bloor', *Philosophy of the Social Sciences*, 12: 71–4.

——(1983). 'The Demise of the Demarcation Problem', in Cohen and Laudan 1983: 111–27.

——(1984*a*). *Science and Values: The Aims of Science and their Role in Scientific Debate*. Berkeley and Los Angeles: University of California Press.

——(1984*b*). 'Explaining the Success of Science: Beyond Epistemic Realism and Relativism', in Cushing, Delaney, and Gutting 1984: 83–105.

——(1984*c*). 'Realism without the Real', *Philosophy of Science*, 51: 156–62.

——(1986). 'Some Problems Facing Intuitionist Meta-methodologies', *Synthese*, 67: 115–29.

——(1987*a*). 'Progress or Rationality? The Prospects for Normative Naturalism', *American Philosophical Quarterly*, 24: 19–31.

——(1987*b*). 'Relativism, Naturalism and Reticulation', *Synthese*, 71: 221–34.

——(1990*a*). 'Demystifying Underdetermination', in Savage 1990: 267–97.

——(1990*b*). *Science and Relativism*. Berkeley and Los Angeles: University of California Press.

——(1996). *Beyond Positivism and Relativism: Theory, Method, and Evidence*. Boulder, Colo.: Westview Press.

——*et al.* (1986). 'Scientific Change: Philosophical Models and Historical Research', *Synthese*, 69: 141–224.

LAURIKAINEN, K. V. (1985). 'Wolfgang Pauli and the Copenhagen Philosophy', in Lahti and Mittelstaedt 1985: 273–87.

——(1987). 'Wolfgang Pauli's Conception of Reality', in Lahti and Mittelstaedt 1987: 209–28.

LAYMON, R. (1982). 'Scientific Realism and the Hierarchical Counterfactual Path from Data to Theory', in P. D. Asquith and T. Nickles (eds.), *PSA*, vol. i. East Lansing, Mich.: Philosophy of Science Association, 107–21.

LEHTI, R. (1986). 'Realism and Fictionalism in the Almagest', in R. Hämäläinen and P. Lahti (eds.), *Essays in Honour of Kalervo Vihtori Laurikainen*, Annales Academiae Scientiarum Fennica A VI 431. Helsinki: Finnish Academy of Science, 116–67.

LEIBNIZ, G. W. (1982). *New Essays on Human Understanding* (abridged edn.). Cambridge: Cambridge University Press.

LENIN, V. I. (1927). *Materialism and Empirio-criticism*. New York: International Publishers.

LEPLIN, J. (1979). 'Reference and Scientific Realism', *Studies in History and Philosophy of Science*, 10: 265–85.

——(ed.) (1984). *Scientific Realism*. Berkeley and Los Angeles: University of California Press.

LEPORE, E. (1983). 'What Model Theoretic Semantics Cannot Do?', *Synthese*, 54: 167–88.

——(ed.) (1986). *Truth and Interpretation: Perspectives in the Philosophy of Donald Davidson*. Oxford: Blackwell.

Levi, I. (1967). *Gambling with Truth: An Essay on Induction and the Aims of Science* (2nd edn. 1973). New York: Harper & Row.

——(1985). 'Messianic vs. Myopic Realism', in P. D. Asquith and P. Kitcher (eds.), *PSA 1984*, vol. ii. East Lansing, Mich.: Philosophy of Science Association, 617–36.

——(1986). 'Estimation and Error-Free Information', *Synthese*, 67: 347–60.

——(1991). *The Fixation of Belief and its Undoing: Changing Beliefs through Inquiry*. Cambridge: Cambridge University Press.

Levin, M. (1984). 'What Kind of Explanation Is Truth?', in Leplin 1984: 124–39.

Lewis, D. (1970). 'How to Define Theoretical Terms', *Journal of Philosophy*, 62: 427–46.

——(1973). *Counterfactuals*. Oxford: Blackwell.

——(1984). 'Putnam's Paradox', *Australasian Journal of Philosophy*, 62: 221–36.

——(1986). *On the Plurality of Worlds*. Oxford: Blackwell.

Lipton, P. (1991). *Inference to the Best Explanation*. London: Routledge.

——(1993). 'Is the Best Good Enough?', *Proceedings of the Aristotelian Society*, 93: 89–104.

Lloyd, E. (1996). 'Science and Anti-science: Objectivity and its Real Enemies', in Nelson and Nelson 1996: 217–59.

——(1997). 'Feyerabend, Mill, and Pluralism', *Philosophy of Science*, 64 (Proceedings): S396–S407.

Lloyd, G. (1984). *The Man of Reason: 'Male' and 'Female' in Western Philosophy*. London: Methuen.

Longino, H. (1989). 'Biological Effects, of Low-Level Radiation: Values, Dose-Response Models, Risk Estimates', *Synthese*, 81: 391–404.

——(1990). *Science as Social Knowledge*. Princeton: Princeton University Press.

——(1996). 'Cognitive and Non-cognitive Values in Science: Rethinking the Distinction', in Nelson and Nelson 1996: 39–58.

Loux, M. (1978). *Substance and Attribute*. Dordrecht: D. Reidel.

Lukács, G. (1971). *History and Class Consciousness*. London: Merlin Press.

Luntley, M. (1988). *Language, Logic, and Experience: The Case for Anti-realism*. London: Duckworth.

Määttänen, P. (1991). *Action and Experience: A Naturalistic Approach to Cognition*, Annales Academiae Scientiarum Fennica, Dissertationes Humanarum Litterarum 68. Helsinki: Societas Scientiarum Fennica.

McAllister, J. W. (1993). 'Scientific Realism and the Criteria of Theory-Choice', *Erkenntnis*, 38: 203–22.

McCormick, P. (ed.) (1996). *Starmaking*. Cambridge, Mass.: MIT Press.

McGinn, C. (1991). *The Problem of Consciousness*. Oxford: Blackwell.

McGuinness, B., and Oliveri, G. (eds.) (1994). *The Philosophy of Michael Dummett*. Dordrecht: Kluwer.

Mach, E. (1959). *The Analysis of Sensations and the Relation of the Physical to the Psychical*. New York: Dover.

——(1960). *The Science of Mechanics*. La Salle, Ill.: Open Court.

318                          REFERENCES

MacIntosh, D. (1994). 'Partial Convergence and Approximate Truth', *British Journal for the Philosophy of Science*, 45: 153–70.

Mackie, J. L. (1974). *The Cement of the Universe: A Study of Causation*. Oxford: Oxford University Press.

——(1977). *Ethics: Inventing Right and Wrong*. Harmondsworth: Penguin Books.

McMullin, E. (ed.) (1967). *Galileo, Man of Science*. New York: Basic Books.

——(1984). 'A Case for Scientific Realism', in Leplin 1984: 8–40.

——(1985). 'Galilean Idealizations', *Studies in the History of Philosophy of Science*, 16: 247–73.

——(1987). 'Review of *Is Science Progressive?*', *Isis*, 78: 200–1.

——(ed.) (1988). *Construction and Constraint: The Shaping of Scientific Rationality*. Notre Dame, Ind.: University of Notre Dame Press.

——(ed.) (1992). *The Social Dimensions of Science*. Notre Dame, Ind.: University of Notre Dame Press.

Maher, P. (1993). *Betting on Theories*. Cambridge: Cambridge University Press.

Mäki, U. (1988). 'How to Combine Rhetoric and Realism in the Methodology of Economics', *Economics and Philosophy*, 4: 89–109.

——(1989). 'On the Problem of Realism in Economics', *Ricerche economiche*, 43: 170–98.

——(1990). *Studies in Realism and Explanation in Economics*, Annales Academiae Scientiarum Fennica, Dissertationes Humanarum Litterarum, 55. Helsinki: Academia Scientiarum Fennica.

Malachowski, A. P. (ed.) (1990). *Reading Rorty: Critical Responses to Philosophy and the Mirror of Nature (and Beyond)*. Oxford: Blackwell.

Margolis, J. (1978). *Persons and Minds: The Prospects of Nonreductive Materialism*. Dordrecht: D. Reidel.

——(1986). *Pragmatism without Foundations: Reconciling Realism and Relativism*. Oxford: Blackwell.

——(1991). *The Truth about Relativism*. Oxford: Blackwell.

Markovic, M. (1968). *Dialektik der Praxis*. Frankfurt am Main: Suhrkamp.

Martens, D. B. (1993). 'Close Enough to Reference', *Synthese*, 95: 357–77.

Martin-Löf, P. (1987). 'Truth of a Proposition, Evidence of a Judgment, Validity of a Proof', *Synthese*, 73: 407–20.

Marx, K. (1975). *Early Writings*, ed. L. Colletti. Harmondsworth: Penguin Books.

Mayo, D. (1996). *Error and the Growth of Experimental Knowledge*. Chicago: University of Chicago Press.

Meiland, J. W., and Krausz, M. (eds.) (1982). *Relativism: Cognitive and Moral*. Notre Dame, Ind.: University of Notre Dame Press.

Merchant, C. (1983). *The Death of Nature: Women, Ecology and the Scientific Revolution*. San Francisco: Harper & Row.

Merton, R. S. (1973). *The Sociology of Science: Theoretical and Empirical Investigations*. Chicago: University of Chicago Press.

Mikenberg, I., da Costa, N. C. A., and Chuaqui, R. (1986). 'Pragmatic Truth and Approximation to Truth', *Journal of Symbolic Logic*, 51: 201–21.

Mill, J. S. (1859). *On Liberty*. (new edn. 1956). London.

MILLER, D. (1974). 'Popper's Qualitative Definition of Verisimilitude', *British Journal for the Philosophy of Science*, 25: 168–77.

——(1994). *Critical Rationalism: A Restatement and Defence*. Chicago: Open Court.

MONK, J. D. (1976). *Mathematical Logic*. New York: Springer-Verlag.

MOORE, G. E. (1929). *Principia Ethica*. Cambridge: Cambridge University Press.

——(1959). *Philosophical Papers*. Oxford: Allen & Unwin.

MORGENBESSER, S. (ed.) (1977). *Dewey and his Critics*. New York: Journal of Philosophy.

MORRIS, C. (1938). *Foundations of the Theory of Signs*. Chicago: University of Chicago Press.

MOSER, P. K. (1990). 'A Dilemma for Internal Realism', *Philosophical Studies*, 59: 101–6.

——and TROUT, J. D. (eds.) (1995). *Contemporary Materialism: A Reader*. London: Routledge.

MOULINES, C. U., and STRAUB, R. (1994). 'Approximation and Idealization from the Structuralist Point of View', in Kuokkanen 1994: 25–48.

MULKAY, M. (1977). 'Some Connections between the Quantitative History of Science, the Social History of Science, and the Sociology of Science', in P. Löppönen (ed.), *Proceedings of the International Seminar on Science Studies*, Publication of the Academy of Finland 4. Helsinki: Academy of Finland, 54–76.

——(1979). *Science and the Sociology of Knowledge*. London: Allen & Unwin.

MUNÉVAR, G. (1991). *Beyond Reason*. Dordrecht: Kluwer.

MUSGRAVE, A. (1979). 'How to Avoid Incommensurability', in Niiniluoto and Tuomela 1979: 336–46.

——(1988). 'The Ultimate Argument for Scientific Realism', in Nola 1988: 229–52.

——(1989). 'Noa's Ark: Fine for Realism', *Philosophical Quarterly*, 39: 383–98.

——(1991). 'The Myth of Astronomical Instrumentalism', in Munévar 1991: 243–80.

——(1993). *Common Sense, Science and Scepticism*. Cambridge: Cambridge University Press.

NAGEL, E. (1961). *The Structure of Science*. New York: Harcourt, Brace & World.

NAGEL, T. (1986). *The View from Nowhere*. Oxford: Oxford University Press.

NELSON, L. H. (1990). *Who Knows: From Quine to a Feminist Empiricism*. Philadelphia: Temple University Press.

——and NELSON, J. (eds.) (1996). *Feminism, Science, and the Philosophy of Science*. Dordrecht: Kluwer.

NEWTON-SMITH, W. (1981). *The Rationality of Science*. London: Routledge & Kegan Paul.

——(1989). 'The Truth in Realism', *Dialectica*, 43: 31–45.

NICHOLSON, L. I. (ed.) (1990), *Feminism/Postmodernism*. London: Routledge.

NICKLES, T. (1992). 'Good Science as Bad History: From Order of Knowing to Order of Being', in McMullin, 1992: 85–129.

NIINILUOTO, I. (1977). 'On the Truthlikeness of Generalizations', in R. E. Butts and J. Hintikka (eds.), *Basic Problems in Methodology and Linguistics*. Dordrecht: D. Reidel, 121–47.

——(1978), 'Truthlikeness: Comments on Recent Discussion', *Synthese*, 38: 281–329.

——(1979). 'Verisimilitude, Theory-Change, and Scientific Progress', in Niiniluoto and Tuomela 1979: 243–64.

——(1980). 'Scientific Progress', *Synthese*, 45: 427–64.

——(1981). 'Language, Norms, and Truth', in I. Pörn (ed.), *Essays in Philosophical Analysis*, Acta Philosophica Fennica 32. Helsinki: Philosophical Society of Finland, 168–89.

——(1982). 'Remarks on the Logic of Perception', in I. Niiniluoto and E. Saarinen (eds.), *Intensional Logic: Theory and Applications*, Acta Philosophica Fennica 35. Helsinki: Philosophical Society of Finland, 116–29.

——(1984). *Is Science Progressive?* Dordrecht: D. Reidel.

——(1985a). 'The Significance of Verisimilitude', in P. D. Asquith and P. Kitcher (eds.), *PSA 1984*, vol. ii. East Lansing, Mich.: Philosophy of Science Association, 591–613.

——(1985b). 'Truth and Legal Norms', in N. MacCormick *et al.* (eds.), *Conditions of Validity and Cognition in Modern Legal Thought*, ARSP 25. Wiesbaden: Franz Steiner Verlag, 168–90.

——(1985c). 'Truthlikeness, Realism, and Progressive Theory-Change', in Pitt 1985: 235–65.

——(1986a). 'Ernst Mach as a Philosopher of Science', in *Essays in Honour of Kalevi Vihtori Laurikainen*, Annales Academiae Scientiarum Fennicae, Series A.VI. Physica 431. Helsinki: Finnish Academy of Science, 190–203.

——(1986b). 'Theories, Approximations, Idealizations', in R. Barcan Marcus, G. J. W. Dorn, and P. Weingartner (eds.), *Logic, Methodology and Philosophy of Science*, vol. vii. Amsterdam: North-Holland, 255–89. (Reprinted in Brzezinski *et al.* 1990: 9–57.)

——(1986c). 'Truthlikeness and Bayesian Estimation', *Synthese*, 67: 321–46.

——(1986d). 'Imagination and Fiction', *Journal of Semantics*, 4: 209–22.

——(1987a). *Truthlikeness*. Dordrecht: D. Reidel.

——(1987b). 'Progress, Realism, and Verisimilitude', in P. Weingartner and G. Schurz (eds.), *Logik, Wissenschaftstheorie und Erkenntnistheorie (Akten des 11. Internationalen Wittgenstein-Symposiums 1986)*. Vienna: Verlag Hölder-Pichler-Tempsky, 151–61.

——(1987c). 'The Varieties of Realism', in Lahti and Mittelstaedt 1987: 459–83.

——(1987d). 'Peer Review: Problems and Prospects', in B. Ståhle (ed.), *Evaluation of Research: Nordic Experiences*. Copenhagen: Nordic Council of Ministers, 7–29.

——(1988a). 'Probability, Possibility, and Plenitude', in J. Fetzer (ed.), *Probability and Causality*. Dordrecht: D. Reidel, 91–108.

——(1988b). 'Analogy and Similarity in Inductive Logic', in D. Helman (ed.), *Analogical Reasoning*. Dordrecht: D. Reidel, 271–98.

——(1989). 'Corroboration, Verisimilitude, and the Success of Science', in Gavroglu, Goudaroulis, and Nicolacopoulos 1989: 229–43.

——(1990*a*). 'Measuring the Success of Science', in A. Fine, M. Forbes, and L. Wessels (eds.), *PSA 1990*, vol. i. East Lansing, Mich.: Philosophy of Science Association, 435–45.

——(1990*b*). 'Science and Epistemic Values', *Science Studies*, 3/1: 21–5.

——(1991*a*). 'Realism, Relativism, and Constructivism', *Synthese*, 89: 135–62.

——(1991*b*). 'Scientific Progress Reconsidered', in E. Deutsch (ed.), *Culture and Modernity*. Honolulu: University of Hawaii Press, 593–614.

——(1991*c*). 'What's Wrong with Relativism', *Science Studies*, 4/2: 17–24.

——(1992*a*). 'Eino Kaila and Scientific Realism', in I. Niiniluoto, M. Sintonen, and G. H. von Wright (eds.), *Eino Kaila and Logical Empiricism*, Acta Philosophica Fennica 52. Helsinki: Philosophical Society of Finland, 102–16.

——(1992*b*). 'Reality, Truth, and Confirmation in Mathematics: Reflections on the Quasi-empiricist Programme', in J. Echeverria, A. Ibarra, and T. Mormann (eds.), *Space of Mathematics*. Berlin: de Gruyter, 60–78.

——(1992*c*). 'Improving Morality: A Reply to Matti Häyry', *Science Studies*, 5/1: 57–9.

——(1993). 'The Aim and Structure of Applied Research', *Erkenntnis*, 1–21.

——(1994*a*). 'Truthlikeness Misapplied: A Reply to Ernest W. Adams', *Synthese*, 101: 291–300.

——(1994*b*). 'Scientific Realism and the Problem of Consciousness', in Kamppinen and Revonsuo 1994: 33–54.

——(1994*c*). 'Defending Tarski against his Critics', in B. Twardowski and J. Wolenski (eds.), *Sixty Years of Tarski's Definition of Truth*. Cracow: Philed, 48–68.

——(1994*d*). 'Approximation in Applied Science', in Kuokkanen 1994: 127–39.

——(1994*e*). 'Descriptive and Inductive Simplicity', in W. Salmon and G. Wolters (eds.), *Logic, Language, and the Structure of Theories*. Pittsburgh: University of Pittsburgh Press, 147–70.

——(1995). 'Is There Progress in Science?', in H. Stachowiak (ed.), *Pragmatik: Handbuch pragmatischen Denken*, vol. v. Hamburg: Felix Meiner Verlag, 30–58.

——(1996*a*). 'Queries about Internal Realism', in Cohen, Hilpinen, and Renzong 1996: 45–54.

——(1996*b*). 'The Relativism Question in Feminist Epistemology', in Nelson and Nelson 1996: 139–57.

——(1997*a*). 'Theoretical Reference and Truthlikeness', in G. Meggle (ed.), *Analyomen 2*. Berlin: de Gruyter, 439–52.

——(1997*b*). 'Reference Invariance and Truthlikeness', *Philosophy of Science*, 64: 546–54.

——(1997*c*). 'Technology Policy in a Democratic State', in S. Hellsten, M. Kopperi, and O. Loukola (eds.), *Taking the Liberal Challenge Seriously: Essays on Contemporary Liberalism at the Turn of the 21st Century*. Aldershot: Ashgate, 192–204.

——(1998). 'Verisimilitude: The Third Period', *British Journal for the Philosophy of Science*, 49: 1–29.

NIINILUOTO, I. (1999*a*). 'Tarskian Truth as Correspondence: Replies to Some Objections', in J. Peregrin (ed.), *Approaches to Truth*. Dordrecht: Kluwer.

——(1999*b*). 'Scepticism, Fallibilism, and Verisimilitude', in J. Sihvola (ed.), *Ancient Scepticism and the Sceptical Tradition*, Acta Philosophica Fennica. Helsinki: Philosophical Society of Finland.

——and TUOMELA, R. (1973). *Theoretical Concepts and Hypothetico-Inductive Inference*. Dordrecht: D. Reidel.

————(eds.) (1979). *The Logic and Epistemology of Scientific Change*, Acta Philosophica Fennica 30. Amsterdam: North-Holland.

NOLA, R. (1980). 'Fixing the Reference of Theoretical Terms', *Philosophy of Science*, 45: 505–31.

——(ed.) (1988). *Realism and Relativism in Science*. Dordrecht: Kluwer.

NORRIS, C. (1996). *Reclaiming Truth: Contribution to a Critique of Cultural Relativism*. London: Lawrence & Wishart.

NOWAK, L. (1980). *The Structure of Idealization: Towards a Systematic Interpretation of the Marxian Idea of Science*. Dordrecht: D. Reidel.

NOWAKOWA, I. (1994). *Idealization, v: The Dynamics of Idealizations*. Amsterdam: Rodopi.

ODDIE, G. (1986). *Likeness to Truth*. Dordrecht: D. Reidel.

O'HEAR, A. (1980). *Karl Popper*. London: Routledge & Kegan Paul.

O'LEARY-HAWTHORNE, J. (1994). 'A Corrective to the Ramsey–Lewis Account of Theoretical Terms', *Analysis*, 54: 105–10.

OLIVÉ, L. (1987). 'Two Conceptions of Truth and their Relationship to Social Theory', *Philosophy of the Social Sciences*, 17: 313–39.

PAPINEAU, D. (1988). 'Does the Sociology of Science Discredit Science?', in Nola 1988: 37–57.

——(ed.) (1996*a*). *The Philosophy of Science*. Oxford: Oxford University Press.

——(1996*b*). 'Theory-Dependent Terms', *Philosophy of Science*, 63: 1–20.

PAPPAS, G., and SWAIN, M. (eds.) (1978). *Essays on Knowledge and Justification*. Ithaca, NY: Cornell University Press.

PEARCE, D. (1983). 'Truthlikeness and Translation: A Comment on Oddie', *British Journal for the Philosophy of Science*, 34: 380–5.

——(1987*a*), *Roads to Commensurability*. Dordrecht: D. Reidel.

——(1987*b*). 'Critical Realism in Progress: Reflections on Ilkka Niiniluoto's Philosophy of Science', *Erkenntnis*, 27: 147–71.

——and RANTALA, V. (1984). 'A Logical Study of the Correspondence Relation', *Journal of Philosophical Logic*, 13: 47–84.

PEIRCE, C. S. (1931–5). *Collected Papers*, ed. C. Hartshorne and P. Weiss, vols. i–vi. Cambridge, Mass.: Harvard University Press.

——(1966). *Selected Writings*, ed. P. P. Wiener. New York: Dover.

PENDLEBURY, M. (1986). 'Facts as Truthmakers', *Monist*, 69: 177–88.

PERA, M. (1985). 'In Praise of Cumulative Progress', in Pitt 1985: 267–82.

PEREGRIN, J. (1995). *Doing Worlds with Words: Formal Semantics without Formal Metaphysics*. Dordrecht: Kluwer.

PETTIT, P. (1992). 'Problem of Rule-Following', in Dancy and Sosa 1992: 386–91.

PIETARINEN, J. (1970). 'Quantitative Tools for Evaluating Scientific Systematizations', in Hintikka and Suppes 1970: 123–47.

PIETILÄ, V. (1981). *Social Practice and the Development of Science*. Tampere: Research Institute for Social Sciences, University of Tampere.

PIHLSTRÖM, S. (1996). *Structuring the World: The Issue of Realism and the Nature of Ontological Problems in Classical and Contemporary Pragmatism*, Acta Philosophica Fennica 59. Helsinki: Philosophical Society of Finland.

——(1998). *Pragmatism and Philosophical Anthropology: Understanding our Human Life in a Human World*. New York: Peter Lang.

PIRON, C. (1985). 'Quantum Mechanics: Fifty Years Later', in Lahti and Mittelstaedt 1985: 207–11.

PITT, J. C. (1981). *Pictures, Images and Conceptual Change: An Analysis of Wilfrid Sellars' Philosophy of Science*. Dordrecht: D. Reidel.

——(ed.) (1985). *Change and Progress in Modern Science*. Dordrecht: Reidel.

POPKIN, R. H. (1979). *The History of Scepticism from Erasmus to Spinoza*. Berkeley and Los Angeles: University of California Press.

POPPER, K. R. (1959). *The Logic of Scientific Discovery*. London: Hutchinson.

——(1963). *Conjectures and Refutations: The Growth of Scientific Knowledge*. London: Hutchinson.

——(1972). *Objective Knowledge: An Evolutionary Approach* (2nd enlarged edn. 1979). Oxford: Oxford University Press.

——(1974). 'Autobiography', in P. A. Schilpp (ed.), *The Philosophy of Karl Popper*, part i. La Salle, Ill.: Open Court, 3–181.

——(1982). *The Open Universe: An Argument for Indeterminism*. Totowa, NJ: Rowman & Littlefield.

——(1985). 'Realism in Quantum Mechanics and a New Version of the EPR Experiment', in G. Tarozzi and A. van der Merwe (eds.), *Open Questions in Quantum Physics*. Dordrecht: D. Reidel, 3–25.

——and ECCLES, J. C. (1977). *The Self and its Brain*. Berlin: Springer International.

POTTER, E. (1993). 'Gender and Epistemic Negotiations', in Alcoff and Potter 1993: 161–86.

PRAWITZ, D. (1977). 'Meaning and Proofs: On the Conflict between Classical and Intuitionistic Logic', *Theoria*, 48: 2–40.

PRESTON, J. (1992). 'On Some Objections to Relativism', *Ratio*, NS 5/1: 57–73.

——(1997). 'Feyerabend's Retreat from Realism', *Philosophy of Science*, 64 (Proceedings): S421–S431.

PRICE, D. DE SOLLA (1963). *Little Science, Big Science*. New York: Columbia University Press.

PRZEŁECKI, M. (1969). *The Logic of Empirical Theories*. London: Routledge & Kegan Paul.

PSILLOS, S. (1994a). 'Science and Realism: A Naturalistic Investigation into Scientific Enquiry', Ph.D. dissertation. King's College, University of London.

——(1994b). 'A Philosophical Study of the Transition from the Caloric Theory of Heat to Thermodynamics: Resisting the Pessimistic Meta-induction', *Studies in History and Philosophy of Science*, 25: 159–90.

PSILLOS, S. (1996). 'On van Fraassen's Critique of Abductive Reasoning: Some Pitfalls of Selective Scepticism', *Philosophical Quarterly*, 46: 31–47.

PUTNAM, H. (1975). *Mind, Language, and Reality*, Philosophical Papers, vol. ii. Cambridge: Cambridge University Press.

——(1978). *Meaning and the Moral Sciences*. London: Routledge & Kegan Paul.

——(1981). *Reason, Truth and History*. Cambridge: Cambridge University Press.

——(1983a). 'On Truth', in L. Cauman *et al.* (eds.), *How Many Questions?* Indianapolis: Hackett, 35–56.

——(1983b). *Realism and Reason*, Philosophical Papers, vol. iii. Cambridge: Cambridge University Press.

——(1987). *The Many Faces of Realism*. La Salle, Ill.: Open Court.

——(1990). *Realism with a Human Face*. Cambridge, Mass.: Harvard University Press.

——(1992). *Renewing Philosophy*. Cambridge, Mass.: Harvard University Press.

——(1994). 'Sense, Nonsense and the Senses: An Inquiry into the Powers of the Human Mind', *Journal of Philosophy*, 91: 445–517.

——(1995). *Pragmatism: An Open Question*. Oxford: Blackwell.

PUTNAM, R. A. (ed.) (1997). *The Cambridge Companion to William James*. Cambridge: Cambridge University Press.

QUINE, W. V. O. (1948). 'On What There Is', *Review of Metaphysics*, 2/5: 21–38.

——(1953). *From a Logical Point of View*. Cambridge, Mass.: Harvard University Press.

——(1960). *Word and Object*. Cambridge, Mass.: MIT Press.

——(1966). 'On Simple Theories of a Complex World', in Foster and Martin 1966: 250–2.

——(1969). *Ontological Relativity and Other Essays*. New York: Columbia University Press.

——(1990). *Pursuit of Truth*. Cambridge, Mass.: Harvard University Press.

RADDER, H. (1996). *In and about the World: Philosophical Studies of Science and Technology*. Albany, NY: State University of New York Press.

RADNITZKY, G., and ANDERSSON, G. (eds.) (1978). *Progress and Rationality in Science*. Dordrecht: D. Reidel.

————(eds.) (1979). *The Structure and Development of Science*. Dordrecht: D. Reidel.

RANTA, A. (1994). *Type-Theoretical Grammar*. Oxford: Oxford University Press.

READHEAD, M. (1987). *Incompleteness, Non-locality, and Realism: A Prolegomena to the Philosophy of Quantum Mechanics*. Oxford: Oxford University Press.

REDLOW, G., *et al.* (1971). *Einführung in dem dialektischen und historischen Materialismus*. Berlin: Dietz Verlag.

REICHENBACH, H. (1938). *Experience and Prediction*. Chicago: University of Chicago Press.

——(1951). *The Rise of Scientific Philosophy*. Berkeley and Los Angeles: University of California Press.

——(1956). *The Direction of Time*. Berkeley and Los Angeles: University of California Press.

RESCHER, N. (1969). *Introduction to Value Theory*. Englewood Cliffs, NJ: Prentice-Hall.

——(1970). *Scientific Explanation*. New York: Free Press.

——(1973). *The Coherence Theory of Truth*. Oxford: Oxford University Press.

——(1977). *Methodological Pragmatism*. Oxford: Blackwell.

——(1978). *Scientific Progress: A Philosophical Essay on the Economics of Research in Natural Science*. Oxford: Blackwell.

——(1980). 'Conceptual Schemes', *Midwest Studies in Philosophy*, 5: 323–45.

——(1982). *Conceptual Idealism*. Washington: University Press of America.

——(1984). *The Limits of Science*. Berkeley and Los Angeles: University of California Press.

——(1987). *Scientific Realism: A Critical Reappraisal*. Dordrecht: D. Reidel.

——(1988). *Rationality*. Oxford: Oxford University Press.

——(ed.) (1990). *Aesthetic Factors in Natural Science*. Lanham, Md.: University Press of America.

RESNIK, D. B. (1992). 'Convergent Realism and Approximate Truth', in D. Hull, M. Forbes, and K. Okruhlik (eds.), *PSA 1992*, vol. i. East Lansing, Mich.: Philosophy of Science Association, 421–34.

RHEINGOLD, H. (1991). *Virtual Reality*. New York: Summit Books.

ROLL-HANSEN, N. (1989). 'The Practice Criterion and the Rise of Lysenkoism', *Science Studies*, 2/1: 3–16.

RORLICH, F. (1985). 'Schrödinger's Criticism of Quantum Mechanics: Fifty Years Later', in Lahti and Mittelstaedt 1985: 555–72.

RORTY, A. O. (ed.) (1980). *Explaining Emotions*. Berkeley and Los Angeles: University of California Press.

RORTY, R. (1980). *Philosophy and the Mirror of Nature*. Princeton: Princeton University Press.

——(1982). *Consequences of Pragmatism*. Minneapolis: University of Minnesota Press.

——(1989). *Contingency, Irony, and Solidarity*. Cambridge: Cambridge University Press.

——(1991). *Objectivity, Relativism, and Truth*, Philosophical Papers, vol. i. Cambridge: Cambridge University Press.

——(1998). *Truth and Progress*, Philosophical Papers, vol. iii. Cambridge: Cambridge University Press.

ROSENBERG, J. (1974). *Linguistic Representation*. Dordrecht: D. Reidel.

——(1980). *One World and our Knowledge of It: The Problematic of Realism in Post-Kantian Perspective*. Dordrecht: Reidel.

ROSENTHAL, D. M. (ed.) (1971). *Materialism and the Mind–Body Problem*. Englewood Cliffs, NJ: Prentice-Hall.

ROUSE, J. (1996). *Engaging Science: How to Understand its Practices Philosophically*. Ithaca, NY: Cornell University Press.

RUSSELL, B. (1940). *An Inquiry into Meaning and Truth* (new edn. 1962). London: Allen & Unwin.

RUSSELL, D. (1983). 'Anything Goes', *Social Studies of Science*, 13: 437–64.

RYLE, G. (1949). *The Concept of Mind*. London: Hutchinson.

SAARKAMP, H. J., JR. (ed.) (1995). *Rorty and Pragmatism: The Philosopher Responds to his Critics*. Nashville: Vanderbilt University Press.

SALMON, W. C. (1984). *Scientific Explanation and the Causal Structure of the World*. Princeton: Princeton University Press.

SANDKÜHLER, H. J. (ed.) (1975). *Marxistische Erkenntnistheorie*. Frankfurt am Main: Fischer Athenäum.

SAVAGE, C. W. (ed.) (1990). *Scientific Theories*. Minneapolis: University of Minnesota Press.

SAYERS, B. (1987). 'Wittgenstein, Relativism, and the Strong Thesis in Sociology', *Philosophy of the Social Sciences*, 17: 133–45.

SAYRE-MCCORD, G. (ed.) (1988). *Essays on Moral Realism*. Ithaca, NY: Cornell University Press.

SCHEFFLER, I. (1965). *Conditions of Knowledge*. Glenview, Ill.: Scott, Foresman & Company.

——(1967). *Science and Subjectivity*. Indianapolis: Hackett.

——(1980). 'The Wonderful Worlds of Goodman', *Synthese*, 45: 201–9.

SCHILLER, F. C. (1912). *Humanism* (new edn. 1970). London: Macmillan.

SCHILPP, P. A. (ed.) (1963). *The Philosophy of Rudolf Carnap*. La Salle, Ill.: Open Court.

SCHLICK, M. (1959). 'Positivism and Realism', in Ayer 1959: 82–107.

——(1979). *Philosophical Papers*, vol. i. Dordrecht: D. Reidel.

——(1985). *General Theory of Knowledge*. La Salle, Ill.: Open Court.

SCHMIDT, A. (1971). *The Concept of Nature in Marx*. London: New Left Books.

SCHRÖDER-HEISTER, P., and SCHÄFER, F. (1989). 'Reduction, Representation and Commensurability of Theories', *Philosophy of Science*, 56: 130–57.

SEARLE, J. (1992). *The Rediscovery of the Mind*. Cambridge, Mass.: MIT Press.

——(1995). *The Construction of Social Reality*. New York: Free Press.

SEGERSTRÅLE, U. (1996). 'Anti-antiscience: The Fight for Science and Reason', *Science Studies*, 9/1: 5–25.

SELLARS, W. (1963). *Science, Perception, and Reality*. London: Routledge & Kegan Paul.

——(1968). *Science and Metaphysics*. London: Routledge & Kegan Paul.

SEXTUS EMPIRICUS (1985). *Selections from the Major Writings on Scepticism, Man, and God*, ed. and introd. P. P. Hallie. Indianapolis: Hackett.

SHAPIN, S. (1994). *A Social History of Truth: Civility and Science in Seventeenth-Century England*. Chicago: University of Chicago Press.

SHOEMAKER, S. (1984). *Identity, Cause, and Mind: Philosophical Essays*. Cambridge: Cambridge University Press.

SHRADER-FRECHETTE, K. (1990). 'Three Arguments against Simplicity', in Rescher 1990: 1–26.

SIEGEL, H. (1987). *Relativism Refuted: A Critique of Contemporary Epistemological Relativism*. Dordrecht: D. Reidel.

——(1988). *Educating Reason: Rationality, Thinking, and Education*. New York: Routledge.

——(1996). 'Instrumental Rationality and Naturalized Philosophy of Science', in

L. Darden (ed.), *PSA 1996*, part i, Supplement to vol. 63/3 of *Philosophy of Science*. Chicago: University of Chicago Press, 116–24.

SINTONEN, M. (1984). *The Pragmatics of Scientific Explanation*, Acta Philosophica Fennica 37. Helsinki: The Philosophical Society of Finland.

SKLAR, L. (1974). *Space, Time, and Spacetime*. Berkeley and Los Angeles: University of California Press.

SMART, J. J. C. (1963). *Philosophy and Scientific Realism*. London: Routledge & Kegan Paul.

——(1968). *Between Science and Philosophy*. New York: Random House.

——(1986). 'Realism vs. Idealism', *Philosophy*, 61: 295–312.

SMITH, P. (1981). *Realism and the Progress of Science*. Cambridge: Cambridge University Press.

SOBER, E. (1975). *Simplicity*. Oxford: Oxford University Press.

——(1990). 'Contrastive Empiricism', in Savage 1990: 392–410.

SOKAL, A., and BRICMONT, J. (1998). *Intellectual Imposters: Postmodern Philosophers' Abuse of Science*. London: Profile Books.

SPENDER, D. (1982). *Man Made Language*. London: Routledge & Kegan Paul.

STALNAKER, R. (1984). *Inquiry*. Cambridge, Mass.: MIT Press.

STANLEY, L., and WISE, S. (1983). *Breaking Out: Feminist Consciousness and Feminist Research*. London: Routledge & Kegan Paul.

STEGMÜLLER, W. (1976). *The Structure and Dynamics of Theories*. New York: Springer-Verlag.

STENIUS, E. (1972). *Critical Essays*, Acta Philosophica Fennica 25. Amsterdam: North-Holland.

STICH, S. (1990). *The Fragmentation of Reason: Preface to a Pragmatic Theory of Cognitive Evaluation*. Cambridge, Mass.: MIT Press.

STINY, G., and GIPS, J. (1978). *Algorithmic Aesthetics: Computer Models for Criticism and Design in the Arts*. Berkeley and Los Angeles: University of California Press.

STRAWSON, P. (1950). 'Truth', *Proceedings of the Aristotelian Society* (supplementary volume), 24: 129–56.

STROUP, T. (ed.) (1982). *Edward Westermarck: Essays on his Life and Works*, Acta Philosophica Fennica 34. Helsinki: The Philosophical Society of Finland.

SUNDHOLM, G. (1994). 'Ontologic versus Epistemologic: Some Strands in the Development of Logic, 1837–1957', in D. Prawitz and D. Westerståhl (eds.), *Logic and Philosophy of Science in Uppsala*. Dordrecht: Kluwer, 373–84.

SUPPE, F. (ed.) (1977). *The Structure of Scientific Theories* (2nd edn.). Urbana, Ill.: University of Illinois Press.

——(1989). *The Semantic Conception of Theories and Scientific Realism*. Urbana, Ill.: University of Illinois Press.

SUPPES, P. (1993). *Models and Methods in the Philosophy of Science: Selected Essays*. Dordrecht: Kluwer.

SWOYER, C. (1982). 'True For', in Meiland and Krausz 1982: 81–104.

TARSKI, A. (1944). 'The Semantic Conception of Truth and the Foundations of Semantics', *Philosophy and Phenomenological Research*, 4: 341–76.

TARSKI, A. (1956). *Logic, Semantics, Metamathematics*. Oxford: Oxford University Press.

TELLER, P. (1981). 'The Projection Postulate and Bohr's Interpretation of Quantum Mechanics', in *PSA 1980*, vol. ii. East Lansing, Mich.: Philosophy of Science Association, 201–23.

THAGARD, P. (1988). *Computational Philosophy of Science*. Cambridge, Mass.: MIT Press.

——(1992). *Conceptual Revolutions*. Princeton: Princeton University Press.

TIBBETS, P. (1986). 'The Sociology of Scientific Knowledge: The Constructivist Thesis and Relativism', *Philosophy of the Social Sciences*, 16: 39–57.

TOMBERLIN, J. E. (ed.) (1987). *Philosophical Perspectives*, i: *Metaphysics*. Atascadero, Calif.: Ridgeview.

TOOLEY, M. (1987). *Causation*. Oxford: Oxford University Press.

TRANÖY, K. E. (1988). *The Moral Import of Science*, ed. A. J. I. Jones. Bergen: Sigma Forlag.

TRIGG, R. (1989). *Reality at Risk: A Defence of Realism in Philosophy and the Sciences* (2nd edn.). New York: Harvester Wheatsheaf.

TUOMELA, R. (1973). *Theoretical Concepts*. Berlin: Springer-Verlag.

——(1977). *Human Action and its Explanation*. Dordrecht: D. Reidel.

——(ed.) (1978). *Dispositions*. Dordrecht: D. Reidel.

——(1985). *Science, Action and Reality*. Dordrecht: Reidel.

——(1990). 'Causal Internal Realism', in G. Pasternack (ed.), *Philosophie und Wissenschaften*. Frankfurt am Main: Peter Lang, 165–79.

TUANA, N. (1996). 'Revaluing Science: Starting from the Practices of Women', in Nelson and Nelson 1996: 17–35.

TYMOCZKO, T. (ed.) (1986). *New Directions in the Philosophy of Mathematics*. Basle: Birkhauser.

UNGER, P. (1975). *Ignorance: A Case for Scepticism*. Oxford: Clarendon Press.

URBACH, P. (1983). 'Intimations of Similarity: The Shaky Basis of Verisimilitude', *British Journal for the Philosophy of Science*, 34: 266–75.

VAN CLEVE, J. (1992). 'Noumenal/Phenomenal', in Dancy and Sosa 1992: 306–8.

VAN FRAASSEN, B. (1980). *The Scientific Image*. Oxford: Oxford University Press.

——(1989). *Laws and Symmetry*. Oxford: Oxford University Press.

VENN, J. (1888). *The Logic of Chance* (3rd edn.). London: Macmillan.

VON WRIGHT, G. H. (1963a). *Norm and Action*. London: Routledge & Kegan Paul.

——(1963b). *The Varieties of Goodness*. London: Routledge & Kegan Paul.

——(1993). *The Tree of Knowledge and Other Essays*. Leiden: E. J. Brill.

WACHBROIT, R. (1986). 'Progress: Metaphysical and Otherwise', *Philosophy of Science*, 53: 354–71.

WALKER, R. C. S. (1989). *The Coherence Theory of Truth: Realism, Anti-realism, Idealism*. London: Routledge.

WANG, S. Y. (1988). 'Niiniluoto's Theory of Progress of Science' (in Chinese), *Journal of Dialectics of Nature*, 10: 7–14.

WARNKE, G. (1987). *Gadamer: Hermeneutics, Tradition and Reason*. Stanford, Calif.: Stanford University Press.

WATKINS, J. (1984). *Science and Scepticism*. Princeton: Princeton University Press.

WESTERMARCK, E. (1932). *Ethical Relativity*. London: Kegan & Paul.

WESTON, T. (1992). 'Approximate Truth and Scientific Realism', *Philosophy of Science*, 55: 53–74.

WHEWELL, W. (1840). *The Philosophy of the Inductive Sciences.* (new edn., ed. G. Buchdahl and L. Laudan, 1967). London: Parker & Sons.

WILLIAMS, B. (1982). 'An Inconsistent Form of Relativism', in Meiland and Krausz 1982: 171–4.

——(1985). *Ethics and the Limits of Philosophy*. London: Fontana Press.

WILLIAMS, D. (1953). 'The Elements of Being', *Review of Metaphysics*, 7: 3–18, 171–92.

WILSON, B. (ed.) (1970). *Rationality*. Oxford: Blackwell.

WINNIE, J. (1975). 'Theoretical Analyticity', in J. Hintikka (ed.), *Rudolf Carnap, Logical Empiricist*. Dordrecht: D. Reidel, 143–59.

WITTGENSTEIN, L. (1922). *Tractatus Logico-Philosophicus*. London: Routledge & Kegan Paul.

——(1969). *On Certainty*. Oxford: Blackwell.

WOLENSKI, J. (1993). 'Tarski as a Philosopher', in F. Coniglione, R. Poli, and J. Wolenski (eds.), *Polish Scientific Philosophy: The Lvov–Warsaw School*, Poznań Studies in the Philosophy of the Sciences and the Humanities 28. Amsterdam: Rodopi, 319–38.

WOLTERSTORFF, N. (1987). 'Are Concept-Users World-Makers?', in Tomberlin 1987: 233–67.

WOOLGAR, S. (1988). *Science: The Very Idea*. London: Tavistock.

WORRALL, J. (1982). 'Scientific Realism and Scientific Change', *Philosophical Quarterly*, 32: 201–31.

——(1989). 'Structural Realism: The Best of Both Worlds', *Dialectica*, 43: 99–124.

WRIGHT, C. (1993). *Realism, Meaning, and Truth* (2nd edn.). Oxford: Blackwell.

ZIMAN, J. (1994). *Prometheus Bound: Science in a Dynamic Steady State*. Cambridge: Cambridge University Press.

ZWART, S. (1998). *Approach to the Truth*, ILLI Dissertation Series. Amsterdam: University of Amsterdam.

# Index of Names

# Index of Subjects

abduction 39, 187
anti-realism v, 7, 18, 105–8, 261
approximate:
  deduction 130
  truth 72, 74n., 99, 128, 140, 188–96
artefact 33, 272n., 277n.
assertability 106, 237, 240
axiology 1–2, 13, 170–4, 234, 290

behaviourism 154
bivalence 3, 64, 106

causality 89
charity 127–32
cognitive problem 68
coherence 50, 66
common sense 7–9, 143–4
concretization 137
confirmation 96, 102, 169
constituent 70–1
constructive empiricism 13, 116–18, 188
corroboration 96, 98, 169
correspondence 49, 63–4, 225–6
  principle 137
counterfactual 134, 137
cultural entity 33
curve fitting 184–5

descriptivism 12, 110
distance 68–71, 99, 185
  Clifford 71
  Euclidian 69
  Minkowskian 69
dualism 22–3

Edinburgh school 253–62
eliminativism 9, 21–2, 156
emergent materialism viii, 21–2, 25, 155
epiphenomenalism 23
epistemic utility 168, 178
epistemological anarchism 11, 293
epistemology 1–2, 79–108
  social 238, 268n. 7
essentialism 32
ethics 1–2
  of science 299–301

event 31
existence 25, 219
externalism 255

fact 34, 64, 221, 234, 276
fallibilism 13, 82–5, 95, 285
feminism 242–51
finitism 263–7
folk psychology 8–9, 143, 156n. 34

geometry 89

hypothetico-deductive method 174–5

icon 45
idealism 22, 37, 90, 207, 260
  conceptual 28, 91, 208–9
  objective 22, 26
  subjective 22, 26, 38–41
  transcendental 88–90
idealization 135–44, 271
incommensurability 121–4
information content 96
instrumentalism 6, 12, 111–19, 135, 144–6,
  155–6, 291–2
interpretation 52, 56
invariance 87, 115, 133

Kantianism 17, 88–92, 209
knowledge 79–85
  maker's 79n., 275

language 42–6, 124, 214, 262
  observational 109, 121
law of nature 133
legisimilitude 75, 135
logical empiricism v, 10, 15, 90, 284

Marxism 206, 231, 246, 248
materialism 21–5, 115
meaning postulate 48, 122
meaning variance 120, 229, 264
metalanguage 47, 55–7
metaphysics 5–7, 35–7
methodology 1–2, 170–4
model theory 47, 51–5